Beginning T-SQL 2012

Scott Shaw
Kathi Kellenberger

Apress®

Beginning T-SQL 2012

ISBN-13 (pbk): 978-1-4302-3704-4

ISBN-13 (electronic): 978-1-4302-3705-1

Trademarked names, logos, an d images may app ear in this book. Rather than us e a trademark s ymbol with every occurrence of a trademarked name, logo, or image we use the names, logos, and images only in an editorial fashion and to the benefit of the trademark owner, with no intention of infringement of the trademark.

The use in this publication of trade names, tr ademarks, service marks, and similar terms, ev en if th ey are not identified as such, is not to be ta ken as an expression of opinion as to whether or not they are subject to proprietary rights.

While the advice and information in this book are believed to be true and accurate at the date of publication, neither the authors nor the editors nor th e publisher can accept any legal responsibility for any errors or o missions that may be made. The publisher makes no warranty, express or implied, with respect to the material contained herein.

President and Publisher: Paul Manning
Lead Editor: Jonathan Gennick
Technical Reviewer: Ken Simmons
Editorial Board: Steve Anglin, Ewan Buckingham, Gary Cornell, Louise Corrigan, Morgan Ertel, Jonathan Gennick, Jonathan Hassell, Robert Hutchin son, Michelle Lowman, James Markham, Matthew Moodie, Jeff Olson, Jeffrey Pepper, Douglas Pundick, Ben Renow-Clarke, Dominic Shakeshaft, Gwenan Spearing, Matt Wade, Tom Welsh
Coordinating Editor: Anita Castro
Copy Editor: Mary Behr
Compositor: Bytheway Publishing Services
Indexer: SPi Global
Artist: SPi Global
Cover Designer: Anna Ishchenko

Distributed to the book trade worldwide by Springer Scic nce+Business Media New York, 233 Spring Street, 6th Floor, New York, NY 10 013. Phone 1-800-SPRINGER, fax (201) 348-4505, e-mail orders-ny@springer-sbm.com, or vi sit www.springeronline.com.

For information on translations, please e-mail rights@apress.com, or visit www.apress.com.

Apress and friends of ED book s may be purchased in bulk for academic, corporate, or promotional use. eBook versions and licenses are also available for most titles. For more information, reference our Special Bulk Sales–eBook Licensing web page at www.apress.com/bulk-sales.

Any source code or other supplementary materials referenced by the author in this text is av ailable to re aders at www.apress.com. For detailed information about how to locate your book's source code, go to www.apress.com/source-code.

I would like to dedicate this book to my family and my co-workers who both had to put up with my diverted attention.

–Scott Shaw

Contents at a Glance

Contents

Foreword

Databases are very important to the modern world. Without them we wouldn't have computers with powerful memories, electronic banking, or even the internet! Many technology experts know that it is software behind the scenes, running everything, but beginners may just assume the process involves magic. But I would like people to know that what is really behind the scenes could be SQL Server.

The idea of a database program can be confusing and daunting to many beginners. While they may be interested in what make modern technology "tick," finding out that they have to learn a complex computer program may scare them away from the topic forever. But I am here to say that SQL Server doesn't need to be scary. Just like any subject, the key to learning this complex process is to start at the beginning.

Students and teachers know that learning the basics is key when learning to read, add, and do regular school work. But then a few years later, students try to jump right in the middle of more advanced concepts, which only confuses them more. When learning a subject like SQL Server, it is extremely important to start with the most basic textbook you can find, and then work your way up. And I believe that I can recommend the best SQL Server basics book.

It is *Beginning T-SQL*, by Scott Shaw and Kathi Kellenberger. I have reviewed this book elsewhere and readers may know that I have nothing but good things to say about it. It breaks down concepts into easy-to-read chapters, with ideas that flow naturally. And every chapter comes with examples and practice problems so that you can get hands-on learning from a textbook. I am very happy to announce that this is an even newer version of one of my favorite books.

Anyone who has read this book before may also notice that it has been updated to include features from Denali T-SQL. These updates are not isolated to a single chapter, but are sprinkled throughout the book wherever it might be important to know what's going on in Denali. This means readers will be picking up extra knowledge without having to read extra pages, or even an extra book.

There is also a brand new chapter (Chapter 8) that covers working with XML. If you are a beginner, don't let the frightening acronyms scare you away. You will have more than enough knowledge under your belt by the time you get to Chapter 8 to master the concept quickly and easily.

And for those of you who might be concerned that there is a whole extra chapter, and extra reading has been added to a book, you are in luck. One chapter has actually been rearranged to appear throughout the book, so that no information has been deleted, but the book has stayed the same length. We all know that we shouldn't skip to the end when reading a textbook, but we all do it anyway. And now we won't be scared by the number of pages remaining in the book, but it will fly by quickly.

There is a reason I think Scott Shaw and Kathi Kellenberger's book is the best introductory book on the market. There are many textbooks that market themselves as "beginner" or "fundamentals" of SQL Server. But if you have picked up any of them, you know that the authors usually assume that you know a little bit about SQL Server. True beginners often have a very hard time picking up one of these books and then beginning their learning immediately, because there is so much background information that the author assumes a beginner should know before attempting to learn.

But I think that is this is the worst thing that can happen to someone trying to learn. Imagine learning to walk, but being knocked down every time you try. This is not going to make you try to skip walking, and jump immediately to running. No – you may never learn to walk or run at all. *Beginning T-SQL* is one of the few books that avoids this problem, I think.

In fact, as proof that Mr. Shaw and Ms. Kellenberger starts the book right where learning needs to start, take a look at the title of chapter number one: Getting Started. It doesn't jump right into writing queries, or using functions, no matter how simple, but walks you through the most basic of all fundamentals. And, of course, if you are already a little bit of an expert – no problem! Just skip this one chapter, and start your learning in Chapter 2.

Ms. Kellenbeger has told me herself that she intends this book to take a beginner to an intermediate T-SQL developer. Many books make wild claims that they can take a beginner and turn them into a database expert by simply reading the book from cover to cover. But like all claims that seem too good to be true, those books often fail to live up to their promises. Often, they really are to take intermediate learners to experts, or are so determined to reach the expert level that they leave off some very important basic concepts, which then just leaves a confused beginner. I appreciate that this book makes solid claims that it can back up with real evidence and actual results.

Best of all, I think this is just an overall well-written book. It is written in easy-to-understand language and presents examples and practice sets at every turn. There has obviously been a lot of care put into making this book the best it can be. Not only is the writing clear, but the entire book is laid out in an orderly fashion, so that you use concepts you have learned before while you master more complex information. But I think the best thing I can say is that I like it because she is easy to read, makes complex subjects easy, and is very thorough in writing and executing.

Now I consider myself a SQL Server expert, and my job as a technology evangelist means that I should have a very firm grasp on the most complex subjects. But I certainly began my early career reading Kathi Kellenberger's books and other writings. She was a huge influence on my career, and thus my life. I cannot recommend this book, and all her writings, more highly than I do right now.

Pinal Dave
Founder, SQLAuthority.com

About the Authors

Scott Shaw has worked with SQL Server for over 10 years in a wide-range of challenging industries. He specializes in SQL virtualization and managing large SQL Server enterprise environments. He also speaks frequently on the role of SQL Server in Healthcare. He has a Masters of Arts in English and Comparative Literature as well as a Masters of Science in Management Information Systems. He works as BI Architect for the Saint Louis based consulting firm Oakwood Systems.

Scott is actively involved in the SQL Community. He has presented at SQLSaturdays, SQLRally, Saint Louis User Group and Virtual PASS chapters. He also has written articles for SSWUG, SQL Server Central, and MSSQLTips. In 2011 he was named as a finalist for the RedGate DBA of the Year Award.

Scott currently lives in Saint Louis and, when not working with SQL Server, he is waiting for instructions from his wife and kids.

CONTACT INFORMATION
Email: spshaw70@gmail.com
Twitter: @shawsql
Blog: www.dbaexperience.wordpress.com

Kathi Kellenberger is a Sr. Consultant with Pragmatic Works after eight years as a database administrator and almost two years with Microsoft in sales. Kathi enjoys writing and speaking about SQL Server having published over two dozen technical articles, writing or contributing to four books and speaking at many SQL Server events. In her spare time, Kathi loves spending time with family and friends, singing and cycling.

About the Technical Reviewer

 **Ken Simmons** is a Database Administrator and Developer specializing in Microsoft SQL Server. He is an author for multiple SQL Server websites and books including Pro SQL Server 2008 Administration, Pro SQL Server 2008 Mirroring, Pro SQL Server 2008 Policy-Based Management, and Pro SQL Server 2012 Administration. He currently holds certifications for MCP, MCAD, MCDBA, MCTS for SQL Server 2005, and MCITP for SQL Server 2008.

Acknowledgments

I would very much like to acknowledge both Apress and Kathi Kellenberger for opening the doors and introducing me to the world of publishing.

–Scott Shaw

For Thomas and Gwen, you keep me young.

-Kathi Kellenberger

Introduction

I never thought I'd be writing a technical book. I have a MA in English Literature so I always pictured myself sitting in an oak paneled room surrounded by books and attentive students listening to me pontificating on the latest criticism of 19th Century novels. It didn't take me long to realize though that path wasn't for me and I really wasn't cut out for a life in academia. But now I was an ex-English major working in a book store, starting a family and with little career prospects.

Working in a bookstore did offer some advantages. One advantage was the easy access to technical books. I had endless access to books just like the one you are reading now. I thought to myself, why not read these books, learn from them, and try working in IT? I didn't see a need to go back to school in order to learn IT. I had the books, I had the computer at home to work on, and I had the goal of acquiring an IT certification. I eventually passed the certification exam and soon after that I got my first break into IT working for a small consulting company.

So, why does any of this matter? The point is that many, if not most, of the people working in IT today didn't plan to be in IT. They come from a diverse background. The one thing that binds them together is their desire to learn and study to become experts in their field. They all started down the path by reading books just like the one you are holding. They made a decision to start an IT career. This is an important book because it's the beginning. The book is the stepping stone to becoming a professional. Although it isn't the great American novel I had hoped to someday write, it was still a pleasure and honor to have been asked by Kathi and Apress to revise it because, unlike a novel, this book has practical, real world applications. I also take pride in the fact I have given back a little for the benefits similar books have given me in the past.

Enjoy the book and never stop learning.

-Scott Shaw

CHAPTER 1

Getting Started

If you are reading this book, you probably know about T-SQL. T-SQL, also known as Transact-SQL, is Microsoft's implementation of the Structured Query Language (SQL) for SQL Server. T-SQL is the language that is most often used to extract or modify data stored in a SQL Server database, regardless of which application or tool you use. SQL Server 2012 T-SQL is based on standards created by the American National Standards Institute (ANSI), but Microsoft has added several functionality enhancements. You will find that T-SQL is a very versatile and powerful programming language.

T-SQL consists of Data Definition Language (DDL) and Data Manipulation Language (DML) statements. This book focuses primarily on the DML statements, which you will use to retrieve and manipulate data. The book also covers DDL statements, which you will use to create and manage objects. You will learn about table creation, for example, in Chapter 9.

In this chapter, you will learn how to install a free edition of SQL Server and get it ready for running the example code and performing the exercises in the rest of the book. This chapter also gives you a quick tour of SQL Server Management Studio (SSMS) and introduces a few concepts to help you become a proficient T-SQL programmer.

Installing SQL Server Express Edition

Microsoft makes SQL Server 2012 available in six different editions, including two that can be installed on a desktop computer or laptop. If you don't have access to SQL Server, you can download and install the SQL Server Express edition from Microsoft's web site at www.microsoft.com/express/sql/download/default.aspx. To fully take advantage of all the concepts covered in this book, download SQL Server 2012 Express with Tools. You may notice a new LocalDB option for SQL Server Express; LocalDB is an extremely lightweight version of SQL Server that doesn't include any configuration options or tools. Since you will need the tools for this book you don't want to download the LocalDB version. Be sure to choose either the 64-bit or 32-bit download according to the operating system that you are running. The Express edition will run on the following operating systems available at the time of this writing: Windows Server 2008 SP2, Windows Server 2008 R2 SP1, Windows 7 SP1, Windows Vista SP2. Note that SQL Server 2012 is not compatible with Windows XP.

■ **Note** SP is shorthand for Service Pack, so SP2 refers to Service Pack 2. A *service pack* is an update to the operating system or to other software that fixes bugs and security issues.

Here are the steps to follow to install SQL Server Express:

1. Once you have downloaded the SQL Server 2012 Express edition installation
   file from Microsoft's site, double-click the file to extract and start up the SQL
   Server Installation Center. Figure 1-1 shows the Planning pane of the SQL
   Server Installation Center once the extraction has completed. You may need to
   click on Planning in the left-hand side to see these options.

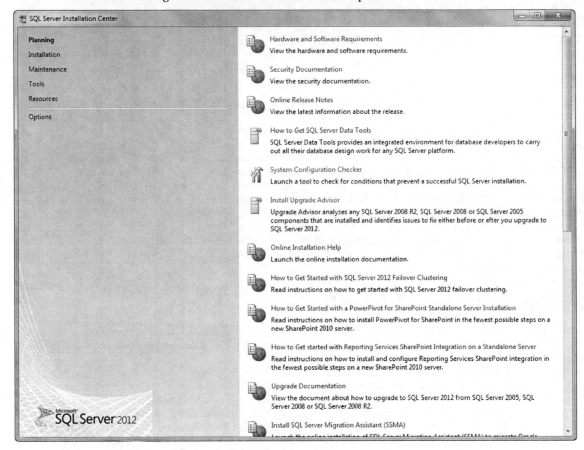

Figure 1-1. SQL Server Installation Center's Planning pane

2. To make sure that your system meets all the requirements to install SQL Server
   Express, click the System Configuration Checker link, which opens the Setup
   Support Rules screen (see Figure 1-2). Click "Show details" or "View detailed
   report" to see more information. Click OK to dismiss the screen when you are
   done.

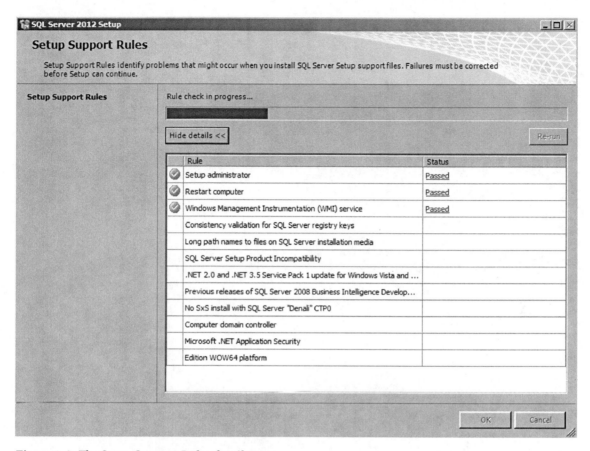

Figure 1-2. *The Setup Support Rules details page*

3. If your system doesn't meet the requirements, click the Hardware and Software Requirements link on the Planning pane of the SQL Server Installation Center, which will take you to a web page on Microsoft's site. Be sure to scroll down the web page to find the information for the Express edition. The hardware requirements are not difficult to meet with today's PCs.

4. Once you are certain that your computer meets all the requirements, switch to the Installation pane, shown in Figure 1-3, and click "New SQL Server stand-alone installation or add features to an existing installation." The Setup Support Rules screen you saw in step 2 will display again, but the behavior will be different this time. Click OK to dismiss the Setup Support Rules screen, and an installation wizard will begin.

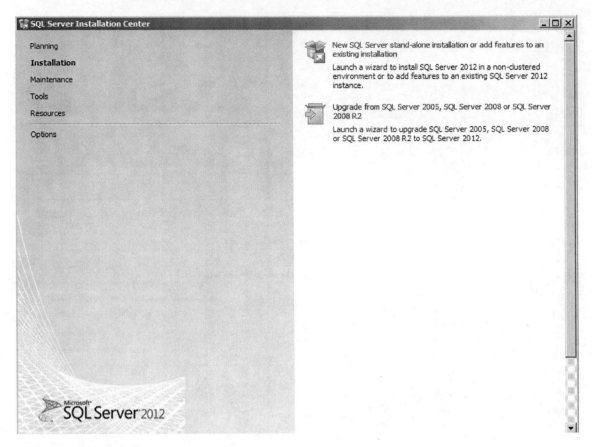

Figure 1-3. The Installation pane

5. You may or may not see a Setup Support Files screen at this point. If you do see it, click Install.

6. Select Express from the drop-down and click Next on the Product Key screen when installing SQL Server Express edition. No need to have a key since this is a free edition! Accept the license terms and click Next.

7. Some more checking of your system will take place. You may get a warning about your firewall (Figure 1-4), especially if you are installing on a workstation. The warning will say to open ports required for other systems to access your SQL Server. You can ignore that warning unless you do really want to open up your system. Click Next to continue.

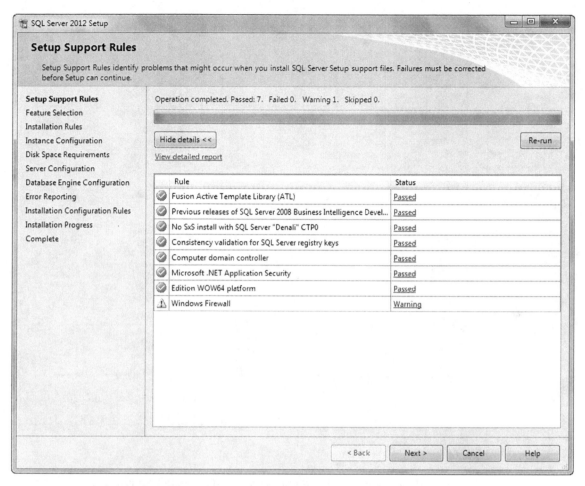

Figure 1-4. More system checks

8. If you have a previously installed instance of SQL Server on your computer, the installation will prompt you to either update an existing instance or install a new instance on the Installation Type screen. Select to install a new instance and click Next. If you don't have a previous install, select the option "SQL Server Feature Installation" and click Next.

9. On the Feature Selection screen (Figure 1-5), make sure that "Database Engine Services," "Full-Text and Semantic Extractions for Search," and "Management Tools – Basic" are selected before clicking Next. If a previous SQL Server 2012 R2 installation is in place, the Management Tools check box might be grayed out since you need to install it only once per computer.

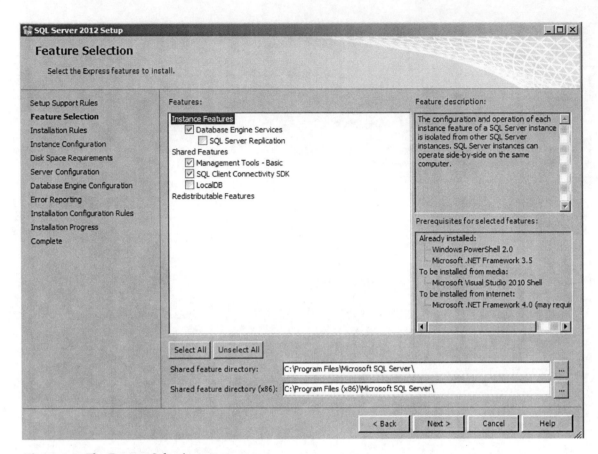

Figure 1-5. The Feature Selection screen

10. Figure 1-6 shows the Instance Configuration screen, and it is very important. Here you can choose to install a default instance or a named instance. If you have any SQL Server instances already installed, possibly an earlier version such as 2008 R2, they will show up in the list on this screen. Each instance must have a unique name, so you must avoid using any existing instance names. See the sidebar "Named Instances" for more information about naming SQL Server instances. The Express edition installation installs the named instance MSSQLSERVER by default. Use the name MSSQLSERVER if you can; otherwise, type in a unique name. Figure 1-6 shows the instance configuration screen. Click Next.

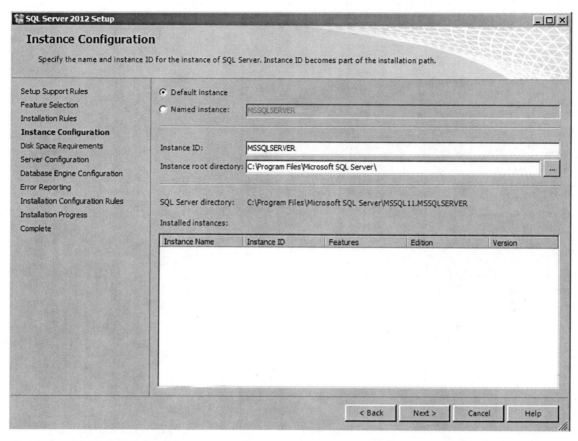

Figure 1-6. The Instance Configuration screen

NAMED INSTANCES

Multiple SQL Server installations can run on one physical computer. Each installation is called an *instance*. You may have only one default instance on a computer. Any additional instances must be named. To connect to SQL Server, you must specify the physical computer name. When working with named instances, you must specify the instance name as well. To connect to a default instance, only the computer name is required. When connecting to name instances, the computer name plus the instance name are required: computer*Name**instanceName*.

11. The Disk Space Requirements screen (Figure 1-7) will ensure that you have enough disk space for the install. However, "space for the install" refers to having space for the executable and other files such as the system databases. The system databases start out small but can grow quite large in a production system. The space requirements don't include any user databases, which are

7

the databases that will store your data, so make sure you also have room for them before clicking Next.

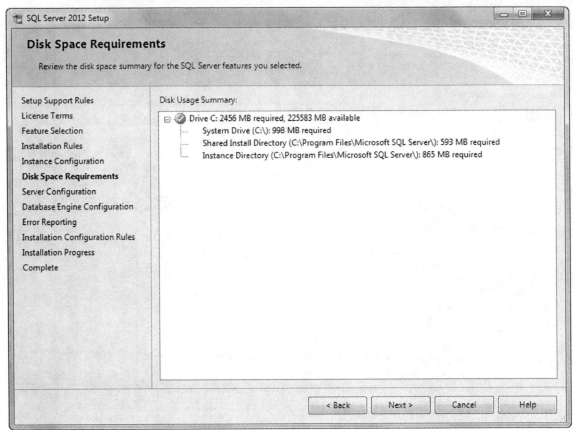

Figure 1-7. *The Disk Space Requirements screen*

12. On the Service Configuration screen, shown in Figure 1-8, you must specify accounts under which SQL Server will run. If you are setting up SQL Server for a production environment, you probably have a special service account to use. Since you are just installing the Express edition for learning purposes here, choose the default for all the services.

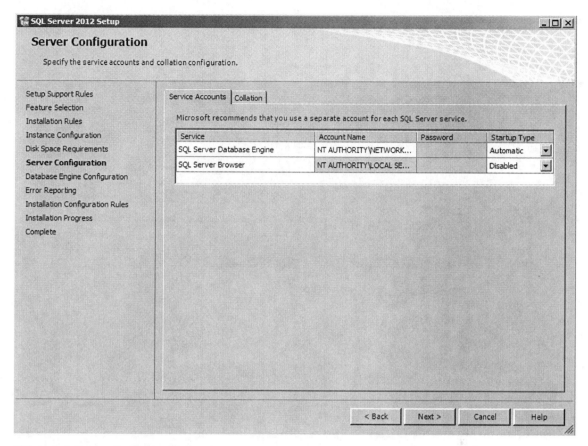

Figure 1-8. Server Configuration screen

13. On the Database Engine Configuration screen's Account Provisioning tab (Figure 1-9), you will either select the "Windows authentication mode" option or the "Mixed Mode" option. If you select "Windows authentication mode," SQL Server can accept connections only from Windows-authenticated accounts; if you selected "Mixed Mode," it can additionally allow accounts set up within SQL Server. For the purposes of the book, you can leave the authentication mode as "Windows authentication mode." Click the Add Current User button near the bottom of the page to make sure that the account you are using is added as an administrator.

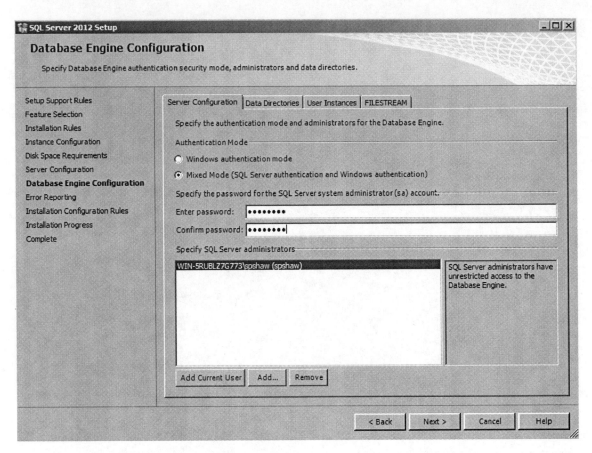

Figure 1-9. The Database Engine Configuration screen

14. On the Data Directories tab, you can specify directories for database and log files as well as all the other directories needed for your SQL Server instance. In a learning environment, the defaults are fine. On a production system, the database administrator will strategically place files for best performance.

15. Click the FILESTREAM tab on the current screen to enable FILESTREAM functionality, as in Figure 1-10. FILESTREAM was introduced in SQL Server 2008 and we will look more closely at it in Chapter 10.

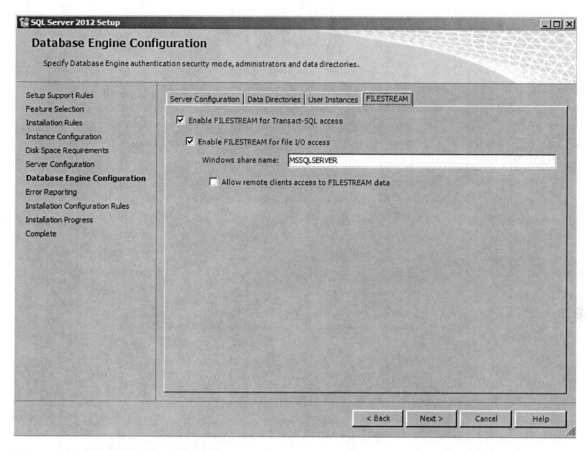

Figure 1-10. FILESTREAM configuration

16. Click Next after configuring FILESTREAM. You'll see an Error and Usage Reporting screen. Check the buttons on that screen to send reports to Microsoft if you choose to do that, and click Next again.

17. The installation performs more checks from the Installation Rules page that appears next, such as making sure that the settings you have selected will work. Click Next to continue.

18. A summary screen of what will be installed displays. Click Install, and the installation begins.

19. Once the install is complete, you can view a report to help you solve any issues with the installation. Figure 1-11 shows the report from a successful installation.

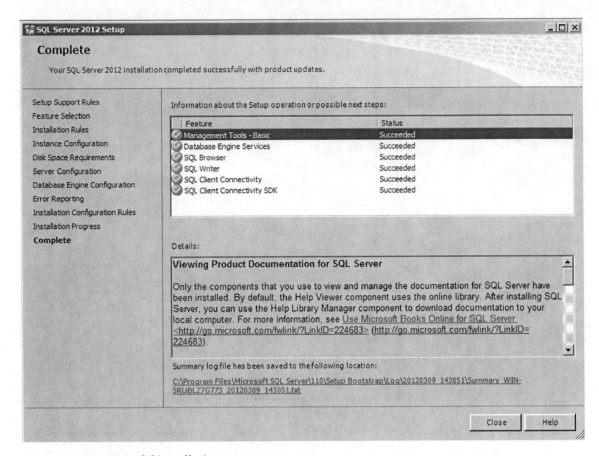

Figure 1-11. A successful installation report

20. Click the Close button. Congratulations! You have just installed SQL Server Express.

After the installation completes, the SQL Server Installation Center displays once more. You may be interested in viewing some of the resources available in this application at a later time. Luckily, you don't have to start the install again. You can run the Installation Center by selecting Start ➤ All Programs ➤ Microsoft SQL Server 2012 ➤ Configuration Tools ➤ SQL Server Installation Center at any time.

Installing the Sample Databases

Sample databases are very useful to help beginners practice writing code. Several databases, such as Pubs, Northwind, and AdventureWorks, have been available for this purpose over the many releases of SQL Server. You can download the sample databases from the CodePlex samples web site at www.codeplex.com. Because the link will change frequently as updated samples become available, search for SQL Server 2012 sample databases. Make sure you are downloading the latest version of the sample databases. Figure 1-12 shows a portion of the download page that was current the day that this section was written.

Figure 1-12. The source for the AdventureWorks databases

The following steps will guide you through installing the sample databases.

1. After clicking the appropriate link for your processor type and operating system, click the I Agree button to accept the license agreement.

2. Click Save to download the files.

3. Navigate to a location that you will remember, and click Save.

4. Once the download completes, open SQL Server Management Studio and start a new query. You can skip ahead in this chapter to see how this is done. In the query windows, execute the command shown in Listing 1-1. You will need to change the path to match the location where you downloaded the AdventureWorks2012 data file. Figure 1-13 shows how your screen should look.

Listing 1-1. Script to Create the AdventureWorks2012 Database

```
CREATE DATABASE AdventureWorks2012 ON (FILENAME = '<drive>:\<file
path>\AdventureWorks2012_Data.mdf') FOR ATTACH_REBUILD_LOG ;
```

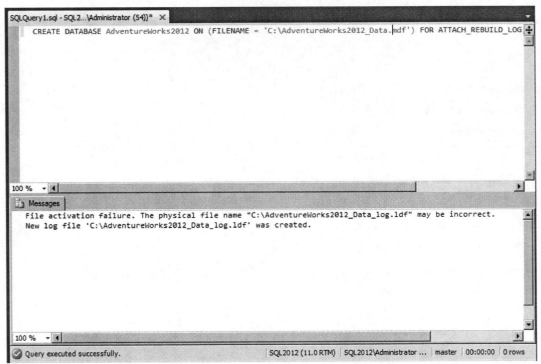

Figure 1-13. The sample database install

You should now have AdventureWorks database installed on your SQL Server instance. Your next step is to install SQL Server's help system, Books Online. Then I'll show you how to look at the AdventureWorks database in the "Using SQL Server Management Studio" section.

Installing Books Online

In SQL Server 2012 you have the choice of accessing Books Online via the Internet or locally. When you first install SQL Server you have the option to install the Books Online components. These components allow for better integration with the web-based documentation. The online components allow for updates to Books Online on the Internet to be applied to your local installation. Follow these steps to install Books Online locally.

1. Open up Management Studio and select Help from the menu. Under Help, select Manage Help Settings.

2. A window will pop up with a list of items. Select "Install Content from Online."

3. Scroll down until you find the entry for SQL Server and click Add, as shown in Figure 1-14, and then click Update.

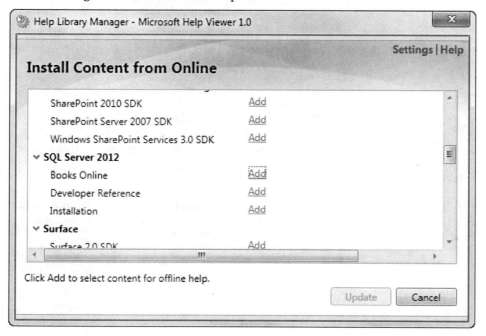

Figure 1-14. Installing Books Online

Using Books Online

Once SQL Server Books Online is installed, you can launch it by opening Management Studio and selecting Help from the top menu. Under the Help menu, select View Help. A new browser window will open up to the first page of MSDN.

Books Online is now part of the standardized Help Viewer. The screen for Microsoft Help Viewer is divided into two sections, as shown in Figure 1-15. The contents are displayed in the left pane. You can expand each entry to see the sections and click a topic to view each article on the right.

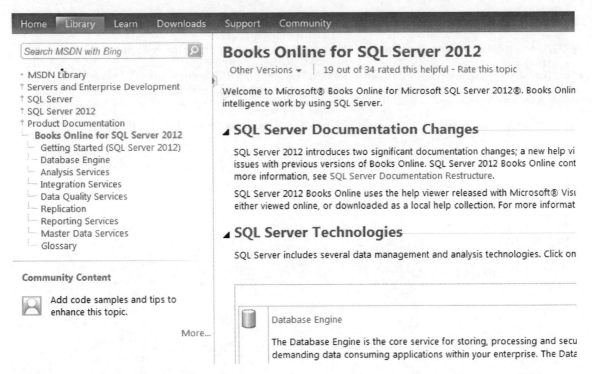

Figure 1-15. The two panes of Microsoft Help Viewer

In the top right corner there is a search bar. Type in a term, such as **query**, to see the results found in the local help system and any articles posted online. On the right you'll see advanced search options (Figure 1-16) and in the main window you'll see the results listed by topic and by location.

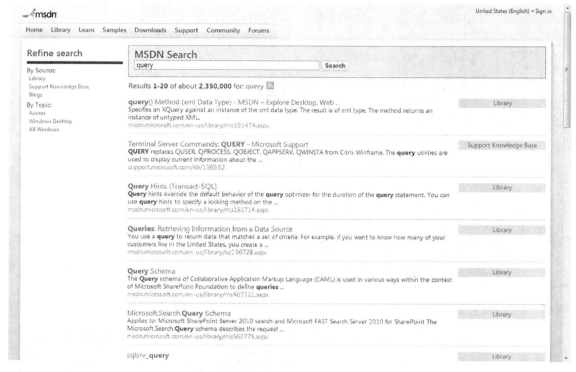

Figure 1-16. Search results in Microsoft Help Viewer

Once you find an article or help topic you think you will want to view periodically, you can click the "Add to Favorites" button as you would for any other web site.

You will learn how to write T-SQL from reading this book, but I recommend that you check Books Online frequently to learn even more!

Using SQL Server Management Studio

Now that you have SQL Server, SQL Server Books Online, and the sample database installed, it's time to get acquainted with SQL Server Management Studio (SSMS). SSMS is the tool that ships with most editions of SQL Server, and you can use it to manage SQL Server and the databases as well as write T-SQL code. If you have installed SQL Server Express with Tools as outlined earlier, you should be able to find SSMS by selecting Start ➤ All Programs ➤ Microsoft SQL Server 2012 ➤ SQL Server Management Studio. SSMS is your window into SQL Server. You can manage your database, create scripts, and—most importantly—execute T-SQL code and see the results.

Launching SQL Server Management Studio

Launch SSMS by selecting Start ➤ All Programs ➤ Microsoft SQL Server 20012 ➤ SQL Server Management Studio. After the splash screen displays, you will be prompted to connect to an instance of SQL Server, as shown in Figure 1-17.

Figure 1-17. Connect to Server dialog box

Notice in this example that the computer name is SQL2012 and we are using the default instance. If you installed a named instance, you will see the computer name followed by a "\" and then the instance name. For the default instance you can also use (local), Localhost, or a period in place of the computer name as long as you are logged on locally and not trying to connect to a remote SQL Server. Make sure that the appropriate server name is filled in, and click Connect.

Once connected to an instance of SQL Server, you can view the databases and all the objects in the Object Explorer. The Object Explorer is located the left side of the screen by default. You can expand each item to see other items underneath. For example, once you expand the Databases folder, you can expand one of the databases. Then you can expand the Tables folder for that database. You can expand a table name and drill down to see the columns, indexes, and other properties. In the right pane, you can see details about the selected item. If you don't see the details, press the F7 key. Figure 1-18 shows the Object Explorer window and details.

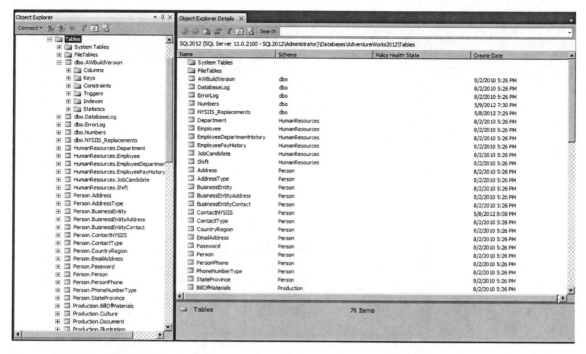

Figure 1-18. *The Object Explorer*

Running Queries

One SSMS feature that you will use extensively during this book is the Query Editor. In this window you will type and run queries as you learn about T-SQL. The following steps will guide you through writing your first query in the Query Editor.

1. Make sure your SQL Server instance is selected in the Object Explorer, and click New Query, which is located right above the Object Explorer, to open the Query Editor window.

2. Select the AdventureWorks2012 database from the drop-down list on the left if it is not already selected, as in Figure 1-19.

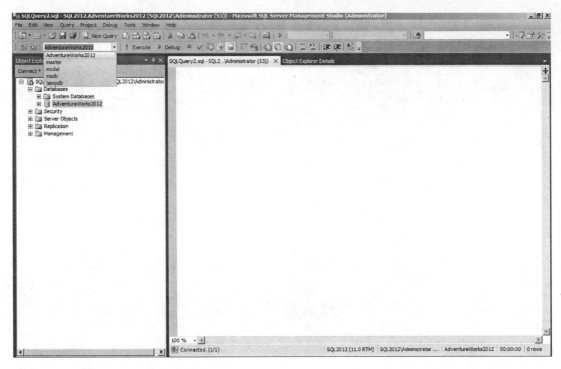

Figure 1-19. The AdventureWorks2012 database

3. Type the following code in the Query Editor window on the right. It's a query to display all the data in the Employee table.

```
SELECT * FROM HumanResources.Employee;
```

4. You will notice as you type that IntelliSense (Figure 1-20) is available in the Query Editor window. IntelliSense helps you by eliminating keystrokes to save you time. It also validates the code before the code is compiled. It doesn't work when connecting to versions earlier than SQL Server 2008.

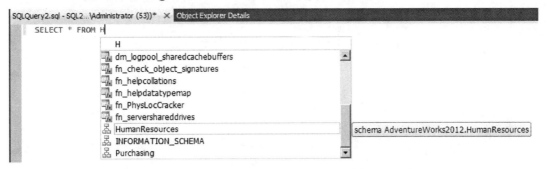

Figure 1-20. IntelliSense

5. Click Execute or press the F5 key to see the results, as in Figure 1-21.

	BusinessEntityID	NationalIDNumber	LoginID	OrganizationNode	OrganizationLevel	JobTitle
1	1	295847284	adventure-works\ken0	0x	0	Chief Executive Officer
2	2	245797967	adventure-works\terri0	0x58	1	Vice President of Engineering
3	3	509647174	adventure-works\roberto0	0x5AC0	2	Engineering Manager
4	4	112457891	adventure-works\rob0	0x5AD6	3	Senior Tool Designer
5	5	695256908	adventure-works\gail0	0x5ADA	3	Design Engineer
6	6	998320692	adventure-works\jossef0	0x5ADE	3	Design Engineer
7	7	134969118	adventure-works\dylan0	0x5AE1	3	Research and Development Manager
8	8	811994146	adventure-works\diane1	0x5AE158	4	Research and Development Engineer
9	9	658797903	adventure-works\gigi0	0x5AE168	4	Research and Development Engineer

The query shown is: `SELECT * FROM HumanResources.Employee`

Figure 1-21. Results of running your first T-SQL query

SSMS has several scripting features to help you write code. Follow these steps to learn how to create a query without typing.

1. Make sure that the Tables folder is expanded, and select the HumanResources.Employee table, as in Figure 1-22.

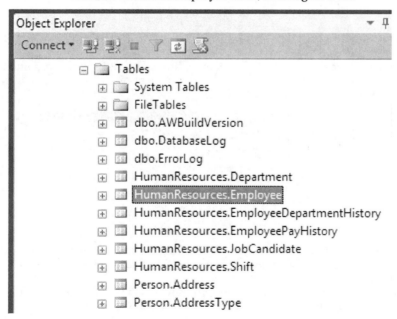

Figure 1-22. The HumanResources.Employee table

2. Right-click the HumanResources.Employee table, and select Script Table as ➤ Select To ➤ New Query Editor Window.

3. A new window will automatically open with some code (Figure 1-23). Click Execute.

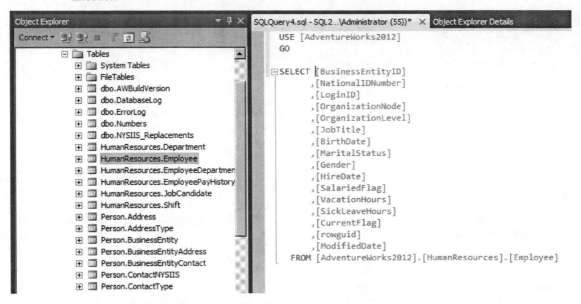

Figure 1-23. Automatically generated code

Sometimes you will end up with multiple statements in one Query Editor window. To run only some of the statements in the window, select what you want to run, and click Execute or press F5. Figure 1-24 shows an example. When you execute, only the first query will run.

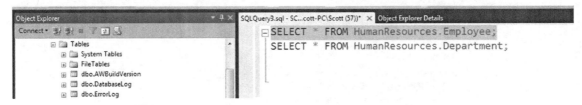

Figure 1-24. Selected code

Sections of code can be collapsed to get them out of your way by clicking the minus sign to the left of the code. You can search and replace just like a regular text editor, and, of course, you have IntelliSense to help you write the code.

Results can be saved to text files by clicking the Results to File icon shown in Figure 1-25 before you execute the code. You can also select and copy the results for pasting into Excel or Notepad.

Figure 1-25. *Results to File icon*

You can add documentation to your code or just keep code from running by adding comments. To comment a section of code, begin the section with /* and end the section with */. You can comment out a line of code or the end of a line of code with two hyphens (--). To automatically comment out code, select the lines you want to comment, and click the Comment button shown in Figure 1-26. Uncomment code by selecting commented lines and clicking the Uncomment button next to the Comment button.

```
/*
I want to comment serveral lines
like this
*/

SELECT 1 -- a comment after the code

-- I want to comment 1 line
```

Figure 1-26. *Commented code*

The Object Explorer allows you to manage the databases, security, maintenance jobs, and other aspects of SQL Server. Most of the tasks that can be performed are in the realm of database administrators, so we will not explore them in this book.

Exploring Database Concepts

In this section, you will learn just what SQL Server is and about the databases and objects that make up databases. You will learn how data is stored in a database, and you'll learn about objects, called *indexes*, that help SQL Server return the results of your queries quickly.

What Is SQL Server?

SQL Server is Microsoft's relational database management system (RDBMS). A relational database management system stores data in tables according to the relational model. The relational model is beyond the scope of this book, but you can learn more by reading *Beginning Relational Data Modeling*, Second Edition, by Sharon Allen and Evan Terry (Apress, 2005).

Editions

Microsoft makes SQL Server available in many editions, including a free edition called Express that can be distributed with applications or used to learn about SQL Server and several expensive, full-featured editions (Standard, Business Intelligence, and Enterprise) that are used to store terabytes of data in the most demanding enterprises. There is even a version that can be installed on smart phones (Compact edition). Search for the article "Features Supported by the Editions of SQL Server 20012" in SQL Server Books Online for more information about the editions and features of each. Table 1-1 gives an overview of the editions available.

Table 1-1. SQL Server 2012 Editions

Edition	Usage	Expense
Compact	Occasionally connected systems including mobile devices	Free
Express	Great for learning SQL Server and can be distributed with applications	Free
Web	Used for small web sites	Inexpensive
Workgroup	Used for workgroups or small database applications	Inexpensive
Developer	Full featured but used for development only	Inexpensive
Standard	Complete data platform with some high-availability and business intelligence features	Expensive
Enterprise	All available features	Very expensive
Business Intelligence	Used in both large and small companies to deploy comprehensive Business Intelligence solutions	Expensive

Many well-known companies trust SQL Server with their data. To read case studies about how some of these companies use SQL Server 20012, visit www.microsoft.com/sqlserver/2008/en/in/case-studies.aspx.

Service vs. Application

SQL Server is a service, not just an application. Even though you can install some of the editions on a regular workstation, it generally runs on a dedicated server and will run when the server starts; in other words, usually no one needs to manually start SQL Server. To minimize or practically eliminate downtime for critical systems, SQL Server boasts high-availability features such as clustering, log shipping, database mirroring, and AlwaysOn. Think about your favorite shopping web site. You expect it to be available any time day or night and every day. Behind the scenes, a database server, possibly a SQL Server instance, must be running and performing well at all times. Even during necessary maintenance—when applying security patches, for example—administrators must keep downtime to a minimum.

SQL Server is feature rich, providing a complete business intelligence suite, impressive management tools, sophisticated data replication features, and much, much more. These features are well beyond the scope of this book, but I invite you to visit www.apress.com to find books to help you learn about these other topics if you are interested.

SQL Server doesn't come with a data-entry interface for regular users or even a way to create a web site or a Windows application. To do that, you will most likely use a programming language such as Visual Basic .NET or C#. Calls to SQL Server via T-SQL can be made within your application code or through a middle tier such as a web service. Regardless of your application architecture, at some point you'll use T-SQL. SQL Server does have a very nice reporting tool called Reporting Services that is part of the business intelligence suite. Otherwise, you will have to use another programming language to create your user interface.

Figure 1-27 shows the architecture of a typical web application. The web server requests data from the database server. The clients communicate with the web server.

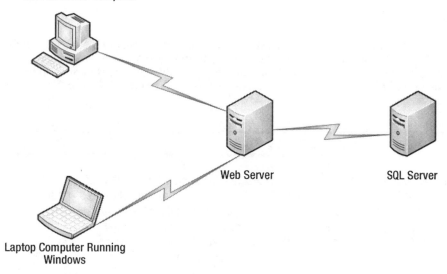

Figure 1-27. The architecture of a typical web application

Database As Container

A database in SQL Server is basically a container that holds several types of objects and data in an organized fashion. Generally, one database is used for a particular application or purpose, though this is not a hard and fast rule. For example, some systems have one database for all the enterprise applications required to run a business. On the other hand, one application could access more than one database.

Start SQL Server Management Studio if it is not already running, and connect to the SQL Server instance you installed in the "Installing SQL Server Express Edition" section. Expand the Databases folder to see the databases installed on the SQL Server. You should be able to see the AdventureWorks2012 database, as in Figure 1-28.

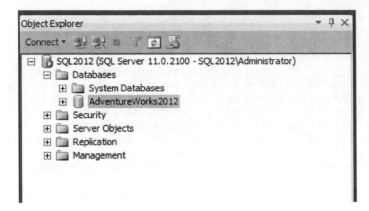

Figure 1-28. The databases

Within a database, you will find several objects, but only one type of object, the table, holds the data that we usually think about. In addition to tables, a database can contain indexes, views, stored procedures, user-defined functions, and user-defined types among other objects. Later chapters in this book will cover most of the other objects that are used to make up a database. You'll find an introduction to indexes later in this chapter.

SQL SERVER FILES

A SQL Server database must be comprised of at least two files. One is the data file with the default extension .mdf, and the other default is the log file with the extension .ldf. Additional data files, if they are used, will usually have the extension .ndf. Technically, the .mdf, .ldf, and .ndf files can have any given extension name though it is not recommended to change them from the defaults. Data files can be organized into multiple file groups. File groups are useful for strategically backing up only portions of the database at a time or to store the data on different drives for increased performance.

The log file in SQL Server stores *transactions*, or changes to the data, to ensure data consistency. Database administrators take frequent backups of the log files to allow the database to be restored to a point in time in case of data corruption, disk failure, or other disaster.

Data Is Stored in Tables

The most important objects in a database are tables because the tables are the objects that store the data and allow you to retrieve the data in an organized fashion. You can represent a table as a grid with columns and rows. The terminology used to describe the data in a database varies depending on the system, but in this book, I will stick with the terms *table, row,* and *column.* The following is an example of a table created to hold data about store owners:

CustomerID	Title	FirstName	MiddleName	LastName	Suffix	CompanyName
1	Mr.	Orlando	N.	Gee	NULL	A Bike Store
2	**Mr.**	**Keith**	**NULL**	**Harris**	**NULL**	**Progressive Sports**
3	Ms.	Donna	F.	Carreras	NULL	Advanced Bike Components
4	Ms.	Janet	M.	Gates	NULL	Modular Cycle Systems

In a normalized database, each table holds information about one type of entity. An entity type might be a student, customer, or vehicle, for example. Each row in a table contains the information about one instance of the entity represented by that table. For example, a row will represent one student, one customer, or one vehicle. Each column in the table will contain one piece of information about the entity. In the vehicle table, there might be a VIN column, a make column, a model column, a color column, and a year column, among others.

Each column within a table has a definition specifying a data type along with rules, called *constraints*, that enforce the values that can be stored. Constraints include whether a column can be left blank, whether it must be unique, whether it is limited to a certain range of values, and so on. You will learn more about constraints in Chapter 9.

In a normalized database, each table will have a primary key that is used to uniquely identify each row. In the previous example, the primary key is CustomerID.

■ **Note** You will learn what NULL means in Chapter 2.

Data Types

SQL Server has a rich assortment of data types for storing strings, numbers, money, XML, binary, and temporal data. Start SQL Server Management Studio if it is not running already, and connect to the SQL Server you installed in the "Installing SQL Server Express Edition" section. Expand the Databases section. Expand the AdventureWorks2012 database and the Tables section. Locate the HumanResources.Employee table, and right-click it. Select the Design option to view the properties (see Figure 1-29).

Column Name	Data Type	Allow Nulls
▶🔑 BusinessEntityID	int	☐
NationalIDNumber	nvarchar(15)	☐
LoginID	nvarchar(256)	☐
OrganizationNode	hierarchyid	☑
OrganizationLevel		☑
JobTitle	nvarchar(50)	☐
BirthDate	date	☐
MaritalStatus	nchar(1)	☐
Gender	nchar(1)	☐
HireDate	date	☐
SalariedFlag	Flag:bit	☐
VacationHours	smallint	☐
SickLeaveHours	smallint	☐
CurrentFlag	Flag:bit	☐
rowguid	uniqueidentifier	☐
ModifiedDate	datetime	☐
		☐

Figure 1-29. The properties of the HumanResources.Employee table

The HumanResources.Employee table contains a variety of data types and one column, OrganizationalLevel, with no data type defined. The OrganizationalLevel column is a computed column consisting of a formula.

SalariedFlag and CurrentFlag have the Flag user-defined data type, which is defined within the database. Developers can create user-defined data types to simplify table creation and to ensure consistency. For example, the AdventureWorks2012 database has a Phone data type used whenever a column contains phone numbers. To see the Phone data type definition, expand the Programmability section, the Type section, and the User Defined Data Types section. Locate and double-click the Phone data type to see the properties (see Figure 1-30).

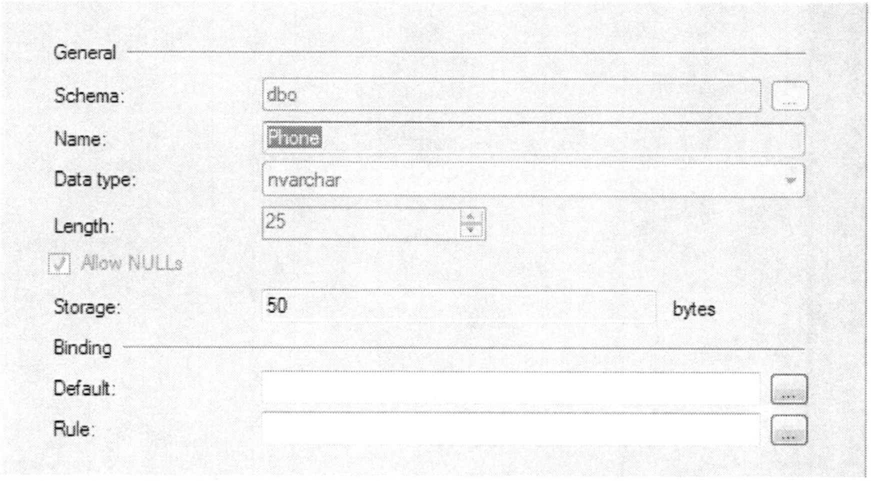

Figure 1-30. The properties of the Phone user-defined data type

Developers can create custom data types, called *CLR data types*, with multiple properties and methods using a .NET language such as C#. Chapter 9 shows how to create a helpful CLR for generating passwords and Chapter 10 covers three built-in CLR data types: HIERARCHYID, GEOMETRY, and GEOGRAPHY. The OrganizationNode column is a HIERARCHYID. You will find a wealth of information about data types in SQL Server Books Online by searching on the data type that interests you.

Normalization

Normalization is the process of designing database tables in a way that makes for efficient use of disk space and that allows the efficient manipulation and updating of the data. Normalization is especially important in online transaction processing (OLTP) databases, such as those used in e-commerce. Database architects usually design reporting-only databases to be denormalized to speed up data retrieval since they don't have to worry about frequent data updates.

The process of normalization is beyond the scope of this book, but it is helpful to understand why databases are normalized. To learn more about normalization, see *Pro SQL Server 2012 Relational Database Design and Implementation* by Louis Davidson and Jessica Moss (Apress, 2012).

Figure 1-31 shows how a database design might look before it is normalized. The example is of an order-entry database. There is one table, and that table consists of data about both customers and orders. One problem that you can probably see straightaway is that there is room only for three items per order and only three orders per customer.

CustomerOrders
CustomerID
Title
FirstName
LastName
CompanyName
AddressLine1
AddressLine2
City
State_Province
Country
PostalCode
OrderID1
OrderDate1
OrderItem1_1
OrderQty1_1
OrderItem1_2
OrderQty1_2
OrderItem1_3
OrderQty1_3
OrderItem2_1
OrderQty2_1
OrderItem2_2
OrderQty2_2
OrderItem2_3
OrderQty2_3
OrderItem3_1
OrderQty3_1
OrderItem3_2
OrderQty3_2
OrderItem3_3

Figure 1-31. *The denormalized database*

Figure 1-32 shows how the database might look once it is normalized. In this case, the database contains a table to hold information about the customer and a table to contain information about the order, such as the order date. The database contains a separate table to hold the items ordered. The order table contains a CustomerID that determines the customer instead of containing all the customer information. The OrderDetail table allows as many items as needed per order. The OrderDetail table contains the OrderID column to specify the correct order.

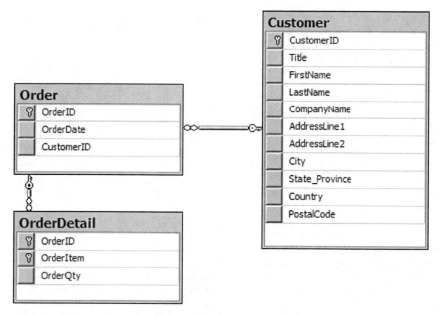

Figure 1-32. *The normalized database*

It may seem like a lot of trouble to properly define a database up front. However, it is well worth the effort to do so. I was called in once to help create reports on one of the most poorly designed databases I have ever seen. This was a small Microsoft Access database that was used to record information from interviewing users at a medium-sized company about the applications that the employees used. Each time a new application was entered into the database, a new Yes/No column for that application was created, and the data-entry form had to be modified. The developer, who should have known better, told me that she just didn't have time to create a properly normalized database. Much more time was spent fighting with this poor design than would have been spent properly designing the database.

Understanding Indexes

When a user runs a query to retrieve a portion of the rows from a table, how does the database engine determine which rows to return? If the table has indexes defined on it, SQL Server may use the indexes to find the appropriate rows.

There are several types of indexes, but this section covers two types: clustered and nonclustered. A *clustered index* stores and organizes the table. A *nonclustered index* is defined on one or more columns of the table, but it is a separate structure that points to the actual table. Both types of indexes are optional, but they can greatly improve the performance of queries when properly designed and maintained. A couple of analogies will help explain how indexes work.

A printed phone directory is a great example of a clustered index. Each entry in the directory represents one row of the table. A table can have only one clustered index. That is because a clustered index is the actual table organized in order of the cluster key. At first glance, you might think that inserting a new row into the table would require all the rows after the inserted row to be moved on the disk. Luckily, this is not the case. The row will have to be inserted into the correct data page. A list of pointers maintains the order between the pages, so the rows in other pages will not have to actually move.

The primary key of the phone directory is the phone number. Usually the primary key is used as the clustering key as well, but this is not the case in our example. The cluster key in the phone directory is a combination of the last name and first name. How would you find a friend's phone number if you knew the last and first name? Easy—you would open the book approximately to the section of the book that contains the entry. If your friend's last name starts with an *F*, you search near the beginning of the book; if it starts with an *S*, you search toward the back. You can use the names printed at the top of the page to quickly locate the page with the listing. You then drill down to the section of the correct page until you find the last name of your friend. Now you can use the first name to choose the correct listing. The phone number is right there next to the name. It probably takes more time to describe the process than to actually do it. Using the last name plus the first name to find the number is called a *clustered index seek*.

The index in the back of a book is an example of a nonclustered index. A nonclustered index has the indexed columns and a pointer or bookmark pointing to the actual row. In the case of our example, it contains a page number. Another example could be a search done on Google, Bing, or another search engine. The results on the page contain links to the original web pages. The thing to remember about nonclustered indexes is that you may have to retrieve part of the required information from the rows in the table. When using a book index, you will probably have to turn to the page of the book. When searching on Google, you will probably have to click the link to view the original page. If all the information you need is included in the index, you have no need to visit the actual data.

Although you can have only one clustered index per table, you can have up to 999 nonclustered indexes per table. If you ever need that many, you might have a design problem! An important thing to keep in mind is that although indexes can improve the performance of queries, indexes take up disk space and require resources to maintain. If a table has four nonclustered indexes, every write to that table may require four additional writes to keep the indexes up-to-date.

I just mentioned that 999 nonclustered indexes is too many. When talking about databases, an answer I hear all the time is "It depends." The number of indexes allowed per table increased with the release of SQL Server 2008 to take advantage of a couple of new features: sparse columns and filtered indexes. You will learn more about sparse columns in Chapter 10.

Database Schemas

A schema is a container that you can use to organize database objects. A schema is a way to organize the tables and object within the database. For example, the AdventureWorks2012 database contains several schemas based on the purpose: HumanResources, Person, Production, Purchasing, and Sales. Each table or other object belongs to one of the schemas.

▧ **Note** Objects in earlier versions of SQL Server were owned by database users. In SQL Server 2005 and later, a user can own a schema, but not individual objects.

A user can have a default schema. When accessing an object in the default schema, the user doesn't have to specify the schema name; however, it's a good practice to do so. If the user has permission to create new objects, the objects will belong to the user's default schema unless specified otherwise. To access objects outside the default schema, the schema name must be used. Table 1-2 shows several objects along with the schema.

Table 1-2. Schemas Found in AdventureWorks2012

Name	Schema	Object
HumanResources.Employee	HumanResources	Employee
Sales.SalesOrderDetail	Sales	SalesOrderDetail
Person.Address	Person	Address

Summary

This chapter provided a quick tour of SQL Server. You learned how databases are structured and designed; you also learned how SQL Server uses indexes to efficiently return data. If you followed the instructions in this chapter, you now have an instance of SQL Server running on your workstation or laptop so that you have a place to practice the queries you are about to learn.

In Chapter 2, you will get a chance to write your own queries. You'll learn the SELECT statement, the next step in your journey to T-SQL mastery.

CHAPTER 2

Writing Simple SELECT Queries

Chapter 1 had you preparing your computer by installing SQL Server 2012 and the AdventureWorks2012 sample database. You learned how to get around in SQL Server Management Studio and a few tips to help make writing queries easier.

Now that you're ready, it's time to learn how to retrieve data from a SQL Server database. You will retrieve data from SQL Server using the SELECT statement, starting with the simplest syntax. This chapter will cover the different parts, called *clauses*, of the SELECT statement so that you will be able to not only retrieve data but also filter and order it. The ultimate goal is to get exactly the data you need from your database—no more, no less.

Beginning in this chapter, you will find many code examples. Even though all the code is available from this book's catalog pages at http://www.apress.com, you will probably find that by typing the examples yourself you will learn more quickly. As they say, practice makes perfect! In addition, exercises follow many of the sections so that you can practice using what you have just learned. You can find the answers for each set of exercises in the appendix.

▨ **Note** If you take a look at SQL Server Books Online, you will find the syntax displayed for each kind of statement. Books Online displays every possible parameter and option, which is not always helpful when learning about a new concept for the first time. In this book, you will find only the syntax that applies to the topic being discussed at the time.

Using the SELECT Statement

You use the SELECT statement to retrieve data from SQL Server. T-SQL requires only the word SELECT followed by at least one item in what is called a *select-list*.

If SQL Server Management Studio is not running, go ahead and start it. When prompted to connect to SQL Server, enter the name of the SQL Server instance you installed while reading Chapter 1 or the name of your development SQL Server. You will need the AdventureWorks2012 sample databases installed to follow along with the examples and to complete the exercises. You will find instructions for installing the sample databases in Chapter 1.

Selecting a Literal Value

Perhaps the simplest form of a SELECT statement is that used to return a literal value that you specify. Begin by clicking New Query to open a new query window. Listing 2-1 shows two SELECT statements that both return a literal value. Notice the single quote mark that is used to designate the string value. Type each line of the code from Listing 2-1 into your query window.

Listing 2-1. Statements Returning Literal Values

```
SELECT 1
SELECT 'ABC'
```

After typing the code in the query window, press F5 or click Execute to run the code. You will see the results displayed in two windows at the bottom of the screen, as shown in Figure 2-1. Because you just ran two statements, two sets of results are displayed.

■ **Tip** By highlighting one or more statements in the query window, you can run just a portion of the code. For example, you may want to run one statement at a time. Use the mouse to select the statements you want to run, and press F5.

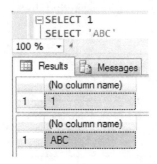

Figure 2-1. The results of running your first T-SQL statements

Notice the Messages tab next to the Results tab. Click Messages, and you will see the number of rows affected by the statements, as well as any error or informational messages. If an error occurs, you will see the Messages tab selected by default instead of the Results tab when the statement execution completes. You can then find the results, if any, by clicking the Results tab.

Retrieving from a Table

You will usually want to retrieve data from a table instead of literal values. After all, if you already know what value you want, you probably don't need to execute a query to get that value.

In preparation for retrieving data from a table, either delete the current code or open a new query window. Change to the example database by typing Use AdventureWorks2012 or by selecting the AdventureWorks2012 database from the drop-down list, as shown in Figure 2-2.

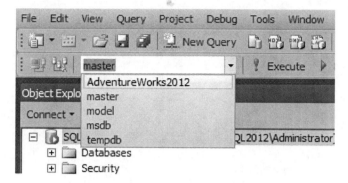

Figure 2-2. Choosing the AdventureWorks2012 database

You use the FROM clause to specify a table name in a SELECT statement. The FROM clause is the first part of the statement that the database engine evaluates and processes. Here is the syntax for the SELECT statement with a FROM clause:

```
SELECT <column1>, <column2> FROM <schema>.<table>;
```

Type in and execute the code in Listing 2-2 to learn how to retrieve data from a table.

Listing 2-2. Writing a Query with a FROM Clause

```
USE AdventureWorks2012;
GO
SELECT BusinessEntityID, JobTitle
FROM HumanResources.Employee;
```

The first statement in Listing 2-2 switches the connection to the AdventureWorks2012 database if it's not already connected to it. The word GO doesn't really do anything except divide the code up into separate distinct code batches.

When retrieving from a table, you still have a select-list as in Listing 2-1; however, your select-list typically contains column names from a table. The select-list in Listing 2-2 requests data from the BusinessEntityID and JobTitle columns, which are both found in the Employee table. The Employee table is in turn found in the HumanResources schema.

Figure 2-3 shows the output from executing the code in Listing 2-2. There is only one set of results, because there is only one SELECT statement.

	BusinessEntityID	Job Title
1	1	Chief Executive Officer
2	2	Vice President of Engineering
3	3	Engineering Manager
4	4	Senior Tool Designer
5	5	Design Engineer
6	6	Design Engineer
7	7	Research and Development Manager
8	8	Research and Development Engineer
9	9	Research and Development Engineer
10	10	Research and Development Manager
11	11	Senior Tool Designer
12	12	Tool Designer
13	13	Tool Designer
14	14	Senior Design Engineer

Figure 2-3. The partial results of running a query with a FROM clause

Notice that the FROM clause in Listing 2-2 specifies the table name in two parts: HumanResources.Employee. The first part—HumanResources—is a schema name. In SQL Server 2012, groups of related tables can be organized together as schemas. You don't always need to provide those schema names, but it's a best practice to do so. Two schemas can potentially each contain a table named Employee, and those would be different tables with different data. Specifying the schema name as part of your table reference eliminates a source of potential confusion and error.

To retrieve all the columns from a table, you can use the * symbol, also known as *asterisk, star,* or *splat.* Run the following statement to try this shortcut: SELECT * FROM HumanResources.Employee. You will see that all the columns from the table are returned.

The asterisk technique is useful for performing a quick query, but you should avoid it in a production application or process. Retrieving more data than you really need may have a negative impact on performance. Why retrieve all the columns from a table and pull more data across the network when you need only a few columns? Using SELECT * also comprises performance by ignoring any indexes created on table columns. This is because indexes are normally based off a WHERE clause filter (see the section call "Filtering Data" later in this chapter). If the SQL Server query optimizer doesn't have a filter, it will default to a full table scan to find the data. Besides performance, application code may break if an additional column is added to or removed from the table. Additionally, there might be security reasons for returning only some of the columns. Best practice is to write select-lists specifying exactly the columns that you need and return only the rows you need.

Generating a Select-List

You might think that typing all the required columns for a select-list is tedious work. Luckily, SQL Server Management Studio provides a shortcut for writing good SELECT statements. Follow these instructions to learn the shortcut:

1. In the Object Explorer, expand Databases.

2. Expand the AdventureWorks2012 database.

3. Expand Tables.

4. Right-click the HumanResources.Employee table.

5. Choose Script Table as ➤ Select To ➤ New Query Editor Window.

You now have a properly formed SELECT statement, as shown in Listing 2-3, that retrieves all the columns from the HumanResources.Employee table. You can easily remove any unneeded columns from the query.

Listing 2-3. A Scripted SELECT Statement

```
SELECT [BusinessEntityID]
      ,[NationalIDNumber]
      ,[LoginID]
      ,[OrganizationNode]
      ,[OrganizationLevel]
      ,[JobTitle]
      ,[BirthDate]
      ,[MaritalStatus]
      ,[Gender]
      ,[HireDate]
      ,[SalariedFlag]
      ,[VacationHours]
      ,[SickLeaveHours]
      ,[CurrentFlag]
      ,[rowguid]
      ,[ModifiedDate]
  FROM [AdventureWorks2012].[HumanResources].[Employee]
GO
```

Notice the brackets around the names in Listing 2-3. Column and table names need to follow specific naming rules so that SQL Server's parser can recognize them. When a table, column, or database has a name that doesn't follow those rules, you can still use that name, but you must enclose it within square brackets ([]). Automated tools often enclose *all* names within square brackets as a "just-in-case" measure.

Also notice that the FROM clause in Listing 2-3 mentions the database name: [AdventureWorks2012]. You need to specify a database name only when accessing a database other than the one to which you are currently connected. For example, if you are currently connected to the master database, you can access data from AdventureWorks2012 by specifying the database name. Again, though, automated tools often specify the database name regardless.

■ **Note** Another shortcut to typing all the column names is to click and drag the column(s) from the left side of Management Studio into the query window. For example, if you click on the Columns folder and drag it to the query window, SQL Server will list all the columns.

Mixing Literals and Column Names

You can mix literal values and column names in one statement. Listing 2-4 shows an example. SQL Server allows you to create or rename a column within a query by using what is known as an *alias*. You use the keyword AS to specify an alias for the column. This is especially useful when using literal values where you create a column name in the T-SQL statement that doesn't exist in the table.

Listing 2-4. Mixing Literal Values and Column Names

```
USE AdventureWorks2012;
GO
SELECT 'A Literal Value' AS "Literal Value",
    BusinessEntityID AS EmployeeID,
    LoginID JobTitle
FROM HumanResources.Employee;
```

Go ahead and execute the query in Listing 2-4. You should see results similar to those in Figure 2-4. Notice the column names in your results. The column names are the aliases that you specified in your query. You can alias any column, giving you complete control over the headers for your result sets.

Results

	Literal Value	EmployeeID	Job Title
1	A Literal Value	225	adventure-works\alan0
2	A Literal Value	193	adventure-works\alejandro0
3	A Literal Value	163	adventure-works\alex0
4	A Literal Value	109	adventure-works\alice0
5	A Literal Value	287	adventure-works\amy0
6	A Literal Value	214	adventure-works\andreas0
7	A Literal Value	47	adventure-works\andrew0
8	A Literal Value	164	adventure-works\andrew1
9	A Literal Value	149	adventure-works\andy0
10	A Literal Value	115	adventure-works\angela0
11	A Literal Value	137	adventure-works\anibal0
12	A Literal Value	260	adventure-works\annette0
13	A Literal Value	33	adventure-works\annik0
14	A Literal Value	252	adventure-works\arvind0
15	A Literal Value	222	adventure-works\ascott0
16	A Literal Value	265	adventure-works\ashvini0
17	A Literal Value	183	adventure-works\barbara0
18	A Literal Value	245	adventure-works\barbara1
19	A Literal Value	131	adventure-works\baris0

Figure 2-4. The results of using aliases

The keyword AS is optional. You can specify an alias name immediately following a column name. If an alias contains a space or is a reserved word, you can surround the alias with square brackets, single quotes, or double quotes. If the alias follows the rules for naming objects, the quotes or square brackets are not required.

Be aware that any word listed immediately after a column within the SELECT list is treated as an alias. If you forget to add the comma between two column names, the second column name will be used as the alias for the first. Omitting this comma is a common error. Look carefully at the query in Listing 2-4, and you'll see that the intent is to display the LoginID and JobTitle columns. Because the comma was left out between those two column names, the name of the LoginID column was changed to JobTitle. JobTitle was treated as an alias rather than as an additional column. Watch for and avoid this common mistake.

Reading about T-SQL and typing in code examples are wonderful ways to learn. The best way to learn, however, is to figure out the code for yourself. Imagine learning how to swim by reading about it instead of jumping into the water. Practice now with what you have learned so far. Follow the instructions in Exercise 2-1, and write a few queries to test what you know.

EXERCISE 2-1

For this exercise, switch to the AdventureWorks2012 database. You can find the solutions in the Appendix.

Remember that you can expand the tables in the Object Explorer to see the list of table names and then expand the table to see the list of column names.

Now, try your hand at writing the following tasks:

1. Write a SELECT statement that lists the customers along with their ID numbers. Include the StoreID and the AccountNumber from the Sales.Customers table.

2. Write a SELECT statement that lists the name, product number, and color of each product from the Production.Product table.

3. Write a SELECT statement that lists the customer ID numbers and sales order ID numbers from the Sales.SalesOrderHeader table.

4. Answer this question: Why should you specify column names rather than an asterisk when writing the select-list? Give at least two reasons.

Filtering Data

Usually an application requires only a fraction of the rows from a table at any given time. For example, an order-entry application that shows the order history will need to display the orders for only one customer at a time. There might be millions of orders in the database, but the operator of the software will view only a handful of rows instead of the entire table. Filtering data is a very important part of T-SQL.

Adding a WHERE Clause

To filter the rows returned from a query, you will add a WHERE clause to your SELECT statement. The database engine processes the WHERE clause second, right after the FROM clause. The WHERE clause will contain expressions, called *predicates*, that can be evaluated to TRUE, FALSE, or UNKNOWN. You will learn more about UNKNOWN in the "Working with Nothing" section later in the chapter. The WHERE clause syntax is as follows:

```
SELECT <column1>,<column2>
FROM <schema>.<table>
WHERE <column> = <value>;
```

Listing 2-5 shows the syntax and some examples demonstrating how to compare a column to a literal value. The following examples are from the AdventureWorks2012 database unless specified otherwise. Be sure to type each query into the query window and execute the statement to see how it works. Make sure you understand how the expression in the WHERE clause affects the results returned by each query. Notice that tick marks, or single quotes, have been used around literal strings and dates.

Listing 2-5. How to Use the WHERE Clause

```
USE AdventureWorks2012;
GO
--1
SELECT CustomerID, SalesOrderID
FROM Sales.SalesOrderHeader
WHERE CustomerID = 11000;

--2
SELECT CustomerID, SalesOrderID
FROM Sales.SalesOrderHeader
WHERE SalesOrderID = 43793;

--3
SELECT CustomerID, SalesOrderID, OrderDate
FROM Sales.SalesOrderHeader
WHERE OrderDate = '2005-07-02';

--4
SELECT BusinessEntityID, LoginID, JobTitle
FROM HumanResources.Employee
WHERE JobTitle = 'Chief Executive Officer';
```

Each query in Listing 2-5 returns rows that are filtered by the expression in the WHERE clause. Be sure to check the results of each query to make sure that the expected rows are returned (see Figure 2-5). Each query returns only the information specified in that query's WHERE clause.

	CustomerID	SalesOrderID
1	11000	43793
2	11000	51522
3	11000	57418

	CustomerID	SalesOrderID
1	11000	43793

	CustomerID	SalesOrderID	OrderDate
1	27645	43702	2005-07-02 00:00:00.000
2	16624	43703	2005-07-02 00:00:00.000
3	11005	43704	2005-07-02 00:00:00.000
4	11011	43705	2005-07-02 00:00:00.000

	BusinessEntityID	LoginID	JobTitle
1	1	adventure-works\ken0	Chief Executive Officer

Figure 2-5. *The results of using the WHERE clause*

Using WHERE Clauses with Alternate Operators

Within WHERE clause expressions, you can use many comparison operators, not just the equal sign. Books Online lists the following operators:

> (greater than)

< (less than)

= (equals)

<= (less than or equal to)

>= (greater than or equal to)

!= (not equal to)

<> (not equal to)

!< (not less than)

!> (not greater than)

Type in and execute the queries in Listing 2-6 to practice using these additional operators in the WHERE clause.

Listing 2-6. Using Operators with the WHERE Clause

```
USE AdventureWorks2012;
GO
--Using a DateTime column
--1
SELECT CustomerID, SalesOrderID, OrderDate
FROM Sales.SalesOrderHeader
WHERE OrderDate > '2005-07-05';

--2
SELECT CustomerID, SalesOrderID, OrderDate
FROM Sales.SalesOrderHeader
WHERE OrderDate < '2005-07-05';

--3
SELECT CustomerID, SalesOrderID, OrderDate
FROM Sales.SalesOrderHeader
WHERE OrderDate >= '2005-07-05';

--4
SELECT CustomerID, SalesOrderID, OrderDate
FROM Sales.SalesOrderHeader
WHERE OrderDate <> '2005-07-05';

--5
SELECT CustomerID, SalesOrderID, OrderDate
FROM Sales.SalesOrderHeader
WHERE OrderDate != '2005-07-05';

--Using a numeric column
--6
SELECT SalesOrderID, SalesOrderDetailID, OrderQty
FROM Sales.SalesOrderDetail
WHERE OrderQty > 10;

--7
SELECT SalesOrderID, SalesOrderDetailID, OrderQty
FROM Sales.SalesOrderDetail
WHERE OrderQty <= 10;

--8
SELECT SalesOrderID, SalesOrderDetailID, OrderQty
FROM Sales.SalesOrderDetail
WHERE OrderQty <> 10;

--9
SELECT SalesOrderID, SalesOrderDetailID, OrderQty
FROM Sales.SalesOrderDetail
WHERE OrderQty != 10;
```

```
--Using a string column
--10
SELECT BusinessEntityID, FirstName
FROM Person.Person
WHERE FirstName <> 'Catherine';

--11
SELECT BusinessEntityID, FirstName
FROM Person.Person
WHERE FirstName != 'Catherine';

--12
SELECT BusinessEntityID, FirstName
FROM Person.Person
WHERE FirstName > 'M';

--13
SELECT BusinessEntityID, FirstName
FROM Person.Person
WHERE FirstName !> 'M';
```

Take a look at the results of each query to make sure that the results make sense and that you understand why you are getting them. Remember that both != and <> mean "not equal to" and are interchangeable. Using either operator should return the same results if all other aspects of a query are the same.

You may find the results of query 12 interesting. At first glance, you may think that only rows with the first name beginning with the letter *N* or later in the alphabet should be returned. However, if any FirstName value begins with *M* followed by at least one additional character, the value is greater than *M*, so the row will be returned. For example, *Ma* is greater than *M*.

Using BETWEEN

BETWEEN is another useful operator to be used in the WHERE clause. You can use it to specify an inclusive range of values. It is frequently used with dates but can be used with string and numeric data as well. Here is the syntax for BETWEEN:

```
SELECT <column1>,<column2>
FROM <schema>.<table>
WHERE <column> BETWEEN <value1> AND <value2>;
```

Type in and execute the code in Listing 2-7 to learn how to use BETWEEN.

Listing 2-7. Using BETWEEN

```
USE AdventureWorks2012
GO
--1
SELECT CustomerID, SalesOrderID, OrderDate
FROM Sales.SalesOrderHeader
WHERE OrderDate BETWEEN '2005-07-02' AND '2005-07-04';
```

```
--2
SELECT CustomerID, SalesOrderID, OrderDate
FROM Sales.SalesOrderHeader
WHERE CustomerID BETWEEN 25000 AND 25005;

--3
SELECT BusinessEntityID, JobTitle
FROM HumanResources.Employee
WHERE JobTitle BETWEEN 'C' and 'E';

--An invalid BETWEEN expression
--4
SELECT CustomerID, SalesOrderID, OrderDate
FROM Sales.SalesOrderHeader
WHERE CustomerID BETWEEN 25005 AND 25000;
```

Pay close attention to the results of Listing 2-7 shown in Figure 2-6. Query 1 returns all orders placed on the two dates specified in the query as well as the orders placed between the dates. You will see the same behavior from the second query—all orders placed by customers with customer IDs within the range specified. What can you expect from query 3? You will see all job titles that start with *C* or *D*. You will not see the job titles beginning with *E*, however. A job title composed of *only* the letter *E* would be returned in the results. Any job title beginning with *E* and at least one other character is greater than *E* and therefore not within the range. For example, the *Ex* in *Executive* is greater than just *E*, so any job titles beginning with *Executive* get eliminated.

	CustomerID	SalesOrderID	OrderDate
1	27645	43702	2005-07-02 00:00:00.000
2	16624	43703	2005-07-02 00:00:00.000
3	11005	43704	2005-07-02 00:00:00.000
4	11011	43705	2005-07-02 00:00:00.000
5	27621	43706	2005-07-03 00:00:00.000
6	27616	43707	2005-07-03 00:00:00.000
7	20042	43708	2005-07-03 00:00:00.000
8	16351	43709	2005-07-03 00:00:00.000

	CustomerID	SalesOrderID	OrderDate
1	25000	73018	2008-06-15 00:00:00.000
2	25001	61662	2008-01-08 00:00:00.000
3	25002	61397	2008-01-03 00:00:00.000
4	25003	60269	2007-12-18 00:00:00.000
5	25004	74889	2008-07-24 00:00:00.000
6	25005	55344	2007-10-01 00:00:00.000

	BusinessEntityID	JobTitle
1	1	Chief Executive Officer
2	5	Design Engineer
3	6	Design Engineer
4	15	Design Engineer
5	217	Document Control M...
6	218	Control Specialist
7	219	Document Control As...
8	220	Document Control As...

CustomerID	SalesOrderID	OrderDate

Figure 2-6. The partial results of queries with BETWEEN

Query 4 returns no rows at all because the values listed in the BETWEEN expression are switched. No values meet the qualification of being greater than or equal to 25,005 and also less than or equal to 25,000. Make sure you always list the lower value first and the higher value second when using BETWEEN.

Using NOT BETWEEN

To find values outside a particular range of values, you write the WHERE clause expression using BETWEEN along with the NOT keyword. In this case, the query returns any rows outside the range. Try the examples in Listing 2-8, and compare them to the results from Listing 2-7.

Listing 2-8. Using NOT BETWEEN

```
Use AdventureWorks2012
GO
--1
SELECT CustomerID, SalesOrderID, OrderDate
FROM Sales.SalesOrderHeader
WHERE OrderDate NOT BETWEEN '2005-07-02' AND '2005-07-04';

--2
SELECT CustomerID, SalesOrderID, OrderDate
FROM Sales.SalesOrderHeader
WHERE CustomerID NOT BETWEEN 25000 AND 25005;

--3
SELECT BusinessEntityID, JobTitle
FROM HumanResources.Employee
WHERE JobTitle NOT BETWEEN 'C' and 'E';

--An invalid BETWEEN expression
--4
SELECT CustomerID, SalesOrderID, OrderDate
FROM Sales.SalesOrderHeader
WHERE CustomerID NOT BETWEEN 25005 AND 25000;
```

Query 1 displays all orders placed before July 2, 2001 (2001-07-02) or after July 4, 2001 (2001-07-04)—in other words, any orders placed outside the range specified (see Figure 2-7). Query 2 displays the orders placed by customers with customer IDs less than 25,000 or greater than 25,005. When using the NOT operator with BETWEEN, the values specified in the expression don't show up in the results. Query 3 returns all job titles beginning with *A* and *B*. It also displays any job titles beginning with *E* and at least one more character, as well as any job titles starting with a letter greater than *E*. If a title consists of just the letter *E*, it will not show up in the results. This is just the opposite of what you saw in Listing 2-7.

Results

	CustomerID	SalesOrderID	OrderDate
1	29825	43659	2005-07-01 00:00:00.000
2	29672	43660	2005-07-01 00:00:00.000
3	29734	43661	2005-07-01 00:00:00.000
4	29994	43662	2005-07-01 00:00:00.000
5	29565	43663	2005-07-01 00:00:00.000

	CustomerID	SalesOrderID	OrderDate
1	29825	43659	2005-07-01 00:00:00.000
2	29672	43660	2005-07-01 00:00:00.000
3	29734	43661	2005-07-01 00:00:00.000
4	29994	43662	2005-07-01 00:00:00.000
5	29565	43663	2005-07-01 00:00:00.000

	BusinessEntityID	Job Title
1	2	Vice President of Engineering
2	3	Engineering Manager
3	4	Senior Tool Designer
4	7	Research and Developmen...
5	8	Research and Developmen...

	CustomerID	SalesOrderID	OrderDate
1	29825	43659	2005-07-01 00:00:00.000
2	29672	43660	2005-07-01 00:00:00.000
3	29734	43661	2005-07-01 00:00:00.000
4	29994	43662	2005-07-01 00:00:00.000
5	29565	43663	2005-07-01 00:00:00.000
6	29898	43664	2005-07-01 00:00:00.000

Figure 2-7. *The partial results of queries with NOT BETWEEN*

Query 4 with the incorrect BETWEEN expression returns all the rows in the table. Since no customer ID values can be less than or equal to 25,005 and also be greater than or equal to 25,000, no rows meet the criteria in the BETWEEN expression. By adding the NOT operator, every row ends up in the results, which is probably not the original intent.

Filtering On Date and Time

Some temporal data columns store the time as well as the date. If you attempt to filter on such a column specifying only the date, you may retrieve incomplete results. Type in and run the code in Listing 2-9 to create and populate a temporary table that will be used to illustrate this issue. Don't worry about trying to understand the table creation code at this point.

Listing 2-9. Table Setup for Date/Time Example

```
CREATE TABLE #DateTimeExample(
    ID INT NOT NULL IDENTITY PRIMARY KEY,
    MyDate DATETIME2(0) NOT NULL,
    MyValue VARCHAR(25) NOT NULL
);
GO
INSERT INTO #DateTimeExample
    (MyDate,MyValue)
VALUES ('1/2/2009 10:30','Bike'),
    ('1/3/2009 13:00','Trike'),
    ('1/3/2009 13:10','Bell'),
    ('1/3/2009 17:35','Seat');
```

Now that the table is in place, type in and execute the code in Listing 2-10 to see what happens when filtering on the MyDate column.

Listing 2-10. Filtering On Date and Time Columns

```
--1
SELECT ID, MyDate, MyValue
FROM #DateTimeExample
WHERE MyDate = '2009-01-03';

--2
SELECT ID, MyDate, MyValue
FROM #DateTimeExample
WHERE MyDate BETWEEN '2009-01-03 00:00:00' AND '2009-01-03 23:59:59';
```

Figure 2-8 shows the results of the two queries. Suppose you want to retrieve a list of entries from January 3, 2009 (2009-01-03). Query 1 tries to do that but returns no results. Results will be returned only for entries where the MyDate value is precisely 2009-01-03 00:00:00, and there are no such entries. The second query returns the expected results—all values where the date is 2009-01-03. It does that by taking the time of day into account. To be even more accurate, the query could be written using two expressions: one filtering for dates greater than or equal to 2009-01-03 and another filtering for dates less than 2009-01-04. You will learn how to write WHERE clauses with multiple expressions in the "Using WHERE Clauses with Two Predicates" section later in this chapter.

Figure 2-8. Results of filtering on a date and time column

So what would happen if you formatted the date differently? Will you get the same results if slashes (/)(/)are used or if the month is spelled out (in other words, as January 3, 2009)? SQL Server does not store the date using any particular character-based format but rather as an integer representing the number of days between 1901-01-01 and the date specified. If the data type holds the time, the time is stored as the number of clock ticks past midnight. As long as you pass a date in an appropriate format, the value will be recognized as a date.

Writing a WHERE clause is as much an art as a skill. Take the time to practice what you have learned so far by completing Exercise 2-2.

EXERCISE 2-2

Use the AdventureWorks2012 database to complete this exercise. Be sure to run each query and check the results. You can go back and review the examples in the section if you don't remember how to write the queries. You can find the solutions in the Appendix.

1.   Write a query using a WHERE clause that displays all the employees listed in the HumanResources.Employee table who have the job title Research and Development Engineer. Display the business entity ID number, the login ID, and the title for each one.

2.   Write a query using a WHERE clause that displays all the names in Person.Person with the middle name J. Display the first, last, and middle names along with the ID numbers.

3.   Write a query displaying all the columns of the Production.ProductCostHistory table from the rows that were modified on June 17, 2005. Be sure to use one of the features in SQL Server Management Studio to help you write this query.

4.   Rewrite the query you wrote in question 1, changing it so that the employees who do not have the title Research and Development Engineer are displayed.

5.   Write a query that displays all the rows from the Person.Person table where the rows were modified after December 29, 2005. Display the business entity ID number, the name columns, and the modified date.

6. Rewrite the last query so that the rows that were not modified on December 29, 2005, are displayed.

7. Rewrite the query from question 5 so that it displays the rows modified during December 2000.

8. Rewrite the query from question 5 so that it displays the rows that were not modified during December 2005.

9. Explain why a WHERE clause should be used in many of your T-SQL queries.

Pattern Matching with LIKE

Sometimes you know only part of the value that will match the data stored in the table. For example, you may need to search for one word within a description. You can perform searches with pattern matching using wildcards to find one value within another value.

Pattern matching is possible by using the keyword LIKE in the expression instead of equal to or one of the other operators. Most of the time, the percent (%) character is used as a wildcard along with LIKE to represent any number of characters. You will also see the underscore (_) used as a wildcard to replace just one character, but it's not used as often. Type in and run the code from Listing 2-11 to learn how to use LIKE.

Listing 2-11. Using LIKE with %

```
USE AdventureWorks2012;
GO
--1
SELECT DISTINCT LastName
FROM Person.Person
WHERE LastName LIKE 'Sand%';

--2
SELECT DISTINCT LastName
FROM Person.Person
WHERE LastName NOT LIKE 'Sand%';

--3
SELECT DISTINCT LastName
FROM Person.Person
WHERE LastName LIKE '%Z%';

--4
SELECT DISTINCT LastName
FROM Person.Person
WHERE LastName LIKE 'Bec_';
```

The queries in Listing 2-11 contain the keyword DISTINCT to eliminate duplicates in the results shown in Figure 2-9. Query 1 returns all rows where the last name starts with *Sand*. Query 2 returns the opposite—it returns all the rows not returned by query 1, which are those rows where the last name does not start with *Sand*. Query 3 returns all rows that contain a *Z* anywhere in the last name. Query 4 will return only the last name *Beck* or any last name starting with *Bec* and one more character, but not the last name *Becker* since the underscore can replace only one character.

	LastName
1	Sandberg
2	Sanders
3	Sandidge
4	Sandoval

	LastName
1	Abbas
2	Abel
3	Abercrombie
4	Abolrous

	LastName
1	Zabokritski
2	Zare
3	Zeman
4	Zeng

	LastName
1	Beck

Figure 2-9. The partial results of queries with LIKE

Restricting the Characters in Pattern Matches

The value replacing a wildcard may be restricted to a list or range of characters. To do this, surround the possible values or range by square brackets ([]). Alternately, include the ^ symbol to list characters or the range of characters that you don't want to use as replacements. Here is the syntax for using brackets as the wildcard:

```
SELECT <column1>,<column2>
FROM <schema>.<table>
WERE <column> LIKE 'value[a-c]';

SELECT <column1>,<column2>
FROM <schema>.<table>
WERE <column> LIKE 'value[a,b,c]';

SELECT <column1>,<column2>
FROM <schema>.<table>
WERE <column> LIKE 'value[^d]';
```

Type in and execute the code from Listing 2-12, which shows some examples. You will probably not encounter the square bracket technique very often, but you should be familiar with the syntax in case you run into it.

Listing 2-12. Using Square Brackets with LIKE

```
USE AdventureWorks2012;
GO

--1
SELECT DISTINCT LastName
FROM Person.Person
WHERE LastName LIKE 'Cho[i-k]';

--2
SELECT DISTINCT LastName
FROM Person.Person
WHERE LastName LIKE 'Cho[i,j,k]';

--3
SELECT DISTINCT LastName
FROM Person.Person
WHERE LastName LIKE 'Cho[^i]';
```

Figure 2-10 displays the results of Listing 2-12. Queries 1 and 2 returns unique rows with a last name of Choi, Choj, or Chok because the pattern specifies the range i to k. Query 1 specifies the range of values, while query 2 explicitly lists the allowable values that may be replaced. Query 3 returns unique rows that have a last name beginning with Cho and ending with any character except for i.

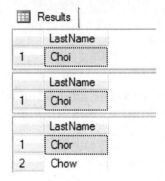

Figure 2-10. The results of queries restricting characters in matches

Combining Wildcards

You may combine wildcards to create even more elaborate patterns. Remember that the percent sign (%) replaces any number of characters, the underscore (_) replaces one character, and the square brackets ([]) replace one character based on the values within the brackets. Listing 2-13 demonstrates some examples. Type in and execute the code to see how this works.

Listing 2-13. Combining Wildcards in One Pattern

```
USE AdventureWorks2012;
GO
--1
SELECT LastName
FROM Person.Person
WHERE LastName LIKE 'Ber[r,g]%';

--2
SELECT LastName
FROM Person.Person
WHERE LastName LIKE 'Ber[^r]%';

--3
SELECT LastName
FROM Person.Person
WHERE LastName LIKE 'Be%n_';
```

View Figure 2-11 to see the results. Query 1 returns all rows with a last name beginning with *Ber* followed by either *r* or *g* (which is signified by the characters within the brackets) and then by any number of characters. Query 2 returns all rows with a last name beginning with *Ber* followed by any letter except for *r* and then by any number of characters. Query 3 returns all rows with a last name beginning with *Be* followed by any number of characters, except that the next-to-last character must be an *n*.

Figure 2-11. The results of queries with multiple wildcards

You will probably find LIKE used frequently in queries, so it's important to understand how it works. Practice the skills you have just learned by completing Exercise 2-3.

EXERCISE 2-3

Use the AdventureWorks2012 database to complete this exercise. Follow the steps in this exercise to test your knowledge of pattern matching and wildcard queries. You can find the solutions in the Appendix.

1. Write a query that displays the product ID and name for each product from the Production.Product table with a name starting with *Chain*.

2. Write a query like the one in question 1 that displays the products with *Paint* in the name.

3. Change the last query so that the products without *Paint* in the name are displayed.

4. Write a query that displays the business entity ID number, first name, middle name, and last name from the Person.Person table for only those rows that have *E* or *B* stored in the middle name column.

5. Explain the difference between the following two queries:

```
SELECT FirstName
FROM Person.Person
WHERE LastName LIKE 'Ja%es';
SELECT FirstName
FROM Person.Person
WHERE LastName LIKE 'Ja_es';
```

Using WHERE Clauses with Two Predicates

So far, the examples have shown only one condition or predicate in the WHERE clause, but the WHERE clause can be much more complex. They can have multiple predicates by using the logical operators OR. Type in and execute the code in Listing 2-14 that demonstrates how to use AND and OR to combine two predicates.

Listing 2-14. How to Use AND and OR

```
USE AdventureWorks2012;
GO

--1
SELECT BusinessEntityID,FirstName,MiddleName,LastName
FROM Person.Person
WHERE FirstName = 'Ken' AND LastName = 'Myer';

--2
SELECT BusinessEntityID,FirstName,MiddleName,LastName
FROM Person.Person
WHERE LastName = 'Myer' OR LastName = 'Meyer';
```

Figure 2-12 shows the results. Query 1 returns any rows with the first name *Ken* and the last name *Myer* because both expressions must evaluate to true. Query 2 returns any rows with either the last name *Myer* or the last name *Meyer* because only one of the expressions must evaluate to true.

	BusinessEntityID	FirstName	MiddleName	LastName
1	1525	Ken	NULL	Myer
2	203	Ken	L	Myer

	BusinessEntityID	FirstName	MiddleName	LastName
1	1459	Deanna	NULL	Meyer
2	1455	Eric	B.	Meyer
3	1457	Helen	M.	Meyer
4	2140	Ken	NULL	Meyer
5	1523	Dorothy	J.	Myer
6	1525	Ken	NULL	Myer
7	203	Ken	L	Myer
8	2319	Linda	NULL	Myer

Figure 2-12. The results of queries with two predicates in the WHERE clause

Using WHERE Clauses with Three or More Predicates

A WHERE clause can contain more than two predicates combined by the logical operators AND and OR. If a WHERE clause contains more than two predicates using both AND and OR, you must be careful to ensure that the query returns the expected results. Type in and execute the code in Listing 2-15 to see how the order of the predicates affects the results and how to use parentheses to enforce the correct logic.

Listing 2-15. WHERE Clauses with Three Predicates

```
USE AdventureWorks2012;
GO

--1
SELECT BusinessEntityID,FirstName,MiddleName,LastName
FROM Person.Person
WHERE FirstName = 'Ken' AND LastName = 'Myer'
    OR LastName = 'Meyer';


--2
SELECT BusinessEntityID,FirstName,MiddleName,LastName
FROM Person.Person
WHERE LastName = 'Myer' OR LastName = 'Meyer'
    AND FirstName = 'Ken';


--3
SELECT BusinessEntityID,FirstName,MiddleName,LastName
FROM Person.Person
WHERE LastName = 'Meyer'
    AND FirstName = 'Ken' OR LastName = 'Myer';
```

```
--4
SELECT BusinessEntityID,FirstName,MiddleName,LastName
FROM Person.Person
WHERE FirstName = 'Ken' AND (LastName = 'Myer'
    OR LastName = 'Meyer');
```

You can see the results of Listing 2-15 in Figure 2-13. Once both logical operators AND and OR are used in the WHERE clause, things can get complicated. The logical operator AND takes precedence over OR; therefore, the database engine evaluates AND first. For example, suppose you want to find a name in the Person.Person table, *Ken Meyer*, but you can't remember the spelling of the last name. It could be *Myer*. Listing 2-15 shows four attempts to solve this problem, but only the last one is correct.

	BusinessEntityID	FirstName	MiddleName	LastName
1	1459	Deanna	NULL	Meyer
2	1455	Eric	B.	Meyer
3	1457	Helen	M.	Meyer
4	2140	Ken	NULL	Meyer
5	1525	Ken	NULL	Myer
6	203	Ken	L	Myer

	BusinessEntityID	FirstName	MiddleName	LastName
1	2140	Ken	NULL	Meyer
2	1523	Dorothy	J.	Myer
3	1525	Ken	NULL	Myer
4	203	Ken	L	Myer
5	2319	Linda	NULL	Myer

	BusinessEntityID	FirstName	MiddleName	LastName
1	2140	Ken	NULL	Meyer
2	1523	Dorothy	J.	Myer
3	1525	Ken	NULL	Myer
4	203	Ken	L	Myer
5	2319	Linda	NULL	Myer

	BusinessEntityID	FirstName	MiddleName	LastName
1	2140	Ken	NULL	Meyer
2	1525	Ken	NULL	Myer
3	203	Ken	L	Myer

Figure 2-13. The results of queries that force precedence to ensure the correct results

Query 1 returns the rows with the name *Ken Myer* but also returns any row with the last name *Meyer*. Queries 2 and 3 return identical results—the row with *Ken Meyer* and any rows with the last name *Myer*. Finally, by using the parentheses, query 4 returns the correct results.

When using multiple conditions, you must be very careful about the *precedence*, or order, that the expressions are evaluated. The database engine evaluates the conditions in the WHERE clause from left to right, but AND takes precedence over OR. Rearranging the terms can produce different but possibly still invalid results as in the previous example. To guarantee that the query is correct, always use parentheses to enforce the logic once the logical operator OR is added to the WHERE clause.

Using NOT with Parentheses

Another interesting twist when using parentheses is that you can negate the meaning of the expression within them by specifying the keyword NOT. For example, you could try to find the rows where the first name is *Ken* and the last name can't be *Myer* or *Meyer*. Type in and execute Listing 2-16 to see two ways to write the query.

Listing 2-16. Using NOT with Parentheses

```
USE AdventureWorks2012;
GO
--1
SELECT BusinessEntityID,FirstName,MiddleName,LastName
FROM Person.Person
WHERE FirstName='Ken' AND LastName <> 'Myer'
    AND LastName <> 'Meyer';

--2
SELECT BusinessEntityID,FirstName,MiddleName,LastName
FROM Person.Person
WHERE FirstName='Ken'
    AND NOT (LastName = 'Myer' OR LastName = 'Meyer');
```

Often multiple ways exist to solve the same problem, as in this case. Query 1 contains three expressions. One expression restricts the rows to those where FirstName is *Ken*. The other two expressions compare LastName to a value using not equal to (<>). In query 2, the expressions within the parentheses are evaluated first. Next, that result is negated by the NOT operator to find all last names that are not *Myer* or *Meyer*. Finally, only the rows that also have the first name *Ken* are returned. You can see the results in Figure 2-14.

As a best practice, always employ parentheses to enforce precedence when the WHERE clause includes the logical operator OR. Not only will this decrease the possibility of an incorrect WHERE clause, but it will increase the readability of the query.

	BusinessEntityID	First Name	MiddleName	LastName
1	2300	Ken	NULL	Kwok
2	1726	Ken	NULL	Sánchez
3	1	Ken	J	Sánchez

	BusinessEntityID	First Name	MiddleName	LastName
1	2300	Ken	NULL	Kwok
2	1726	Ken	NULL	Sánchez
3	1	Ken	J	Sánchez

Figure 2-14. The identical results of two queries with different techniques

Using the IN Operator

The IN operator is very useful when multiple values must be compared to the same column. Query 4 in Listing 2-15 could have been written in a more straightforward way using the IN operator. Follow the IN operator with a list of possible values for a column within parentheses. Here is the syntax:

```
SELECT <column1>,<column2>
FROM <schema>.<table>
WHERE <column> IN (<value1>,<value2>);
```

Type in and execute the code from Listing 2-17. The queries in this listing demonstrate how to use the IN operator. Review the results to be sure that you understand them.

Listing 2-17. Using the IN Operator

```
USE AdventureWorks2012
GO


--1
SELECT BusinessEntityID,FirstName,MiddleName,LastName
FROM Person.Person
WHERE FirstName = 'Ken' AND
    LastName IN ('Myer','Meyer');

--2
SELECT TerritoryID, Name
FROM Sales.SalesTerritory
WHERE TerritoryID IN (2,1,4,5);

--3
SELECT TerritoryID, Name
FROM Sales.SalesTerritory
WHERE TerritoryID NOT IN (2,1,4,5);
```

You will probably find that the operator IN can simplify many queries. Query 1 solves the same problem as in Listing 2-15. The original query used two expressions to compare two values to the same column within parentheses: (LastName = 'Myer' OR LastName = 'Meyer'). By using the IN operator, you were able to eliminate one expression by including both values in the IN list. You can also use IN with numbers and dates. Query 2 returns all rows with TerritoryID 2, 1, 4, or 5. By using NOT, query 3 returns the opposite results. Figure 2-15 shows the results of the three queries from Listing 2-17.

Results

	BusinessEntityID	FirstName	MiddleName	LastName
1	2140	Ken	NULL	Meyer
2	1525	Ken	NULL	Myer
3	203	Ken	L	Myer

	TerritoryID	Name
1	1	Northwest
2	2	Northeast
3	4	Southwest
4	5	Southeast

	TerritoryID	Name
1	9	Australia
2	6	Canada
3	3	Central
4	7	France
5	8	Germany
6	10	United Kingdom

Figure 2-15. The results of queries using the IN operator

As the WHERE clause becomes more complicated, it becomes very easy to make a mistake. Complete Exercise 2-4 to practice writing multiple predicates, WHERE clauses with multiple predicates, and the IN operator.

EXERCISE 2-4

Use the AdventureWorks2012 database to complete this exercise. Be sure to check your results to assure that they make sense. You can find the solutions in the Appendix.

1. Write a query displaying the order ID, order date, and total due from the Sales.SalesOrderHeader table. Retrieve only those rows where the order was placed during the month of September 2005 and the total due exceeded $1,000.

2. Change the query in question so that only the dates September 1–3, 2005, are retrieved. See whether you can figure out three different ways to write this query.

3. Write a query displaying the sales orders where the total due exceeds $1,000. Retrieve only those rows where the salesperson ID is 279 or the territory ID is 6.

4. Change the query in question 3 so that territory 4 is included.

5. Explain when it makes sense to use the IN operator.

Working with Nothing

Probably nothing causes more aggravation to T-SQL developers than NULL values. NULL means that a value has not been entered for a particular column in a row. Suppose you have an e-commerce application that requires the customer to fill in information such as name and address. In this example, the phone number is optional. What does it mean if the customer does not enter a phone number and the table ends up with NULL in the PhoneNumber column of the Customer table? Does it mean that the customer does not have a phone? That's one possibility. Another is that the customer has at least one phone number but chose not to supply it since it was not required. Either way, the end result is that you have =.

Think now about what would happen if you had a list of 1,000,000 phone numbers and tried to figure out whether any of the phone numbers belonged to the customer. Even if you compared each phone number to the customer's row, one by one, you would never know whether any of the phone numbers were the right one. You would never know because you would be comparing 1,000,000 values to nothing. Conversely, can you guarantee that every one of your 1,000,000 phone numbers is not the missing phone number? No, you can't do that either, since the customer's phone number is unknown.

This example should give you an idea about the challenges of working with NULL values. Type in and execute the code in Listing 2-18 to work on some examples using real data.

Listing 2-18. An Example Illustrating NULL

```
USE AdventureWorks2012;
GO

--1) Returns 19,972 rows
SELECT MiddleName
FROM Person.Person;

--2) Returns 291 rows
SELECT MiddleName
FROM Person.Person
WHERE MiddleName = 'B';

--3) Returns 11,182 but 19,681 were expected
SELECT MiddleName
FROM Person.Person
WHERE MiddleName != 'B';

--4) Returns 19,681
SELECT MiddleName
FROM Person.Person
WHERE MiddleName IS NULL
    OR MiddleName !='B';
```

Query 1 with no WHERE clause returns 19,972 rows, the total number of rows in the table. Query 2 returns 291 rows with the middle name *B*. Logic follows that query 3 will return the difference of the two numbers: 19,681 rows. When you check the results of query 3, you will find that more than 8,000 rows are not accounted for. That is because the rows with NULL values can't be found by the expression containing not equal. Comparing NULL to *B* returns UNKNOWN, so the rows are not returned. You must specifically check for NULL values by using the IS NULL operator, as shown in query 4, which returns the correct number of rows.

Usually comparing the data in a column to a value or comparing the values from two columns returns either TRUE or FALSE. If the expression evaluates to TRUE, then the row is returned. If the expression evaluates to FALSE, then the row is not returned. If a value in the expression contains NULL, then the expression is resolved to UNKNOWN. In some ways, the behavior is like FALSE. When an expression resolves to UNKNOWN, the row is not returned. The problems begin when using any operator except for equal to (=). The opposite of FALSE is TRUE, but the opposite of UNKNOWN is still UNKNOWN.

■ **Note** Be aware that NULL is not a numeric value so it can't equal itself or any other value. T-SQL instead provides specific expressions and functions to test for NULL values. To test for a NULL value you will want to use the IS [NOT] NULL expression (http://msdn.microsoft.com/en-us/library/ms188795(v=SQL.110).aspx). The function ISNULL will replace a NULL value with a value specified in the query (see Chapter 3).

Neglecting to take possible NULL values into consideration can often cause incorrect results. Always remember to think about NULL values, especially when writing any expression containing NOT. Do the NULL values belong in the results? If so, you will have to check for NULL. You will also need to keep NULL values in mind when using the less than operator. NULL values will be left out of those results as well. Chapter 3 will show you some other options for working with NULL.

Understanding how NULL values can affect the results of your queries is one of the most important skills you will learn. Even experienced T-SQL developers struggle from time to time when working with NULL values. Be sure to complete Exercise 2-5 to practice what you have just learned.

EXERCISE 2-5

Use the AdventureWorks2012 database to complete this exercise. Make sure you consider how NULL values will affect your results. You can find the solutions in the Appendix.

1. Write a query displaying the ProductID, Name, and Color columns from rows in the Production.Product table. Display only those rows where no color has been assigned.

2. Write a query displaying the ProductID, Name, and Color columns from rows in the Production.Product table. Display only those rows in which the color is *known* not to be blue.

3. Write a query displaying ProductID, Name, Style, Size, and Color from the Production.Product table. Include only the rows where at least one of the Style, Size, or Color columns contains a value.

Performing a Full-Text Search

You have learned how to use LIKE to find a character match in data. Full-text search provides the ability to search for words or phrases within string or binary data columns similar to a web search such as Google or Bing. You can use LIKE for pattern matching only and not for searching binary data. Full-text search has support for multiple languages and other features such as synonym searches. Full-text search is especially beneficial for documents stored as binary data in the database.

Full-text search must be installed during the SQL Server setup, and a special full-text index needs to be created on the table. This book doesn't intend to teach you how to set up and manage full-text search, but it will show you how to write some of the basic queries. For more information about full-text search, see the book *Pro Full-Text Search in SQL Server 2008* by Hillary Cotter and Michael Coles (Apress, 2008). The AdventureWorks2012 database ships with three full-text indexes already in place. Table 2-1 lists the columns with full-text indexes included by default in AdventureWorks2012.

Table 2-1. Tables with Full-Text Indexes

Table Name	Column Name
Production.ProductReview	Comments
Production.Document	DocumentSummary
Production.Document	Document
HumanResources.JobCandidate	Resume

Using CONTAINS

CONTAINS is one of the functions used to search full-text indexes. You will learn more about functions in Chapter 3. The simplest way to use CONTAINS is to search a column for a particular word or phrase. Here is the syntax for CONTAINS:

```
SELECT <column1>,<column2>
FROM <schema>.<tablename>
WHERE CONTAINS(<indexed column>,<searchterm>);
```

Listing 2-19 shows how to use CONTAINS. Notice that the second query has a regular predicate in the WHERE clause as well. Be sure to type in and execute the code to learn how to use CONTAINS.

Listing 2-19. Using CONTAINS

```
USE AdventureWorks2012;
GO

--1
SELECT FileName
FROM Production.Document
WHERE Contains(Document,'important');

--2
SELECT FileName
FROM Production.Document
WHERE Contains(Document,' "service guidelines " ')
    AND DocumentLevel = 2;
```

Figure 2-16 displays the results. Notice how double quotes are used within single quotes to designate a phrase in query 2. Query 2 also demonstrates that both a full-text predicate and a regular predicate can be used in the same query. You may be wondering why the Document column is not part of the results since that is the search term. The document is actually a binary file, such as a Microsoft Word document, that must be opened by the appropriate application.

Results	
	FileName
1	Repair and Service Guidelines.doc
2	Crank Arm and Tire Maintenance.doc
3	Lubrication Maintenance.doc

	FileName
1	Repair and Service Guidelines.doc

Figure 2-16. *The results of a full-text search operation*

Using Multiple Terms with CONTAINS

You can use CONTAINS to find words in data that are not even next to each other by using AND, OR, and NEAR. You can use the operator AND NOT to find results with one term and not another. This syntax is similar to searches with Google or other search engines. Listing 2-20 demonstrates this technique.

Listing 2-20. *Multiple Terms in CONTAINS*

```
USE AdventureWorks2012;
GO

--1
SELECT FileName, DocumentSummary
FROM Production.Document
WHERE Contains(DocumentSummary,'bicycle AND reflectors');

--2
SELECT FileName, DocumentSummary
FROM Production.Document
WHERE CONTAINS(DocumentSummary,'bicycle AND NOT reflectors');

--3
SELECT FileName, DocumentSummary
FROM Production.Document
WHERE CONTAINS(DocumentSummary,'maintain NEAR bicycle AND NOT reflectors');
```

Figure 2-17 shows the results. In this case, a regular string data column, DocumentSummary, is searched so that you can verify the results.

	FileName	Document Summary
1	Front Reflector Bracket Installation.doc	Reflectors are vital safety components of your b...

	FileName	Document Summary
1	Repair and Service Guidelines.doc	It is important that you maintain your bicycle and ...
2	Lubrication Maintenance.doc	Guidelines and recommendations for lubricating t...
3	Installing Replacement Pedals.doc	Detailed instructions for replacing pedals with Ad...

	FileName	Document Summary
1	Repair and Service Guidelines.doc	It is important that you maintain your bicycle a...

Figure 2-17. The results from using multiple search terms

Searching Multiple Columns

You can search multiple columns or all full-text indexed columns at once without multiple CONTAINS predicates in the WHERE clause. Use the asterisk to specify that all possible columns are searched, or use a comma-delimited list in parentheses to specify a list of columns. Type in and execute the code in Listing 2-21, which demonstrates these techniques.

Listing 2-21. Using Multiple Columns

```
USE AdventureWorks2012;
GO

--1
SELECT FileName, DocumentSummary
FROM Production.Document
WHERE CONTAINS((DocumentSummary,Document),'maintain');

--2
SELECT FileName, DocumentSummary
FROM Production.Document
WHERE CONTAINS((DocumentSummary),'maintain')
      OR CONTAINS((Document),'maintain')

--3
SELECT FileName, DocumentSummary
FROM Production.Document
WHERE CONTAINS(*,'maintain');
```

The list of columns to be searched in query 1 is explicitly listed and contained within an inner set of parentheses. Query 2 is equivalent to query 1 by using two CONTAINS expressions, each searching a different column for the same term. By using the asterisk in query 3 within the CONTAINS expression, all columns with a full-text index are searched.

Using FREETEXT

FREETEXT is similar to CONTAINS except that it returns rows that don't exactly match. It will return rows that have terms with similar meanings to your search terms by using a thesaurus. FREETEXT is less precise than CONTAINS, and it is less flexible. The keywords AND, OR, and NEAR can't be used with CONTAINS. Avoid using double quotes that specify an exact phrase with FREETEXT, because then SQL Server won't use the thesaurus and will search only for the exact phrase. The same rules about multiple columns apply. Type in and execute the code in Listing 2-22, which compares FREETEXT to LIKE.

Listing 2-22. Using FREETEXT

```
USE AdventureWorks2012
GO

--1
SELECT FileName, DocumentSummary
FROM Production.Document
WHERE FREETEXT((DocumentSummary),'provides');

--2
SELECT FileName, DocumentSummary
FROM Production.Document
WHERE DocumentSummary LIKE '%provides%'
```

Figure 2-18 displays the results from Listing 2-22. The DocumentSummary value in the rows returned from query 1 do not contain the word *provides*. Query 1 returns the rows anyway because FREETEXT will find similar words as well as exact matches.

Figure 2-18. The results from using FREETEXT

Full-text search operations can get much more complicated than the information provided here. This was meant to be an overview of the basic syntax. Be sure to see the book *Pro Full-Text Search in SQL Server 2008* by Hillary Cotter and Michael Coles (Apress, 2008) to learn more about full-text search. Practice what you have just learned about full-text search by completing Exercise 2-6.

EXERCISE 2-6

Use the AdventureWorks2012 database to complete the following tasks. Be sure to take advantage of the full-text indexes in place when writing the queries. You can find the solutions in the Appendix.

---

1. Write a query using the Production.ProductReview table. Use CONTAINS to find all the rows that have the word *socks* in the Comments column. Return the ProductID and Comments columns.

2. Write a query using the Production.Document table. Use CONTAINS to find all the rows that have the word *reflector* in any column that is indexed with full-text search. Display the Title and FileName columns.

3. Change the query in question 2 so that the rows containing *seat* are not returned in the results.

4. Answer this question: when searching a VARBINARY(MAX) column that contains Word documents, a LIKE search can be used, but the performance will be worse. True or false?

Sorting Data

So far, you have learned how to retrieve a list of columns from a table and filter the results. This section covers how to sort the data that is retrieved using the ORDER BY clause. The ORDER BY clause is the last part of the SELECT statement that the database engine will process.

You can specify one or more columns in the ORDER BY clause separated by commas. The sort order is ascending by default, but you can specify descending order by using the keyword DESCENDING or DESC after the column name. Here is the syntax for ORDER BY:

```
SELECT <column1>,<column2>
FROM <schema>.<tablename>
ORDER BY <column1>[<sort direction>],<column2> [<sort direction>]
```

Type in and execute the code in Listing 2-23 to learn how to use the ORDER BY clause.

Listing 2-23. How to Use ORDER BY

```
USE AdventureWorks2012;
GO

--1
SELECT ProductID, LocationID
FROM Production.ProductInventory
ORDER BY LocationID;

--2
SELECT ProductID, LocationID
FROM Production.ProductInventory
ORDER BY ProductID, LocationID DESC
```

Figure 2-19 shows the partial results. The rows from query 1 display in order of LocationID. Query 2 returns the results ordered first by ProductID, and then the results are further sorted by LocationID in descending order.

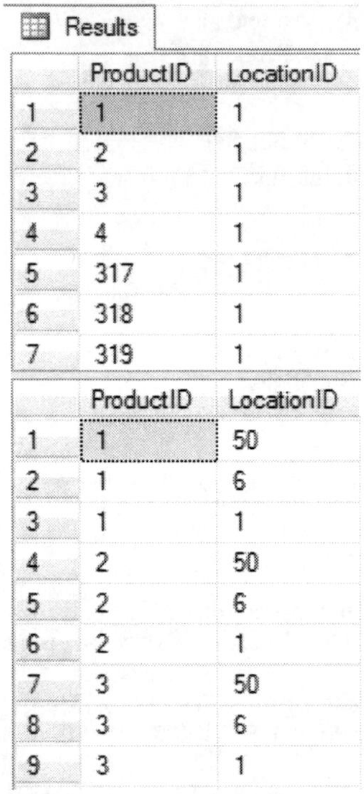

	ProductID	LocationID
1	1	1
2	2	1
3	3	1
4	4	1
5	317	1
6	318	1
7	319	1

	ProductID	LocationID
1	1	50
2	1	6
3	1	1
4	2	50
5	2	6
6	2	1
7	3	50
8	3	6
9	3	1

Figure 2-19. The results when using the ORDER BY clause

You can also use the ORDER BY clause to reduce the dataset returned by the query. This is helpful when you have a large table but only need a subset of the rows or your application only requires a small portion of a given dataset. There are two key words used to return only a subset of the selected rows. The first is OFFSET and it determines at what row count to start returning data. Type in the code in Listing 2-24 and execute in the query window.

Listing 2-24. How to Use ORDER BY OFFSET

```
SELECT ProductID, LocationID
FROM Production.ProductInventory
ORDER BY LocationID
OFFSET 10 ROWS;
```

Figure 2-20 shows the partial results of using the OFFSET command. If you compare the results of ProductID with the similar query from 2-23 you will notice the result skips the first 10 rows and begins showing data starting at row 11.

	ProductID	LocationID
1	323	1
2	324	1
3	325	1
4	326	1
5	341	1
6	342	1
7	343	1
8	344	1
9	345	1
10	346	1
11	347	1
12	348	1

Figure 2-20. Results when using the OFFSET clause

An additional feature allows you to also limit the total rows returned. To do this you use the FETCH NEXT…ONLY command. To use the command, type the keywords and specify the amount of rows you want to return. In Listing 2-25, you will run the same query as before but this time it will only return 10 rows.

Listing 2-25. How to Use ORDER BY FETCH NEXT…ONLY

```
SELECT ProductID, LocationID
FROM Production.ProductInventory
ORDER BY LocationID
OFFSET 10 ROWS
FETCH NEXT 10 ROWS ONLY;
```

The results in Figure 2-21 are the same as in Figure 2-20 but you restricted the dataset to only 10 rows.

	ProductID	LocationID
1	323	1
2	324	1
3	325	1
4	326	1
5	341	1
6	342	1
7	343	1
8	344	1
9	345	1
10	346	1

Figure 2-21. Results when using the FETCH NEXT…ONLY clause

■ **Note** Although you used the words NEXT and ROWS in the OFFSET and the FETCH NEXT clause, you can replace these with the words FIRST and ROW and still maintain the same results. Those key words are interchangeable and do not affect the resultset.

You may find the ORDER BY clause easy to use, but you should still practice what you have learned about sorting the results of your queries by completing Exercise 2-7.

EXERCISE 2-7

Use the AdventureWorks2012 database to complete this exercise and practice sorting the results of your queries. You can find the solutions in the Appendix.

1. Write a query that returns the business entity ID and name columns from the Person.Person table. Sort the results by LastName, FirstName, and MiddleName.

2. Modify the query written in question 1 so that the data is returned in the opposite order.

3. Modify the query written in question 1 so that you return only 10 rows starting at row 20.

Thinking About Performance

Reading this book and performing the exercises found in each chapter will enable you to become a proficient T-SQL programmer. You will learn how to write the queries, often in more than one way, to get results. Often T-SQL developers don't learn the best way to write a query, and the performance of their applications and reports suffer. As a result, several chapters of this book, beginning with this chapter, feature a section on performance to get you thinking about how the statements you write can affect performance.

Taking Advantage of Indexes

Indexes help the database engine locate the rows that must be returned by a query. In fact, the database engine will retrieve all the required columns from the index instead of accessing the table if possible. I am not advocating creating an index on every column, but strategically designed indexes immensely improve the performance of queries.

When a table contains an index on a column, the database engine will usually use that index to find the rows for the results if the column appears in the WHERE clause. For example, the Person.Person table contains an index called IX_Person_LastName_FirstName_MiddleName, which consists of the LastName, FirstName, and MiddleName columns. To see the index properties, follow these steps:

1. Using SQL Server Management Studio, connect to your SQL Server instance if you aren't connected already.

2. Expand Databases.

3. Expand AdventureWorks2012.

4. Expand Tables.

5. Expand Person.Person.

6. Expand Indexes.

7. Locate the IX_Person_LastName_FirstName_MiddleName index, and double-click it to view the properties.

View the index properties in Figure 2-22. Notice that the LastName column appears first in the list. To take full advantage of this index, the WHERE clause must filter on LastName. Imagine searching a phone book by first name when you don't know the last name! SQL Server must do the same thing, looking at each entry in the index, when the query filters on FirstName but not LastName.

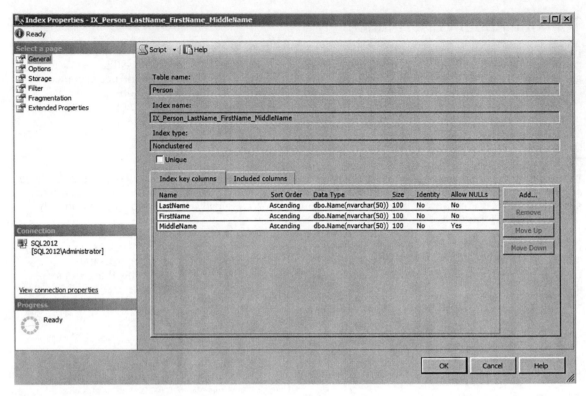

Figure 2-22. The properties of an index

What happens when you filter on only a nonindexed column? The database engine must check the value of the column in each row of the table to find the rows meeting the criteria. Again, I'm not advocating creating an index on every column, and index creation and tuning are both well beyond the scope of this book. I just want to make you aware that the indexes defined on the table will affect the performance of your queries.

Viewing Execution Plans

By using execution plans, you can determine whether the database engine utilizes an index to return the rows in the query. You can also compare the performance of two or more queries to see which one performs the best. Again, this book doesn't intend to make you an expert on execution plans but instead just gets you started using them to help you understand how your query performs.

■ **Note** To learn more about execution plans, see the book *SQL Server 2008 Query Performance Tuning Distilled* by Grant Fritchey and Sajal Dam (Apress, 2009).

While you have a query window open, click the Include Actual Execution Plan icon (see Figure 2-23) to turn on this feature for the current session. The setting must be toggled on for each query window; it is not a permanent setting.

Figure 2-23. *Clicking the Include Actual Execution Plan icon*

Listing 2-26 contains three queries to demonstrate the differences in performance found depending on whether SQL Server can take advantage of an index to return the results. Type in and execute the code in Listing 2-26.

Listing 2-26. *Learning How to View Execution Plans*

```
USE AdventureWorks2012;
GO

--1
SELECT LastName, FirstName
FROM Person.Person
WHERE LastName = 'Smith';

--2
SELECT LastName, FirstName
FROM Person.Person
WHERE FirstName = 'Ken';

--3
SELECT ModifiedDate
FROM Person.Person
WHERE ModifiedDate BETWEEN '2005-01-01' and '2005-01-31';
```

Once the query execution completes, click the Execution Plan tab. Figure 2-24 shows the graphical execution plans for the three queries. First, take a look at the query cost for each query shown at the top of each section. The query cost gives you an estimated weight of each query compared to the total. The numbers should add up to 100 percent.

Query 1, which has a relative query cost of 0 percent, filters the results on the LastName column. Recall that an index comprised of the LastName, FirstName, and MiddleName columns exists on the Person.Person table. Because the query filters on the first column in the index, the database engine can take full advantage of the index; it performs an *index seek* without scanning the entire index. This is similar to looking at the phone book when you know the last name; you don't need to look at every page or every entry to find the name you are looking for. Query 2, which has a relative query cost of 3 percent, filters the results on the FirstName column. The table has an index that contains the FirstName column, but since it appears second in the index, SQL Server must perform an *index scan*. This means that the database engine must compare the string *Ken* to every FirstName value in the index. The database was able to take advantage of the index but not to the fullest extent. Because the index contains both columns found in the results, the database engine didn't have to touch the actual table, pulling all the needed data from the index. The execution plan also suggests a new index that will make this query perform better.

Query 3, which has a relative query cost of 96 percent, filters the results on the ModifiedDate column. The table doesn't have an index containing this column. To filter the rows, the database engine must perform a *clustered index scan*. The *clustered index* is the actual table. In this case, the database engine had to look at each row of the table to retrieve the results, which causes the worst possible performance. Review the "Understanding Indexes" section in Chapter 1 to learn more about clustered indexes and indexes in general.

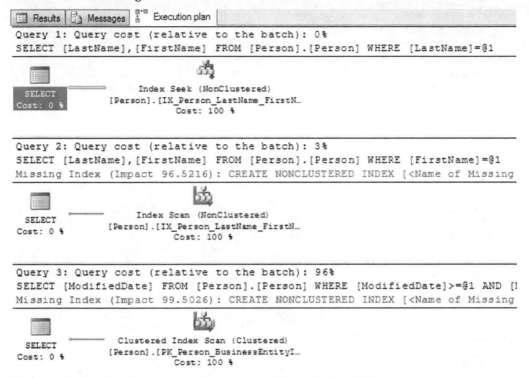

Figure 2-24. The actual execution plans generated from Listing 2-26

Viewing and understanding execution plans will help you learn how writing queries will affect the performance of your applications and reports. Don't rush to your database administrator demanding changes to the database indexes in your production database; this section doesn't intend to teach index tuning. Think of execution plans as another tool you can use to write better code. To learn more about how execution plans affect performance, complete Exercise 2-8.

EXERCISE 2-8

Use the AdventureWorks2012 database to complete this exercise. Be sure to turn on the Include Actual Execution Plan setting before you begin. Type the following code into the query window, and then complete each question. You can find the solutions in the Appendix.

```
USE AdventureWorks2012;
GO
```

```
--1
SELECT LastName
FROM Person.Person
WHERE LastName = 'Smith';

--2
SELECT LastName
FROM Person.Person
WHERE LastName LIKE 'Sm%';

--3
SELECT LastName
FROM Person.Person
WHERE LastName LIKE '%mith';

--4
SELECT ModifiedDate
FROM Person.Person
WHERE ModifiedDate BETWEEN '2005-01-01' and '2005-01-31';
```

1. Highlight and run queries 1 and 2. Explain why there is no difference in performance between the two queries.

2. Highlight and run queries 2 and 3. Determine which query performs the best, and explain why you think so.

3. Highlight and run queries 3 and 4. Determine which query performs the best, and explain why you think so.

Summary

The SELECT statement is used to retrieve data from tables stored in SQL Server databases. The statement can be broken down into several parts called *clauses*. The FROM clause specifies the table where the data is stored. The SELECT clause contains a list of columns to be retrieved. To filter the data, use the WHERE clause. To sort the data, use the ORDER BY clause.

This chapter covered a lot of ground, especially all the nuances of the WHERE clause. Make sure you really understand the material covered in the chapter before continuing. Everything you learn throughout the rest of the book will depend on a thorough knowledge of the basics. The next chapter explores many of the built-in functions you can use to make data retrieval even more interesting.

CHAPTER 3

Using Functions and Expressions

Now that you have the knowledge to write simple SELECT statements, it is time to explore some of the other features of T-SQL that allow you to manipulate how the data is displayed, filtered, or ordered. To create expressions in T-SQL, you use functions and operators along with literal values and columns. The reasons for using expressions in T-SQL code are many. For example, you may want to display only the year of a column of the DATETIME data type on a report, or you may need to calculate a discount based on the order quantity in an order-entry application. Any time the data must be displayed, filtered, or ordered in a way that is different from how it is stored, you can use expressions and functions to manipulate it.

You will find a very rich and versatile collection of functions and operators available to create expressions that manipulate strings and dates and much more. You can use expressions in the SELECT, WHERE, and ORDER BY clauses as well as in other clauses you will learn about in Chapter 5.

Expressions Using Operators

You learned how to use several comparison operators in the WHERE clause in Chapter 2. In this section, you will learn how to use operators to concatenate strings and perform mathematical calculations in T-SQL queries.

Concatenating Strings

The concatenation operator (+) allows you to add together two strings. The syntax is simple: `<string or column name> + <string or column name>`. Start up SQL Server Management Studio if it is not already running, and connect to your development server. Open a new query window, and type in and execute the code in Listing 3-1.

Listing 3-1. Concatenating Strings

```
USE AdventureWorks2012;
GO

--1
SELECT 'ab' + 'c';
```

```
--2
SELECT BusinessEntityID, FirstName + ' ' + LastName AS "Full Name"
FROM Person.Person;
--3
SELECT BusinessEntityID, LastName + ', ' + FirstName AS "Full Name"
FROM Person.Person;
```

Figure 3-1 shows the results of Listing 3-1. Query 1 shows that you can concatenate two strings. Queries 2 and 3 demonstrate concatenating the LastName and FirstName columns along with either a space or a comma and space. Notice that you specified the alias, Full Name, to provide a column header for the result of the expressions combining FirstName and LastName. If you did not provide the alias, the column header would be (No column name), as in query 1.

	(No column name)
1	abc

	BusinessEntityID	Full Name
1	285	Syed Abbas
2	293	Catherine Abel
3	295	Kim Abercrombie
4	2170	Kim Abercrombie
5	38	Kim Abercrombie

	BusinessEntityID	Full Name
1	285	Abbas, Syed
2	293	Abel, Catherine
3	295	Abercrombie, Kim
4	2170	Abercrombie, Kim
5	38	Abercrombie, Kim
6	211	Abolrous, Hazem
7	2357	Abolrous, Sam
8	297	Acevedo, Humberto
9	291	Achong, Gustavo

Figure 3-1. The results of queries concatenating strings

Concatenating Strings and NULL

In Chapter 2 you learned about the challenges when working with NULL in WHERE clause expressions. When concatenating a string with a NULL, NULL is returned. Listing 3-2 demonstrates this problem. Type the code in Listing 3-2 into a new query window, and execute it.

Listing 3-2. Concatenating Strings with NULL Values

```
USE AdventureWorks2012;
GO

SELECT BusinessEntityID, FirstName + ' ' + MiddleName +
    ' ' + LastName AS "Full Name"
FROM Person.Person;
```

Figure 3-2 shows the results of Listing 3-2. The query combines the FirstName, MiddleName, and LastName columns into a Full Name column. The MiddleName column is optional; that is, NULL values are allowed. Only the rows where the MiddleName value has been entered show the expected results. The rows where MiddleName is NULL return NULL.

Results

	BusinessEntityID	Full Name
1	285	Syed E Abbas
2	293	Catherine R. Abel
3	295	NULL
4	2170	NULL
5	38	Kim B Abercrombie
6	211	Hazem E Abolrous
7	2357	NULL
8	297	NULL
9	291	NULL
10	299	NULL
11	121	Pilar G Ackerman
12	16867	Aaron B Adams
13	16901	NULL
14	16724	Alex C Adams
15	10263	Alexandra J Adams
16	10312	Allison L Adams
17	10274	Amanda P Adams

Figure 3-2. The results of concatenating a string with NULL

CONCAT

SQL 2012 introduces another powerful tool for concatenating strings. The CONCAT statement takes any number of strings as arguments and automatically concatenates them together. The values can be passed to the CONCAT statement as variables or as regular strings. The output is always implicitly converted to a string datatype. Run the code in listing 3-3 to see how to use the CONCAT statement.

Listing 3-3. CONCAT Examples

```
-- Simple CONCAT statement
SELECT CONCAT ('I ', 'love', ' writing', ' T-SQL') AS RESULT;

--Using variable with CONCAT
DECLARE @a VARCHAR(30) = 'My birthday is on '
DECLARE @b DATE = '08/25/1980'
SELECT CONCAT (@a, @b) AS RESULT;

--Using CONCAT with table rows
USE AdventureWorks2012
SELECT CONCAT (AddressLine1, PostalCode) AS Address
FROM Person.Address;
```

The first command simply concatenates four separate string values. The second example declares two variables and then concatenates those into a single result. The final example uses the CONCAT statement in a SELECT clause to concatenate table rows. Figure 3-3 shows the output. I've only showed the partial results for the final example.

	RESULT
1	I love writing T-SQL

	RESULT
1	My birthday is on 1980-08-25

	Address
1	#500-75 O'Connor Street K4B 1S2
2	#9900 2700 Production Way V5A 4X1
3	00, rue Saint-Lazare 59140
4	02, place de Fontenoy 91370
5	035, boulevard du Montparnasse 91370
6	081, boulevard du Montparnasse 93400
7	081, boulevard du Montparnasse 98104
8	084, boulevard du Montparnasse 91940
9	1 Corporate Center Drive 33127
10	1 Mt. Dell Drive 97205
11	1 Smiling Tree Court 90012

Figure 3-3. Partial Results of CONCAT Statements

ISNULL and COALESCE

Two functions are available to replace NULL values with another value. The first function, ISNULL, requires two parameters: the value to check and the replacement for NULL values. COALESCE works a bit differently. COALESCE will take any number of parameters and return the first non-NULL value. T-SQL developers often prefer COALESCE over ISNULL because COALESCE meets ANSI standards, while ISNULL does not. Also, COALESCE is more versatile. Here is the syntax for the two functions:

```
ISNULL(<value>,<replacement>)
COALESCE(<value1>,<value2>,...,<valueN>)
```

Type in and execute the code in Listing 3-4 to learn how to use ISNULL and COALESCE.

Listing 3-4. Using ISNULL and COALESCE

```
USE AdventureWorks2012;
GO

--1
SELECT BusinessEntityID, FirstName + ' ' + ISNULL(MiddleName,'') +
    ' ' + LastName AS "Full Name"
FROM Person.Person;
--2
SELECT BusinessEntityID, FirstName + ISNULL(' ' + MiddleName,'') +
    ' ' + LastName AS "Full Name"
FROM Person.Person;

--3
SELECT BusinessEntityID, FirstName + COALESCE(' ' + MiddleName,'') +
    ' ' + LastName AS "Full Name"
FROM Person.Person;
```

Figure 3-4 shows a partial result of running the code. Query 1 uses the ISNULL function to replace any missing MiddleName values with an empty string in order to build Full Name. Notice in the results that whenever MiddleName is missing, you end up with two spaces between FirstName and LastName. Line 3 in the results of query 1 contains two spaces between Kim and Ambercrombie because a space is added both before and after the ISNULL function. To correct this problem, move the space inside the ISNULL function instead of before it: ISNULL(' ' + MiddleName,''). Concatenating a space with NULL returns NULL. When the MiddleName value is NULL, the space is eliminated, and no extra spaces show up in your results. Instead of ISNULL, query 3 contains the COALESCE function. If MiddleName is NULL, the next non-NULL value, the empty string, is returned.

Results

	BusinessEntityID	Full Name
1	285	Syed E Abbas
2	293	Catherine R. Abel
3	295	Kim Abercrombie
4	2170	Kim Abercrombie
5	38	Kim B Abercrombie

	BusinessEntityID	Full Name
1	285	Syed E Abbas
2	293	Catherine R. Abel
3	295	Kim Abercrombie
4	2170	Kim Abercrombie
5	38	Kim B Abercrombie
6	211	Hazem E Abolrous

	BusinessEntityID	Full Name
1	285	Syed E Abbas
2	293	Catherine R. Abel
3	295	Kim Abercrombie
4	2170	Kim Abercrombie
5	38	Kim B Abercrom…
6	211	Hazem E Abolr…
7	2357	Sam Abolrous

Figure 3-4. *The results of using ISNULL and COALESCE when concatenating strings*

Concatenating Other Data Types to Strings

To concatenate nonstring values to strings, the nonstring value must be converted to a string. If the string value can be implicitly converted to a number, the values will be added together instead. Run this statement to see what happens: SELECT 1 + '1';. If the desired result is 11 instead of 2, the numeric value must be converted to a string using either the CAST or CONVERT function. If you attempt to concatenate a non-numeric string and a number without converting, you will receive an error message. Run this example to see the error: SELECT 1 + 'a';.

Use one of the functions, CAST or CONVERT, to convert a numeric or temporal value to a string. Here is the syntax:

```
CAST(<value> AS <new data type>)
CONVERT(<new data type>,<value>)
```

Listing 3-5 demonstrates how to use these functions. Type in and execute the code in a query window.

Listing 3-5. Using CAST and CONVERT

```
USE AdventureWorks2012
GO

--1
SELECT CAST(BusinessEntityID AS NVARCHAR) + ': ' + LastName
    + ', ' + FirstName AS ID_Name
FROM Person.Person;

--2
SELECT CONVERT(NVARCHAR(10),BusinessEntityID) + ': ' + LastName
    + ', ' + FirstName AS ID_Name
FROM Person.Person;

--3
SELECT BusinessEntityID, BusinessEntityID + 1 AS "Adds 1",
    CAST(BusinessEntityID AS NVARCHAR(10)) + '1'AS "Appends 1"
FROM Person.Person;
```

Figure 3-5 shows the partial results of running the code. The functions in queries 1 and 2 have very different syntaxes, but they accomplish the same result.. They both change the BusinessEntityID values from integers into a string data type (NVARCHAR) so that it can be concatenated to a string. Many programmers prefer CAST over CONVERT because CAST is compliant with the ANSI SQL-99 standard. Query 1 specifies just NVARCHAR as the data type without a size. By default, the maximum length will be 30 characters. If you need to cast TO a value more than 30 characters, you must specify a length argument greater than 30. Query 3 demonstrates the difference between converting the numeric value and not converting it. For more information about CONVERT, take a look at the "CONVERT" section later in the chapter.

Results

	ID_Name
1	285: Abbas, Syed
2	293: Abel, Catherine
3	295: Abercrombie, Kim
4	2170: Abercrombie, Kim
5	38: Abercrombie, Kim
6	211: Abolrous, Hazem

	ID_Name
1	285: Abbas, Syed
2	293: Abel, Catherine
3	295: Abercrombie, Kim
4	2170: Abercrombie, Kim
5	38: Abercrombie, Kim
6	211: Abolrous, Hazem

	BusinessEntityID	Adds 1	Appends 1
1	16496	16497	164961
2	12506	12507	125061
3	11390	11391	113901
4	10798	10799	107981
5	963	964	9631
6	12283	12284	122831

Figure 3-5. The partial results of using CAST and CONVERT

Developers must often concatenate strings for reports or for loading data from one system to another. Now practice what you have learned about concatenating strings within a T-SQL query by completing Exercise 3-1.

EXERCISE 3-1

Use the AdventureWorks2012 database to complete this exercise. You can find the solutions in the Appendix.

1. Write a query that displays in the "AddressLine1 (City PostalCode)" format from the Person.Address table.

2. Write a query using the Production.Product table displaying the product ID, color, and name columns. If the color column contains a NULL value, replace the color with *No Color*.

3. Modify the query written in question 2 so that the description of the product is displayed in the "Name: Color" format. Make sure that all rows display a value even if the Color value is missing.

4. Write a query using the Production.Product table displaying a description with the "ProductID: Name" format. Hint: You will need to use a function to write this query.

5. Explain the difference between the ISNULL and COALESCE functions.

Using Mathematical Operators

You can use several operators to perform simple mathematical operations on numeric values. Use the plus symbol (+) to perform addition, the minus symbol (–) to perform subtraction, the asterisk (*) to perform multiplication, and the slash (/) to perform division. One operator that may be new to you is the modulo (%) operator. The modulo operator returns the remainder when division is performed on the two values. For example, 5 % 2 returns 1 because 1 is the remainder when you divide 5 by 2. One common use for modulo is to determine whether a number is odd or even when the second value in the expression is 2. If the result is 1, then the value is odd; if the result is 0, then the value is even. Listing 3-6 shows how to use some of the mathematical operators. Type in and execute the code to see the results.

Listing 3-6. Using Mathematical Operators

```
USE AdventureWorks2012;
GO

--1
SELECT 1 + 1;

--2
SELECT 10 / 3 AS DIVISION, 10 % 3 AS MODULO;

--3
SELECT OrderQty, OrderQty * 10 AS Times10
FROM Sales.SalesOrderDetail;

--4
SELECT OrderQty * UnitPrice * (1.0 - UnitPriceDiscount)
    AS Calculated, LineTotal
FROM Sales.SalesOrderDetail;

--5
SELECT SpecialOfferID,MaxQty,DiscountPct,
    DiscountPct * ISNULL(MaxQty1000) AS MaxDiscount
FROM Sales.SpecialOffer;
```

Take a look at the results shown in Figure 3-6. Queries 1 and 2 show how to perform calculations on literal values. Query 3 shows the result of multiplying the values stored in the OrderQty column by 10. Query 4 compares the precalculated LineTotal column to calculating the value by using an expression.

The LineTotal column is a "computed column." Computed columns have a property, PERSISTED, that allows the calculated value to be stored in the table. If the PERSISTED property of the column is set to FALSE, the value is calculated each time the data is accessed. The advantage of storing the calculated value is that you can add an index on the computed column. The actual formula used in the table definition looks a bit more complicated than the one I used since it checks for NULL values. The simplified formula I used requires parentheses to enforce the logic, causing subtraction to be performed before multiplication. Since multiplication has a higher precedence than subtraction, use parentheses to enforce the intended logic. Query 5 shows how to use the ISNULL function to substitute the value 1000 when the MaxQty is NULL before multiplying by the DiscountPct value.

Results

	(No column name)
1	2

	DIVISION	MODULO
1	3	1

	OrderQty	Times10
1	1	10
2	3	30
3	1	10
4	1	10
5	1	10
6	2	20

	Calculated	LineTotal
1	2024.994000	2024.994000
2	6074.982000	6074.982000
3	2024.994000	2024.994000
4	2039.994000	2039.994000
5	2039.994000	2039.994000
6	4079.988000	4079.988000

	SpecialOfferID	MaxQty	DiscountPct	MaxDiscount
1	1	NULL	0.00	0.00
2	2	14	0.02	0.28
3	3	24	0.05	1.20
4	4	40	0.10	4.00
5	5	60	0.15	9.00
6	6	NULL	0.20	200.00

Figure 3-6. The results of using mathematical operators

Practice what you have learned about mathematical operators to complete Exercise 3-2.

```
                                 EXERCISE 3-2
```

Use the AdventureWorks2012 database to complete this exercise. You can find the solutions in the Appendix.

1. Write a query using the Sales.SpecialOffer table. Display the difference between the MinQty and MaxQty columns along with the SpecialOfferID and Description columns.

2. Write a query using the Sales.SpecialOffer table. Multiply the MinQty column by the DiscountPct column. Include the SpecialOfferID and Description columns in the results.

3. Write a query using the Sales.SpecialOffer table that multiplies the MaxQty column by the DiscountPct column. If the MaxQty value is NULL, replace it with the value 10. Include the SpecialOfferID and Description columns in the results.

4. Describe the difference between division and modulo.

Data Type Precedence

When using operators, you must keep the data types of the values in mind. When performing an operation that involves two different data types, the expression will return values with the data type with the highest precedence if possible. What value can be rolled into the other value? For example, an INT can be converted to a BIGINT, but not the other way around. In other words, if a value can be a valid INT, it is also a valid BIGINT. However, many valid BIGINT values are too big to be converted to INT. Therefore, when an operation is performed on a BIGINT and an INT, the result will be a BIGINT.

It is not always possible to convert the lower precedence data type to the higher precedence data type. A character can't always be converted to a numeric value. For a list of possible data types in order of precedence, see the article "Data Type Precedence" in SQL Server's help system, Books Online.

Using Functions

So far, this chapter has covered using operators along with columns and literal values to create expressions. To get around issues concerning NULL values and incompatible data types within an expression, you were introduced to several functions: ISNULL, COALESCE, CAST, and CONVERT. This section covers many other built-in functions available with SQL Server 2012.

The functions you will learn about in this chapter return a single value. The functions generally require one or more parameters. The data to be operated on can be a literal value, a column name, or the results of another function. This section covers functions to manipulate strings, dates, and numeric data. You will also learn about several system functions and how to nest one function within another function.

Using String Functions

You will find a very rich set of T-SQL functions for manipulating strings. You often have a choice of where a string will be manipulated. If the manipulation will occur on one of the columns in the select-list, it might make sense to utilize the client to do the work if the manipulation is complex, but it is possible to do quite a bit of manipulation with T-SQL. You can use the string functions to clean up data before loading it into a database. This section covers many of the commonly used string functions. You can find many more in Books Online.

RTRIM and LTRIM

The RTRIM and LTRIM functions remove spaces from the right side (RTRIM) or left side (LTRIM) of a string. You may need to use these functions when working with fixed-length data types (CHAR and NCHAR) or to clean up flat-file data before it is loaded from a staging database into a data warehouse. The syntax is simple.

```
RTRIM(<string>)
LTRIM(<string>)
```

Type in and execute the code in Listing 3-7. AdventureWorks2012The first part of the code creates and populates a temporary table. Don't worry about understanding that part of the code at this point.

Listing 3-7. Using RTRIM and LTRIM

```
--Create the temp table
CREATE TABLE #trimExample (COL1 VARCHAR(10));
GO
--Populate the table
INSERT INTO #trimExample (COL1)
VALUES ('a '),('b '),(' c'),('  d ');

--Select the values using the functions
SELECT COL1, '*' + RTRIM(COL1) + '*' AS "RTRIM",
    '*' + LTRIM(COL1) + '*' AS "LTRIM"
FROM #trimExample;

--Clean up
DROP TABLE #trimExample;
```

Figure 3-7 shows the results of the code. The INSERT statement added four rows to the table with no spaces (a), spaces on the right (b), spaces on the left (c), and spaces on both (d). Inside the SELECT statement, you will see that asterisks surround the values to make it easier to see the spaces in the results. The RTRIM function removed the spaces from the right side; the LTRIM function removed the spaces from the left side. T-SQL doesn't contain a native function that removes the spaces from both sides of the string, but you will learn how to get around this problem in the section "Nesting Functions" later in the chapter.

	COL1	RTRIM	LTRIM
1	a	*a*	*a*
2	b	*b*	*b *
3	c	* c*	*c*
4	d	* d*	*d *

Figure 3-7. The results of using RTRIM and LTRIM

LEFT and RIGHT

The LEFT and RIGHT functions return a specified number of characters on the left or right side of a string. Developers use these functions to parse strings. For example, you may need to retrieve the three-character extension from file path data by using RIGHT. Take a look at the syntax.

```
LEFT(<string>,<number of characters)
RIGHT(<string>,<number of characters)
```

Listing 3-8 demonstrates how to use these functions. Type in and execute the code.

Listing 3-8. The LEFT and RIGHT Functions

```
USE AdventureWorks2012;
GO
SELECT LastName,LEFT(LastName,5) AS "LEFT",
    RIGHT(LastName,4) AS "RIGHT"
FROM Person.Person
WHERE BusinessEntityID IN (293,295,211,297,299,3057,15027);
```

Figure 3-8 shows the results. Notice that even if the value contains fewer characters than the number specified in the second parameter, the function still works to return as many characters as possible.

	LastName	LEFT	RIGHT
1	Abolrous	Abolr	rous
2	Abel	Abel	Abel
3	Abercrombie	Aberc	mbie
4	Acevedo	Aceve	vedo
5	Ackerman	Acker	rman
6	Alexander	Alexa	nder
7	Bell	Bell	Bell

Figure 3-8. The results of using LEFT and RIGHT

LEN and DATALENGTH

Use LEN to return the number of characters in a string. Developers sometimes use another function, DATALENGTH, incorrectly in place of LEN. DATALENGTH returns the number of bytes in a string. DATALENGTH returns the same value as LEN when the string is a CHAR or VARCHAR data type, which takes one byte per character. The problem occurs when using DATALENGTH on NCHAR or NVARCHAR data types, which take two byes per characters. In this case, the DATALENGTH value is two times the LEN value. This is not incorrect; the two functions measure different things. The syntax is very simple.

```
LEN(<string>)
DATALENGTH(<string>)
```

Type in and execute the code in Listing 3-9 to learn how to use LEN and DATALENGTH.

Listing 3-9. Using the LEN and DATALENGTH Functions

```
USE AdventureWorks2012;
GO

SELECT LastName,LEN(LastName) AS "Length",
    DATALENGTH(LastName) AS "Data Length"
FROM Person.Person
WHERE BusinessEntityID IN (293,295,211,297,299,3057,15027);
```

Figure 3-9 shows the results. The Length column displays a count of the characters, while the Data Length column displays the number of bytes.

	LastName	Length	Data Length
1	Abolrous	8	16
2	Abel	4	8
3	Abercrombie	11	22
4	Acevedo	7	14
5	Ackerman	8	16
6	Alexander	9	18
7	Bell	4	8

Figure 3-9. The results of using LEN and DATALENGTH

CHARINDEX

Use CHARINDEX to find the numeric starting position of a search string inside another string. By checking to see whether the value returned by CHARINDEX is greater than zero, you can use the function to just determine whether the search string exists inside the second value. Developers often use CHARINDEX to locate a particular character, such as the at symbol (@) in an e-mail address column, along with other functions when parsing strings. You will learn more about this in the "Nesting Functions" section later in the chapter. The CHARINDEX function requires two parameters: the search string and the string to be searched. An optional parameter, the start location, instructs the function to ignore a given number of characters at the beginning of the string to be searched. The following is the syntax; remember that the third parameter is optional (square brackets surround optional parameters in the syntax):

```
CHARINDEX(<search string>,<target string>[,<start location>])
```

Listing 3-10 demonstrates how to use CHARINDEX. Type in and execute the code to learn how to use this function.

Listing 3-10. *Using CHARINDEX*

```
USE AdventureWorks2012;
GO
SELECT LastName, CHARINDEX('e',LastName) AS "Find e",
    CHARINDEX('e',LastName,4) AS "Skip 4 Characters",
    CHARINDEX('be',LastName) AS "Find be",
    CHARINDEX('Be',LastName) AS "Find B"
FROM Person.Person
WHERE BusinessEntityID IN (293,295,211,297,299,3057,15027);
```

Figure 3-10 shows the results. The Find e column in the results displays the first location of the letter e in the LastName value. The Skip 4 Characters column displays the first location of the letter e when the first four characters of the LastName value are ignored. Finally, the Find be column demonstrates that you can use the function with search strings that are more than one character in length. Notice how "Be" returns a value of "Bell". This is due to the case sensitivity of the AdventureWorks2012 database, which differentiates between an upper and lowercase "b."

▦ Results

	LastName	Find e	Skip 4 Characters	Find be	Find Be
1	Abolrous	0	0	0	0
2	Abel	3	0	2	0
3	Abercrombie	3	11	2	0
4	Acevedo	3	5	0	0
5	Ackerman	4	4	0	0
6	Alexander	3	8	0	0
7	Bell	2	0	0	1

Figure 3-10. *The results of using CHARINDEX*

SUBSTRING

Use SUSTRING to return a portion of a string starting at a given position and for a specified number of characters. For example, an order-entry application may assign a customer ID based on the first seven letters of the customer's last name plus digits 4–9 of the phone number. The SUBSTRING function requires three parameters: the string, a starting location, and the number of characters to retrieve. If the number of characters to retrieve is greater than the length of the string, the function will return as many characters as possible. Here is the syntax of SUBSTRING:

```
SUBSTRING(<string>,<start location>,<length>)
```

Type in and execute the code in Listing 3-11 to learn how to use SUBSTRING.

Listing 3-11. Using SUBSTRING

```
USE AdventureWorks2012;
GO
SELECT LastName, SUBSTRING(LastName,1,4) AS "First 4",
    SUBSTRING(LastName,5,50) AS "Characters 5 and later"
FROM Person.Person
WHERE BusinessEntityID IN (293,295,211,297,299,3057,15027);
```

Notice in the results (Figure 3-11) that if the starting point is located after the available characters (Abel and Bell), an empty string is returned. Otherwise, in this example, the FirstName column is divided into two strings.

Results

	LastName	First 4	Characters 5 and later
1	Abolrous	Abol	rous
2	Abel	Abel	
3	Abercrombie	Aber	crombie
4	Acevedo	Acev	edo
5	Ackerman	Acke	rman
6	Alexander	Alex	ander
7	Bell	Bell	

Figure 3-11. The results of using SUBSTRING

CHOOSE

CHOOSE is a new function in SQL 2012 which allows you to select a value in an array based off an index. The CHOOSE function requires an index value and list of values for the array. Here is the basic syntax for the CHOOSE function.

```
CHOOSE ( index, val_1, val_2 [, val_n ] )
```

The index simply points to the position in the array that you want to return. Listing 3-12 shows a basic example.

Listing 3-12. Using the CHOOSE Function

```
SELECT CHOOSE (4, 'a', 'b', c, 'd', 'e', 'f', 'g', 'h', 'i')
```

Figure 3-12 shows the results. Keep in mind that the results take the highest datatype precendence. This means if there is an integer in the list then the CHOOSE function will try to convert any results to an integer. If the value is a string then the CHOOSE command will throw an error. You will need to convert any interger values in the array to varchar to avoid this error.

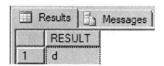

Figure 3-12. Result from CHOOSE Function

REVERSE

REVERSE returns a string in reverse order. I often use it along with the RIGHT function to find a file name from the file's path. I use REVERSE to find the last backslash in the path, which then tells me how many characters, minus 1, on the right side of the string I need to grab. The same method can be used to parse an e-mail address. To see how to do this, see the example in the "Nesting Functions" later in the chapter. Type in and execute this code to learn how to use REVERSE:

```
SELECT REVERSE('!dlroW ,olleH')
```

UPPER and LOWER

Use UPPER and LOWER to change a string to either uppercase or lowercase. You may need to display all uppercase data in a report, for example. The syntax is very simple.

```
UPPER(<string>)
LOWER(<string>)
```

Type in and execute the code in Listing 3-13.

Listing 3-13. Using UPPER and LOWER

```
USE AdventureWorks2012;
GO
SELECT LastName, UPPER(LastName) AS "UPPER",
    LOWER(LastName) AS "LOWER"
FROM Person.Person
WHERE BusinessEntityID IN (293,295,211,297,299,3057,15027);
```

Take a look at the results in Figure 3-13. All LastName values appear in uppercase in the UPPER column, while they appear in lowercase in the LOWER column.

	LastName	UPPER	LOWER
1	Abolrous	ABOLROUS	abolrous
2	Abel	ABEL	abel
3	Abercrombie	ABERCROMBIE	abercrombie
4	Acevedo	ACEVEDO	acevedo
5	Ackerman	ACKERMAN	ackerman
6	Alexander	ALEXANDER	alexander
7	Bell	BELL	bell

Figure 3-13. The partial results of using UPPER and LOWER

■ **Note** You may think that you will use UPPER or LOWER often in the WHERE clause to make sure that the case of the value does not affect the results, but usually you don't need to do this. By default, searching in T-SQL is case insensitive. The collation of the column determines whether the search will be case sensitive. This is defined at the server, but you can specify a different collation of the database, table, or column. See "Working with Collations" in Books Online for more information.

REPLACE

Use REPLACE to substitute one string value for another. REPLACE has three required parameters, but it is very easy to use. Use REPLACE to clean up data; for example, you may need to replace slashes (/) in a phone number column with hyphens (-) for a report. Here is the syntax:

```
REPLACE(<string value>,<string to replace>,<replacement>)
```

Type in and execute the code in Listing 3-14 to learn how to use REPLACE.

Listing 3-14. Using REPLACE

```
USE AdventureWorks2012;
GO

--1
SELECT LastName, REPLACE(LastName,'A','Z') AS "Replace A",
    REPLACE(LastName,'A','ZZ') AS "Replace with 2 characters",
    REPLACE(LastName,'ab','') AS "Remove string"
FROM Person.Person
WHERE BusinessEntityID IN (293,295,211,297,299,3057,15027);
```

```
--2
SELECT BusinessEntityID,LastName,MiddleName,
    REPLACE(LastName,'a',MiddleName) AS "Replace with MiddleName",
    REPLACE(LastName,MiddleName,'a') AS "Replace MiddleName"
FROM Person.Person
WHERE BusinessEntityID IN (285,293,10314);
```

Notice in the results (Figure 3-14) that the REPLACE function replaces every instance of the string to be replaced. It doesn't matter if the strings in the second and third parameter are not the same length, as shown in Replace with 2 characters. The Remove string example shows a convenient way to remove a character or characters from a string by replacing with an empty string represented by two single quotes. Because the last name *Bell* doesn't contain any of the values to be replaced, the value doesn't change.

Query 2 demonstrates that the second and third parameters don't have to be literal values by using the MiddleName column either as the string to replace in the Replace MiddleName column or as the replacement in the Replace with MiddleName column.

	LastName	Replace A	Replace with 2 characters	Remove string
1	Abolrous	Zbolrous	ZZbolrous	Abolrous
2	Abel	Zbel	ZZbel	Abel
3	Abercrombie	Zbercrombie	ZZbercrombie	Abercrombie
4	Acevedo	Zcevedo	ZZcevedo	Acevedo
5	Ackerman	Zckerman	ZZckerman	Ackerman
6	Alexander	Zlexander	ZZlexander	Alexander
7	Bell	Bell	Bell	Bell

	BusinessEntityID	LastName	MiddleName	Replace with MiddleName	Replace MiddleName
1	285	Abbas	E	AbbEs	Abbas
2	293	Abel	R.	Abel	Abel
3	10314	Adams	M	AdMms	Adams

Figure 3-14. The partial results of using REPLACE

Nesting Functions

The previous section showed how to use one function at a time to manipulate strings. If the results of one expression must be used as a parameter of another function call, you can nest functions. For example, you can nest the LTRIM and RTRIM functions to remove the spaces from the beginning and ending of a string like this: LTRIM(RTRIM(' test ')). Keep in mind when writing nested functions you work from the inside out. The inner-most function is executed first and the outer functions execute against the results. Let's look at some examples. Type in and execute the example shown in Listing 3-15 to display the domains in a list of e-mail addresses and the file name from a list of file paths.

Listing 3-15. Nesting Functions

```
USE AdventureWorks2012;
GO

--1
SELECT EmailAddress,
    SUBSTRING(EmailAddress,CHARINDEX('@',EmailAddress) + 1,50) AS DOMAIN
FROM Production.ProductReview;

--2
SELECT EmailAddress,
RIGHT(EmailAddress, CHARINDEX('@', REVERSE(EmailAddress))-1) AS DOMAIN
FROM Production.ProductReview;
```

Figure 3-15 shows the results. Query 1 first uses the CHARINDEX function to find the location of the at symbol (@). The results of that expression are used as a parameter to the outer SUBSTRING function. To display the characters after the @ symbol, add 1 to the position of the @ symbol.

Query 2 produces the same results but uses different commands. The query performs a SELECT command from the Production.ProductReview table. After the SELECT the inner REVERSE function reverses the string value. Then the outer CHARINDEX finds the location of the @ symbol and subtracts one character to remove it from the results. By using that result as the second parameter of the RIGHT function, the query returns the domain name. When writing a query like this, take it a step at a time and work from the inside out. You may have to experiment a bit to get it right.

Results

	EmailAddress	DOMAIN
1	john@fourthcoffee.com	fourthcoffee.com
2	david@graphicdesigninstitute.com	graphicdesigninstitute.com
3	jill@margiestravel.com	margiestravel.com
4	laura@treyresearch.net	treyresearch.net

	EmailAddress	DOMAIN
1	john@fourthcoffee.com	fourthcoffee.com
2	david@graphicdesigninstitute.com	graphicdesigninstitute.com
3	jill@margiestravel.com	margiestravel.com
4	laura@treyresearch.net	treyresearch.net

Figure 3-15. The results of using nested functions

This section covered a sample of the many functions available to manipulate strings in T-SQL. Complete Exercise 3-3 to practice using these functions.

```
                           EXERCISE 3-3
```

Use the AdventureWorks2012 database to complete this exercise. If you need help, refer to the discussion of the functions to help you figure out which ones to use. You can find the solutions to these questions in the Appendix.

1. Write a query that displays the first 10 characters of the AddressLine1 column in the Person.Address table.

2. Write a query that displays characters 10 to 15 of the AddressLine1 column in the Person.Address table.

3. Write a query displaying the first and last names from the Person.Person table all in uppercase.

4. The ProductNumber in the Production.Product table contains a hyphen (-). Write a query that uses the SUBSTRING function and the CHARINDEX function to display the characters in the product number following the hyphen. Note: there is also a second hyphen in many of the rows; ignore the second hyphen for this question. Hint: Try writing this statement in two steps, the first using the CHARINDEX function and the second adding the SUBSTRING function.

Using Date Functions

Just as T-SQL features a rich set of functions for working with string data, it also boasts an impressive list of functions for working with date and time data types. In this section, you'll take a look at some of the most commonly used functions for date and time data.

GETDATE and SYSDATETIME

Use GETDATE or SYSDATETIME to return the current date and time of the server. The difference is that SYSDATETIME returns seven decimal places after the second, while GETDATE returns only three places. You may see zeros filling in some of the right digits if your SQL Server is installed on Vista-64 instead of another operating system.

GETDATE and SYSDATETIME are *nondeterministic* functions. This means that they return different values each time they are called. Most of the functions in this chapter are *deterministic*, which means that a function always returns the same value when called with the same parameters and database settings. For example, the code CHARINDEX('B','abcd') will always return 2 if the collation of the database is case insensitive. In a case-sensitive database, the expression will return 0.

Run this code several times to see how these functions work:

```
SELECT GETDATE(), SYSDATETIME();
```

DATEADD

Use DATEADD to add a number of time units to a date. The function requires three parameters: the date part, the number, and a date. T-SQL doesn't have a DATESUBTRACT function, but you can use a negative number to accomplish the same thing. You might use DATEADD to calculate an expiration date or a date that a payment is due, for example. Table 3-1 from Books Online lists the possible values for the date part parameter in the DATADD function and other date functions. Here is the syntax for DATEADD:

```
DATEADD(<date part>,<number>,<date>)
```

Table 3-1. The Values for the Date Part Parameter

Date Part	Abbreviation
Year	yy, yyyy
Quarter	qq, q
Month	mm, m
Dayofyear	dy, y
Day	dd, d
Week	wk, ww
Weekday	Dw
Hour	Hh
Minute	mi, n
Second	ss, s
Millisecond	Ms
Microsecond	Mcs
Nanosecond	Ns

Type in and execute the code in Listing 3-16 to learn how to use the DATEADD function.

Listing 3-16. Using the DATEADD Function

```
Use AdventureWorks2012
GO
--1
SELECT OrderDate, DATEADD(year,1,OrderDate) AS OneMoreYear,
    DATEADD(month,1,OrderDate) AS OneMoreMonth,
    DATEADD(day,-1,OrderDate) AS OneLessDay
FROM Sales.SalesOrderHeader
WHERE SalesOrderID in (43659,43714,60621);
--2
SELECT DATEADD(month,1,'1/29/2009') AS FebDate;
```

Figure 3-16 shows the results of Listing 3-16. In query 1, the DATEADD function adds exactly the time unit specified in each expression to the OrderDate column from the Sales.SalesOrderHeader table. Notice in the results of query 2 that since there is no 29th day of February 2009, adding one month to January 29, 2009, returns February 28, the last possible day in February that year.

	OrderDate	OneMoreYear	OneMoreMonth	OneLessDay
1	2005-07-01 00:00:00.000	2006-07-01 00:00:00.000	2005-08-01 00:00:00.000	2005-06-30 00:00:00.000
2	2005-07-05 00:00:00.000	2006-07-05 00:00:00.000	2005-08-05 00:00:00.000	2005-07-04 00:00:00.000
3	2007-12-23 00:00:00.000	2008-12-23 00:00:00.000	2008-01-23 00:00:00.000	2007-12-22 00:00:00.000

	FebDate
1	2009-02-28 00:00:00.000

Figure 3-16. The results of using the DATEADD function

DATEDIFF

The DATEDIFF function allows you to find the difference between two dates. The function requires three parameters: the date part and the two dates. The DATEDIFF function might be used to calculate how many days have passed since unshipped orders were taken, for example. Here is the syntax:

```
DATEDIFF(<datepart>,<early date>,<later date>)
```

See Table 3-1 for the list of possible date parts. Listing 3-17 demonstrates how to use DATEDIFF. Be sure to type in and execute the code.

Listing 3-17. Using DATEDIFF

```
Use AdventureWorks2012;
GO

--1
SELECT OrderDate, GETDATE() CurrentDateTime,
    DATEDIFF(year,OrderDate,GETDATE()) AS YearDiff,
    DATEDIFF(month,OrderDate,GETDATE()) AS MonthDiff,
    DATEDIFF(day,OrderDate,GETDATE()) AS DayDiff
FROM Sales.SalesOrderHeader
WHERE SalesOrderID in (43659,43714,60621);

--2
SELECT DATEDIFF(year,'12/31/2008','1/1/2009') AS YearDiff,
    DATEDIFF(month,'12/31/2008','1/1/2009') AS MonthDiff,
    DATEDIFF(day,'12/31/2008','1/1/2009') AS DayDiff;
```

Figure 3-17 shows the results. Your results from query 1 will be different from mine since the query uses GETDATE(), a nondeterministic function, instead of hard-coded dates or dates from a table. Even though query 2 compares the difference between two dates that are just one day apart, the differences in years and months are both 1. The DATEDIFF rounds up the result to the nearest integer and doesn't display decimal results.

	OrderDate	CurrentDateTime	YearDiff	MonthDiff	DayDiff
1	2005-07-01 00:00:00.000	2011-03-23 07:31:46.513	6	68	2091
2	2005-07-05 00:00:00.000	2011-03-23 07:31:46.513	6	68	2087
3	2007-12-23 00:00:00.000	2011-03-23 07:31:46.513	4	39	1186

	YearDiff	MonthDiff	DayDiff
1	1	1	1

Figure 3-17. The results of using DATEDIFF

DATENAME and DATEPART

The DATENAME and DATEPART functions return the part of the date specified. Developers use the DATENAME and DATEPART functions to display just the year or month on reports, for example. DATEPART always returns a numeric value. DATENAME returns the actual name when the date part is the month or the day of the week. Again, you can find the possible date parts in Table 3-1. The syntax for the two functions is similar.

```
DATENAME(<datepart>,<date>)
DATEPART(<datepart>,<date>)
```

Type in and execute the code in Listing 3-18 to learn how to use DATENAME.

Listing 3-18. Using DATENAME and DATEPART

```
Use AdventureWorks2012
GO
--1
SELECT OrderDate, DATEPART(year,OrderDate) AS OrderYear,
    DATEPART(month,OrderDate) AS OrderMonth,
    DATEPART(day,OrderDate) AS OrderDay,
    DATEPART(weekday,OrderDate) AS OrderWeekDay
FROM Sales.SalesOrderHeader
WHERE SalesOrderID in (43659,43714,60621);

--2
SELECT OrderDate, DATENAME(year,OrderDate) AS OrderYear,
    DATENAME(month,OrderDate) AS OrderMonth,
    DATENAME(day,OrderDate) AS OrderDay,
    DATENAME(weekday,OrderDate) AS OrderWeekDay
FROM Sales.SalesOrderHeader
WHERE SalesOrderID in (43659,43714,60621);
```

Figure 3-18 displays the results. You will see that the results are the same except for spelling out the month and weekday in query 2. One other thing to keep in mind is that the value returned from DATEPART is always an integer, while the value returned from DATENAME is always a string, even when the expression returns a number.

	OrderDate	OrderYear	OrderMonth	OrderDay	OrderWeekDay
1	2005-07-01 00:00:00.000	2005	7	1	6
2	2005-07-05 00:00:00.000	2005	7	5	3
3	2007-12-23 00:00:00.000	2007	12	23	1

	OrderDate	OrderYear	OrderMonth	OrderDay	OrderWeekDay
1	2005-07-01 00:00:00.000	2005	July	1	Friday
2	2005-07-05 00:00:00.000	2005	July	5	Tuesday
3	2007-12-23 00:00:00.000	2007	December	23	Sunday

Figure 3-18. Results of using DATENAME and DATEPART

DAY, MONTH, and YEAR

The DAY, MONTH, and YEAR functions work just like DATEPART. These functions are just alternate ways to get the day, month, or year from a date. Here is the syntax:

```
DAY(<date>)
MONTH(<date>)
YEAR(<date>)
```

Type in and execute the code in Listing 3-19 to see that this is just another way to get the same results as using the DATEPART function.

Listing 3-19. Using the DAY, MONTH, and YEAR Functions

```
Use AdventureWorks2012
GO

SELECT OrderDate, YEAR(OrderDate) AS OrderYear,
    MONTH(OrderDate) AS OrderMonth,
    DAY(OrderDate) AS OrderDay
FROM Sales.SalesOrderHeader
WHERE SalesOrderID in (43659,43714,60621);
```

Figure 3-19 displays the results of the code from Listing 3-19. If you take a look at the results of query 1 from Listing 3-18 that used the DATEPART function, you will see that they are the same.

	OrderDate	OrderYear	OrderMonth	OrderDay
1	2005-07-01 00:00:00.000	2005	7	1
2	2005-07-05 00:00:00.000	2005	7	5
3	2007-12-23 00:00:00.000	2007	12	23

Figure 3-19. The result of using YEAR, MONTH, and DAY

CONVERT

You learned about CONVERT earlier in the chapter when I talked about concatenating strings. To append a number or a date to a string, the number or date must first be cast to a string. The CONVERT function has an optional parameter called style that can be used to format a date.

I have frequently seen code that used the DATEPART function to break a date into its parts and then cast the parts into strings and concatenate them back together to format the date. It is so much easier just to use CONVERT to accomplish the same thing! Here is the syntax:

```
CONVERT(<data type, usually varchar>,<date>,<style>)
```

Type in and execute the code in Listing 3-20 to compare both methods of formatting dates. Take a look at the SQL Server Books Online article "CAST and CONVERT" for a list of all the possible formats.

Listing 3-20. Using CONVERT to Format a Date/Time Value

```
--1 The hard way!
SELECT CAST(DATEPART(YYYY,GETDATE()) AS VARCHAR) + '/' +
    CAST(DATEPART(MM,GETDATE()) AS VARCHAR) +
    '/' + CAST(DATEPART(DD,GETDATE()) AS VARCHAR) AS DateCast;
--2 The easy way!
SELECT CONVERT(VARCHAR,GETDATE(),111) AS DateConvert;
--3
USE AdventureWorks2012
GO
```

```
SELECT CONVERT(VARCHAR,OrderDate,1) AS "1",
    CONVERT(VARCHAR,OrderDate,101) AS "101",
    CONVERT(VARCHAR,OrderDate,2) AS "2",
    CONVERT(VARCHAR,OrderDate,102) AS "102"
FROM Sales.SalesOrderHeader
WHERE SalesOrderID in (43659,43714,60621);
```

Figure 3-20 shows the results of Listing 3-20. Notice in query 1 that you not only had to use DATEPART three times, but you also had to cast each result to a VARCHAR in order to concatenate the pieces back together. Query 2 shows the easy way to accomplish the same thing. This method is often used to remove the time from a DATETIME data type. Query 3 demonstrates four different formats. Notice that the three-digit formats always produce four-digit years.

	DateCast
1	2011/3/23

	DateConvert
1	2011/03/23

	1	101	2	102
1	07/01/05	07/01/2005	05.07.01	2005.07.01
2	07/05/05	07/05/2005	05.07.05	2005.07.05
3	12/23/07	12/23/2007	07.12.23	2007.12.23

Figure 3-20. The results of formatting dates

FORMAT

SQL Server 2012 introduces the FORMAT function. The primary purpose is to simplify the conversion of date/time values as string values. Another purpose of the format function is to convert date/time values to their cultural equivalencies. Here is the syntax:

```
FORMAT ( value, format [, culture ] )
```

The FORMAT function greatly simplifies how date/time values are converted, and it should be used for date/time values instead of the CAST or CONVERT functions. Listing 3-21 shows some examples.

Listing 3-21. FORMAT Function Examples

```
DECLARE @d DATETIME = GETDATE();

SELECT FORMAT( @d, 'dd', 'en-US' ) AS Result;
SELECT FORMAT( @d, 'd/M/y', 'en-US' ) AS Result;
SELECT FORMAT( @d, 'dd/MM/yyyy', 'en-US' ) AS Result;
```

Figure 3-21 shows the results. Keep in mind the letters for each part of the date are case sensitive. For example if you switch mm for MM you will get back minutes instead of months.

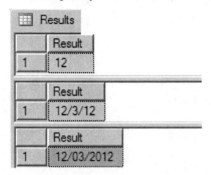

Figure 3-21. FORMAT Function Results

SQL 2012 also introduces a simple method to derive a date, time, or date and time from a list of values. The primary function is called DATEFROMPARTS but there is also a version of the function for time, and date and time. Listing 3-22 shows some examples.

Listing 3-22. DATEFROMPARTS Examples

```
SELECT DATEFROMPARTS(2012, 3, 10) AS RESULT;
SELECT TIMEFROMPARTS(12, 10, 32, 0, 0) AS RESULT;
SELECT DATETIME2FROMPARTS (2012, 3, 10, 12, 10, 32, 0, 0) AS RESULT;
```

Figure 3-22 shows the results from each function. The first function returns only the date. The TIMEFROMPARTS function returns a time. Finally, the DATETIME2FROMPARTS returns both a date and a time. If a value is out of the range of either a date or time, for example you put 13 for the month value, the function will throw an error.

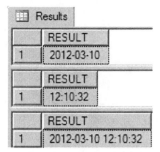

Figure 3-22. Results from DATEFROMTIME functions

This section covered a sample of the functions available for manipulating dates. Practice what you have learned by completing Exercise 3-4.

EXERCISE 3-4

Use the AdventureWorks2012 database to complete this exercise. You can find the solutions to the questions in the Appendix.

1. Write a query that calculates the number of days between the date an order was placed and the date that it was shipped using the Sales.SalesOrderHeader table. Include the SalesOrderID, OrderDate, and ShipDate columns.

2. Write a query that displays only the date, not the time, for the order date and ship date in the Sales.SalesOrderHeader table.

3. Write a query that adds six months to each order date in the Sales.SalesOrderHeader table. Include the SalesOrderID and OrderDate columns.

4. Write a query that displays the year of each order date and the numeric month of each order date in separate columns in the results. Include the SalesOrderID and OrderDate columns.

5. Change the query written in question 4 to display the month name instead.

Using Mathematical Functions

You can use several mathematical functions on numeric values. These include trigonometric functions such as SIN and TAN and logarithmic functions that are not used frequently in business applications. This section discusses some of the more commonly used mathematical functions.

ABS

The ABS function returns the absolute value of the number—the difference between the number and zero. Type in and execute this code to see how to use ABS:

```
SELECT ABS(2) AS "2", ABS(-2) AS "-2"
```

POWER

The POWER function returns the power of one number to another number. The syntax is simple.

```
POWER(<number>,<power>)
```

There may not be many uses for POWER in business applications, but you may use it in scientific or academic applications. Type in and execute the code in Listing 3-23.

Listing 3-23. Using POWER

```
SELECT POWER(10,1) AS "Ten to the First",
    POWER(10,2) AS "Ten to the Second",
    POWER(10,3) AS "Ten to the Third";
```

Figure 3-23 displays the results. The POWER function returns a FLOAT value. Caution must be taken, however, with this function. The results will increase in size very quickly and can cause an overflow error. Try finding the value of 10 to the 10th power to see what can happen.

	Ten to the First	Ten to the Second	Ten to the Third
1	10	100	1000

Figure 3-23. The results of using POWER

SQUARE and SQRT

The SQUARE function returns the square of a number, or the number multiplied to itself. The SQRT function returns the opposite, the square root of a number. Type in and execute the code in Listing 3-24 to see how to use these functions.

Listing 3-24. Using the SQUARE and SQRT Functions

```
SELECT SQUARE(10) AS "Square of 10",
    SQRT(10) AS "Square Root of 10",
    SQRT(SQUARE(10)) AS "The Square Root of the Square of 10";
```

Figure 3-24 shows the results. Notice that the third expression in the query is a nested function that squares 10 and then takes the square root of that result.

Results

	Square of 10	Square Root of 10	The Square Root of the Square of 10
1	100	3.16227766016838	10

Figure 3-24. The results of using SQUARE and SQRT

ROUND

The ROUND function allows you to round a number to a given precision. The ROUND function is used frequently to display only the number of decimal places required in the report or application. The ROUND function requires two parameters, the number and the length, which can be either positive or negative. It also has an optional third parameter that causes the function to just truncate instead of rounding if a nonzero value is supplied. Here is the syntax:

```
ROUND(<number>,<length>[,<function>])
```

Type in and execute the code in Listing 3-25 to learn how to use ROUND.

Listing 3-25. Using ROUND

```
SELECT ROUND(1234.1294,2) AS "2 places on the right",
    ROUND(1234.1294,-2) AS "2 places on the left",
    ROUND(1234.1294,2,1) AS "Truncate 2",
    ROUND(1234.1294,-2,1) AS "Truncate -2";
```

You can view the results in Figure 3-25. When the expression contains a negative number as the second parameter, the function rounds on the left side of the decimal point. Notice the difference when 1 is used as the third parameter, causing the function to truncate instead of rounding. When rounding 1234.1294, the expression returns 1234.1300. When truncating 1234.1294, the expression returns 1234.1200. It doesn't round the value; it just changes the specified digits to zero.

Results

	2 places on the right	2 places on the left	Truncate 2	Truncate -2
1	1234.1300	1200.0000	1234.1200	1200.0000

Figure 3-25. The results of using ROUND

RAND

RAND returns a float value between 0 and 1. RAND can be used to generate a random value. This might be used to generate data for testing an application, for example. The RAND function takes one optional integer parameter, @seed. When the RAND expression contains the seed value, the function returns the same value each time. If the expression doesn't contain a seed value, SQL Server randomly assigns a seed, effectively providing a random number. Type in and execute the code in Listing 3-26 to generate a random numbers.

Listing 3-26. Using RAND

```
SELECT CAST(RAND() * 100 AS INT) + 1 AS "1 to 100",
    CAST(RAND()* 1000 AS INT) + 900 AS "900 to 1900",
    CAST(RAND() * 5 AS INT)+ 1 AS "1 to 5";
```

Since the function returns a float value, multiply by the size of the range, and add the lower limit (see Figure 3-26). The first expression returns random numbers between 1 and 100. The second expression returns random numbers between 900 and 1,900. The third expression returns random values between 1 and 5.

	1 to 100	900 to 1900	1 to 5
1	89	1658	5

Figure 3-26. The results of generating random numbers with RAND

If you supply a seed value to one of the calls to RAND within a batch of statements, that seed affects the other calls. The value is not the same, but the values are predictable. Run this statement several times to see what happens when a seed value is used:

```
SELECT RAND(3),RAND(),RAND().
```

Just like strings and dates, you will find several functions that manipulate numbers. Practice using these functions by completing Exercise 3-5.

EXERCISE 3-5

Use the AdventureWorks2012 database to complete this exercise. You can find the solutions to the questions in the Appendix.

1. Write a query using the Sales.SalesOrderHeader table that displays the SubTotal rounded to two decimal places. Include the SalesOrderID column in the results.

2. Modify the query from question 1 so that the SubTotal is rounded to the nearest dollar but still displays two zeros to the right of the decimal place.

3. Write a query that calculates the square root of the SalesOrderID value from the Sales.SalesOrderHeader table.

4. Write a statement that generates a random number between 1 and 10 each time it is run.

System Functions

T-SQL features many other built-in functions. Some are specific for administering SQL Server, while others are very useful in regular end user applications, returning information such as the database and current usernames. Be sure to review the "Functions" topic in Books Online often to discover functions that will make your life easier.

The CASE Function

Use the CASE function to evaluate a list of expressions and return the first one that evaluates to true. For example, a report may need to display the season of the year based on one of the date columns in the table. CASE is similar to Select Case or Switch used in other programming languages, but it is used inside the statement.

There are two ways to write a CASE expression: simple or searched. The following sections will explain the differences and how to use them.

Simple CASE

To write the simple CASE statement, come up with an expression that you want to evaluate, often a column name, and a list of possible values. Here is the syntax:

```
CASE <test expression>
    WHEN <comparison expression1> THEN <return value1>
    WHEN <comparison expression2> THEN <return value2>
    [ELSE <value3>] END
```

Type in and execute the code in Listing 3-27 to learn how to use the simple version of CASE.

Listing 3-27. Using Simple CASE

```
USE AdventureWorks2012;
GO
SELECT Title,
    CASE Title
    WHEN 'Mr.' THEN 'Male'
    WHEN 'Ms.' THEN 'Female'
    WHEN 'Mrs.' THEN 'Female'
    WHEN 'Miss' THEN 'Female'
    ELSE 'Unknown' END AS Gender
FROM Person.Person
WHERE BusinessEntityID IN (1,5,6,357,358,11621,423);
```

Figure 3-27 shows the results. Even though the CASE statement took up a lot of room in the query, it is producing only one column in the results. For each row returned, the expression evaluates the Title column to see whether it matches any of the possibilities listed and returns the appropriate value. If the value from Title doesn't match or is NULL, then whatever is in the ELSE part of the expression is returned. If no ELSE exists, the expression returns NULL.

	Title	Gender
1	NULL	Unknown
2	Ms.	Female
3	Mr.	Male
4	Ms.	Female
5	Sr.	Unknown
6	Mrs.	Female

Figure 3-27. The results of using simple CASE

Searched CASE

Developers often used the searched CASE syntax when the expression is too complicated for the simple CASE syntax. For example, you might want to compare the value from a column to several IN lists or use greater-than or less-than operators. The CASE statement returns the first expression that returns true. This is the syntax for the searched CASE:

```
CASE WHEN <test expression1> THEN <value1>
WHEN <test expression2> THEN <value2>
[ELSE <value3>] END
```

Type in and execute the code in Listing 3-28 to learn how to use this more flexible method of using CASE.

Listing 3-28. Using Searched CASE

```
SELECT Title,
    CASE WHEN Title IN ('Ms.','Mrs.','Miss') THEN 'Female'
    WHEN Title = 'Mr.' THEN 'Male'
    ELSE 'Unknown' END AS Gender
FROM Person.Person
WHERE BusinessEntityID IN (1,5,6,357,358,11621,423);
```

This query returns the same results (see Figure 3-28) as the one in Listing 3-27. The CASE function evaluates each WHEN expression independently until finding the first one that returns true. It then returns the appropriate value. If none of the expressions returns true, the function returns the value from the ELSE part or NULL if no ELSE is available.

	Title	Gender
1	NULL	Unknown
2	Ms.	Female
3	Mr.	Male
4	Ms.	Female
5	Sr.	Unknown
6	Mrs.	Female

Figure 3-28. The results of using searched CASE

One very important note about using CASE is that the return values must be of compatible data types. For example, you can't have one part of the expression returning an integer while another part returns a non-numeric string. Precedence rules apply as with other operations.

Listing a Column as the Return Value

It is also possible to list a column name instead of hard-coded values in the THEN part of the CASE function. This means that you can display one column for some of the rows and another column for other rows. Type in and execute the code in Listing 3-29 to see how this works.

Listing 3-29. Returning a Column Name in CASE

```
USE AdventureWorks2012;
GO

SELECT VacationHours,SickLeaveHours,
    CASE WHEN VacationHours > SickLeaveHours THEN VacationHours
    ELSE SickLeaveHours END AS 'More Hours'
FROM HumanResources.Employee;
```

In this example (see Figure 3-29), if there are more VacationHours than SickLeaveHours, the query displays the VacationHours column from the HumanResources.Empoyee table in the More Hours column. Otherwise, the query returns the SickLeaveHours.

▦ Results

	VacationHours	SickLeaveHours	More Hours
1	99	69	99
2	1	20	20
3	2	21	21
4	48	80	80
5	5	22	22
6	6	23	23
7	61	50	61
8	62	51	62
9	63	51	63
10	16	64	64

Figure 3-29. The results of returning a column from CASE

IIF

SQL 2012 introduces one easier method of writing a simple CASE statement. In SQL 2012 you can now use an IIF statement to return a result based on whether or not a Boolean expression is true or false. To create an IFF statement you need a Boolean expression and the values to return based on the results. Here is the basic syntax for the IIF statement.

```
IIF ( boolean_expression, true_value, false_value )
```

Execute the code in Listing 3-30. The first IIF statement is a simple execution while the second IFF shows how you can introduce varibles into the statement.

Listing 3-30. IIF Statement

```
--IIF Statement without variables

SELECT IIF (50 > 20, 'TRUE', 'FALSE') AS RESULT;

--IIF Statement with variables

DECLARE @a INT = 50
DECLARE @b INT = 25
SELECT IIF (@a > @b, 'TRUE', 'FALSE') AS RESULT;
```

Figure 3-30 shows the results. Keep in mind that all rules which apply to CASE statements also apply to IIF statements.

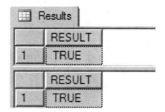

Figure 3-30. Results of IFF Statements

COALESCE

You learned about COALESCE earlier in the chapter in the "Concatenating Strings and NULL" section. You can use COALESCE with other data types as well and with any number of arguments to return the first non-NULL value. You can use the COALESCE function in place of ISNULL. If a list of values must be evaluated instead of one value, you must use COALESCE instead of ISNULL. COALESCE may be used when concatenating strings or any time that a replacement for NULL must be found. Type in and execute the code in Listing 3-31 to learn more about COALESCE.

Listing 3-31. Using COALESCE

```
USE AdventureWorks2012;
GO

SELECT ProductID,Size, Color,
    COALESCE(Size, Color,'No color or size') AS 'Description'
FROM Production.Product
where ProductID in (1,2,317,320,680,706);
```

Figure 3-31 displays the results. The COALESCE expression first checks the Size value and then the Color value to find the first non-NULL value. If both values are NULL, then the string No color or size is returned.

	ProductID	Size	Color	Description
1	1	NULL	NULL	No color or size
2	2	NULL	NULL	No color or size
3	317	NULL	Black	Black
4	320	NULL	Silver	Silver
5	680	58	Black	58
6	706	58	Red	58

Figure 3-31. The results of using COALESCE

115

Admin Functions

T-SQL contains many administrative functions that are useful for developers. SQL Server also has many functions that help database administrators manage SQL Server; these functions are beyond the scope of this book. Listing 3-32 shows a few examples of functions that return information about the current connection such as the database name and application.

Listing 3-32. A Few System Functions

```
SELECT DB_NAME() AS "Database Name",
    HOST_NAME() AS "Host Name",
    CURRENT_USER AS "Current User",
    USER_NAME() AS "User Name",
    APP_NAME() AS "App Name";
```

Take a look at Figure 3-32 for my results; your results will probably be different. When I ran the query, I was connected to the AdventureWorks2012 database on a computer named WIN-5RUBLZ7G773 as the dbo (database owner) user while using Management Studio.

	Database Name	Host Name	Current User	User Name	App Name
1	AdventureWorks2012	WIN-5RUBLZ7G773	dbo	dbo	Microsoft SQL Server Management Studio - Query

Figure 3-32. The results of using system functions

In addition to the functions used to manipulate strings, dates, and numbers, you will find many system functions. Some of these work on different types of data, such as CASE, while others provide information about the current connection. Administrators can manage SQL Server using dozens of system functions not covered in this book. Complete Exercise 3-6 to practice using the system functions covered in this section.

EXERCISE 3-6

Use the AdventureWorks2012 database to complete this exercise. You can find the solutions to the questions in the Appendix.

1. Write a query using the HumanResources.Employee table to display the BusinessEntityID column. Also include a CASE statement that displays "Even" when the BusinessEntityID value is an even number or "Odd" when it is odd. Hint: Use the modulo operator.

2. Write a query using the Sales.SalesOrderDetail table to display a value ("Under 10" or "10–19" or "20–29" or "30–39" or "40 and over") based on the OrderQty value by using the CASE function. Include the SalesOrderID and OrderQty columns in the results.

3. Using the Person.Person table, build the full names using the Title, FirstName, MiddleName, LastName, and Suffix columns. Check the table definition to see

which columns allow NULL values and use the COALESCE function on the appropriate columns.

4. Look up the SERVERPROPERTY function in Books Online. Write a statement that displays the edition, instance name, and machine name using this function.

Using Functions in the WHERE and ORDER BY Clauses

So far you have seen functions used in the SELECT list. You may also use functions in the WHERE and ORDER BY clauses. Take a look at Listing 3-33 for several examples.

Listing 3-33. Using Functions in WHERE and ORDER BY

```
USE AdventureWorks2012;
GO

--1
SELECT FirstName
FROM Person.Person
WHERE CHARINDEX('ke',FirstName) > 0;

--2
SELECT LastName,REVERSE(LastName)
FROM Person.Person
ORDER BY REVERSE(LastName);

--3
SELECT BirthDate
FROM HumanResources.Employee
ORDER BY YEAR(BirthDate);
```

Figure 3-33 shows the results of Listing 3-34. Even though it is very easy to use a function on a column in the WHERE clause, it is important to note that performance may suffer. If the database designer created an index on the searched column, the database engine must evaluate each row one at a time when a function is applied to a column.

Results

	FirstName
1	Blake
2	Luke
3	Mackenzie
4	Luke
5	Blake
6	Luke

	LastName	(No column name)
1	Skjønaa	aanøjkS
2	Lyeba	abeyL
3	Vaca	acaV
4	Okada	adakO
5	Osada	adasO
6	Osada	adasO

	BirthDate
1	1945-11-17
2	1946-06-13
3	1946-10-29
4	1946-04-03
5	1947-06-01
6	1948-05-25
7	1949-03-02

Figure 3-33. The results of using functions in the WHERE and ORDER BY clauses

Practice using functions in the WHERE and ORDER by clauses by completing Exercise 3-7.

EXERCISE 3-7

Use the AdventureWorks2012 database to complete this exercise. You will find the solutions to the questions in the Appendix.

1. Write a query using the Sales.SalesOrderHeader table to display the orders placed during 2001 by using a function. Include the SalesOrderID and OrderDate columns in the results.

2. Write a query using the Sales.SalesOrderHeader table listing the sales in order of the month the order was placed and then the year the order was placed. Include the SalesOrderID and OrderDate columns in the results.

3. 3. Write a query that displays the `PersonType` and the name columns from the Person.Person table. Sort the results so that rows with a `PersonType` of IN, SP, or SC sort by `LastName`. The other rows should sort by FirstName. Hint: Use the CASE function.

The TOP Keyword

Use the TOP keyword to limit the number or percentage of rows returned from a query. TOP has been around for a long time, but beginning with the release of SQL Server 2005, Microsoft has added several enhancements. TOP originally could be used in SELECT statements only. You could not use TOP in a DELETE, UPDATE, or INSERT statement. The number or percentage specified had to be a hard-coded value. SQL Server 2012You can use TOP in data manipulation statements and use a variable to specify the number or percentage or rows. Here is the syntax:

```
SELECT TOP(<number>) [PERCENT] [WITH TIES] <col1>,<col2>
FROM <table1> [ORDER BY <col1>]

DELETE TOP(<number>) [PERCENT] [FROM] <table1>

UPDATE TOP(<number>) [PERCENT] <table1> SET <col1> = <value>

INSERT TOP(<number>) [PERCENT] [INTO] <table1> (<col1>,<col2>)
SELECT <col3>,<col4> FROM <table2>

INSERT [INTO] <table1> (<col1>,<col2>)
SELECT TOP(<numbers>) [PERCENT] <col3>,<col4>
FROM <table2>
ORDER BY <col1>
```

The ORDER BY clause is optional with the SELECT statement, but most of the time, you will use it to determine which rows the query returns. A scenario you may want to select random rows is if you need to select sample data in order to populate a test environment. Otherwise, it rarely makes sense to request the TOP N random rows. Usually one sorts by some criteria in order to get the TOP N rows in that sequence.

The ORDER BY clause is not valid with DELETE and UPDATE. The WITH TIES option is valid only with the SELECT statement. It means that, if there are rows that have identical values in the ORDER BY clause, the results will include all the rows even though you now end up with more rows than you expect. Type in and execute the code in Listing 3-34 to learn how to use TOP.

Listing 3-34. Limiting Results with TOP

```
USE AdventureWorks2012;
GO

--1
IF OBJECT_ID('dbo.Sales') IS NOT NULL BEGIN
    DROP TABLE dbo.Sales;
END;

--2
CREATE TABLE dbo.Sales (CustomerID INT, OrderDate DATE,
    SalesOrderID INT NOT NULL PRIMARY KEY);
GO

--3
INSERT TOP(5) INTO dbo.Sales(CustomerID,OrderDate,SalesOrderID)
SELECT CustomerID, OrderDate, SalesOrderID
FROM Sales.SalesOrderHeader;

--4
SELECT CustomerID, OrderDate, SalesOrderID
FROM dbo.Sales
ORDER BY SalesOrderID;

--5
DELETE TOP(2) dbo.Sales

--6
UPDATE TOP(2) dbo.Sales SET CustomerID = CustomerID + 10000;

--7
SELECT CustomerID, OrderDate, SalesOrderID
FROM dbo.Sales
ORDER BY SalesOrderID;

--8
DECLARE @Rows INT = 2;
SELECT TOP(@Rows) CustomerID, OrderDate, SalesOrderID
FROM dbo.Sales
ORDER BY SalesOrderID;
```

Figure 3-34 shows the results. Code section 1 drops the dbo.Sales table if it exists. Statement 2 creates the table. Statement 3 inserts five rows into the dbo.Sales table. Using TOP in the INSERT part of the statement doesn't allow you to use ORDER BY to determine which rows to insert. To control which rows get inserted, move TOP to the SELECT statement. Query 4 shows the inserted rows. Statement 5 deletes two of the rows. Statement 6 updates the CustomerID of two of the rows. Query 7 shows how the data looks after the delete and update. Code section 8 shows how to use a variable with TOP.

	CustomerID	OrderDate	SalesOrderID
1	29825	2005-07-01	43659
2	29672	2005-07-01	43660
3	29734	2005-07-01	43661
4	29994	2005-07-01	43662
5	29565	2005-07-01	43663

	CustomerID	OrderDate	SalesOrderID
1	39734	2005-07-01	43661
2	39994	2005-07-01	43662
3	29565	2005-07-01	43663

	CustomerID	OrderDate	SalesOrderID
1	39734	2005-07-01	43661
2	39994	2005-07-01	43662

Figure 3-34. *The results of using TOP*

■ **Note** Microsoft recommends using the OFFSET and FETCH clauses instead of TOP as a paging solution and to limit the amount of data sent to a client. OFFSET and FETCH also allow more options, including the use of variables.

Ranking Functions

Ranking functions introduced with SQL Server 2005 allow you to assign a number to each row returned from a query. For example, suppose you need to include a row number with each row for display on a web page. You could come up with a method to do this, such as inserting the query results into a temporary table that includes an IDENTITY column, but now you can create the numbers by using the ROW_NUMBER function. During your T-SQL programming career, you will probably find you can solve many query problems by including ROW_NUMBER. Recently I needed to insert several thousand rows into a table that included a unique ID. I was able to add the maximum ID value already in the table to the result of the ROW_NUMBER function to successfully insert the new rows. Along with ROW_NUMBER, this section covers RANK, DENSE_RANK, and NTILE.

Using ROW_NUMBER

The ROW_NUMBER function returns a sequential numeric value along with the results of a query. The ROW_NUMBER function contains the OVER clause, which the function uses to determine the numbering behavior. You must include the ORDER BY option, which determines the order in which the function applies the numbers. You have the option of starting the numbers over whenever the values of a specified column change, called *partitioning*, with the PARTITION BY clause. One limitation with using ROW_NUMBER is that you can't include it in the WHERE clause. To filter the rows, include the query containing

ROW_NUMBER in a CTE (you will learn about common table expressions in Chapter 10), and then filter on the ROW_NUMBER alias in the outer query. Here is the syntax:

```
SELECT <col1>,<col2>,
    ROW_NUMBER() OVER([PARTITION BY <col1>,<col2>]
        ORDER BY <col1>,<col2>) AS <RNalias>
FROM <table1>

WITH <cteName> AS (
    SELECT <col1>,<col2>,
        ROW_NUMBER() OVER([PARTITION BY <col1>,<col2>]
            ORDER BY <col1>,<col2>) AS <RNalias>
    FROM <table1>)
SELECT <col1>,<col2>,<RNalias>
FROM <table1>
WHERE <criteria including RNalias>
```

Type in and execute Listing 3-35 to learn how to use ROW_NUMBER.

Listing 3-35. Using ROW_NUMBER

```
USE AdventureWorks2012;
GO

--1
SELECT CustomerID, FirstName + ' ' + LastName AS Name,
    ROW_NUMBER() OVER (ORDER BY LastName, FirstName) AS Row
FROM Sales.Customer AS c INNER JOIN Person.Person AS p
ON c.PersonID = p.BusinessEntityID;

--2
WITH customers AS (
    SELECT CustomerID, FirstName + ' ' + LastName AS Name,
        ROW_NUMBER() OVER (ORDER BY LastName, FirstName) AS Row
    FROM Sales.Customer AS c INNER JOIN Person.Person AS p
    ON c.PersonID = p.BusinessEntityID
    )
SELECT CustomerID, Name, Row
FROM customers
WHERE Row > 50
ORDER BY Row;

--3
SELECT CustomerID, FirstName + ' ' + LastName AS Name, c.TerritoryID,
    ROW_NUMBER() OVER (PARTITION BY c.TerritoryID
        ORDER BY LastName, FirstName) AS Row
FROM Sales.Customer AS c INNER JOIN Person.Person AS p
ON c.PersonID = p.BusinessEntityID;
```

Figure 3-35 shows the partial results. Query 1 assigns the row numbers in order of LastName, FirstName to the query joining the Sales.Customer table to the Person.Person table. Each row in the results contains a unique row number.

Results

	CustomerID	Name	Row
1	29485	Catherine Abel	1
2	29486	Kim Abercrombie	2
3	29487	Humberto Acevedo	3
4	29484	Gustavo Achong	4
5	29488	Pilar Ackerman	5

	CustomerID	Name	Row
1	29030	Jeremy Adams	51
2	17172	Jesse Adams	52
3	28247	Jonathan Adams	53
4	16377	Jordan Adams	54
5	20387	Jordan Adams	55

	CustomerID	Name	TerritoryID	Row
1	21139	Alex Adams	1	1
2	13280	Bailey Adams	1	2
3	28678	Ben Adams	1	3
4	26598	Charles Adams	1	4
5	19410	Chloe Adams	1	5

Figure 3-35. The partial results of using ROW_NUMBER

Query 2 demonstrates how you can include the row number in the WHERE clause by using a CTE. The CTE in query 2 contains the same code as query 1. Now the Row column is available to you to use in the WHERE clause just like any other column. By using this technique, you can apply the WHERE clause to the results of the ROW_NUMBER function, and only the rows with a row number exceeding 50 appear in the results.

Query 3 uses the PARTITION BY option to start the row numbers over on each TerritoryID. The results shown in Figure 3-30 show the end of TerritoryID 1 and the beginning of TerritoryID 2.

Using RANK and DENSE_RANK

RANK and DENSE_RANK are very similar to ROW_NUMBER. The difference is how the functions deal with ties in the ORDER BY values. RANK assigns the same number to the duplicate rows and skips numbers not used. DENSE_RANK doesn't skip numbers. For example, if rows 2 and 3 are duplicates, RANK will supply the values 1, 3, 3, and 4, and DENSE_RANK will supply the values 1, 2, 2, and 3. Here is the syntax:

```
--1 RANK exampple
SELECT <col1>, RANK() OVER([PARTITION BY <col2>,<col3>] ORDER BY <col1>,<col2>)
FROM <table1>

--2 DENSE_RANK example
SELECT <col2>, DENSE_RANK() OVER([PARTITION BY <col2>,<col3>]
    ORDER BY <col1>,<col2>)
FROM <table1>
```

Type in and execute the code in Listing 3-36 to learn how to use RANK and DENSE_RANK.

Listing 3-36. Using RANK and DENSE_RANK

```
USE AdventureWorks2012;
GO

SELECT CustomerID,COUNT(*) AS CountOfSales,
    RANK() OVER(ORDER BY COUNT(*) DESC) AS Ranking,
    ROW_NUMBER() OVER(ORDER BY COUNT(*) DESC) AS Row,
    DENSE_RANK() OVER(ORDER BY COUNT(*) DESC) AS DenseRanking
FROM Sales.SalesOrderHeader
GROUP BY CustomerID
ORDER BY COUNT(*) DESC;
```

Figure 3-36 shows the partial results. The query compares ROW_NUMBER to RANK and DENSE_RANK. In each expression, the count of the sales for each customer determines the order of the numbers.

	CustomerID	CountOfSales	Ranking	Row	DenseRanking
1	11091	28	1	1	1
2	11176	28	1	2	1
3	11185	27	3	3	2
4	11200	27	3	4	2
5	11223	27	3	5	2
6	11262	27	3	6	2
7	11276	27	3	7	2
8	11277	27	3	8	2
9	11287	27	3	9	2
10	11300	27	3	10	2
11	11330	27	3	11	2
12	11331	27	3	12	2
13	11711	27	3	13	2
14	11566	25	14	14	3
15	11211	17	15	15	4
16	11212	17	15	16	4
17	11203	17	15	17	4

Figure 3-36. The partial results of using RANK and DENSE_RANK

Using NTILE

While the other ranking functions supply a row number or rank to each row, the NTILE function assigns buckets to groups of rows. For example, suppose the AdventureWorks company wants to divide up bonus money for the sales staff. You can use the NTILE function to divide up the money based on the sales by each employee. Here is the syntax:

```
SELECT <col1>, NTILE(<buckets>) OVER([PARTITION BY <col1>,<col1>]
    ORDER BY <col1>,<col2>) AS <alias>
FROM <table1>
```

Type in and execute Listing 3-37 to learn how to use NTILE.

Listing 3-37. Using NTILE

```
USE AdventureWorks2012;
GO

SELECT SalesPersonID,SUM(TotalDue) AS TotalSales,
    NTILE(10) OVER(ORDER BY SUM(TotalDue)) * 10000/COUNT(*) OVER() AS Bonus
FROM Sales.SalesOrderHeader
WHERE SalesPersonID IS NOT NULL
    AND OrderDate BETWEEN '1/1/2005' AND '12/31/2005'
GROUP BY SalesPersonID
ORDER BY TotalSales;
```

Figure 3-37 shows the results. The query returns the sum of the total sales grouped by the SalesPersonID for 2005. The NTILE function divides the rows into 10 groups, or buckets, based on the sales for each salesperson. The query multiplies the value returned by the NTILE expression by 10,000 divided by the number of rows to determine the bonus amount. The query uses the COUNT(*) OVER() expression to determine the number of rows in the results. See "The OVER Clause" in Chapter 5 to review how this works.

	SalesPersonID	TotalSales	Bonus
1	274	32567.9155	1000
2	278	532111.8814	2000
3	283	570467.7098	3000
4	280	684031.4513	4000
5	275	846580.2377	5000
6	281	999685.163	6000
7	282	1170079.0677	7000
8	276	1288179.9682	8000
9	277	1404871.479	9000
10	279	1555332.8072	10000

Figure 3-37. The results of using NTILE

The salespeople with the lowest sales get the smallest bonuses. The salespeople with the highest sales get the biggest bonuses. Notice that the smaller values have two rows in each bucket, but the last three buckets each have one row. The query must produce ten buckets, but there are not enough rows to divide the buckets up evenly.

Thinking About Performance

In Chapter 2 you learned how to use execution plans to compare two or more queries and determine which query uses the least resources or, in other words, performs the best. In this chapter, you will see how using functions can affect performance. Review the "Thinking About Performance" section in Chapter 2 if you need to take another look at how to use execution plans or to brush up on how SQL Server uses indexes.

Using Functions in the WHERE Clause

In the section "Using Functions in the WHERE and ORDER BY Clauses," you learned that functions can be used in the WHERE clause to filter out unneeded rows. Although I am not saying that you should never include a function in the WHERE clause, you need to realize that including a function that operates on a column may cause a decrease in performance.

The Sales.SalesOrderHeader table does not contain an index on the OrderDate column. Run the following code to create an index on the column. Don't worry about trying to understand the code at this point.

```
USE AdventureWorks2012
GO
--Add an index
IF  EXISTS (SELECT * FROM sys.indexes WHERE object_id =
    OBJECT_ID(N'[Sales].[SalesOrderHeader]')
    AND name = N'DEMO_SalesOrderHeader_OrderDate')
DROP INDEX [DEMO_SalesOrderHeader_OrderDate]
    ON [Sales].[SalesOrderHeader] WITH ( ONLINE = OFF );
GO
CREATE NONCLUSTERED INDEX [DEMO_SalesOrderHeader_OrderDate]
    ON [Sales].[SalesOrderHeader]
([OrderDate] ASC);
```

Toggle on the Include Actual Execution Plan setting before typing and executing the code in Listing 3-38.

Listing 3-38. Compare the Performance When Using a Function in the WHERE Clause

```
USE AdventureWorks2012;
GO

--1
SELECT SalesOrderID, OrderDate
FROM Sales.SalesOrderHeader
WHERE OrderDate >= '2005-01-01 00:00:00'
    AND OrderDate <= '2006-01-01 00:00:00';
```

```
--2
SELECT SalesOrderID, OrderDate
FROM Sales.SalesOrderHeader
WHERE YEAR(OrderDate) = 2005;
```

Query 1 finds all the orders placed in 2005 without using a function. Query 2 uses the YEAR function to return the same results. Take a look at the execution plans (Figure 3-38) to see that query 1 performs much better with a query cost of 7 percent. When executing query 2, the database engine performs a scan of the entire index to see whether the result of the function applied to each value meets the criteria. The database engine performs a seek of the index in query 1 because it just has to compare the actual values, not the results of the function for each value.

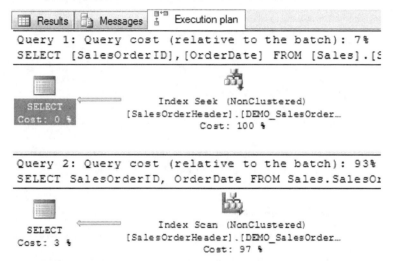

Figure 3-38. *The execution plans showing that using a function in the WHERE clause can affect performance*

Remove the index you created for this demonstration by running this code:

```
IF  EXISTS (SELECT * FROM sys.indexes WHERE object_id =
    OBJECT_ID(N'[Sales].[SalesOrderHeader]')
    AND name = N'DEMO_SalesOrderHeader_OrderDate')
DROP INDEX [DEMO_SalesOrderHeader_OrderDate]
    ON [Sales].[SalesOrderHeader] WITH ( ONLINE = OFF );
```

Run Listing 3-38 again now that the index is gone. Figure 3-39 shows that with no index on the OrderDate column, the performance is almost identical. Now the database engine must perform a scan of the table (in this case, the clustered index) to find the correct rows in both of the queries. Notice that the execution plan suggests an index to help the performance of query 1. It doesn't suggest an index for query 2 since an index won't help.

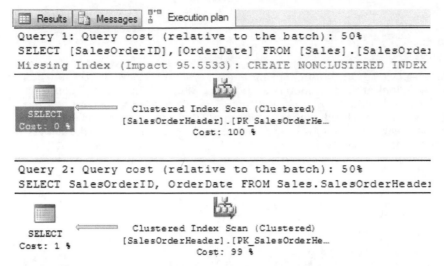

Figure 3-39. The execution plans after removing the index

You can see from these examples that writing queries is more than just getting the correct results; performance is important, too. Complete Exercise 3-8 to learn how using a function compares to a wildcard search.

EXERCISE 3-8

Use the AdventureWorks2012 database to complete this exercise. Make sure you have the Include Actual Execution Plan setting toggled on before starting this exercise. You can find the solutions in the Appendix.

1. Type in and execute the following code. View the execution plans once query execution completes, and explain whether one query performs better than the other and why.

```
USE AdventureWorks2012;
GO

--1
SELECT Name
FROM Production.Product
WHERE Name LIKE 'B%';

--2
SELECT Name
FROM Production.Product
WHERE CHARINDEX('B',Name) = 1;
```

2. Type in and execute the following code. View the execution plans once query execution completes, and explain whether one query performs better than the other and why.

```
USE AdventureWorks2012;
GO

--1
SELECT LastName
FROM Person.Person
WHERE LastName LIKE '%i%';

--2
SELECT LastName
FROM Person.Person
WHERE CHARINDEX('i',LastName) > 0;
```

Summary

Using expressions in T-SQL with the built-in functions and operators can be very convenient. There is a rich collection of functions for string and date manipulation as well as mathematical and system functions and more. It's possible to use expressions and functions in the SELECT, WHERE, and ORDER BY clauses. You must use caution when using functions in the WHERE clause; it is possible to decrease performance.

CHAPTER 4

Querying Multiple Tables

Now that you know how to write simple queries using one table and how to use functions and expressions in queries, it is time to learn how to write queries involving two or more tables. In a properly designed relational database, a table contains data about one thing or entity. For example, an order-entry application will have a table storing customer information, a table containing data about orders, and a table containing detail information about each item ordered. The order table has a column, called a *foreign key*, that points to a row in the customer table. The detail table has a foreign key column that points to the order table. By using *joins*, you can link these tables together so that you can display columns from each table in the same result set.

You can also use multiple tables with subqueries and union queries. You might use a subquery in place of an IN list in the WHERE clause, for example. A union query allows you to combine the result of two or more queries into one result set. For example, a database may contain archive tables with old sales data. By using a UNION query, you can combine the data from both the production tables and the archived tables so that it looks like the results are from the same table.

Finally, this chapter demonstrates two useful techniques: derived tables and common table expressions. These techniques allow you to isolate the logic used to query one table from the rest of the main query.

Learning how to join tables is a critical skill for T-SQL developers because it allows you to combine the relational data stored in multiple tables and present it as a single result set. Make sure you understand all the example code and complete the exercises in this chapter before moving on to the next chapter.

Writing INNER JOINS

Most of the time, to join tables together, you will use INNER JOIN. When connecting two tables with INNER JOIN, only the rows from the tables that match on the joining columns will show up in the results. If you join the customer and order tables, the query will return only the customers who have placed orders, along with the orders that have been placed. Only the rows where the customer ID is common in both tables will show up in the results.

Joining Two Tables

To join tables together, you might think that another clause will be added to the SELECT statement. This is not the case. Instead, the FROM clause contains information about how the tables join together. Here is the syntax for joining two tables (the keyword INNER is optional):

```
SELECT <select list>
FROM <table1>
[INNER] JOIN <table2> ON <table1>.<col1> = <table2>.<col2>
```

Figure 4-1 shows how the Sales.SalesOrderHeader and Sales.SalesOrderDetail tables connect and shows some of the columns in the tables. You will see these tables joined in the first example query, so make sure you understand how they connect before typing Listing 4-1.

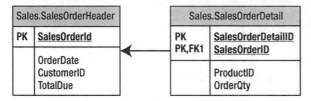

***Figure 4-1.** The Sales.SalesOrderHeader and Sales.SalesOrderDetail tables*

The Sales.SalesOrderHeader table has a primary key called SalesOrderID. The Sales.SalesOrderDetail table has a composite primary key, one that is made up of more than one column, consisting of SalesOrderDetailID and SalesOrderID. The SalesOrderID column in the Sales.SalesOrderDetail table is also a foreign key pointing back to the Sales.SalesOrderHeader table. The arrow points from the foreign key in the Sales.SalesOrderDetail table to the primary key in the Sales.SalesOrderHeader table.

Take a look at the code in Listing 4-1. Type in and execute the code to learn how to join the two tables.

***Listing 4-1.** Joining Two Tables*

```
USE AdventureWorks2012;
GO
SELECT s.SalesOrderID, s.OrderDate, s.TotalDue, d.SalesOrderDetailID,
    d.ProductID, d.OrderQty
FROM Sales.SalesOrderHeader AS s
INNER JOIN Sales.SalesOrderDetail AS d ON s.SalesOrderID = d.SalesOrderID;
```

Figure 4-2 displays the results. The SELECT list may contain columns from either of the tables. In the FROM clause, you list one of the tables followed by the words INNER JOIN and the second table name. To define how the two tables join together, use the keyword ON and an equality expression. Each Sales.OrderHeader row contains a unique SalesOrderID. Each Sales.SalesOrderDetail row contains a SalesOrderID column that determines to which order the detail belongs. When you join these two tables together, the query displays every row from the Sales.SalesOrderHeader table that matches a row in the Sales.SalesOrderDetail table.

Results

	SalesOrderID	OrderDate	TotalDue	SalesOrderDetailID	ProductID	OrderQty
1	43659	2005-07-01 00:00:00.000	23153.2339	1	776	1
2	43659	2005-07-01 00:00:00.000	23153.2339	2	777	3
3	43659	2005-07-01 00:00:00.000	23153.2339	3	778	1
4	43659	2005-07-01 00:00:00.000	23153.2339	4	771	1
5	43659	2005-07-01 00:00:00.000	23153.2339	5	772	1
6	43659	2005-07-01 00:00:00.000	23153.2339	6	773	2
7	43659	2005-07-01 00:00:00.000	23153.2339	7	774	1
8	43659	2005-07-01 00:00:00.000	23153.2339	8	714	3
9	43659	2005-07-01 00:00:00.000	23153.2339	9	716	1
10	43659	2005-07-01 00:00:00.000	23153.2339	10	709	6
11	43659	2005-07-01 00:00:00.000	23153.2339	11	712	2
12	43659	2005-07-01 00:00:00.000	23153.2339	12	711	4
13	43660	2005-07-01 00:00:00.000	1457.3288	13	762	1
14	43660	2005-07-01 00:00:00.000	1457.3288	14	758	1
15	43661	2005-07-01 00:00:00.000	36865.8012	15	745	1
16	43661	2005-07-01 00:00:00.000	36865.8012	16	743	1

Figure 4-2. The partial results of joining two tables

Take a look at the data from the Sales.SalesOrderHeader columns in the query results. The information from the Sales.SalesOrderHeader table repeats for each matching row in the Sales.SalesOrderDetail table. If a row exists in the Sales.SalesOrderHeader table with no matches in the Sales.SalesOrderDetail table, the Sales.SalesOrderHeader row will not show up in the results.

Because the column name, SalesOrderID, is the same in both tables, it must be fully qualified with the table name anywhere it is used in the query. To save typing, use an alias for each table. Notice that the query uses the table alias for all the columns in the SELECT list. Fully qualifying the column name is not required except for the columns with the same name; however, fully qualifying all of the column names will make the query more readable. Six months after you write a query, you can immediately see which table each column comes from without spending a lot of time figuring it out.

Avoiding an Incorrect Join Condition

Although you must specify join criteria with ON in the FROM clause when using INNER JOIN, nothing keeps you from writing the join incorrectly. Take a look at Listing 4-2. If you decide to run the code, you may have to click the red, square Cancel Executing Query icon to the right of the Execute icon to stop query execution, or the query will run for several minutes.

Listing 4-2. Writing an Incorrect Query

```
USE AdventureWorks2012;
GO
SELECT s.SalesOrderID, OrderDate, TotalDue, SalesOrderDetailID,
    d.ProductID, d.OrderQty
FROM Sales.SalesOrderHeader AS s
INNER JOIN Sales.SalesOrderDetail d ON 1 = 1;
```

Figure 4-3 displays a portion of the results after scrolling down more than 3,000 rows. When comparing the results to those in Figure 4-2, you will see that the rows from Sales.SalesOrderHeader join inappropriate rows from Sales.SalesOrderDetail. Both sets of results show SalesOrderID 43659, but the results are correct only in Figure 4-2. Because 1=1 is always true, *every* row from the first table joins *every* row from the second table to produce these incorrect results, which is also called a *Cartesian product*.

Results

	SalesOrderID	OrderDate	TotalDue	SalesOrderDetailID	ProductID	OrderQty
31462	43659	2005-07-01 00:00:00.000	23153.2339	31462	793	3
31463	43659	2005-07-01 00:00:00.000	23153.2339	31463	760	1
31464	43659	2005-07-01 00:00:00.000	23153.2339	31464	761	3
31465	43659	2005-07-01 00:00:00.000	23153.2339	31465	759	1
31466	43659	2005-07-01 00:00:00.000	23153.2339	31466	738	2
31467	43659	2005-07-01 00:00:00.000	23153.2339	31467	826	1
31468	43659	2005-07-01 00:00:00.000	23153.2339	31468	764	1
31469	43659	2005-07-01 00:00:00.000	23153.2339	31469	796	4
31470	43659	2005-07-01 00:00:00.000	23153.2339	31470	820	1
31471	43659	2005-07-01 00:00:00.000	23153.2339	31471	819	1
31472	43659	2005-07-01 00:00:00.000	23153.2339	31472	725	5
31473	43659	2005-07-01 00:00:00.000	23153.2339	31473	801	3
31474	43659	2005-07-01 00:00:00.000	23153.2339	31474	769	4

Figure 4-3. The partial results of an incorrect join

Whenever you write a query with INNER JOIN, make sure you understand the relationship between the two tables. For example, you could join the OrderQty column from the Sales.SalesOrderDetail table to the SalesOrderID column in the Sales.SalesOrderHeader table. The query would run, but the results would not make any sense at all.

Joining on a Different Column Name

In the previous two examples, the key column names happen to be the same, but this is not a requirement. The Person.Person table contains information about people from several tables in the AdventureWorks2012 database. Figure 4-4 shows how the Person.Person and the Sales.Customer table connect. The PersonID from the Sales.Customer table joins to the BusinessEntityID in the Person.Person table. The PersonID column in the Sales.Customer table is the foreign key.

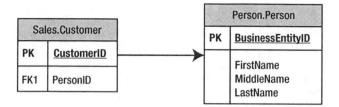

Figure 4-4. How to connect the Sales.Customer and Person.Person tables

Listing 4-3 shows an example that joins these two tables.

Listing 4-3. Joining Two Tables with Different Column Names

```
USE AdventureWorks2012;
GO
SELECT c.CustomerID, c.PersonID, p.BusinessEntityID, p.LastName
FROM Sales.Customer AS c
INNER JOIN Person.Person AS p ON c.PersonID = p.BusinessEntityID;
```

Figure 4-5 shows the partial results. The Person.Person table contains information about people from several tables in the database. In this case, the columns joining the two tables have different names. The PersonID from the Sales.Customer table joins to the BusinessEntityID in the Person.Person table. This works even though the columns have different names.

	CustomerID	PersonID	BusinessEntityID	LastName
1	29485	293	293	Abel
2	29486	295	295	Abercrombie
3	29487	297	297	Acevedo
4	29484	291	291	Achong
5	29488	299	299	Ackerman
6	28866	16867	16867	Adams
7	13323	16901	16901	Adams
8	21139	16724	16724	Adams
9	29170	10263	10263	Adams
10	19419	10312	10312	Adams

Figure 4-5. The partial results of joining tables with different key column names

Joining on More Than One Column

Although a JOIN frequently involves joining a column from one table to a column from another table, sometimes you must join multiple columns. The AdventureWorks2012 database contains only one example in which multiple columns must be used in a single JOIN: Sales.SalesOrderDetail to Sales.SpecialOfferProduct. Figure 4-6 shows how these two tables connect.

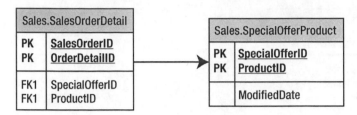

Figure 4-6. How to connect the Sales.SalesOrderDetail table to the Sales.SpecialOfferProduct table

The Sales.SalesSpecialOfferProduct table has a composite primary key composed of SpecialOfferID plus ProductID. To identify a row in this table, you must use both columns. When joining Sales.SalesOrderDetail to the Sales.SpecialOfferProduct table, you specify both columns in the join. Here is the syntax for joining on more than one column:

```
SELECT <SELECT list>
FROM <table1>
[INNER] JOIN <table2> ON <table1>.<col1> = <table2><col2>
    AND <table1>.<col3> = <table2>.<col4>
```

Type in and execute the code in Listing 4-4 to learn how to join on two columns.

Listing 4-4. Joining on Two Columns

```
USE AdventureWorks2012;
GO

SELECT sod.SalesOrderID, sod.SalesOrderDetailID,
    so.ProductID, so.SpecialOfferID, so.ModifiedDate
FROM Sales.SalesOrderDetail AS sod
INNER JOIN Sales.SpecialOfferProduct AS so
    ON so.ProductID = sod.ProductID AND
    so.SpecialOfferID = sod.SpecialOfferID
WHERE sod.SalesOrderID IN (51116,51112);
```

Take a look at the results (see Figure 4-7). Two columns, ProductID and SpecialOfferID, comprise the join condition. To determine which row matches the rows from Sales.SalesOrderDetail, both columns are used in the join condition. If the join contained only one of the columns, the results would be similar to the incorrect results in the section "Avoiding an Incorrect Join." If the join contained only the ProductID, the results would show every possible SpecialOfferID row for each ProductID, not just the correct rows. Try modifying the join yourself by leaving out one of the conditions to see what happens.

Results

	SalesOrderID	SalesOrderDetailID	ProductID	SpecialOfferID	ModifiedDate
1	51112	36341	956	14	2007-06-01 00:00:00.000
2	51112	36342	965	13	2007-06-01 00:00:00.000
3	51112	36343	885	1	2005-05-02 00:00:00.000
4	51112	36344	948	1	2005-05-02 00:00:00.000
5	51112	36345	960	13	2007-06-01 00:00:00.000
6	51112	36346	886	1	2005-05-02 00:00:00.000
7	51112	36347	994	1	2005-05-02 00:00:00.000
8	51112	36348	966	1	2005-05-02 00:00:00.000
9	51112	36349	959	13	2007-06-01 00:00:00.000
10	51112	36350	978	13	2007-06-01 00:00:00.000
11	51112	36351	970	1	2005-05-02 00:00:00.000

Figure 4-7. The partial results of joining on two columns

Joining Three or More Tables

Sometimes you will need to join only two tables together in a query, but more frequently, you will need to join three or more tables. You will often join three tables when there is a *many-to-many* relationship between two of the tables. For example, suppose you have a table listing college courses and a table listing students. You would need a third table that records which students take which courses. To join courses to students, your query will join all three tables.

In the AdventureWorks2012 database, you will find many reasons to join more than two tables in one query. For example, suppose you want to see a list of the product names for each order, along with the OrderDate column. This query requires the Sales.SalesOrderHeader, Sales.SalesOrderDetail, and Production.Product tables. Figure 4-8 shows how to connect these three tables.

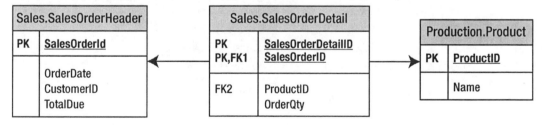

Figure 4-8. How to join Sales.SalesOrderHeader to Production.Product

To add a third or more tables, just continue the FROM clause. Take a look at the syntax.

```
SELECT <SELECT list> FROM <table1>
[INNER] JOIN <table2> ON <table1>.<col1> = <table2>.<col2>
[INNER] JOIN <table3> ON <table2>.<col2> = <table3>.<col3>
```

Type in and execute the query in Listing 4-5 to learn how to join more than two tables in one query.

Listing 4-5. Joining Three Tables

```
USE AdventureWorks2012;
GO

SELECT soh.SalesOrderID, soh.OrderDate, p.ProductID, p.Name
FROM Sales.SalesOrderHeader as soh
INNER JOIN Sales.SalesOrderDetail AS sod ON soh.SalesOrderID = sod.SalesOrderID
INNER JOIN Production.Product AS p ON sod.ProductID = p.ProductID
ORDER BY soh.SalesOrderID;
```

Figure 4-9 shows the results. Notice that even though the query joins three tables, the query displays columns from only two of the tables. To get from Sales.SalesOrderHeader to the names of the products ordered in the Production.Product table, the query must include the Sales.SalesOrderDetail table to connect the other two tables. Depending on the goal of the query, you may want to include columns from all tables involved in the query.

Results

	SalesOrderID	OrderDate	ProductID	Name
1	43659	2005-07-01 00:00:00.000	711	Sport-100 Helmet, Blue
2	43659	2005-07-01 00:00:00.000	712	AWC Logo Cap
3	43659	2005-07-01 00:00:00.000	709	Mountain Bike Socks, M
4	43659	2005-07-01 00:00:00.000	716	Long-Sleeve Logo Jersey, XL
5	43659	2005-07-01 00:00:00.000	714	Long-Sleeve Logo Jersey, M
6	43659	2005-07-01 00:00:00.000	771	Mountain-100 Silver, 38
7	43659	2005-07-01 00:00:00.000	778	Mountain-100 Black, 48
8	43659	2005-07-01 00:00:00.000	772	Mountain-100 Silver, 42
9	43659	2005-07-01 00:00:00.000	773	Mountain-100 Silver, 44
10	43659	2005-07-01 00:00:00.000	774	Mountain-100 Silver, 48
11	43659	2005-07-01 00:00:00.000	776	Mountain-100 Black, 42
12	43659	2005-07-01 00:00:00.000	777	Mountain-100 Black, 44
13	43660	2005-07-01 00:00:00.000	762	Road-650 Red, 44

Figure 4-9. The partial results of joining three tables

Take another look at the FROM clause. The Sales.SalesOrderHeader table joins to the Sales.SalesOrderDetail table on the SalesOrderID column. Then the Sales.SalesOrderDetail table joins the Production.Product table on the ProductID column. If you have trouble figuring out how to join the tables, take it a step at a time. Join two tables first, and then add the third table.

Joining tables is a very important skill for T-SQL developers. Before you move on to the next section, make sure you are comfortable with what the chapter has covered so far by completing Exercise 4-1.

EXERCISE 4-1

Use the AdventureWorks2012 database to complete this exercise. You can find the solutions in the Appendix.

1. The HumanResources.Employee table does not contain the employee names. Join that table to the Person.Person table on the BusinessEntityID column. Display the job title, birth date, first name, and last name.

2. The customer names also appear in the Person.Person table. Join the Sales.Customer table to the Person.Person table. The BusinessEntityID column in the Person.Person table matches the PersonID column in the Sales.Customer table. Display the CustomerID, StoreID, and TerritoryID columns along with the name columns.

3. Extend the query written in question 2 to include the Sales.SalesOrderHeader table. Display the SalesOrderID column along with the columns already specified. The Sales.SalesOrderHeader table joins the Sales.Customer table on CustomerID.

4. Write a query that joins the Sales.SalesOrderHeader table to the Sales.SalesPerson table. Join the BusinessEntityID column from the Sales.SalesPerson table to the SalesPersonID column in the Sales.SalesOrderHeader table. Display the SalesOrderID along with the SalesQuota and Bonus.

5. Add the name columns to the query written in step 4 by joining on the Person.Person table. See whether you can figure out which columns will be used to write the join.

6. The catalogue description for each product is stored in the Production.ProductModel table. Display the columns that describe the product such as the color and size, along with the catalogue description for each product.

7. Write a query that displays the names of the customers along with the product names that they have purchased. Hint: Five tables will be required to write this query!

Writing Outer Joins

When joining two tables with INNER JOIN, there must be an exact match between the two tables for a row to show up in the results. Occasionally, you'll need to retrieve all the rows from one of the tables even if the other table doesn't contain a match for every row. For example, you may want to display all the customers along with their orders, including the customers who have not placed orders yet. By using OUTER JOIN, you can retrieve all the rows from one table along with any rows that match from the other table.

Using LEFT OUTER JOIN

When writing OUTER JOIN, you must specify either LEFT or RIGHT. If the main table, the table that you want to see all the rows even if there is not a match, is on the left side of the join, you will specify LEFT. Figure 4-10 shows how the Sales.Customer and Sales.SalesOrderHeader tables connect when using LEFT OUTER JOIN so that all customers show up in the results even if they have not placed any orders. The gray area of the Venn diagram illustrates how all the CustomerID values in the Sales.Customer table will be returned whether or not there is a matching CustomerID value in the Sales.SalesOrderHeader table. Additionally, all matching CustomerID values (this is where the circles intersect in the diagram) will also be returned.

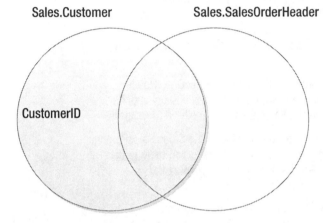

Sales.Customer   Sales.SalesOrderHeader

CustomerID

Figure 4-10. How to perform LEFT JOIN

Here is the syntax for LEFT OUTER JOIN:

```
SELECT <SELECT list>
FROM <table1>
LEFT [OUTER] JOIN <table2> ON <table1>.<col1> = <table2>.<col2>
```

Type in and execute the code in Listing 4-6 to learn how to write a LEFT OUTER JOIN query. Note that the word OUTER is optional.

Listing 4-6. Using LEFT OUTER JOIN

```
USE AdventureWorks2012;
GO
SELECT c.CustomerID, s.SalesOrderID, s.OrderDate
FROM Sales.Customer AS c
LEFT OUTER JOIN Sales.SalesOrderHeader AS s ON c.CustomerID = s.CustomerID
WHERE c.CustomerID IN (11028,11029,1,2,3,4);
```

Figure 4-11 displays the results. Just like INNER JOIN, you must determine which column or columns from one table join the column or columns from the other table. All the rows from the table on the left side of the join, the Sales.Customer table, that meet the criteria in the WHERE clause, show up in the results. The query returns rows from the right side of the join, the Sales.SalesOrderHeader table, only if they match on CustomerID. All of the columns from the Sales.SalesOrderHeader rows that don't match return NULL values. The query returns the customers along with the orders even for customers with no orders, customers 1–4.

▦ Results

	CustomerID	SalesOrderID	OrderDate
1	1	NULL	NULL
2	2	NULL	NULL
3	3	NULL	NULL
4	4	NULL	NULL
5	11028	43831	2005-07-29 00:00:00.000
6	11028	57943	2007-11-14 00:00:00.000
7	11028	67961	2008-04-09 00:00:00.000
8	11029	43794	2005-07-22 00:00:00.000
9	11029	57294	2007-11-02 00:00:00.000
10	11029	70593	2008-05-14 00:00:00.000

Figure 4-11. The results of using LEFT OUTER JOIN

Using OUTER JOIN is not difficult, but it seems to be confusing to people when they first try to use it. If the tables have the primary and foreign keys defined, the table joining with the primary key will usually be the table on the left side in a LEFT OUTER JOIN. Figure out which table must have rows returned even if there is not a match. That table must show up on the left side of a LEFT OUTER JOIN.

Using RIGHT OUTER JOIN

RIGHT OUTER JOIN differs from LEFT OUTER JOIN in just the location of the tables. If the main table, the table in which you want to see all the rows even if there is not a match, is on the right side of the join, you will specify RIGHT. Here is the syntax:

```
SELECT <SELECT list>
FROM <table2>
RIGHT [OUTER] JOIN <table1> ON <table1>.<col1> = <table2>.<col2>
```

Type in and execute the code in Listing 4-7 to learn how to write a query using RIGHT OUTER JOIN.

Listing 4-7. Using RIGHT OUTER JOIN

```
USE AdventureWorks2012;
GO
SELECT c.CustomerID, s.SalesOrderID, s.OrderDate
FROM Sales.SalesOrderHeader AS s
RIGHT OUTER JOIN Sales.Customer AS c ON c.CustomerID = s.CustomerID
WHERE c.CustomerID IN (11028,11029,1,2,3,4);
```

Figure 4-12 shows the results; they are identical to the results in Figure 4-11. The only difference between this query and the one from Listing 4-6 is the order of the tables within the FROM clause and the direction keyword. Again, all of the customers who meet the criteria display along with any orders that were placed. For customers with no orders, NULL values are returned in the Sales.SalesOrderHeader columns.

Results

	CustomerID	SalesOrderID	OrderDate
1	1	NULL	NULL
2	2	NULL	NULL
3	3	NULL	NULL
4	4	NULL	NULL
5	11028	43831	2005-07-29 00:00:00.000
6	11028	57943	2007-11-14 00:00:00.000
7	11028	67961	2008-04-09 00:00:00.000
8	11029	43794	2005-07-22 00:00:00.000
9	11029	57294	2007-11-02 00:00:00.000
10	11029	70593	2008-05-14 00:00:00.000

Figure 4-12. Result of using RIGHT OUTER JOIN

Using OUTER JOIN to Find Rows with No Match

Sometimes it's useful to find all the rows in one table that don't have corresponding rows in another table. For example, you may want to find all the customers who have never placed an order. Since the columns from the nonmatching rows contain NULL values, you can use OUTER JOIN to find rows with no match by checking for NULL. The syntax is as follows:

```
SELECT <SELECT list>
FROM <table1>
LEFT [OUTER] JOIN <table2> ON <table1>.<col1> = <table2>.<col2>
WHERE <col2> IS NULL
```

Type in and execute the code in Listing 4-8 to see how this works.

Listing 4-8. Using LEFT OUTER JOIN to Find the Rows with No Matches

```
USE AdventureWorks2012;
GO

SELECT c.CustomerID, s.SalesOrderID, s.OrderDate
FROM Sales.Customer AS c
LEFT OUTER JOIN Sales.SalesOrderHeader AS s ON c.CustomerID = s.CustomerID
WHERE s.SalesOrderID IS NULL;
```

Figure 4-13 shows the partial results. The query in Listing 4-8 returns a list of all customers who have not placed an order. After you run the query, scroll down to see that every row in the results contains NULL in the SalesOrderID column.

The LEFT JOIN returns all rows from Sales.Customer even if the customer has no orders. The customer rows with no orders contain NULL in the Sales.SalesOrderHeader columns. By checking for

NULL, the customers with no orders show up in the results. Again, this might be complicated to understand at first. Just take it a step at a time when writing your own queries.

	CustomerID	SalesOrderID	OrderDate
1	215	NULL	NULL
2	46	NULL	NULL
3	169	NULL	NULL
4	507	NULL	NULL
5	630	NULL	NULL
6	338	NULL	NULL
7	229	NULL	NULL
8	567	NULL	NULL
9	461	NULL	NULL
10	398	NULL	NULL
11	292	NULL	NULL

Figure 4-13. The partial results of finding rows with no match

Adding a Table to the Right Side of a Left Join

The next step is to understand what to do when additional tables are added to the query. For example, you might want to display all the customers and their orders even if an order has not been placed, along with the ProductID from those orders that were placed. To keep the customers with no orders from dropping out of the results, you must continue to use LEFT JOIN. Figure 4-14 shows how these three tables can be joined to produce the correct results. Notice the Venn diagram shows the SalesOrderHeader and the SalesOrderDetail tables joining on the SalesOrderID. Those results are matched with the CustomerID to get a resultset that includes all of the customers in the Customer table including those without orders. The diagram in Figure 4-14 shows the SalesOrderHeader as the circle linking the Customer and SalesOrderDetail together because it is the only table containing both the CustomerID and the SalesOrderID. These types of linking tables are normally referred to as *junction* tables. The junction table allows you to combine in a single query output SalesOrderDetail and Customer data.

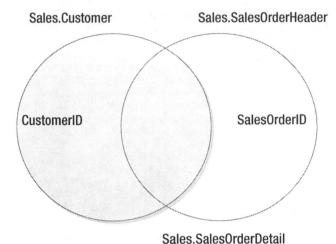

Figure 4-14. *How to connect the tables with two LEFT OUTER JOINs*

Take a look at the syntax.

```
SELECT <SELECT list>
FROM <table1> LEFT [OUTER]JOIN <table2> ON <table1>.<col1> = <table2>.<col2>
LEFT [OUTER] JOIN <table3> ON <table2>.<col3> = <table3>.<col4>
```

Listing 4-9 contains an example query. Type in and execute the code to learn how to write this type of join.

Listing 4-9. *Joining Three Tables with LEFT JOIN*

```
USE AdventureWorks2012;
GO

SELECT C.CustomerID, SOH.SalesOrderID, SOD.SalesOrderDetailID, SOD.ProductID
FROM Sales.Customer AS C
LEFT OUTER JOIN Sales.SalesOrderHeader AS SOH ON C.CustomerID = SOH.CustomerID
LEFT OUTER JOIN Sales.SalesOrderDetail AS SOD ON SOH.SalesOrderID = SOD.SalesOrderID
WHERE C.CustomerID IN (11028,11029,1,2,3,4);
```

Figure 4-15 shows the results. Because the columns from the nonmatching rows from Sales.SalesOrderHeader contain NULL, they can't join to the Sales.SalesOrderDetail table. If you must join another table to the Sales.SalesOrderHeader table, you must use LEFT OUTER JOIN because you can't join on the NULL values. On your own, change the query by removing the words LEFT OUTER in the join between Sales.SalesOrderHeader and Sales.SalesOrderDetail. The customers with no orders will drop out of the results.

Results

	CustomerID	SalesOrderID	SalesOrderDetailID	ProductID
1	1	NULL	NULL	NULL
2	2	NULL	NULL	NULL
3	3	NULL	NULL	NULL
4	4	NULL	NULL	NULL
5	11028	43831	487	776
6	11028	57943	65072	779
7	11028	57943	65073	930
8	11028	57943	65074	873
9	11028	67961	98619	962
10	11029	43794	450	774
11	11029	57294	63489	779
12	11029	57294	63490	711
13	11029	57294	63491	882
14	11029	70593	107626	962
15	11029	70593	107627	872
16	11029	70593	107628	870

Figure 4-15. *The results of a querying multiple tables with* LEFT JOIN

I prefer listing the main table first and using left joins over right joins. If you list the main table first and you start down the LEFT OUTER JOIN path, you can continue to use LEFT. If you start out with RIGHT, you may have to switch to LEFT when you add more tables, which can be confusing.

Adding a Table to the Left Side of a Left Join

You may be wondering what kind of join you must use if you join another table to the left side of the join, in other words, to your main table. To be on the safe side, use LEFT OUTER JOIN to ensure that you will not lose any rows from the main table.

Figure 4-16 shows how to add the Sales.Territory table to the example started in the previous section. The Sales.Territory table joins to the main table, the Sales.Customer table. Since you want to make sure that all customers show up in the results, use LEFT OUTER JOIN to join this new table.

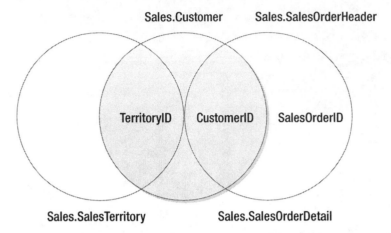

Figure 4-16. How to add another table to the left side of the join

Listing 4-10 shows two example queries that add another table to the main table. Type in and execute the code.

Listing 4-10. Adding Another Table to the Left Side of the Join

```
USE AdventureWorks2012;
GO

SELECT C.CustomerID, SOH.SalesOrderID, SOD.SalesOrderDetailID,
    SOD.ProductID, T.Name
FROM Sales.Customer AS C
LEFT OUTER JOIN Sales.SalesOrderHeader AS SOH ON C.CustomerID = SOH.CustomerID
LEFT OUTER JOIN Sales.SalesOrderDetail AS SOD ON SOH.SalesOrderID = SOD.SalesOrderID
LEFT OUTER JOIN Sales.SalesTerritory AS T ON C.TerritoryID = T.TerritoryID
WHERE C.CustomerID IN (11028,11029,1,2,3,4);
```

Figure 4-17 shows the results. The Sales.SalesTerritory table joins the Sales.Customer table on TerritoryID. Because you don't want to lose any rows from the Sales.Customer table, use LEFT OUTER JOIN.

Results

	CustomerID	SalesOrderID	SalesOrderDetailID	ProductID	Name
1	1	NULL	NULL	NULL	Northwest
2	2	NULL	NULL	NULL	Northwest
3	3	NULL	NULL	NULL	Southwest
4	4	NULL	NULL	NULL	Southwest
5	11028	43831	487	776	Australia
6	11028	57943	65072	779	Australia
7	11028	57943	65073	930	Australia
8	11028	57943	65074	873	Australia
9	11028	67961	98619	962	Australia
10	11029	43794	450	774	Australia
11	11029	57294	63489	779	Australia
12	11029	57294	63490	711	Australia
13	11029	57294	63491	882	Australia
14	11029	70593	107626	962	Australia
15	11029	70593	107627	872	Australia
16	11029	70593	107628	870	Australia

Figure 4-17. The results of joining to the left side of LEFT OUTER JOIN

FULL OUTER JOIN

FULL OUTER JOIN is similar to LEFT OUTER JOIN and RIGHT OUTER JOIN, but in this case, all the rows from each side of the join are returned. In other words, all rows from the left side of the join, even if there is not a match, and all rows from the right side, even if there is not a match, show up in the results. This type of join is rare and could indicate some problems with the database design or the data. For example, this type of join might be necessary if the Sales.SalesOrderHeader table contains orders with invalid CustomerID values. Here is the syntax:

```
SELECT <column list>
FROM <table1>
FULL [OUTER] JOIN <table2> ON <table1>.<col1>  = <table2>.<col2>
```

Because no good example exists in the AdventureWorks2012 database, Listing 4-11 includes a script that creates and populates a table of colors that can be used in the Production.Product table. After populating the table, it contains colors that don't appear in the Production.Product table, and it is missing a color that should be there. Don't worry about understanding the table creation and population part of the script at this point.

Listing 4-11. FULL OUTER JOIN Demonstration

```
USE AdventureWorks2012;
GO
IF OBJECT_ID('Production.ProductColor') IS NOT NULL BEGIN
    DROP TABLE Production.ProductColor;
END
CREATE table Production.ProductColor
    (Color nvarchar(15) NOT NULL PRIMARY KEY)
GO
--Insert most of the existing colors
INSERT INTO Production.ProductColor
SELECT DISTINCT Color
FROM Production.Product
WHERE Color IS NOT NULL and Color <> 'Silver'
--Insert some additional colors
INSERT INTO Production.ProductColor
VALUES ('Green'),('Orange'),('Purple');

--Here is the query:
SELECT c.Color AS "Color from list", p.Color, p.ProductID
FROM Production.Product AS p
FULL OUTER JOIN Production.ProductColor AS c ON p.Color = c.Color
ORDER BY p.ProductID;
```

Figure 4-18 displays the results. When colors from the Production.ProductColor table have no matches in the Production.Product table, the query returns NULL values in the second and third columns, which are from Production.Product (rows 1–3). When colors from the Production.Product table don't match the Production.ProductColor table (in this case, silver) or no color for a product is specified, the query returns NULL values in the first column, which is from Production.ProductColor (rows 12–13). Finally, when a product has a color that matches one found in the Production.ProductColor table, the query returns all non-NULL values (rows 9–11). A query like this might be used to find problems in data so that it can be cleaned up before loading it into a production system or data warehouse.

	Color from list	Color	ProductID
1	Green	NULL	NULL
2	Purple	NULL	NULL
3	Orange	NULL	NULL
4	NULL	NULL	1
5	NULL	NULL	2
6	NULL	NULL	3
7	NULL	NULL	4
8	NULL	NULL	316
9	Black	Black	317
10	Black	Black	318
11	Black	Black	319
12	NULL	Silver	320

Figure 4-18. The partial results of using FULL OUTER JOIN

CROSS JOIN

Another type of rarely used join is CROSS JOIN. This is actually the same as the Cartesian product mentioned in the "Avoiding an Incorrect Join Condition" section. In this case, use CROSS JOIN when you intend to multiply two tables together—every row from one table matched to every row from another table. You might write a CROSS JOIN query to populate a table for a special purpose such as an inventory. You may need a list of every product in every possible location to create forms for the inventory crew. Here is the syntax:

```
SELECT <SELECT list> FROM <table1> CROSS JOIN <table2>
```

Notice that the FROM clause doesn't contain a join condition. Every possible row from one table joins every possible row from another table, so you don't have to specify a join condition. Listing 4-12 demonstrates how to write this type of query. Type in and execute the code.

Listing 4-12. A CROSS JOIN

```
USE AdventureWorks2012;
GO
--1
SELECT p.ProductID, l.LocationID
FROM Production.Product AS p
CROSS JOIN Production.Location AS l
ORDER BY ProductID;
--2
SELECT p.ProductID, l.LocationID
FROM Production.Product AS p
CROSS JOIN Production.Location AS l
ORDER BY LocationID;
```

Figure 4-19 shows the partial results. These queries, just sorted differently, each produce a row for every possible product and every possible location. Query 1 shows that product 1 displays along with every location. Query 2 shows that location 1 displays along with every product.

	ProductID	LocationID
1	1	1
2	1	2
3	1	3
4	1	4
5	1	5
6	1	6
7	1	7
8	1	10
9	1	20
10	1	30

	ProductID	LocationID
1	980	1
2	365	1
3	771	1
4	404	1
5	977	1
6	818	1
7	474	1
8	748	1
9	975	1
10	884	1

Figure 4-19. The partial results of a CROSS JOIN

Self-Joins

A self-join is a special type of query that joins a table back to itself. In this example, you will first create a temporary table named #Employee. Normally the EmployeeID would be a primary key column and the ManagerID would be a foreign key pointing back to the same table. This would ensure that only an existing EmployeeID could be added to the ManagerID column. Every employee, except for one, has a manager—another employee appearing in the same table. The one employee with no manager is the CEO of Adventure Works. The SQL Server team chose to eliminate the self-join when creating AdventureWorks2012 in favor of a new feature first introduced with SQL Server 2008, the HIERARCHYID data type. You will learn about HIERARCHYID in Chapter 10.

You can actually join any table to itself even if it doesn't have a foreign key pointing back to the primary key. This relationship is called a *unary relationship*. Here is the syntax for a self-join:

```
SELECT <a.col1>, <b.col1>
FROM <table1> AS a
LEFT [OUTER] JOIN <table1> AS b ON a.<col1> = b.<col2>
```

Listing 4-13 demonstrates how to write a self-join. Be sure to type in and execute the code.

Listing 4-13. Using Self-Join

```
USE AdventureWorks2012;
GO

CREATE TABLE #Employee (
EmployeeID  int,
ManagerID int,
Title nvarchar(50));

INSERT INTO #Employee
VALUES (1, NULL, 'Chief Executive Officer')
INSERT INTO #Employee
VALUES (2, 1, 'Engineering Manager')
INSERT INTO #Employee
VALUES (3, 2, 'Senior Tool Designer')
INSERT INTO #Employee
VALUES (4, 2, 'Design Engineer')
INSERT INTO #Employee
VALUES (5, 2, 'Research and Development')
INSERT INTO #Employee
VALUES (6, 1, 'Marketing Manager')
INSERT INTO #Employee
VALUES (7, 6, 'Marketing Specialist');

SELECT a.EmployeeID AS Employee,
    a.Title AS EmployeeTitle,
    b.EmployeeID AS ManagerID,
    b.Title AS ManagerTitle
FROM #Employee AS a
LEFT OUTER JOIN #Employee AS b ON a.ManagerID = b.EmployeeID;

DROP TABLE #Employee;
```

Take a look at the results shown in Figure 4-20. Each employee, except for one, has a manager who is also an employee in the same table. The table has ManagerID, which points back to the EmployeeID. Since employee 1 doesn't have a manager, the query uses LEFT OUTER JOIN. Be sure to keep track of which table each column is supposed to come from. Even though the query uses the same table twice, it has two separate roles.

Results

	Employee	EmployeeTitle	ManagerID	ManagerTitle
1	1	Chief Executive Officer	NULL	NULL
2	2	Engineering Manager	1	Chief Executive Officer
3	3	Senior Tool Designer	2	Engineering Manager
4	4	Design Engineer	2	Engineering Manager
5	5	Research and Development	2	Engineering Manager
6	6	Marketing Manager	1	Chief Executive Officer
7	7	Marketing Specialist	6	Marketing Manager

Figure 4-20. The results of using a self-join

The important thing to remember is that one table is used twice in the query. At least one of the table names must be aliased; it is not an option because you can't have two tables with the same name in the query. You will have to qualify all the column names, so you may want to alias both table names to save typing.

This section covered several advanced joining techniques. Understanding how the techniques work and when to use them are very important skills. Practice what you have learned by completing Exercise 4-2.

EXERCISE 4-2

Use the AdventureWorks2012 database to complete this exercise. You can find the solutions in the Appendix.

1. Write a query that displays all the products along with the SalesOrderID even if an order has never been placed for that product. Join to the Sales.SalesOrderDetail table using the ProductID column.

2. Change the query written in step 1 so that only products that have not been ordered show up in the query.

3. Write a query that returns all the rows from the Sales.SalesPerson table joined to the Sales.SalesOrderHeader table along with the SalesOrderID column even if no orders match. Include the SalesPersonID and SalesYTD columns in the results.

4. Change the query written in question 3 so that the salesperson's name also displays from the Person.Person table.

5. The Sales.SalesOrderHeader table contains foreign keys to the Sales.CurrencyRate and Purchasing.ShipMethod tables. Write a query joining all three tables, and make sure it contains all rows from Sales.SalesOrderHeader. Include the CurrencyRateID, AverageRate, SalesOrderID, and ShipBase columns.

6. Write a query that returns the `BusinessEntityID` column from the `Sales.SalesPerson` table along with every `ProductID` from the `Production.Product` table.

7. Starting with the query written in Listing 4-13, join the table `a` to the `Person.Person` table to display the employee's name. The `EmployeeID` column joins the `BusinessEntityID` column. Note that you will need to recreate the `#Employee` table.

Writing Subqueries

The previous examples in this chapter demonstrated how to write queries using `JOIN`. This section demonstrates using subqueries in the `WHERE` clause. A *subquery* is a nested query—a query within a query. One reason to use a subquery is to find the rows in one table that match another table without actually joining the second table. For example, without actually joining the order table, you could use a subquery to display a list of the customers who have placed an order. Another technique, correlated subqueries, will be shown in Chapter 5.

Using a Subquery in an IN List

Using a subquery in an `IN` list is similar to the hard-coded `IN` list you learned to use in a `WHERE` clause in Chapter 2. Here is the syntax:

```
SELECT <select list> FROM <table1>
WHERE <col1> IN (SELECT <col2> FROM <table2>)
```

Listing 4-14 demonstrates this technique. Type in and execute the code.

Listing 4-14. Using a Subquery in the IN List

```
USE AdventureWorks2012;
GO
SELECT CustomerID, AccountNumber
FROM Sales.Customer
WHERE CustomerID IN (SELECT CustomerID FROM Sales.SalesOrderHeader);
```

This query returns a list of the customers who have placed an order (see Figure 4-21). The difference between this example and other examples in this chapter that join these tables is that the columns from the Sales.SalesOrderHeader table don't show up in the results. Each customer displays only once in the results, not once for each order placed. The subquery produces a list of possible values from one, and only one, column. The outer query compares a column to that list.

	CustomerID	AccountNumber
1	11000	AW00011000
2	11001	AW00011001
3	11002	AW00011002
4	11003	AW00011003
5	11004	AW00011004
6	11005	AW00011005
7	11006	AW00011006
8	11007	AW00011007
9	11008	AW00011008
10	11009	AW00011009

Figure 4-21. The results of using a subquery in an IN list

Using a Subquery and NOT IN

A subquery in the WHERE clause can also be used to find rows that don't match the values from another table by adding the NOT operator. You can find the customers who have not placed an order by adding the word NOT to the previous query. Type in and execute the code in Listing 4-15, which demonstrates using NOT IN.

Listing 4-15. A Subquery with NOT IN

```
USE AdventureWorks2012;
GO

SELECT CustomerID, AccountNumber
FROM Sales.Customer
WHERE CustomerID NOT IN
    (SELECT CustomerID FROM Sales.SalesOrderHeader);
```

This query returns the opposite results of Listing 4-14 (see Figure 4-22). The subquery returns a list of all the CustomerID values found in Sales.SalesOrderHeader. By using NOT IN, the query returns all the rows from Sales.Customer that don't match.

Results

	CustomerID	AccountNumber
1	1	AW00000001
2	2	AW00000002
3	3	AW00000003
4	4	AW00000004
5	5	AW00000005
6	6	AW00000006
7	7	AW00000007
8	8	AW00000008
9	9	AW00000009
10	10	AW00000010

Figure 4-22. The partial results of using a subquery with NOT IN

Using a Subquery Containing NULL with NOT IN

Recall that you will often get incorrect results if you don't take NULL values into account. If the subquery contains any NULL values, using NOT IN will incorrectly produce no rows. For example, the values returned by a subquery are NULL, 1, 2, and 3. The values from the outer query (1, 2, and 10) must each be compared to that list. The database engine can tell that 10 is not 1, 2, or 3, but it can't tell whether it is the same as NULL. The intended result is 10 since it doesn't match any of the values from the subquery, but because of the NULL, the comparison returns no results at all. Type in and execute the code in Listing 4-16, which shows incorrect results and how to correct the problem.

Listing 4-16. A Subquery with NOT IN

```
USE AdventureWorks2012;
GO

--1
SELECT CurrencyRateID, FromCurrencyCode, ToCurrencyCode
FROM Sales.CurrencyRate
WHERE CurrencyRateID NOT IN
    (SELECT CurrencyRateID
     FROM Sales.SalesOrderHeader);

--2
SELECT CurrencyRateID, FromCurrencyCode, ToCurrencyCode
FROM Sales.CurrencyRate
WHERE CurrencyRateID NOT IN
    (SELECT CurrencyRateID
     FROM Sales.SalesOrderHeader
     WHERE CurrencyRateID IS NOT NULL);
```

Figure 4-23 shows the results. Query 1 does not return any results because NULL values exist in the values returned by the subquery. Since any value from CurrencyRateID compared to NULL returns

UNKNOWN, it is impossible to know whether any of the values meet the criteria. Query 2 corrects the problem by adding a WHERE clause to the subquery that eliminates NULL values.

Using a subquery in the WHERE clause is a very popular technique. Just make sure that you always eliminate the possibility of NULL values in the subquery.

	CurrencyRateID	FromCurrencyCode	ToCurrencyCode

	CurrencyRateID	FromCurrencyCode	ToCurrencyCode
1	1	USD	ARS
2	3	USD	BRL
3	5	USD	CNY
4	6	USD	DEM
5	7	USD	EUR
6	9	USD	GBP
7	10	USD	JPY
8	11	USD	MXN

Figure 4-23. The results of code that corrects the NULL problem with NOT IN

Writing UNION Queries

A UNION query is not really a join, but it is a way to merge the results of two or more queries together. I like to think of it as "folding" one table into another table. One reason for using a UNION query is to view data with one query that combines data from a production table along with data that has been archived into another table. A UNION query combines two or more queries, and the results are returned in one result set. Here is the syntax:

```
SELECT <col1>, <col2>,<col3>
FROM <table1>
UNION [ALL]
SELECT <col4>,<col5>,<col6>FROM <table2>
```

Figure 4-24 shows a diagram of how a UNION query might look. Each individual query must contain the same number of columns and be of compatible data types. For example, you could have an INT column and a VARCHAR column line up as long as the VARCHAR column contains only numbers.

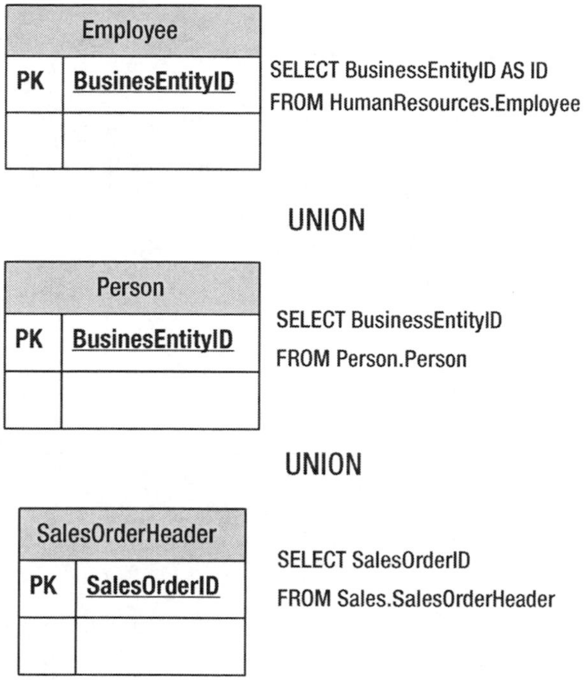

Employee	
PK	**BusinesEntityID**

SELECT BusinessEntityID AS ID
FROM HumanResources.Employee

UNION

Person	
PK	**BusinesEntityID**

SELECT BusinessEntityID
FROM Person.Person

UNION

SalesOrderHeader	
PK	**SalesOrderID**

SELECT SalesOrderID
FROM Sales.SalesOrderHeader

Figure 4-24. *The diagram of a UNION query*

Type in and execute the code in Listing 4-17 to learn how to use UNION.

Listing 4-17. *Using UNION*

```
USE AdventureWorks2012;
GO

--1
SELECT BusinessEntityID AS ID
FROM HumanResources.Employee
UNION
SELECT BusinessEntityID
FROM Person.Person
UNION
SELECT SalesOrderID
FROM Sales.SalesOrderHeader
ORDER BY ID;

--2
SELECT BusinessEntityID AS ID
FROM HumanResources.Employee
UNION ALL
SELECT BusinessEntityID
```

```
FROM Person.Person
UNION ALL
SELECT SalesOrderID
FROM Sales.SalesOrderHeader
ORDER BY ID;
```

Notice the difference in the two queries in Listing 4-17. Figure 4-25 shows the results. Query 2 uses UNION ALL, which returns all rows, even if they are duplicates. Leaving out the keyword ALL eliminates the duplicates. The first query in the UNION query determines the number of columns and the name of each column. When using a UNION query, only one ORDER BY clause can be used, and it will be located at the end of the statement.

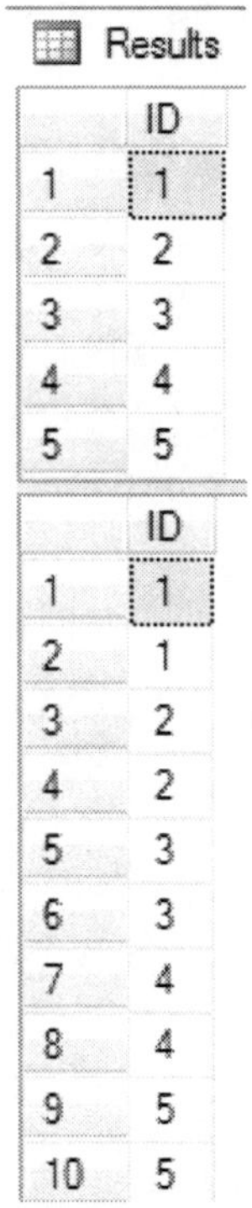

	ID
1	1
2	2
3	3
4	4
5	5

	ID
1	1
2	1
3	2
4	2
5	3
6	3
7	4
8	4
9	5
10	5

Figure 4-25. The results of UNION queries

A UNION query is often used to combine the results of two tables so that they look the same. For example, a database has separate customer tables for each division of the company. By using a UNION query, the customers can be displayed together as if they were in the same table. It is also possible to write UNION queries using the same table.

When writing a UNION query, you must make sure that both queries contain the same number of columns in the results and that the data types are compatible. The first query sets the number of columns and the name of each column. The second and later queries must match up to the first query. The data type of each column follows precedence rules, so you can't allow one query to return an integer where the other query returns a string. Run these practice queries to see what happens when a UNION query doesn't follow these rules:

```
--Incompatible types
SELECT 1
UNION ALL
SELECT 'a'
--Number of columns don't match up
SELECT 1
UNION ALL
SELECT 1,2
```

This section covered some alternate ways to utilize more than one table within a query. Practice these techniques by completing Exercise 4-3.

EXERCISE 4-3

Use the AdventureWorks2012 database to complete this exercise. You can find the solutions in the Appendix.

1. Using a subquery, display the product names and product ID numbers from the Production.Product table that have been ordered.

2. Change the query written in question 1 to display the products that have not been ordered.

3. If the Production.ProductColor table is not part of the AdventureWorks2012 database, run the code in Listing 4-11 to create it. Write a query using a subquery that returns the rows from the Production.ProductColor table that are not being used in the Production.Product table.

4. Write a query that displays the colors used in the Production.Product table that are not listed in the Production.ProductColor table using a subquery. Use the keyword DISTINCT before the column name to return each color only once.

5. Write a UNION query that combines the ModifiedDate from Person.Person and the HireDate from HumanResources.Employee.

Exploring Derived Tables and Common Table Expressions

Using derived tables and common table expressions allows T-SQL developers to solve some complicated query problems. You will find these techniques useful as you learn about aggregate queries (Chapter 5) and updating data (Chapter 6). With only the skills you have learned so far, using these techniques does not actually make writing queries any easier, but you will appreciate learning about them before you progress to more advanced skills.

Using Derived Tables

If you still work with some SQL Server 2000 systems, you may work with derived tables. A *derived table* is a subquery that appears in the FROM clause. Actually, you may see derived tables with SQL Server 2005 and 2008 code, but starting with 2005, another option, common table expressions, is available. You will learn about common table expressions in the next section.

Derived tables allow developers to join to queries instead of tables so that the logic of the query is isolated. At this point, I just want you to learn how to write a query using a derived table. This technique will be very useful as you learn to write more advanced queries. Here is the syntax:

```
SELECT <select list> FROM <table1>
[INNER] JOIN (SELECT <select list>
              FROM <table2>) AS B ON <table1>.<col1> = B.<col2>
```

The syntax shows INNER JOIN, but this could also be done with OUTER JOIN as well. Figure 4-26 shows a diagram representing a LEFT OUTER JOIN query joining the Sales.Customer table to a *query* of the Sales.SalesOrderHeader table as a derived table.

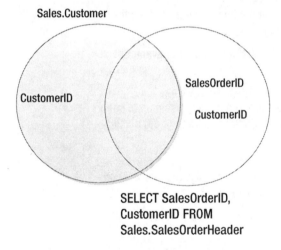

Figure 4-26. The diagram of a derived query

Listing 4-18 demonstrates how to use a derived table. Type in and execute the code. Make sure you take the time to understand how this works with these simple examples even though a regular join makes more sense at this point.

Listing 4-18. Using a Derived Table

```
USE AdventureWorks2012;
GO

SELECT c.CustomerID, s.SalesOrderID
FROM Sales.Customer AS c
INNER JOIN (SELECT SalesOrderID, CustomerID
            FROM Sales.SalesOrderHeader) AS s ON c.CustomerID = s.CustomerID;
```

Obviously, you could write this query using a regular INNER JOIN. Figure 4-27 shows the results. Keep in mind three rules when using derived tables. First, any columns that will be needed outside the derived table must be included in its SELECT list. Even though only SalesOrderID appears in the main SELECT list, CustomerID is required for joining. Second, the derived table requires an alias. Use the alias to refer to columns from the derived table in the outer query. Finally, the derived table may contain multiple tables, a WHERE clause, and even another derived table.

▦ Results

	CustomerID	SalesOrderID
1	11000	43793
2	11000	51522
3	11000	57418
4	11001	43767
5	11001	51493
6	11001	72773
7	11002	43736
8	11002	51238
9	11002	53237
10	11003	43701
11	11003	51315
12	11003	57783
13	11004	43810

Figure 4-27. *The results of a query with a virtual table*

Using Common Table Expressions

Microsoft introduced the common table expression (CTE) feature with SQL Server 2005. This gives developers another way to separate out the logic of one part of the query. When writing a CTE, you define one or more queries up front, which you can then immediately use. This technique will come in handy when learning more advanced skills. For simple problems, there is no advantage over derived tables, but CTEs have several advanced features covered in Chapter 11 that are not available with derived tables. Here is the simplest syntax:

```
WITH <CTE Name> AS (SELECT <select list> FROM <table1>)
SELECT <select list> FROM <table2>
[INNER] JOIN <CTE Name> ON <table2>.<col1> = <CTE Name>.<col2>
```

Type in and execute the code in Listing 4-19. Again, the example is very simple but should help you learn the technique.

Listing 4-19. Using a Common Table Expression

```
USE AdventureWorks2012;
GO

WITH orders AS (
    SELECT SalesOrderID, CustomerID
    FROM Sales.SalesOrderHeader
    )
SELECT c.CustomerID, orders.SalesOrderID
FROM Sales.Customer AS c
INNER JOIN orders ON c.CustomerID = orders.CustomerID;
```

You can see the results in Figure 4-28. The CTE begins with the word WITH. Because WITH is a keyword in several T-SQL commands, it must be either the first word in the batch, as in this example, or proceeded by a semicolon. The word GO begins a new batch. Supply the CTE name followed by the definition. The main query immediately follows the CTE definition. Treat the CTE as a regular table in the main query. Once the query completes executing, the CTE goes out of scope and can no longer be used.

	CustomerID	SalesOrderID
1	11000	43793
2	11000	51522
3	11000	57418
4	11001	43767
5	11001	51493
6	11001	72773
7	11002	43736
8	11002	51238
9	11002	53237
10	11003	43701
11	11003	51315
12	11003	57783
13	11004	43810

Figure 4-28. The results of a query using a CTE

Using a CTE to Solve a Complicated Join Problem

The examples in the previous sections on joining tables demonstrated very simple join conditions, one or two columns from one table equal to the same number of columns in another table. Join conditions may be much more complicated. For example, suppose you wanted to produce a list of all customers along with the orders, if any, placed on a certain date. Figure 4-29 shows a diagram of this query. The left-hand circle represents the Customer table in the AdventureWorks2012 database while the right-hand circle represents the CTE. The Customer table is then joined to the results of the CTE query.

Sales.Customer

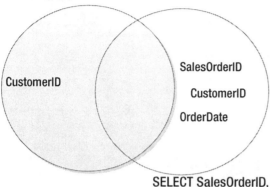

SELECT SalesOrderID,
CustomerID, OrderDate FROM
Sales.SalesOrderHeader WHERE
OrderDate = '2005/07/01'

Figure 4-29. *A diagram of a CTE query*

Listing 4-20 demonstrates the problem and how to solve it with a CTE.

Listing 4-20. *Using a CTE to Solve a Problem*

```
USE AdventureWorks2012;
GO

--1
SELECT c.CustomerID, s.SalesOrderID, s.OrderDate
FROM Sales.Customer AS c
LEFT OUTER JOIN Sales.SalesOrderHeader AS s ON c.CustomerID = s.CustomerID
WHERE s.OrderDate = '2005/07/01';

--2
WITH orders AS (
    SELECT SalesOrderID, CustomerID, OrderDate
    FROM Sales.SalesOrderHeader
    WHERE OrderDate = '2005/07/01'
    )
SELECT c.CustomerID, orders.SalesOrderID, orders.OrderDate
FROM Sales.Customer AS c
LEFT OUTER JOIN orders ON c.CustomerID = orders.CustomerID
ORDER BY orders.OrderDate DESC;
```

Take a look at the results in Figure 4-30. Query 1 returns only the 43 rows with the specified order date. The nonmatching rows dropped out of the query because of the NULLs and values other than 2005/07/01 in the OrderDate column. If you want to show all customers even if there is not an order placed on the specified date, then by adding the WHERE clause to the CTE instead, the NULL values and other OrderDate values do not cause any problems, and the correct results are returned.

	CustomerID	SalesOrderID	OrderDate
37	29958	43695	2005-07-01 00:00:00.000
38	29849	43696	2005-07-01 00:00:00.000
39	21768	43697	2005-07-01 00:00:00.000
40	28389	43698	2005-07-01 00:00:00.000
41	25863	43699	2005-07-01 00:00:00.000
42	14501	43700	2005-07-01 00:00:00.000
43	11003	43701	2005-07-01 00:00:00.000

	CustomerID	SalesOrderID	OrderDate
33	29811	43676	2005-07-01 00:00:00.000
34	29825	43659	2005-07-01 00:00:00.000
35	29958	43695	2005-07-01 00:00:00.000
36	29614	43668	2005-07-01 00:00:00.000
37	29849	43696	2005-07-01 00:00:00.000
38	29596	43674	2005-07-01 00:00:00.000
39	29761	43679	2005-07-01 00:00:00.000
40	29824	43677	2005-07-01 00:00:00.000
41	29994	43662	2005-07-01 00:00:00.000
42	29734	43661	2005-07-01 00:00:00.000
43	29912	43684	2005-07-01 00:00:00.000
44	29945	NULL	NULL
45	29740	NULL	NULL

Figure 4-30. The results of using a CTE to solve a tricky query

This section demonstrated how to use derived tables and common table expressions. The examples, except for the last one, covered queries that you could have easily written using joins. In Chapter 5, you will learn more examples of how to use these techniques when regular joins will not work. Practice writing queries with derived tables and common table expressions by completing Exercise 4-4.

EXERCISE 4-4

Use the AdventureWorks2012 database to complete this exercise. You can find the solutions in the Appendix.

1. Using a derived table, join the Sales.SalesOrderHeader table to the Sales.SalesOrderDetail table. Display the SalesOrderID, OrderDate, and ProductID columns in the results. The Sales.SalesOrderDetail table should be inside the derived table query.

2. Rewrite the query in question 1 with a common table expression.

3. Write a query that displays all customers along with the orders placed in 2005. Use a common table expression to write the query and include the CustomerID, SalesOrderID, and OrderDate columns in the results.

Thinking About Performance

Often, using different query techniques can produce the same execution plan, or at least similar performance. To see an example of this, toggle on the Include Actual Execution Plan setting, and run Listing 4-21, which shows two techniques to get the same results.

Listing 4-21. Comparing the Performance of Two Techniques

```
USE AdventureWorks2012;
GO

--1
SELECT DISTINCT c.CustomerID
FROM Sales.Customer AS c
INNER JOIN Sales.SalesOrderHeader AS o ON c.CustomerID = o.CustomerID;

--2
SELECT CustomerID
FROM Sales.Customer
WHERE CustomerID IN (SELECT CustomerID FROM Sales.SalesOrderHeader);
```

Figure 4-31 shows the identical execution plans. These queries produce identical results but with very different techniques.

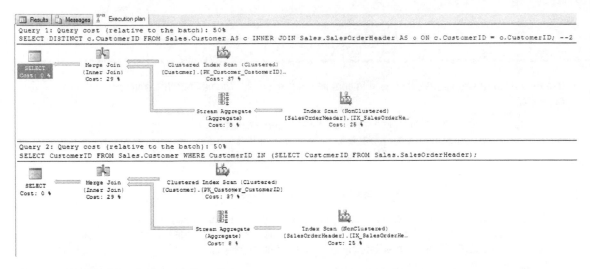

Figure 4-31. The identical execution plans

As you learn to write more complicated queries, especially using aggregate functions in Chapter 5, you will learn that how you join the tables can make a big difference in performance. To experiment a bit more with performance, complete Exercise 4-5.

EXERCISE 4-5

Use the AdventureWorks2012 database to complete this exercise. You can find the solutions in the Appendix.

1. Run the following code to add and populate a new column, OrderID, to the Sales.SalesOrderDetail table. After running the code, the new column will contain the same data as the SalesOrderID column.

```
USE AdventureWorks2012;
GO
ALTER TABLE Sales.SalesOrderDetail ADD OrderID INT NULL;
GO
UPDATE Sales.SalesOrderDetail SET OrderID = SalesOrderID;
```

2. Make sure that the Include Actual Execution Plan is turned on before running the code below. View the execution plan, and explain why one query performs better than the other.

```
--1
SELECT o.SalesOrderID, d.SalesOrderDetailID
FROM Sales.SalesOrderHeader AS o
INNER JOIN Sales.SalesOrderDetail AS d ON o.SalesOrderID = d.SalesOrderID;
```

```
--2
SELECT o.SalesOrderID,d.SalesOrderDetailID
FROM Sales.SalesOrderHeader AS o
INNER JOIN Sales.SalesOrderDetail AS d ON o.SalesOrderID = d.OrderID;
```

3. Compare the execution plans of the derived table example (Listing 4-18) and the CTE example (Listing 4-19). Explain why the query performance is the same or why one query performs better than the other.

Summary

For the data to make sense in reports and applications, tables must be joined together. As you can see from the number of topics in this chapter, there are many ways to do it. Most queries will use the INNER JOIN syntax, but for returning all the rows even if there is not a match, use an OUTER JOIN. After learning about joins, you learned about subqueries in the WHERE clause using IN and UNION queries. Finally, the chapter covered derived tables and common table expressions, which will help you solve more intriguing query puzzles as you learn more advanced techniques.

CHAPTER 5

Grouping and Summarizing Data

So far, you have learned to write simple queries that include filtering and ordering. You can also work with expressions built with operators and functions. The previous chapter taught you how to write queries with multiple tables so that the data makes sense in applications and reports. Now it's time to learn about a special type of query, *aggregate queries*, used to group and summarize data. You may find that writing aggregate queries is more challenging than the other queries you have learned so far, but by taking a step-by-step approach, you will see that they are not difficult to write at all. Be sure to take the time to understand the examples and complete all the exercises before moving on to the next section.

Aggregate Functions

You use aggregate functions to summarize data in queries. The functions that you worked with in Chapter 3 operate on one value at a time. These functions operate on sets of values from multiple rows all at once. For example, you may need to supply information about how many orders were placed and the total amount ordered for a report. Here are the most commonly used aggregate functions:

- COUNT: Counts the number of rows or the number of non-NULL values in a column.

- SUM: Adds up the values in numeric or money data.

- AVG: Calculates the average in numeric or money data.

- MIN: Finds the lowest value in the set of values. This can be used on string data as well as numeric, money, or date data.

- MAX: Finds the highest value in the set of values. This can be used on string data as well as numeric, money, or date data.

Keep the following in mind when working with these aggregate functions:

- The functions AVG and SUM will operate only on numeric and money data columns.

- The functions MIN, MAX, and COUNT will work on numeric, money, string, and temporal data columns.

- The aggregate functions will not operate on TEXT, NTEXT, and IMAGE columns. These data types are deprecated, meaning that they may not be supported in future versions of SQL Server.

- The aggregate functions ignore NULL values.

- COUNT can be used with an asterisk (*) to give the count of the rows even if all the columns are NULL.

- Once an aggregate function is used in a query, the query becomes an aggregate query.

Here is the syntax for the simplest type of aggregate query where the aggregate function is used in the SELECT list:

```
SELECT <aggregate function>(<col1>)
FROM <table>
```

Listing 5-1 shows an example of using aggregate functions. Type in and execute the code to learn how these functions are used over the entire result set.

Listing 5-1. *Using Aggregate Functions*

```
USE AdventureWorks2012;
GO

--1
SELECT COUNT(*) AS CountOfRows,
    MAX(TotalDue) AS MaxTotal,
    MIN(TotalDue) AS MinTotal,
    SUM(TotalDue) AS SumOfTotal,
    AVG(TotalDue) AS AvgTotal
FROM Sales.SalesOrderHeader;

--2
SELECT MIN(Name) AS MinName,
    MAX(Name) AS MaxName,
    MIN(SellStartDate) AS MinSellStartDate
FROM Production.Product;
```

Take a look at the results in Figure 5-1. The aggregate functions operate on all the rows in the Sales.SalesOrderHeader table in query 1 and return just one row of results. The first expression, CountOfRows, uses an asterisk (*) to count all the rows in the table. The other expressions perform calculations on the TotalDue column. Query 2 demonstrates using the MIN and MAX functions on string and date columns. In these examples, the SELECT clause lists only aggregate expressions. You will learn how to add columns that are not part of aggregate expressions in the next section.

	CountOfRows	MaxTotal	MinTotal	SumOfTotal	AvgTotal
1	31465	187487.825	1.5183	123216786.1159	3915.9951

	MinName	MaxName	MinSellStartDate
1	Adjustable Race	Women's Tights, S	2002-06-01 00:00:00.000

Figure 5-1. *The results of using aggregate functions*

Now that you know how to use aggregate functions to summarize a result set, practice what you have learned by completing Exercise 5-1.

EXERCISE 5-1

Use the AdventureWorks2012 database to complete this exercise. You can find the solutions in the Appendix.

1. Write a query to determine the number of customers in the Sales.Customer table.

2. Write a query that lists the total number of products ordered. Use the OrderQty column of the Sales.SalesOrderDetail table and the SUM function.

3. Write a query to determine the price of the most expensive product ordered. Use the UnitPrice column of the Sales.SalesOrderDetail table.

4. Write a query to determine the average freight amount in the Sales.SalesOrderHeader table.

5. Write a query using the Production.Product table that displays the minimum, maximum, and average ListPrice.

The GROUP BY Clause

The previous example query and exercise questions listed only aggregate expressions in the SELECT list. The aggregate functions operated on the entire result set in each query. By adding more nonaggregated columns to the SELECT list, you add grouping levels to the query, which requires the use of the GROUP BY clause. The aggregate functions then operate on the grouping levels instead of on the entire set of results. This section covers grouping on columns and grouping on expressions.

Grouping on Columns

You can use the GROUP BY clause to group data so that the aggregate functions apply to groups of values instead of the entire result set. For example, you may want to calculate the count and sum of the orders placed, grouped by order date or grouped by customer. Here is the syntax for the GROUP BY clause:

```
SELECT <aggregate function>(<col1>), <col2>
FROM <table>
GROUP BY <col2>
```

One big difference you will notice once the query contains a GROUP BY clause is that additional nonaggregated columns may be included in the SELECT list. Once nonaggregated columns are in the SELECT list, you must add the GROUP BY clause and include all the nonaggregated columns. Run this code example, and view the error message:

```
USE AdventureWorks2012;
GO
SELECT CustomerID,SUM(TotalDue) AS TotalPerCustomer
FROM Sales.SalesOrderHeader;
```

Figure 5-2 shows the error message. To get around this error, add the GROUP BY clause and include nonaggregated columns in that clause. Make sure that the SELECT list includes only those columns that you really need in the results, because the SELECT list directly affects which columns will be required in the GROUP BY clause.

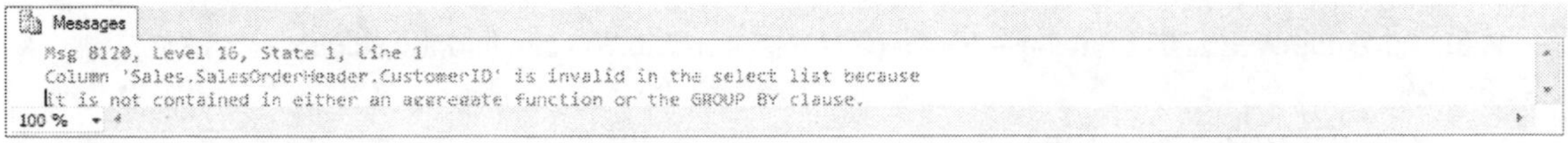

> **Messages**
>
> Msg 8120, Level 16, State 1, Line 1
> Column 'Sales.SalesOrderHeader.CustomerID' is invalid in the select list because
> it is not contained in either an aggregate function or the GROUP BY clause.
> 100 % ▾ ◂

Figure 5-2. *The error message that results when the required GROUP BY clause is missing*

Type in and execute the code in Listing 5-2, which demonstrates how to use GROUP BY.

Listing 5-2. *Using the GROUP BY Clause*

```
USE AdventureWorks2012;
GO

--1
SELECT CustomerID,SUM(TotalDue) AS TotalPerCustomer
FROM Sales.SalesOrderHeader
GROUP BY CustomerID;

--2
SELECT TerritoryID,AVG(TotalDue) AS AveragePerTerritory
FROM Sales.SalesOrderHeader
GROUP BY TerritoryID;
```

Take a look at the results in Figure 5-3. Query 1 displays every customer with orders along with the sum of the TotalDue for each customer. The results are grouped by the CustomerID, and the sum is applied over each group of rows. Query 2 returns the average of the TotalDue values grouped by the TerritoryID. In each case, the nonaggregated column in the SELECT list must appear in the GROUP BY clause.

	CustomerID	TotalPerCustomer
1	14324	5659.1783
2	22814	5.514
3	11407	59.659
4	28387	645.2869
5	19897	659.6408
6	15675	7963.05
7	24165	3366.7583
8	27036	8.0444

	TerritoryID	AveragePerTerritory
1	9	1726.4907
2	3	23151.4266
3	6	4523.956
4	7	3038.8283
5	1	3931.576
6	10	2663.5752
7	4	4362.242
8	5	18280.0398

Figure 5-3. The results of using the GROUP BY clause

Any columns listed that are not part of an aggregate expression must be used to group the results. Those columns must be included in the GROUP BY clause. If you don't want to group on a column, don't list it in the SELECT list. This is where developers struggle when writing aggregate queries, so I can't stress it enough.

Grouping on Expressions

The previous examples demonstrated how to group on columns, but it is possible to also group on expressions. You must include the exact expression from the SELECT list in the GROUP BY clause. Listing 5-3 demonstrates how to avoid incorrect results caused by adding a column instead of the expression to the GROUP BY clause.

Listing 5-3. How to Group on an Expression

```
Use AdventureWorks2012;
GO

--1
SELECT COUNT(*) AS CountOfOrders, YEAR(OrderDate) AS OrderYear
FROM Sales.SalesOrderHeader
GROUP BY OrderDate;
```

```
--2
SELECT COUNT(*) AS CountOfOrders, YEAR(OrderDate) AS OrderYear
FROM Sales.SalesOrderHeader
GROUP BY YEAR(OrderDate);
```

You can find the results in Figure 5-4. Notice that query 1 will run, but instead of returning one row per year, the query returns multiple rows with unexpected values. Because the GROUP BY clause contains OrderDate, the grouping is on OrderDate. The CountOfOrders expression is the count by OrderDate, not OrderYear. The expression in the SELECT list just changes how the data displays; it doesn't affect the calculations.

Query 2 fixes this problem by including the exact expression from the SELECT list in the GROUP BY clause. Query 2 returns only one row per year, and CountOfOrders is correctly calculated.

Results

	CountOfOrders	OrderYear
1	12	2006
2	10	2007
3	52	2008
4	57	2008
5	10	2006
6	8	2007
7	67	2007
8	70	2006

	CountOfOrders	OrderYear
1	12443	2007
2	13951	2008
3	1379	2005
4	3692	2006

Figure 5-4. Using an expression in the GROUP BY clause

You use aggregate functions along with the GROUP BY clause to summarize data over groups of rows. Be sure to practice what you have learned by completing Exercise 5-2.

EXERCISE 5-2

Use the AdventureWorks2012 database to complete the exercise. You can find the solutions in the Appendix.

1. Write a query that shows the total number of items ordered for each product. Use the Sales.SalesOrderDetail table to write the query.

2. Write a query using the Sales.SalesOrderDetail table that displays a count of the detail lines for each SalesOrderID.

3. Write a query using the Production.Product table that lists a count of the products in each product line.

4. Write a query that displays the count of orders placed by year for each customer using the Sales.SalesOrderHeader table.

The ORDER BY Clause

You already know how to use the ORDER BY clause, but special rules exist for using the ORDER BY clause in aggregate queries. If a nonaggregate column appears in the ORDER BY clause, it must also appear in the GROUP BY clause, just like the SELECT list. Here is the syntax:

```
SELECT <aggregate function>(<col1>),<col2>
FROM <table1>
GROUP BY <col2>
ORDER BY <col2>
```

Type in the following code to see the error that results when a column included in the ORDER BY clause is missing from the GROUP BY clause:

```
USE AdventureWorks2012;
GO

SELECT CustomerID,SUM(TotalDue) AS TotalPerCustomer
FROM Sales.SalesOrderHeader
GROUP BY CustomerID
ORDER BY TerritoryID;
```

Figure 5-5 shows the error message that results from running the code. To avoid this error, make sure that you add only those columns to the ORDER BY clause that you intend to be grouping levels.

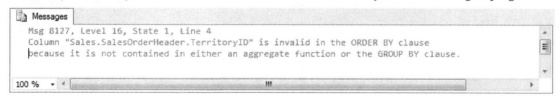

Figure 5-5. The error message resulting from including a column in the ORDER BY clause that is not a grouping level

Listing 5-4 demonstrates how to use the ORDER BY clause within an aggregate query. Be sure to type in and execute the code.

Listing 5-4. Using ORDER BY

```
USE AdventureWorks2012;
GO

--1
SELECT CustomerID,SUM(TotalDue) AS TotalPerCustomer
FROM Sales.SalesOrderHeader
GROUP BY CustomerID
ORDER BY CustomerID;

--2
SELECT TerritoryID,AVG(TotalDue) AS AveragePerTerritory
FROM Sales.SalesOrderHeader
GROUP BY TerritoryID
ORDER BY TerritoryID;

--3
SELECT CustomerID,SUM(TotalDue) AS TotalPerCustomer
FROM Sales.SalesOrderHeader
GROUP BY CustomerID
ORDER BY SUM(TotalDue) DESC;
```

View the results of Listing 5-4 in Figure 5-6. As you can see, the ORDER BY clause follows the same rules as the SELECT list. Queries 1 and 2 return the results in the order of the nonaggregated column that is listed in the GROUP BY clause. Query 3 displays the results in the order of the sum of TotalDue in descending order.

	CustomerID	TotalPerCustomer
1	11000	9115.1341
2	11001	7054.1875
3	11002	8966.0143
4	11003	8993.9155
5	11004	9056.5911
6	11005	8974.0698
7	11006	8971.5283
8	11007	9073.1551

	TerritoryID	AveragePerTerritory
1	1	3931.576
2	2	22216.5046
3	3	23151.4266
4	4	4362.242
5	5	18280.0398
6	6	4523.956
7	7	3038.8283
8	8	2089.142

	CustomerID	TotalPerCustomer
1	29818	989184.082
2	29715	961675.8596
3	29722	954021.9235
4	30117	919801.8188
5	29614	901346.856
6	29639	887090.4106
7	29701	841866.5522
8	29617	834475.9271

Figure 5-6. Using ORDER BY

The WHERE Clause

The WHERE clause in an aggregate query may contain anything allowed in the WHERE clause in any other query type. It may not, however, contain an aggregate expression. You use the WHERE clause to eliminate rows before the groupings and aggregates are applied. To filter after the groupings are applied, you will use the HAVING clause. You'll learn about HAVING in the next section. Type in and execute the code in Listing 5-5, which demonstrates using the WHERE clause in an aggregate query.

***Listing 5-5.** Using the WHERE Clause*

```
USE AdventureWorks2012;
GO
SELECT CustomerID,SUM(TotalDue) AS TotalPerCustomer
FROM Sales.SalesOrderHeader
WHERE TerritoryID in (5,6)
GROUP BY CustomerID;
```

The results in Figure 5-7 contain only those rows where the TerritoryID is either 5 or 6. The query eliminates the rows before the grouping is applied. Notice that TerritoryID doesn't appear anywhere in the query except for the WHERE clause. The WHERE clause may contain any of the columns in the table as long as it doesn't contain an aggregate expression.

	CustomerID	TotalPerCustomer
1	11739	5257.6232
2	18237	2562.4508
3	26040	3335.2547
4	18546	32.5754
5	29761	68068.6803
6	30093	111168.3274
7	28101	87.2729
8	17026	288.836
9	18523	177.8388
10	18855	1276.8054

Figure 5-7. *The results of using the WHERE clause in an aggregate query*

The HAVING Clause

To eliminate rows based on an aggregate expression, use the HAVING clause. The HAVING clause may contain aggregate expressions that do or do not appear in the SELECT list. For example, you could write a query that returns the sum of the total due for customers who have placed at least ten orders. The count of the orders doesn't have to appear in the SELECT list. Alternately, you could include only those customers who have spent at least $10,000 (sum of total due), which does appear in the list.

You can also include nonaggregate columns in the HAVING clause as long as the columns appear in the GROUP BY clause. In other words, you can eliminate some of the groups with the HAVING clause. Behind the scenes, however, the database engine may move that criteria to the WHERE clause because it is more efficient to eliminate those rows first. Criteria involving nonaggregate columns actually belongs in the WHERE clause, but the query will still work with the criteria appearing in the HAVING clause.

Most of the operators such as equal to (=), less than (<), and between that are used in the WHERE clause will work. Here is the syntax:

```
SELECT <aggregate function1>(<col1>),<col2>
FROM <table1>
GROUP BY <col2>
HAVING <aggregate function2>(<col3>) = <value>
```

Like the GROUP BY clause, the HAVING clause will be in aggregate queries only. Listing 5-6 demonstrates the HAVING clause. Be sure to type in and execute the code.

Listing 5-6. Using the HAVING Clause

```
USE AdventureWorks2012;
GO

--1
SELECT CustomerID,SUM(TotalDue) AS TotalPerCustomer
FROM Sales.SalesOrderHeader
GROUP BY CustomerID
HAVING SUM(TotalDue) > 5000;

--2
SELECT CustomerID,SUM(TotalDue) AS TotalPerCustomer
FROM Sales.SalesOrderHeader
GROUP BY CustomerID
HAVING COUNT(*) = 10 AND SUM(TotalDue) > 5000;

--3
SELECT CustomerID,SUM(TotalDue) AS TotalPerCustomer
FROM Sales.SalesOrderHeader
GROUP BY CustomerID
HAVING CustomerID > 27858;
```

You can find the results in Figure 5-8. Query 1 shows only the rows where the sum of the TotalDue exceeds 5,000. The TotalDue column appears within an aggregate expression in the SELECT list. Query 2 demonstrates how an aggregate expression not included in the SELECT list may be used (in this case, the count of the rows) in the HAVING clause. Query 3 contains a nonaggregated column, CustomerID, in the HAVING clause, but it is a column in the GROUP BY clause. In this case, you could have moved the criteria to the WHERE clause instead and received the same results.

	CustomerID	TotalPerCustomer
1	14324	5659.1783
2	15675	7963.05
3	11453	9035.563
4	14155	6622.5524
5	12804	6572.7942
6	30030	68644.5658
7	13050	6244.6309
8	28264	6627.0497

	CustomerID	TotalPerCustomer
1	29830	38452.4651
2	29842	156413.2374
3	29622	262408.3464
4	29588	17361.1884
5	29508	10227.5269
6	29569	24082.9023
7	29961	79847.8229
8	29606	16030.152

	CustomerID	TotalPerCustomer
1	28719	2634.3974
2	28055	83.4054
3	28387	645.2869
4	28032	83.3944
5	29761	68068.6803
6	28765	3953.9884
7	30093	111168.3274
8	28101	87.2729

Figure 5-8. The partial results of using the HAVING clause

Developers often struggle when trying to figure out whether the filter criteria belongs in the WHERE clause or in the HAVING clause. Here's a tip: you must know the order in which the database engine processes the clauses. First, review the order in which you write the clauses in an aggregate query.

- SELECT
- FROM
- WHERE
- GROUP BY
- HAVING

- ORDER BY

The database engine processes the WHERE clause before the groupings and aggregates are applied. Here is the order that the database engine actually processes the query:

- FROM

- WHERE

- GROUP BY

- HAVING

- ORDER BY

- SELECT

The database engine processes the WHERE clause before it processes the groupings and aggregates. Use the WHERE clause to completely eliminate rows from the query. For example, your query might eliminate all the orders except those placed in 2011. The database engine processes the HAVING clause after it processes the groupings and aggregates. Use the HAVING clause to eliminate rows based on aggregate expressions or groupings. For example, use the HAVING clause to remove the customers who have placed fewer than ten orders. Practice what you have learned about the HAVING clause by completing Exercise 5-3.

EXERCISE 5-3

Use the AdventureWorks2012 to complete this exercise. You can find the solutions in the Appendix.

1. Write a query that returns a count of detail lines in the Sales.SalesOrderDetail table by SalesOrderID. Include only those sales that have more than three detail lines.

2. Write a query that creates a sum of the LineTotal in the Sales.SalesOrderDetail table grouped by the SalesOrderID. Include only those rows where the sum exceeds 1,000.

3. Write a query that groups the products by ProductModelID along with a count. Display the rows that have a count that equals 1.

4. Change the query in question 3 so that only the products with the color blue or red are included.

DISTINCT

You can use the keyword DISTINCT in any SELECT list. For example, you can use DISTINCT to eliminate duplicate rows in a regular query. This section discusses using DISTINCT and aggregate queries.

Using DISTINCT vs. GROUP BY

Developers often use the DISTINCT keyword to eliminate duplicate rows from a regular query. Be careful when tempted to do this; using DISTINCT to eliminate duplicate rows may be a sign that there is a problem with the query. Assuming that the duplicate results are valid, you will get the same results by using GROUP BY instead. Type in and execute the code in Listing 5-7 to see how this works.

Listing 5-7. Using DISTINCT and GROUP BY

```
Use AdventureWorks2012;
GO

--1
SELECT DISTINCT SalesOrderID
FROM Sales.SalesOrderDetail;

--2
SELECT SalesOrderID
FROM Sales.SalesOrderDetail
GROUP BY SalesOrderID;
```

Queries 1 and 2 return identical results (see Figure 5-9). Even though query 2 contains no aggregate expressions, it is still an aggregate query because GROUP BY has been added. By grouping on SalesOrderID, only the unique values show up in the returned rows.

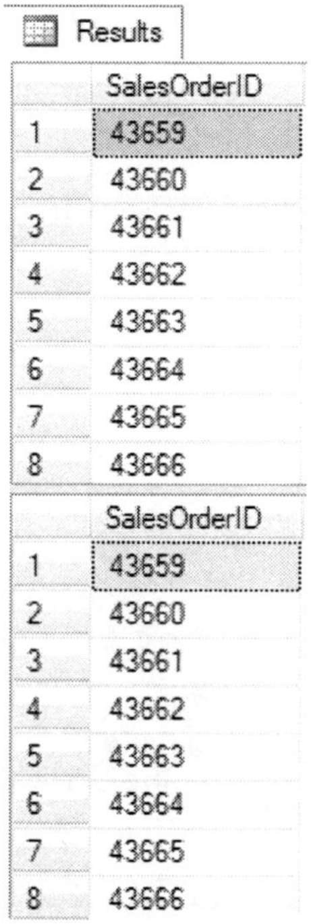

Figure 5-9. *The results of DISTINCT vs. GROUP BY*

DISTINCT Within an Aggregate Expression

You may also use DISTINCT within an aggregate query to cause the aggregate functions to operate on unique values. For example, instead of the count of rows, you could write a query that counts the number of unique values in a column. Type in and execute the code in Listing 5-8 to see how this works.

Listing 5-8. *Using DISTINCT in an Aggregate Expression*

```
USE AdventureWorks2012;
GO

--1
SELECT COUNT(*) AS CountOfRows,
    COUNT(SalesPersonID) AS CountOfSalesPeople,
    COUNT(DISTINCT SalesPersonID) AS CountOfUniqueSalesPeople
FROM Sales.SalesOrderHeader;

--2
SELECT SUM(TotalDue) AS TotalOfAllOrders,
    SUM(Distinct TotalDue) AS TotalOfDistinctTotalDue
FROM Sales.SalesOrderHeader;
```

Take a look at the results in Figure 5-10. Query 1 contains three aggregate expressions all using COUNT. The first one counts all rows in the table. The second expression counts the values in SalesPersonID. The expression returns a much smaller value because the data contains many NULL values, which are ignored by the aggregate function. Finally, the third expression returns the count of unique SalesPersonID values by using the DISTINCT keyword.

Query 2 demonstrates that DISTINCT works with other aggregate functions, not just COUNT. The first expression returns the sum of TotalDue for all rows in the table. The second expression returns the sum of unique TotalDue values.

	CountOfRows	CountOfSalesPeople	CountOfUniqueSalesPeople
1	31465	3806	17

	TotalOfAllOrders	TotalOfDistinctTotalDue
1	123216786.1159	91735344.3814

Figure 5-10. Using DISTINCT in an aggregate expression

You can use DISTINCT either to return unique rows from your query or to make your aggregate expression operate on unique values in your data. Practice what you have learned by completing Exercise 5-4.

EXERCISE 5-4

Use the AdventureWorks2012 database to complete this exercise. You can find the solutions in the Appendix.

1. Write a query using the Sales.SalesOrderDetail table to come up with a count of unique ProductID values that have been ordered.

2. Write a query using the Sales.SalesOrderHeader table that returns the count of unique TerritoryID values per customer.

Aggregate Queries with More Than One Table

So far, the examples have demonstrated how to write aggregate queries involving just one table. You may use aggregate expressions and the GROUP BY and HAVING clauses when joining tables as well; the same rules apply. Type in and execute the code in Listing 5-9 to learn how to do this.

Listing 5-9. Writing Aggregate Queries with Two Tables

```
USE AdventureWorks2012;
GO

--1
SELECT c.CustomerID, c.AccountNumber, COUNT(*) AS CountOfOrders,
    SUM(TotalDue) AS SumOfTotalDue
FROM Sales.Customer AS c
INNER JOIN Sales.SalesOrderHeader AS s ON c.CustomerID = s.CustomerID
GROUP BY c.CustomerID, c.AccountNumber
ORDER BY c.CustomerID;

--2
SELECT c.CustomerID, c.AccountNumber, COUNT(*) AS CountOfOrders,
    SUM(TotalDue) AS SumOfTotalDue
FROM Sales.Customer AS c
LEFT OUTER JOIN Sales.SalesOrderHeader AS s ON c.CustomerID = s.CustomerID
GROUP BY c.CustomerID, c.AccountNumber
ORDER BY c.CustomerID;

--3
SELECT c.CustomerID, c.AccountNumber,COUNT(s.SalesOrderID) AS CountOfOrders,
    SUM(COALESCE(TotalDue,0)) AS SumOfTotalDue
FROM Sales.Customer AS c
LEFT OUTER JOIN Sales.SalesOrderHeader AS s ON c.CustomerID = s.CustomerID
GROUP BY c.CustomerID, c.AccountNumber
ORDER BY c.CustomerID;
```

You can see the results of Listing 5-9 in Figure 5-11. All three queries join the Sales.Customer and Sales.SalesOrderHeader tables together and attempt to count the orders placed and calculate the sum of the total due for each customer.

	CustomerID	AccountNumber	CountOfOrders	SumOfTotalDue
1	11000	AW00011000	3	9115.1341
2	11001	AW00011001	3	7054.1875
3	11002	AW00011002	3	8966.0143
4	11003	AW00011003	3	8993.9155
5	11004	AW00011004	3	9056.5911

	CustomerID	AccountNumber	CountOfOrders	SumOfTotalDue
1	1	AW00000001	1	NULL
2	2	AW00000002	1	NULL
3	3	AW00000003	1	NULL
4	4	AW00000004	1	NULL
5	5	AW00000005	1	NULL

	CustomerID	AccountNumber	CountOfOrders	SumOfTotalDue
1	1	AW00000001	0	0.00
2	2	AW00000002	0	0.00
3	3	AW00000003	0	0.00
4	4	AW00000004	0	0.00
5	5	AW00000005	0	0.00

Figure 5-11. The partial results of using aggregates with multiple tables

Using an INNER JOIN, query 1 includes only the customers who have placed an order. By changing to a LEFT OUTER JOIN, query 2 includes all customers but incorrectly returns a count of 1 for customers with no orders and returns a NULL for the SumOfTotalDue when you probably want to see 0. Query 3 solves the first problem by changing COUNT(*) to COUNT(s.SalesOrderID), which eliminates the NULL values and correctly returns 0 for those customers who have not placed an order. Query 3 solves the second problem by using COALESCE to change the NULL value to 0.

Remember that writing aggregate queries with multiple tables is really not different from with just one table; the same rules apply. You can use your knowledge from the previous chapters, such as how to write a WHERE clause and how to join tables to write aggregate queries. Practice what you have learned by completing Exercise 5-5.

EXERCISE 5-5

Use the AdventureWorks2012 database to complete this exercise. You can find the solutions in the Appendix.

1. Write a query joining the Person.Person, Sales.Customer, and Sales.SalesOrderHeader tables to return a list of the customer names along with a count of the orders placed.

2. Write a query using the Sales.SalesOrderHeader, Sales.SalesOrderDetail, and Production.Product tables to display the total sum of products by ProductID and OrderDate.

Isolating Aggregate Query Logic

Several techniques exist that allow you to separate an aggregate query from the rest of the statement. Sometimes this is necessary because the grouping levels and the columns that must be displayed are not compatible. This section will demonstrate these techniques.

Using a Correlated Subquery in the WHERE Clause

In Chapter 4 you learned how to add subqueries to the WHERE clause. Developers often use another type of subquery, the *correlated subquery*, to isolate an aggregate query. In a correlated subquery, the subquery refers to the outer query within the subquery's WHERE clause.

You will likely see this query type used, so I want you to be familiar with it, but other options shown later in the section will be better choices for your own code. Here is the syntax:

```
SELECT <select list>
FROM <table1>
WHERE <value or column> = (SELECT <aggregate function>(<col1>)
    FROM <table2>
    WHERE <col2> = <table1>.<col3>)
```

Notice that the predicate in the WHERE clause contains an equal to (=) operator instead of the IN operator. Recall that the subqueries described in the "Using a Subquery in an IN List" section in Chapter 4 require the IN operator because the subquery returns multiple rows. The query compares the value from a column in the outer query to a list of values in the subquery when using the IN operator. When using a correlated subquery, the subquery returns only one value for each row of the outer query, and you can use the other operators, such as equal to. In this case, the query compares a value or column from one row to one value returned by the subquery. Take a look at Listing 5-10, which demonstrates this technique.

Listing 5-10. Using a Correlated Subquery in the WHERE Clause

```
Use AdventureWorks2012;
GO

--1
SELECT CustomerID, SalesOrderID, TotalDue
FROM Sales.SalesOrderHeader AS soh
WHERE 10 =
    (SELECT COUNT(*)
     FROM Sales.SalesOrderDetail
     WHERE SalesOrderID = soh.SalesOrderID);
```

```
--2
SELECT CustomerID, SalesOrderID, TotalDue
FROM Sales.SalesOrderHeader AS soh
WHERE 10000 <
    (SELECT SUM(TotalDue)
     FROM Sales.SalesOrderHeader
     WHERE CustomerID = soh.CustomerID);

--3
SELECT CustomerID
FROM Sales.Customer AS c
WHERE CustomerID > (
    SELECT SUM(TotalDue)
    FROM Sales.SalesOrderHeader
    WHERE CustomerID = c.CustomerID);
```

You can see the partial results in Figure 5-12. Query 1 displays the Sales.SalesOrderHeader rows where there are ten matching detail rows. Inside the subquery's WHERE clause, the SalesOrderID from the subquery must match the SalesOrderID from the outer query. Usually when the same column name is used, both must be qualified with the table name or alias. In this case, if the column is not qualified, it refers to the tables in the subquery. Of course, if the subquery contains more than one table, you may have to qualify the column name.

	CustomerID	SalesOrderID	TotalDue
1	29580	43665	16158.6961
2	29491	43693	23126.45
3	29955	43843	37106.2915
4	29888	43845	9661.1367
5	30107	43869	55408.1581
6	29925	43877	23223.5397
7	29901	43901	25575.00
8	29487	44131	23095.3463

	CustomerID	SalesOrderID	TotalDue
1	29825	43659	23153.2339
2	29734	43661	36865.8012
3	29994	43662	32474.9324
4	29898	43664	27510.4109
5	29580	43665	16158.6961
6	30052	43666	5694.8564
7	29974	43667	6876.3649
8	29614	43668	40487.7233

	CustomerID
1	11012
2	11013
3	11014
4	11021
5	11022
6	11040
7	11062
8	11063

Figure 5-12. A correlated subquery in the WHERE clause

Query 2 displays rows from the Sales.SalesOrderHeader table but only for customers who have the sum of TotalDue greater than 10,000. In this case, the CustomerID from the outer query must equal the CustomerID from the subquery. Query 3 demonstrates how you can compare a column to the results of the aggregate expression in the subquery. The query compares the CustomerID to the sum of the orders and displays the customers who have ordered less than the CustomerID. Of course, this particular example may not make sense from a business rules perspective, but it shows that you can compare a column to the value of an aggregate function using a correlated subquery.

Inline Correlated Subqueries

You may also see correlated subqueries used within the SELECT list. I really don't recommend this technique because if the query contains more than one correlated subquery, performance deteriorates quickly. You will learn about better options later in this section. Here is the syntax for the inline correlated subquery:

```
SELECT <select list>,
    (SELECT <aggregate function>(<col1>)
     FROM <table2> WHERE <col2> = <table1>.<col3>) AS <alias name>
FROM <table1>
```

The subquery must produce only one row for each row of the outer query, and only one expression may be returned from the subquery. Listing 5-11 shows two examples of this query type.

Listing 5-11. Using an Inline Correlated Subquery

```
USE AdventureWorks2012;
GO

--1
SELECT CustomerID,
    (SELECT COUNT(*)
     FROM Sales.SalesOrderHeader
     WHERE CustomerID = C.CustomerID) AS CountOfSales
FROM Sales.Customer AS C
ORDER BY CountOfSales DESC;

--2
SELECT CustomerID,
    (SELECT COUNT(*) AS CountOfSales
     FROM Sales.SalesOrderHeader
     WHERE CustomerID = C.CustomerID) AS CountOfSales,
    (SELECT SUM(TotalDue)
     FROM Sales.SalesOrderHeader
     WHERE CustomerID = C.CustomerID) AS SumOfTotalDue,
    (SELECT AVG(TotalDue)
     FROM Sales.SalesOrderHeader
     WHERE CustomerID = C.CustomerID) AS AvgOfTotalDue
FROM Sales.Customer AS C
ORDER BY CountOfSales DESC;
```

You can see the results in Figure 5-13. Query 1 demonstrates how an inline correlated subquery returns one value per row. Notice the WHERE clause in the subquery. The CustomerID column must be equal to the CustomerID in the outer query. The alias for the column must be added right after the subquery definition, not the column definition.

Results

	CustomerID	CountOfSales
1	11091	28
2	11176	28
3	11185	27
4	11200	27
5	11223	27

	CustomerID	CountOfSales	SumOfTotalDue	AvgOfTotalDue
1	11176	28	1458.6118	52.0932
2	11091	28	1314.2103	46.936
3	11277	27	1585.6648	58.7283
4	11200	27	1617.0356	59.8902
5	11223	27	1331.9455	49.3313

Figure 5-13. *Using an inline correlated subquery*

Normally, when working with the same column name from two tables, both must be qualified. Within the subquery, if the column is not qualified, the column is assumed to be from the table within the subquery. If the subquery involves multiple tables, well, then you will probably have to qualify the columns.

Notice that Query 2 contains three correlated subqueries because three values are required. Although one correlated subquery doesn't usually cause a problem, performance quickly deteriorates as additional correlated subqueries are added to the query. Luckily, other techniques exist to get the same results with better performance.

Using Derived Tables

In Chapter 4 you learned about derived tables. You can use derived tables to isolate the aggregate query from the rest of the query, especially when working with SQL Server 2000, without a performance hit. Here is the syntax:

```
SELECT <col1>,<col4>,<col3> FROM <table1> AS a
INNER JOIN
    (SELECT <aggregate function>(<col2>) AS <col4>,<col3>
     FROM <table2> GROUP BY <col3>) AS b ON a.<col1> = b.<col3>
```

Listing 5-12 shows how to use this technique. Type in and execute the code.

Listing 5-12. *Using a Derived Table*

```
USE AdventureWorks2012;
GO

SELECT c.CustomerID,CountOfSales,
    SumOfTotalDue, AvgOfTotalDue
FROM Sales.Customer AS c INNER JOIN
    (SELECT CustomerID, COUNT(*) AS CountOfSales,
```

```
            SUM(TotalDue) AS SumOfTotalDue,
            AVG(TotalDue) AS AvgOfTotalDue
        FROM Sales.SalesOrderHeader
        GROUP BY CustomerID) AS s
ON c.CustomerID = s.CustomerID;
```

You can see the results in Figure 5-14. This query has much better performance than the second query in Listing 5-11, but it produces the same results. Remember that any column required in the outer query must be listed in the derived table. You must also supply an alias for the derived table.

	CustomerID	CountOfSales	SumOfTotalDue	AvgOfTotalDue
1	11012	2	89.7923	44.8961
2	11013	2	125.9258	62.9629
3	11014	2	152.9873	76.4936
4	11021	1	2621.0158	2621.0158
5	11022	1	2566.1194	2566.1194
6	11040	1	2597.8108	2597.8108
7	11062	1	2598.9158	2598.9158
8	11063	1	2622.1098	2622.1098

Figure 5-14. The partial results of using a derived table

Besides the increase in performance, the derived table may return more than one row for each row of the outer query, and multiple aggregates may be included. If you are working with some legacy SQL Server 2000 systems, keep derived tables in mind for solving complicated T-SQL problems.

Common Table Expressions

You learned about common table expressions (CTEs) in Chapter 4. A CTE also allows you to isolate the aggregate query from the rest of the statement. The CTE is not stored as an object; it just makes the data available during the query. Here is the syntax:

```
WITH <cteName> AS (SELECT <aggregate function>(<col2>) AS <col4>, <col3>
    FROM <table2> GROUP BY <col3>)
SELECT <col1>,<col4>,<col3>
FROM <table1> INNER JOIN b ON <cteName>.<col1> = <table1>.<col3>
```

Type in and execute the code in Listing 5-13 to learn how to use a CTE with an aggregate query.

Listing 5-13. Using a Common Table Expression

```
USE AdventureWorks2012;
GO

WITH s AS
    (SELECT CustomerID, COUNT(*) AS CountOfSales,
        SUM(TotalDue) AS SumOfTotalDue,
        AVG(TotalDue) AS AvgOfTotalDue
```

```
    FROM Sales.SalesOrderHeader
    GROUP BY CustomerID)
SELECT c.CustomerID,CountOfSales,
    SumOfTotalDue, AvgOfTotalDue
FROM Sales.Customer AS c INNER JOIN s
ON c.CustomerID = s.CustomerID;
```

Figure 5-15 displays the results. This query looks a lot like the one in Listing 5-12, just rearranged a bit. At this point, there is no real advantage to the CTE over the derived table, but it is easier to read, in my opinion. CTEs have several extra features that you will learn about in Chapter 11.

	CustomerID	CountOfSales	SumOfTotalDue	AvgOfTotalDue
1	11012	2	89.7923	44.8961
2	11013	2	125.9258	62.9629
3	11014	2	152.9873	76.4936
4	11021	1	2621.0158	2621.0158
5	11022	1	2566.1194	2566.1194
6	11040	1	2597.8108	2597.8108
7	11062	1	2598.9158	2598.9158
8	11063	1	2622.1098	2622.1098

Figure 5-15. Using a common table expression

Using Derived Tables and CTEs to Display Details

Suppose you want to display several nonaggregated columns along with some aggregate expressions that apply to the entire result set or to a larger grouping level. For example, you may need to display several columns from the Sales.SalesOrderHeader table and calculate the percent of the TotalDue for each sale compared to the TotalDue for all the customer's sales. If you group by CustomerID, you can't include other nonaggregated columns from Sales.SalesOrderHeader unless you group by those columns. To get around this, you can use a derived table or a CTE. Type in and execute the code in Listing 5-14 to learn this technique.

Listing 5-14. Displaying Details

```
USE AdventureWorks2012;
GO

--1
SELECT c.CustomerID, SalesOrderID, TotalDue, AvgOfTotalDue,
    TotalDue/SumOfTotalDue * 100 AS SalePercent
FROM Sales.SalesOrderHeader AS soh
INNER JOIN
    (SELECT CustomerID, SUM(TotalDue) AS SumOfTotalDue,
     AVG(TotalDue) AS AvgOfTotalDue
     FROM Sales.SalesOrderHeader
     GROUP BY CustomerID) AS c ON soh.CustomerID = c.CustomerID
ORDER BY c.CustomerID;
```

```
--2
WITH c AS
    (SELECT CustomerID, SUM(TotalDue) AS SumOfTotalDue,
        AVG(TotalDue) AS AvgOfTotalDue
     FROM Sales.SalesOrderHeader
     GROUP BY CustomerID)
SELECT c.CustomerID, SalesOrderID, TotalDue,AvgOfTotalDue,
    TotalDue/SumOfTotalDue * 100 AS SalePercent
FROM Sales.SalesOrderHeader AS soh
INNER JOIN c ON soh.CustomerID = c.CustomerID
ORDER BY c.CustomerID;
```

Take a look at the results in Figure 5-16. The queries return the same results and just use different techniques. Inside the derived table or CTE, the data is grouped by CustomerID. The outer query contains no grouping at all, and any columns can be used. Either of these techniques performs much better than the equivalent query written with correlated subqueries.

	CustomerID	SalesOrderID	TotalDue	AvgOfTotalDue	SalePercent
1	11000	43793	3756.989	3038.378	41.21
2	11000	51522	2587.8769	3038.378	28.39
3	11000	57418	2770.2682	3038.378	30.39
4	11001	51493	2674.0227	2351.3958	37.90
5	11001	43767	3729.364	2351.3958	52.86
6	11001	72773	650.8008	2351.3958	9.22
7	11002	43736	3756.989	2988.6714	41.90
8	11002	51238	2535.964	2988.6714	28.28

	CustomerID	SalesOrderID	TotalDue	AvgOfTotalDue	SalePercent
1	11000	43793	3756.989	3038.378	41.21
2	11000	51522	2587.8769	3038.378	28.39
3	11000	57418	2770.2682	3038.378	30.39
4	11001	51493	2674.0227	2351.3958	37.90
5	11001	43767	3729.364	2351.3958	52.86
6	11001	72773	650.8008	2351.3958	9.22
7	11002	43736	3756.989	2988.6714	41.90
8	11002	51238	2535.964	2988.6714	28.28

Figure 5-16. The results of displaying details with a derived table and a CTE

The OVER Clause

The OVER clause provides a way to add aggregate values to a nonaggregate query. For example, you may need to write a report that compares the total due of each order to the total due of the average order. The query is not really an aggregate query, but one aggregate value from the entire results set or a grouping level is required to perform the calculation. Here is the syntax:

```
SELECT <col1>,<aggregate function>(<col2>) OVER([PARTITION BY <col3>])
FROM <table1>
```

Type in and execute the code in Listing 5-15 to learn how to use OVER.

Listing 5-15. Using the OVER Clause

```
USE AdventureWorks2012;
GO

SELECT CustomerID, SalesOrderID, TotalDue,
    AVG(TotalDue) OVER(PARTITION BY CustomerID) AS AvgOfTotalDue,
    SUM(TotalDue) OVER(PARTITION BY CustomerID) AS SumOfTOtalDue,
    TotalDue/(SUM(TotalDue) OVER(PARTITION BY CustomerID)) * 100
        AS SalePercentPerCustomer,
    SUM(TotalDue) OVER() AS SalesOverAll
FROM Sales.SalesOrderHeader
ORDER BY CustomerID;
```

Figure 5-17 displays the results. The PARTITION BY part of the expressions specifies the grouping over which the aggregate is calculated. In this example, when partitioned by CustomerID, the function calculates the value grouped over CustomerID. When no PARTITION BY is specified, as in the SalesOverAll column, the aggregate is calculated over the entire result set.

	CustomerID	SalesOrderID	TotalDue	AvgOfTotalDue	SumOfTOtalDue	SalePercentPerCustomer	SalesOverAll
1	11000	43793	3756.989	3038.378	9115.1341	41.21	123216786.1159
2	11000	57418	2770.2682	3038.378	9115.1341	30.39	123216786.1159
3	11000	51522	2587.8769	3038.378	9115.1341	28.39	123216786.1159
4	11001	43767	3729.364	2351.3958	7054.1875	52.86	123216786.1159
5	11001	72773	650.8008	2351.3958	7054.1875	9.22	123216786.1159
6	11001	51493	2674.0227	2351.3958	7054.1875	37.90	123216786.1159
7	11002	51238	2535.964	2988.6714	8966.0143	28.28	123216786.1159
8	11002	43736	3756.989	2988.6714	8966.0143	41.90	123216786.1159

Figure 5-17. Using the OVER clause

You can also include a GROUP BY in the overall query. Be careful here because any columns that are part of the OVER clause aggregate must be grouped. If you need to do this, you are probably better off solving the problem with a CTE.

The OVER clause allows you to add an aggregate function to an otherwise nonaggregate query. Practice using the OVER clause by completing Exercise 5-65.

EXERCISE 5-6

Use the AdventureWorks2012 database to complete this exercise. You can find the solutions in the Appendix.

1.   Write a query that joins the HumanResources.Employee table to the Person.Person table so that you can display the FirstName, LastName, and HireDate columns for

each employee. Display the JobTitle along with a count of employees for the title. Use a derived table to solve this query.

2. Rewrite the query from question 1 using a CTE.

3. Rewrite the query from question 1 using the OVER clause.

4. Display the CustomerID, SalesOrderID, and OrderDate for each Sales.SalesOrderHeader row as long as the customer has placed at least five orders. Use any of the techniques from this section to come up with the query.

GROUPING SETS

GROUPING SETS, when added to an aggregate query, allows you to combine different grouping levels within one statement. This is equivalent to combining multiple aggregate queries with UNION. For example, suppose you want the data summarized by one column combined with the data summarized by a different column. Just like MERGE, this feature is very valuable for loading data warehouses and data marts. When using GROUPING SETS instead of UNION, you can see increased performance, especially when the query includes a WHERE clause and the number of columns specified in the GROUPING SETS clause increases. Here is the syntax:

```
SELECT <col1>,<col2>,<aggregate function>(<col3>)
FROM <table1>
WHERE <criteria>
GROUP BY GROUPING SETS (<col1>,<col2>)
```

Listing 5-16 compares the equivalent UNION query to a query using GROUPING SETS. Type in and execute the code to learn more.

Listing 5-16. Using GROUPING SETS

```
USE AdventureWorks2012;
GO

--1
SELECT NULL AS SalesOrderID,SUM(UnitPrice)AS SumOfPrice,ProductID
FROM Sales.SalesOrderDetail
WHERE SalesOrderID BETWEEN 44175 AND 44180
GROUP BY ProductID
UNION
SELECT SalesOrderID,SUM(UnitPrice), NULL
FROM Sales.SalesOrderDetail
WHERE SalesOrderID BETWEEN 44175 AND 44180
GROUP BY SalesOrderID;

--2
SELECT SalesOrderID,SUM(UnitPrice) AS SumOfPrice,ProductID
FROM Sales.SalesOrderDetail
WHERE SalesOrderID BETWEEN 44175 AND 44180
GROUP BY GROUPING SETS(SalesOrderID,ProductID);
```

Figure 5-18 shows the partial results. Query 1 is a UNION query that calculates the sum of the UnitPrice. The first part of the query supplies a NULL value for SalesOrderID. That is because SalesOrderID is just a placeholder. The query groups by ProductID, and SalesOrderID is not needed. The second part of the query supplies a NULL value for ProductID. In this case, the query groups by SalesOrderID, and ProductID is not needed. The UNION query combines the results. Query 2 demonstrates how to write the equivalent query using GROUPING SETS.

	SalesOrderID	SumOfPrice	ProductID
1	NULL	3578.27	751
2	NULL	3578.27	752
3	NULL	3578.27	753
4	NULL	3399.99	774
5	NULL	6749.98	777
6	44175	3578.27	NULL
7	44176	3578.27	NULL
8	44177	3374.99	NULL

	SalesOrderID	SumOfPrice	ProductID
1	NULL	3578.27	751
2	NULL	3578.27	752
3	NULL	3578.27	753
4	NULL	3399.99	774
5	NULL	6749.98	777
6	44175	3578.27	NULL
7	44176	3578.27	NULL
8	44177	3374.99	NULL

Figure 5-18. The partial results of comparing UNION to GROUPING SETS

CUBE and ROLLUP

You can add subtotals to your aggregate queries by using CUBE or ROLLUP in the GROUP BY clause. CUBE and ROLLUP are very similar, but there is a subtle difference. CUBE will give subtotals for every possible combination of the grouping levels. ROLLUP will give subtotals for the hierarchy. For example, if you are grouping by three columns, CUBE will provide subtotals for every grouping column. ROLLUP will provide subtotals for the first two columns but not the last column in the GROUP BY list. Here is the syntax:

```
SELECT <col1>, <col2>, <aggregate expression>
    FROM <table>
GROUP BY <CUBE or ROLLUP>(<col1>,<col2>)
```

The following example demonstrates how to use CUBE and ROLLUP. Run the code in Listing 5-17 to see how this works.

Listing 5-17. CUBE and ROLLUP

```
--1
USE AdventureWorks2012
GO
SELECT COUNT(*) AS CountOfRows, Color,
       ISNULL(Size,CASE WHEN GROUPING(Size) = 0 THEN 'UNK' ELSE 'ALL' END) AS Size
FROM Production.Product
GROUP BY CUBE(Color,Size)
ORDER BY Size;

--2
SELECT COUNT(*) AS CountOfRows, Color,
       ISNULL(Size,CASE WHEN GROUPING(Size) = 0 THEN 'UNK' ELSE 'ALL' END) AS Size
FROM Production.Product
GROUP BY ROLLUP(Color,Size)
ORDER BY Size;
```

Figure 5-19 shows the partial results. Query 1 returns 98 rows while Query 2 returns only 79 rows. Notice that Query 2 doesn't have an ALL row for size 38. Query 2 returns a subtotal row for every color but not every size. Query 1 returns a subtotal row for every color and every size.

In this example, the subtotal row for Red contains a NULL in the size column. In order to distinguish the subtotal rows from legitimate NULLs in the data, use the GROUPING function. The GROUPING function returns a 1 in the subtotal rows. Combine GROUPING with the ISNULL function to handle this.

Results			
	CountOfRows	Color	Size
1	5	Black	38
2	5	Silver	38
3	2	Yellow	38
4	12	ALL	38
5	4	Black	40
	CountOfRows	Color	Size
1	5	Black	38
2	5	Silver	38
3	2	Yellow	38
4	3	Yellow	40
5	4	Silver	40
6	4	Black	40
7	5	Black	42

Figure 5-19. The partial results of CUBE and ROLLUP

Thinking About Performance

Inline correlated subqueries are very popular among developers. Unfortunately, the performance is poor compared to other techniques, such as derived tables and CTEs. Toggle on the Include Actual Execution Plan setting before typing and executing the code in Listing 5-18.

Listing 5-18. Comparing a Correlated Subquery to a Common Table Expression

```
USE AdventureWorks2012;
GO

--1
SELECT CustomerID,
    (SELECT COUNT(*) AS CountOfSales
     FROM Sales.SalesOrderHeader
     WHERE CustomerID = c.CustomerID) AS CountOfSales,
    (SELECT SUM(TotalDue)
     FROM Sales.SalesOrderHeader
     WHERE CustomerID = c.CustomerID) AS SumOfTotalDue,
    (SELECT AVG(TotalDue)
     FROM Sales.SalesOrderHeader
     WHERE CustomerID = c.CustomerID) AS AvgOfTotalDue
FROM Sales.Customer AS c
ORDER BY CountOfSales DESC;

--2
WITH Totals AS
    (SELECT COUNT(*) AS CountOfSales,
        SUM(TotalDue) AS SumOfTotalDue,
        AVG(TotalDue) AS AvgOfTotalDue,
        CustomerID
    FROM Sales.SalesOrderHeader
    GROUP BY CustomerID)
SELECT c.CustomerID, CountOfSales,SumOfTotalDue, AvgOfTotalDue
FROM Totals
LEFT OUTER JOIN Sales.Customer AS c ON Totals.CustomerID = c.CustomerID
ORDER BY CountOfSales DESC;
```

Figure 5-20 displays a portion of the execution plan windows. These plans are pretty complex, but the important thing to note is that query 1, with the correlated subqueries, takes up 62 percent of the resources. Query 2, with the CTE, produces the same results but requires only 38 percent of the resources.

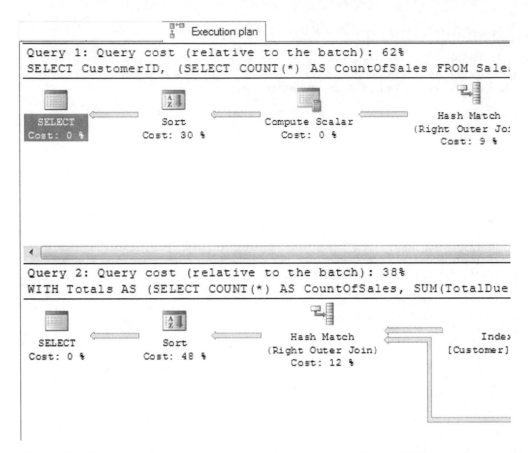

Query 1: Query cost (relative to the batch): 62%
SELECT CustomerID, (SELECT COUNT(*) AS CountOfSales FROM Sale:

SELECT   Sort   Compute Scalar   Hash Match
Cost: 0 %   Cost: 30 %   Cost: 0 %   (Right Outer Jo:
                                                   Cost: 9 %

Query 2: Query cost (relative to the batch): 38%
WITH Totals AS (SELECT COUNT(*) AS CountOfSales, SUM(TotalDue

SELECT   Sort   Hash Match   Inde>
Cost: 0 %   Cost: 48 %   (Right Outer Join)   [Customer]
                               Cost: 12 %

Figure 5-20. The execution plans when comparing a derived table to a CTE

As you can see, the way you write a query can often have a big impact on the performance. Complete Exercise 5-7 to learn more about the performance of aggregate queries.

EXERCISE 5-7

Use the AdventureWorks2012 database to complete this exercise. You can find the solutions in the Appendix.

1. Make sure that the Include Actual Execution Plan setting is turned on before typing and executing the following code. Compare the execution plans to see whether the CTE query performs better than the OVER clause query.

```
USE AdventureWorks2012;
GO

--1
WITH SumSale AS
    (SELECT SUM(TotalDue) AS SumTotalDue,
        CustomerID
     FROM Sales.SalesOrderHeader
     GROUP BY CustomerID)
SELECT o.CustomerID, TotalDue,
    TotalDue / SumTotalDue * 100 AS PercentOfSales
FROM SumSale INNER JOIN Sales.SalesOrderHeader AS o
ON SumSale.CustomerID = o.CustomerID
ORDER BY CustomerID;

--2
SELECT CustomerID, TotalDue,
    TotalDue / SUM(TotalDue) OVER(PARTITION BY CustomerID) * 100
      AS PercentOfSales
FROM Sales.SalesOrderHeader
ORDER BY CustomerID;
```

2. The following queries each contain two calculations: percent of sales by customer and percent of sales by territory. Type in and execute the code to see the difference in performance. Make sure the Include Actual Execution Plan setting is turned on before running the code.

```
USE AdventureWorks2012;
GO

--1
WITH SumSale AS
    (SELECT SUM(TotalDue) AS SumTotalDue,
        CustomerID
     FROM Sales.SalesOrderHeader
     GROUP BY CustomerID),
 TerrSales AS
     (SELECT SUM(TotalDue) AS SumTerritoryTotalDue, TerritoryID
      FROM Sales.SalesOrderHeader
      GROUP BY TerritoryID )
SELECT o.CustomerID, TotalDue,
    TotalDue / SumTotalDue * 100 AS PercentOfCustSales,
    TotalDue / SumTerritoryTotalDue * 100 AS PercentOfTerrSales
FROM SumSale
INNER JOIN Sales.SalesOrderHeader AS o ON SumSale.CustomerID = o.CustomerID
INNER JOIN TerrSales ON TerrSales.TerritoryID = o.TerritoryID
ORDER BY CustomerID;
```

```
--2
SELECT CustomerID, TotalDue,
    TotalDue / SUM(TotalDue) OVER(PARTITION BY CustomerID) * 100
    AS PercentOfCustSales,
    TotalDue / SUM(TotalDue) OVER(PARTITION BY TerritoryID) * 100
    AS PercentOfTerrSales
FROM Sales.SalesOrderHeader
ORDER BY CustomerID;
```

Summary

If you follow the steps outlined in the preceding sections, you will be able to write aggregate queries. With practice, you will become proficient. Keep the following rules in mind when writing an aggregate query:

- Any column not contained in an aggregate function in the SELECT list or ORDER BY clause must be part of the GROUP BY clause.

- Once an aggregate function, the GROUP BY clause, or the HAVING clause appears in a query, it is an aggregate query.

- Use the WHERE clause to filter out rows before the grouping and aggregates are applied. The WHERE clause doesn't allow aggregate functions.

- Use the HAVING clause to filter out rows using aggregate functions.

- Don't include anything in the SELECT list or ORDER BY clause that you don't want as a grouping level.

- Use common table expressions or derived tables instead of correlated subqueries to solve tricky aggregate query problems.

- To combine more than one grouping combination, use GROUPING SETS.

- Use CUBE and ROLLUP to produce subtotal rows.

- Remember that aggregate functions ignore NULL values except for COUNT(*).

CHAPTER 6

Manipulating Data

The data stored in most databases is not static. The application users constantly add data to tables as customers place orders, the company hires employees, and the payroll department writes checks. Automated processes periodically load new data into reporting databases, such as data warehouses, and into production systems. Users and processes also update existing rows or delete rows from tables.

In Chapters 1 through 5, you learned how to retrieve data from SQL Server. These skills are important for generating reports and displaying data. These skills will come in handy as you learn to insert new rows, update the values in existing rows, and delete rows from tables. This chapter covers how to manipulate data in many different scenarios, such as by using one table, joins, and subqueries.

Inserting New Rows

There are many ways to add new rows to tables in SQL Server databases. Be aware that there are other tools such as SQL Server Integration Services (SSIS) that you can use to load data into SQL Server, but because this book is about T-SQL, this section covers the T-SQL statements to insert data. To learn more about SSIS, read *Pro SQL Server 2011 Integration Services* by Francis Rodrigues and Michael Coles (Apress, 2012), and also *SSIS Design Patterns* by Andy Leonard, Tim Mitchell, Jessica Moss, and Michelle Ufford (Apress, 2012).

Run the following code to create a table that you will populate with data in this section:

```
USE AdventureWorks2012;
GO
IF OBJECT_ID('demoCustomer') IS NOT NULL BEGIN
    DROP TABLE demoCustomer;
END;
CREATE TABLE demoCustomer(CustomerID INT NOT NULL PRIMARY KEY,
    FirstName NVARCHAR(50) NOT NULL, MiddleName NVARCHAR(50) NULL,
    LastName NVARCHAR(50) NOT NULL);
```

Note You may notice that I have used two different techniques to check for the existence of a table before dropping it. When using SQL Server Management Studio to create the script, the code checks for the table in the sys.objects table. When I write the code myself, I check the results of the OBJECT_ID function. Either technique works.

Adding One Row with Literal Values

Adding one row with literal values is the simplest way to add data to an existing table. For example, a user may fill out a Windows or web form in an application and click Save. At that point, the application builds and sends a single INSERT statement to SQL Server containing the values that the user entered in the form. To insert new rows, you will use the INSERT statement. The syntax of the INSERT statement, which has two variations, is simple.

```
INSERT [INTO] <table1> [(<col1>,<col2>)] SELECT <value1>,<value2>;
INSERT [INTO] <table1> [(<col1>,<col2>)] VALUES (<value1>,<value2>);
```

The INTO keyword is optional, but I like to include it. Type in and execute the code in Listing 6-1 to learn this technique. The last statement displays the inserted data.

Listing 6-1. *Adding One Row at a Time with Literal Values*

```
USE AdventureWorks2012;
GO

--1
INSERT INTO dbo.demoCustomer (CustomerID, FirstName, MiddleName, LastName)
VALUES (1,'Orlando','N.','Gee');

--2
INSERT INTO dbo.demoCustomer (CustomerID, FirstName, MiddleName, LastName)
SELECT 3, 'Donna','F.','Cameras';

--3
INSERT INTO dbo.demoCustomer
VALUES (4,'Janet','M.','Gates');

--4
INSERT INTO dbo.demoCustomer
SELECT 6,'Rosmarie','J.','Carroll';

--5
INSERT INTO dbo.demoCustomer (CustomerID, FirstName, MiddleName, LastName)
VALUES (2,'Keith',NULL,'Harris');

--6
INSERT INTO dbo.demoCustomer (CustomerID, FirstName, LastName)
VALUES (5,'Lucy','Harrington');

--7
SELECT CustomerID, FirstName, MiddleName, LastName
FROM dbo.demoCustomer;
```

Figure 6-1 shows the results of query 7. The INSERT INTO clause specifies the table name and optionally the column names. Statement 1 inserts the row using the VALUES clause. Notice that parentheses surround the literal values in the statement. Statement 2 uses a slightly different syntax with the keyword SELECT. In this case, you could successfully run the SELECT part of the statement because it is a valid statement by itself.

	CustomerID	First Name	Middle Name	Last Name
1	1	Orlando	N.	Gee
2	2	Keith	NULL	Harris
3	3	Donna	F.	Cameras
4	4	Janet	M.	Gates
5	5	Lucy	NULL	Harrington
6	6	Rosmarie	J.	Carroll

Figure 6-1. The results after inserting six rows

■ **Note** This book uses the word *query* for T-SQL commands that return data. It uses the word *statement* for other T-SQL commands.

Both statements 1 and 2 specify the column names in parentheses. The order of the values must match the order of the column names. Statements 3 and 4 look very similar to the first two statements, but these statements don't specify the column names. Although not specifying the column names will work some of the time, the best practice is to specify the columns. Not only does this help clarify the code, it often, but not always, keeps the code from breaking if new nonrequired columns are added to the table later.

Notice that statement 5 inserts NULL into the MiddleName column. Statement 6 just leaves MiddleName out of the statement altogether. Both of these statements work because the MiddleName column is optional.

Avoiding Common Insert Errors

The statements in the previous section successfully added six rows to the dbo.demoCustomer table because they were carefully written to avoid breaking any of the constraints and column requirements. Listing 6-2 demonstrates several invalid statements. Type in and execute the code to learn about some of the things that can go wrong when inserting data into tables.

Listing 6-2. Attempting to Insert Rows with Invalid INSERT Statements

```
USE AdventureWorks2012;
GO

PRINT '1';
--1
INSERT INTO dbo.demoCustomer (CustomerID, FirstName, MiddleName, LastName)
VALUES (1, 'Dominic','P.','Gash');
```

```
PRINT '2';
--2
INSERT INTO dbo.demoCustomer (CustomerID, MiddleName, LastName)
VALUES (10,'M.','Garza');

GO
PRINT '3';
GO

--3
INSERT INTO dbo.demoCustomer
VALUES (11,'Katherine','Harding');

GO
PRINT '4';
GO

--4
INSERT INTO dbo.demoCustomer (CustomerID, FirstName, LastName)
VALUES (11, 'Katherine', NULL,'Harding');

GO
PRINT '5';
GO

--5
INSERT INTO dbo.demoCustomer (CustomerID, FirstName, LastName)
VALUES ('A','Katherine','Harding');
```

Figure 6-2 shows the error messages that result from running Listing 6-2. Statement 1 attempts to add another row with the CustomerID value 1. Since a row with CustomerID 1 already exists in the table, the INSERT statement violates the primary key constraint. Because the primary key of a table uniquely identifies a row, you may not insert duplicate values. If the primary key is a composite key, however, you can have duplicate values in any of the columns but not duplicates of the entire key. A primary key may not contain any NULL values in the key columns.

```
 Messages
1
Msg 2627, Level 14, State 1, Line 4
Violation of PRIMARY KEY constraint 'PK__demoCust__A4AE64B85EAFE411'. Cannot insert duplicate key in
  object 'dbo.demoCustomer'. The duplicate key value is (1).
The statement has been terminated.
2
Msg 515, Level 16, State 2, Line 9
Cannot insert the value NULL into column 'FirstName', table 'AdventureWorks2008R2.dbo.demoCustomer';
column does not allow nulls. INSERT fails.
The statement has been terminated.
3
Msg 213, Level 16, State 1, Line 3
Column name or number of supplied values does not match table definition.
4
Msg 110, Level 15, State 1, Line 3
There are fewer columns in the INSERT statement than values specified in the VALUES clause. The number
of values in the VALUES clause must match the number of columns specified in the INSERT statement.
5
Msg 245, Level 16, State 1, Line 3
Conversion failed when converting the varchar value 'A' to data type int.
```

Figure 6-2. The results of attempting to insert rows with invalid INSERT statements

Statement 2 violates the NOT NULL constraint on the FirstName column. Every row must contain a non-NULL value in the FirstName and LastName columns.

The database engine doesn't discover problems with statements 1 and 2 until the code runs. The problems with statements 3 and 4 are compile errors that cause the entire batch to fail. To show all the error messages for the listing, the word GO separates statements 3 and 4 into their own batches. In fact, even the PRINT statement will not run if it is contained in the same batch as these statements. The intent of statements 3 and 4 is to insert a row with a NULL MiddleName. Because statement 3 doesn't specify the column names, the database engine expects a value for each of the four columns in the table definition. Since the statement supplies only three values, the statement fails. Statement 4 does supply the column names, but the VALUES clause doesn't supply the same number of values. Once again, the statement fails. Statement 5 also contains a compile error. It attempts to insert a string value when the column, CustomerID, accepts only an integer.

Inserting Multiple Rows with One Statement

You can write one statement using a feature called *row constructors* to insert multiple rows. With versions prior to SQL Server 2008, you could write an INSERT statement with a UNION query to avoid writing multiple INSERT statements. Type in and execute Listing 6-3 to learn how to use both techniques.

Listing 6-3. Inserting Multiple Rows with One INSERT

```
USE AdventureWorks2012;
GO

--1
INSERT INTO dbo.demoCustomer (CustomerID, FirstName, MiddleName, LastName)
SELECT 7,'Dominic','P.','Gash'
UNION
SELECT 10,'Kathleen','M.','Garza'
UNION
SELECT 11, 'Katherine', NULL,' Harding';
```

```
--2
INSERT INTO dbo.demoCustomer (CustomerID, FirstName, MiddleName, LastName)
VALUES (12,'Johnny','A.','Capino'),
       (16,'Christopher','R.','Beck'),
       (18,'David','J.','Liu');

--3
SELECT CustomerID, FirstName, MiddleName, LastName
FROM dbo.demoCustomer
WHERE CustomerID >= 7;
```

Figure 6-3 displays the rows inserted by Listing 6-3. Statement 1 uses the UNION query technique. You can successfully select just the five lines that make up the UNION query part of the INSERT statement and run it by itself. Statement 2 demonstrates how to use the row constructor technique. By using row constructors, you can specify multiple lists of values, separated by commas, in one VALUES clause.

	CustomerID	First Name	Middle Name	Last Name
1	7	Dominic	P.	Gash
2	10	Kathleen	M.	Garza
3	11	Katherine	NULL	Harding
4	12	Johnny	A.	Capino
5	16	Christopher	R.	Beck
6	18	David	J.	Liu

Figure 6-3. Inserting multiple rows with one INSERT statement

Inserting Rows from Another Table

So far, you have learned how to insert literal values into a table. Often you will need to insert data from one table or query into another table. For example, you may need to load production data into a data warehouse. Often application programmers think about data in terms of individual rows and so insert data one row at a time when it is possible, and almost always more efficient, to insert more rows at once. They will often loop through one table, saving the values in variables, and then insert the values in the second table.

My favorite analogy involves 2 boxes and 100 car keys. How would you move the keys from one box to the other most efficiently without picking up either of the boxes? Would you pick up one key at a time and move it? No, you would probably grab up all the keys if you could and just move them all at once. If you could not pick up all the keys in one trip, you could at least move them in two or three batches. Listing 6-4 shows how to import rows from one table into another all within one statement. This example demonstrates "moving all the car keys at once." Type in and execute the code to see how this works.

Listing 6-4. Inserting Rows from Another Table

```
USE AdventureWorks2012;
GO
```

```
--1
INSERT INTO dbo.demoCustomer (CustomerID, FirstName, MiddleName, LastName)
SELECT BusinessEntityID, FirstName, MiddleName, LastName
FROM Person.Person
WHERE BusinessEntityID BETWEEN 19 AND 35;

--2
INSERT INTO dbo.demoCustomer (CustomerID, FirstName, MiddleName, LastName)
SELECT DISTINCT c.BusinessEntityID, c.FirstName, c.MiddleName, c.LastName
FROM Person.Person AS c
INNER JOIN Sales.SalesOrderHeader AS s ON c.BusinessEntityID = s.SalesPersonID

--3
SELECT CustomerID, FirstName, MiddleName, LastName
FROM dbo.demoCustomer
WHERE CustomerID > 18;
```

Figure 6-4 shows some of the rows added to the dbo.demoCustomer table by Listing 6-4. Statement 1 inserts the rows from the Person.Person table where the BusinessEntityID is between 19 and 35. Statement 2 inserts the rows from a query that joins the Person.Person and Sales.SalesOrderHeader tables. The SELECT parts of the statements are valid queries that you can run without the INSERT clauses. You can use any of the techniques you have learned so far to write SELECT statements to insert data into a table as long as the data selected meets the constraints and requirements of the target table.

	CustomerID	FirstName	MiddleName	LastName
1	19	Mary	A	Dempsey
2	20	Wanida	M	Benshoof
3	21	Terry	J	Eminhizer
4	22	Sariya	E	Hampadoungsataya
5	23	Mary	E	Gibson
6	24	Jill	A	Williams
7	25	James	R	Hamilton
8	26	Peter	J	Krebs
9	27	Jo	A	Brown
10	28	Guy	R	Gilbert
11	29	Mark	K	McArthur
12	30	Britta	L	Simon
13	31	Margie	W	Shoop
14	32	Rebecca	A	Laszlo
15	33	Annik	O	Stahl
16	34	Suchitra	O	Mohan

Figure 6-4. The partial results of adding rows from another table

Inserting Missing Rows

You have seen what can happen when you attempt to insert a new row that violates the primary key. You can use the technique in the "Using OUTER JOIN to Find Rows with No Match" section of Chapter 4 to insert rows into one table that don't exist in the source table. Type in and execute the code in Listing 6-5 to learn how this works.

***Listing 6-5.** Inserting Missing Rows*

```
USE AdventureWorks2012;
GO

--1
INSERT INTO dbo.demoCustomer (CustomerID, FirstName, MiddleName, LastName)
SELECT c.BusinessEntityID, c.FirstName, c.MiddleName, c.LastName
FROM Person.Person AS c
LEFT OUTER JOIN dbo.demoCustomer AS d ON c.BusinessEntityID = d.CustomerID
WHERE d.CustomerID IS NULL;

--2
SELECT COUNT(CustomerID) AS CustomerCount
FROM dbo.demoCustomer;
```

Figure 6-5 shows the customer count after adding the missing rows. By using the LEFT OUTER JOIN and checking for NULL values in the target table, the SELECT part of the INSERT statement finds the missing rows and inserts those rows into the table. As mentioned in the "Inserting Rows from Another Table" section, any valid SELECT statement may be used to insert rows into a table. If you run the same code a second or third time, you will find that the row count doesn't change. Since the code inserted all the missing rows, there are no new rows to insert after the first time.

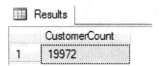

***Figure 6-5.** The results of checking the row count after adding the missing rows*

Creating and Populating a Table in One Statement

The SELECT INTO statement allows you to create a table and populate it with one statement. Developers often use this technique to create temporary tables, or *work tables*.

```
SELECT <col1>,<col2>
INTO <table2>
FROM <table1>;
```

Type in and execute the code in Listing 6-6 to learn how to use this technique. The first part of the code drops the dbo.demoCustomer table because the SELECT INTO statement will fail if the table already exists.

Listing 6-6. Using SELECT INTO to Create and Populate a Table

```
USE AdventureWorks2012;
GO

IF EXISTS (SELECT * FROM sys.objects
            WHERE object_id = OBJECT_ID(N'[dbo].[demoCustomer]')
                AND type in (N'U'))
DROP TABLE dbo.demoCustomer;

GO

--1
SELECT BusinessEntityID, FirstName, MiddleName, LastName,
    FirstName + ISNULL(' ' + MiddleName,'') + ' ' +  LastName AS FullName
INTO dbo.demoCustomer
FROM Person.Person;


--2
SELECT BusinessEntityID, FirstName, MiddleName, LastName, FullName
FROM dbo.demoCustomer;
```

Figure 6-6 displays the partial results. Statement 1 lists the columns and an expression along with the word INTO and the name of the table to create. The resulting table contains a column, FullName, that the statement created with the expression. Even though you could write a query that doesn't specify an alias for the expression, you must specify the alias for the expression when writing SELECT INTO statements. The database engine uses the column and alias names when creating the new table.

	BusinessEntityID	FirstName	MiddleName	LastName	FullName
1	285	Syed	E	Abbas	Syed E Abbas
2	293	Catherine	R.	Abel	Catherine R. Abel
3	295	Kim	NULL	Abercrombie	Kim Abercrombie
4	2170	Kim	NULL	Abercrombie	Kim Abercrombie
5	38	Kim	B	Abercrombie	Kim B Abercrombie
6	211	Hazem	E	Abolrous	Hazem E Abolrous
7	2357	Sam	NULL	Abolrous	Sam Abolrous
8	297	Humberto	NULL	Acevedo	Humberto Acevedo
9	291	Gustavo	NULL	Achong	Gustavo Achong
10	299	Pilar	NULL	Ackerman	Pilar Ackerman
11	121	Pilar	G	Ackerman	Pilar G Ackerman
12	16867	Aaron	B	Adams	Aaron B Adams

Figure 6-6. The partial results of creating and populating a table with SELECT INTO

Figure 6-7 shows the table definition of the dbo.demoCustomer table found by navigating to the table in the Object Explorer window of SQL Server Management Studio. You may have to right-click Tables and select Refresh to see the new table. Except for the missing primary key, the column definitions match the columns from the Person.Person table, which was the source of the data. The data in the FullName column can be 152 characters—the three name columns plus the two spaces.

- AdventureWorks2012
  - Tables
    - System Tables
    - dbo.AWBuildVersion
    - dbo.DatabaseLog
    - dbo.demoAutoPopulate
    - dbo.demoCustomer
      - Columns
        - BusinessEntityID (int, not null)
        - FirstName (Name(nvarchar(50)), not null)
        - MiddleName (Name(nvarchar(50)), null)
        - LastName (Name(nvarchar(50)), not null)
        - FullName (nvarchar(152), not null)

Figure 6-7. The dbo.demoCustomer table definition

Developers often use the SELECT INTO statement to create an empty table by adding 1=2 to the WHERE clause. Because one never equals two, the statement creates the table but doesn't add any rows. Even if you want to create and populate a work table, the performance of the entire system is often better by creating the empty table first and then populating it with a regular INSERT statement when you are working with a large number of rows. This is because the SELECT INTO statement locks system tables that can cause problems for other connections. Using a CREATE TABLE first and then populating it locks the system tables only momentarily. Using the SELECT INTO syntax locks the tables until the entire statement completes.

Inserting Rows into Tables with Default Column Values

Column definitions often specify a default value, called a *default constraint*, if the INSERT statement doesn't supply a value for the column. This is different from inserting NULL. When inserting NULL, you specify NULL in the INSERT statement, or the NULL value is a result of the SELECT statement used to insert the data. You might also omit the column from the INSERT statement to insert NULL. If the column definition specifies a default constraint, you can just leave that column out of the INSERT statement to automatically insert the default value. Run the code in Listing 6-7 to learn how to insert data into tables when one or more of the columns have a default value. The first part of the code creates the table and adds the default constraints.

Listing 6-7. Inserting Data with a Column Default Constraint

```
USE AdventureWorks2012;
GO
IF  EXISTS (SELECT * FROM sys.objects
            WHERE object_id = OBJECT_ID(N'[dbo].[demoDefault]')
                AND type in (N'U'))
DROP TABLE [dbo].[demoDefault]
GO

CREATE TABLE [dbo].[demoDefault](
    [KeyColumn] [int] NOT NULL PRIMARY KEY,
        [HasADefault1] [DATETIME2](1) NOT NULL,
        [HasADefault2] [NVARCHAR](50) NULL,
)
GO
ALTER TABLE [dbo].[demoDefault] ADD  CONSTRAINT [DF_demoDefault_HasADefault]
    DEFAULT (GETDATE()) FOR [HasADefault1]
GO
ALTER TABLE [dbo].[demoDefault] ADD  CONSTRAINT [DF_demoDefault_HasADefault2]
    DEFAULT ('the default') FOR [HasADefault2]
GO

--1
INSERT INTO dbo.demoDefault(HasADefault1,HasADefault2,KeyColumn)
VALUES ('2009-04-24','Test 1',1),('2009-10-1',NULL,2);

--2
INSERT INTO dbo.demoDefault (HasADefault1,HasADefault2,KeyColumn)
VALUES (DEFAULT,DEFAULT,3),(DEFAULT,DEFAULT,4);

--3
INSERT INTO dbo.demoDefault (KeyColumn)
VALUES (5),(6);

--4
SELECT HasADefault1,HasADefault2,KeyColumn
FROM dbo.demoDefault;
```

Figure 6-8 shows the results. Statement 1 inserts literal values into the HasADefault1 and HasADefault2 columns. Even though the two columns have default constraints, you can still override them and insert your own values. Notice that the row inserted with KeyColumn value 2 contains a NULL value in the HasADefault2 column. The statement specified and inserted NULL, not the default value.

	HasADefault1	HasADefault2	KeyColumn
1	2009-04-24 00:00:00.0	Test 1	1
2	2009-10-01 00:00:00.0	NULL	2
3	2011-05-30 06:11:56.9	the default	3
4	2011-05-30 06:11:56.9	the default	4
5	2011-05-30 06:11:56.9	the default	5
6	2011-05-30 06:11:56.9	the default	6

Figure 6-8. The results of inserting rows into a table with column default constraints

Statements 2 and 3 take advantage of the default constraints. Statement 2 specifies the keyword DEFAULT instead of a value. Statement 3 just omits the two columns. Whenever using the keyword DEFAULT or omitting the columns, the default definition determines the values to be inserted. The GETDATE function provides default values for the HasDefault1 column. The literal value "the default" is filled in for HasADefault2.

Inserting Rows into Tables with Automatically Populating Columns

In addition to default constraints, four types of columns exist that can be autopopulated. In other words, you should not specify values for these columns. The columns types are as follows:

- *rowversion*: Formerly called TIMESTAMP, this contains a binary number that is unique within a database. Developers generally use ROWVERSION to determine whether changes have been made to a row.

- *identity*: This contains an autoincrementing numeric value. Developers often use INDENITY columns when an ID number is needed for a table.

- *Computed columns*: These have a definition that is usually based on the values of other columns in the same row. The values in a computed column can be stored in the table by specifying the keyword PERSISTED in the column definition. If the table definition doesn't contain PERSISTED, it will be calculated each time it is accessed.

- *Sequences*: These are user-defined objects and act like identity columns but are not restricted to a specific table. Unlike identity numbers, sequence numbers can be reused and created across multiple tables and rows and you need to reference the sequence object in the insert statement.

Be sure to always specify the column names, avoiding the automatically populated columns when you write an INSERT statement to avoid causing an error.

▓ **Note** There is an exception to the rule about inserting data into IDENTITY columns. You can change a session-specific setting called IDENTITY_INSERT that will allow you to insert a value into an IDENTITY column. Developers and database administrators often do this when loading data and the IDENTITY values must be preserved. After loading the data, the IDENTITY column will work as before after you turn off IDENTITY_INSERT in that session or insert into the table from a different session.

Type in and execute the code in Listing 6-8. The first part of the code creates a table with the special column types.

Listing 6-8. Inserting Rows into Tables with Autopopulated Columns

```
USE [AdventureWorks2012]
GO

IF  EXISTS (SELECT * FROM sys.objects
            WHERE object_id = OBJECT_ID(N'[dbo].[demoAutoPopulate]')
                AND type in (N'U'))
DROP TABLE [dbo].[demoAutoPopulate];

IF  EXISTS (SELECT * FROM sys.objects
            WHERE object_id = OBJECT_ID(N'[dbo].[demoSequence]'))
DROP SEQUENCE [dbo].[demoSequence];

CREATE SEQUENCE dbo.demoSequence
AS INT
START WITH 1
INCREMENT BY 1;

CREATE TABLE [dbo].[demoAutoPopulate](
    [RegularColumn] [NVARCHAR](50) NOT NULL PRIMARY KEY,
    [IdentityColumn] [INT] IDENTITY(1,1) NOT NULL,
    [RowversionColumn] [ROWVERSION] NOT NULL,
    [SequenceColumn] [INT] NOT NULL,
    [ComputedColumn] AS ([RegularColumn]+CONVERT([NVARCHAR],
    [IdentityColumn],(0))) PERSISTED)
GO

--1
INSERT INTO dbo.demoAutoPopulate (RegularColumn, SequenceColumn)
VALUES ('a', NEXT VALUE FOR dbo.demoSequence),
('b', NEXT VALUE FOR dbo.demoSequence),
('c', NEXT VALUE FOR dbo.demoSequence);
```

```
--2
SELECT RegularColumn, IdentityColumn, RowversionColumn, SequenceColumn, ComputedColumn
FROM demoAutoPopulate;
```

Figure 6-9 shows the results. Statement 1 specified values for RegularColumn only. The database engine automatically determined the values for the other columns. Notice that the IdentityColumn contains an incrementing value. The ComputedColumn contains the result of the expression RegularColumn + CAST(IdentityColumn AS NVARCHAR).

Results

	RegularColumn	IdentityColumn	RowversionColumn	SequenceColumn	ComputedColumn
1	a	1	0x000000000000ADFF	1	a1
2	b	2	0x000000000000AE01	2	b2
3	c	3	0x000000000000AE02	3	c3

Figure 6-9. The results of inserting rows into a table with autopopulating columns

Notice that the SequenceColumn, like the IdentityColumn, starts with one and increments by one. A difference between the two is you have the ability to reference the same demoSequence object when inserting values into another table. You can also set the command referencing the sequence object as a column default and this would allow the column to autopopulate. Another benefit to sequence numbers over identity values is you can determine the next number prior to inserting the value. SQL Server generates an identity number when a value is inserted but determines sequence numbers only when an application executes the NEXT VALUE FOR statement.

You have learned how to insert new rows into tables by using literal values or data from a query. Before moving on to the next section, where you will learn how to delete data, practice inserting new rows into a table by completing Exercise 6-1.

EXERCISE 6-1

Use the AdventureWorks2012 database to complete this exercise. You can find the solutions in the Appendix.

Run the following code to create required tables. You can also download the code from this book's page at www.apress.com to save typing time.

```
USE AdventureWorks2012;
GO
IF  EXISTS (SELECT * FROM sys.objects
            WHERE object_id = OBJECT_ID(N'[dbo].[demoProduct]')
                AND type in (N'U'))
DROP TABLE [dbo].[demoProduct]
GO

CREATE TABLE [dbo].[demoProduct](
    [ProductID] [INT] NOT NULL PRIMARY KEY,
    [Name] [dbo].[Name] NOT NULL,
    [Color] [NVARCHAR](15) NULL,
```

```
        [StandardCost] [MONEY] NOT NULL,
        [ListPrice] [MONEY] NOT NULL,
        [Size] [NVARCHAR](5) NULL,
        [Weight] [DECIMAL](8, 2) NULL,
);
IF  EXISTS (SELECT * FROM sys.objects
            WHERE object_id = OBJECT_ID(N'[dbo].[demoSalesOrderHeader]')
                AND type in (N'U'))
DROP TABLE [dbo].[demoSalesOrderHeader]
GO

CREATE TABLE [dbo].[demoSalesOrderHeader](
    [SalesOrderID] [INT] NOT NULL PRIMARY KEY,
    [SalesID] [INT] NOT NULL IDENTITY,
    [OrderDate] [DATETIME] NOT NULL,
    [CustomerID] [INT] NOT NULL,
    [SubTotal] [MONEY] NOT NULL,
    [TaxAmt] [MONEY] NOT NULL,
    [Freight] [MONEY] NOT NULL,
    [DateEntered] [DATETIME],
    [SalesNumber] [INT] NOT NULL,
    [TotalDue]  AS (ISNULL((([SubTotal]+[TaxAmt])+[Freight],(0)))),
    [RV] ROWVERSION NOT NULL);
GO

ALTER TABLE [dbo].[demoSalesOrderHeader] ADD  CONSTRAINT
    [DF_demoSalesOrderHeader_DateEntered]
DEFAULT (getdate()) FOR [DateEntered];

IF  EXISTS (SELECT * FROM sys.objects
            WHERE object_id = OBJECT_ID(N'[dbo].[demoSalesSequence]'))
DROP SEQUENCE [dbo].[demoSalesSequence]
GO

CREATE SEQUENCE demoSalesSequence
AS INT
START WITH 1
INCREMENT BY 1;

GO
IF  EXISTS (SELECT * FROM sys.objects
    WHERE object_id = OBJECT_ID(N'[dbo].[demoAddress]')
    AND type in (N'U'))
DROP TABLE [dbo].[demoAddress]
GO

CREATE TABLE [dbo].[demoAddress](
    [AddressID] [INT] NOT NULL IDENTITY PRIMARY KEY,
    [AddressLine1] [NVARCHAR](60) NOT NULL,
    [AddressLine2] [NVARCHAR](60) NULL,
    [City] [NVARCHAR](30) NOT NULL,
```

```
    [PostalCode] [NVARCHAR](15) NOT NULL
);
```

1. Write a SELECT statement to retrieve data from the Sales.Product table. Use these values to insert five rows into the dbo.demoProduct table using literal values. Write five individual INSERT statements.

2. Insert five more rows into the dbo.demoProduct table. This time write one INSERT statement.

3. Write an INSERT statement that inserts all the rows into the dbo.demoSalesOrderHeader table from the Sales.SalesOrderHeader table. Hint: Pay close attention to the properties of the columns in the dbo.demoSalesOrderHeader table.

4. Write a SELECT INTO statement that creates a table, dbo.tempCustomerSales, showing every CustomerID from the Sales.Customer along with a count of the orders placed and the total amount due for each customer.

5. Write an INSERT statement that inserts all the products into the dbo.demoProduct table from the Production.Product table that have not already been inserted. Don't specify literal ProductID values in the statement.

6. Write an INSERT statement that inserts all the addresses into the dbo.demoAddress table from the Sales.Address table. Before running the INSERT statement, type in and run the following command so that you can insert values into the AddressID column:

```
SET IDENTITY_INSERT dbo.demoAddress ON;
```

Deleting Rows

You now know how to add new rows to tables. This section covers deleting existing rows, which is an important but dangerous task. Many developers and database administrators have accidentally removed the data from an entire table when intending to remove just one row. Care must be taken whenever deleting rows, especially when writing ad hoc queries.

Using DELETE

The DELETE statement is very simple. At a minimum, you need the word DELETE and the table name. This will remove all rows from the table. Most of the time, your goal will be to remove just a portion of the rows. Here is the syntax:

```
DELETE [FROM] <table1>
[WHERE <condition>]
```

If you omit the WHERE clause, the statement removes every row from the table. The table still exists, just without any rows. When writing ad hoc DELETE statements, always test your WHERE clause with a SELECT statement first to make sure you know exactly which rows you are deleting. Type in and execute the code in Listing 6-9. The listing creates several copies of the main tables from the AdventureWorks2012 database. To avoid typing the table creation portion, you can download the code from the book's page at www.apress.com.

Listing 6-9. Creating Demo Tables

```
USE AdventureWorks2012;
GO

IF  EXISTS (SELECT * FROM sys.objects
            WHERE object_id = OBJECT_ID(N'[dbo].[demoProduct]')
              AND type in (N'U'))
DROP TABLE [dbo].[demoProduct];
GO

SELECT * INTO dbo.demoProduct FROM Production.Product;

IF  EXISTS (SELECT * FROM sys.objects
            WHERE object_id = OBJECT_ID(N'[dbo].[demoCustomer]')
              AND type in (N'U'))
DROP TABLE [dbo].[demoCustomer];
GO

SELECT * INTO dbo.demoCustomer FROM Sales.Customer;
IF  EXISTS (SELECT * FROM sys.objects
            WHERE object_id = OBJECT_ID(N'[dbo].[demoAddress]')
              AND type in (N'U'))
DROP TABLE [dbo].[demoAddress];
GO

SELECT * INTO dbo.demoAddress FROM Person.Address;

IF  EXISTS (SELECT * FROM sys.objects
            WHERE object_id = OBJECT_ID(N'[dbo].[demoSalesOrderHeader]')
              AND type in (N'U'))
DROP TABLE [dbo].[demoSalesOrderHeader];
GO

SELECT * INTO dbo.demoSalesOrderHeader FROM Sales.SalesOrderHeader;

IF  EXISTS (SELECT * FROM sys.objects
            WHERE object_id = OBJECT_ID(N'[dbo].[demoSalesOrderDetail]')
              AND type in (N'U'))
DROP TABLE [dbo].[demoSalesOrderDetail];
GO

SELECT * INTO dbo.demoSalesOrderDetail FROM Sales.SalesOrderDetail;
```

You should now have several tables that you can use to practice deleting data. Type in and execute the code in Listing 6-10 to learn how to delete rows from tables.

Listing 6-10. *Deleting Rows from Tables*

```
USE AdventureWorks2012;
GO
--1
SELECT CustomerID
FROM dbo.demoCustomer;

--2
DELETE dbo.demoCustomer;

--3
SELECT CustomerID
FROM dbo.demoCustomer;

--4
SELECT ProductID
FROM dbo.demoProduct
WHERE ProductID > 900;

--5
DELETE dbo.demoProduct
WHERE ProductID > 900;

--6
SELECT ProductID
FROM dbo.demoProduct
WHERE ProductID > 900;
```

Figure 6-10 shows the rows before and after running the DELETE statements affecting the dbo.demoCustomer and dbo.demoProduct tables. Running a SELECT statement before deleting data is a good idea and enables you to test your WHERE clause. Make sure you know which rows will be deleted before you delete them. Statement 2 removes every row from dbo.demoCustomer. Statement 5 removes the rows from dbo.demoProduct where the ProductID was greater than 900. The word FROM is optional.

	CustomerID
46	46
47	47
48	48
49	49
50	50

	CustomerID

	ProductID
1	901
2	902
3	903
4	904

	ProductID

Figure 6-10. The partial results before and after rows deleted

Deleting from a Table Using a Join or a Subquery

Listing 6-10 demonstrated how to remove rows from a table when the statement contains just one table. You can also remove rows from a table that is involved in a join to restrict which rows the statement deletes. You may delete rows from only one of the tables. Often developers will use a subquery instead of a join to accomplish the same thing. Here is the syntax:

```
DELETE <alias>
FROM <table1> AS <alias>
INNER JOIN <table2> ON <alias>.<col1> = <table2>.<col2>
[WHERE <condition>]

DELETE [FROM] <table1>
WHERE <col1> IN (SELECT <col2> FROM <table2>)
```

The syntax shows INNER JOIN, but you could use an OUTER JOIN if that makes sense for the particular deletion. Type in and execute the code in Listing 6-11 to learn how to use both of these techniques. If you didn't run the code in Listing 6-9 that creates the tables used in these examples and the code in Listing 6-10 that deletes some of the data, do that first.

Listing 6-11. Deleting When Joining or Using a Subquery

```
USE AdventureWorks2012;
GO
```

```
--1
SELECT d.SalesOrderID, SalesOrderNumber
FROM dbo.demoSalesOrderDetail AS d
INNER JOIN dbo.demoSalesOrderHeader AS h ON d.SalesOrderID = h.SalesOrderID
WHERE h.SalesOrderNumber = 'SO71797'

--2
DELETE d
FROM dbo.demoSalesOrderDetail AS d
INNER JOIN dbo.demoSalesOrderHeader AS h ON d.SalesOrderID = h.SalesOrderID
WHERE h.SalesOrderNumber = 'SO71797'

--3
SELECT d.SalesOrderID, SalesOrderNumber
FROM dbo.demoSalesOrderDetail AS d
INNER JOIN dbo.demoSalesOrderHeader AS h ON d.SalesOrderID = h.SalesOrderID
WHERE h.SalesOrderNumber = 'SO71797'

--4
SELECT SalesOrderID, ProductID
FROM dbo.demoSalesOrderDetail
WHERE ProductID NOT IN
    (SELECT ProductID FROM dbo.demoProduct WHERE ProductID IS NOT NULL);

--5
DELETE FROM dbo.demoSalesOrderDetail
WHERE ProductID NOT IN
    (SELECT ProductID FROM dbo.demoProduct WHERE ProductID IS NOT NULL);

--6
SELECT SalesOrderID, ProductID
FROM dbo.demoSalesOrderDetail
WHERE ProductID NOT IN
    (SELECT ProductID FROM dbo.demoProduct WHERE ProductID IS NOT NULL);
```

Figure 6-11 shows the results before and after deleting. Again, write SELECT statements first to test your WHERE clause and to make sure you will delete the correct rows. Statement 2 joins the dbo.demoSalesOrderDetail table to the dbo.demoSalesOrderHeader table. The statement deletes the rows from the dbo.demoSalesOrderDetail table that have a SalesOrderNumber of SO71797 in the dbo.demoSalesOrderHeader table. The value in one table determines which rows in another table will be deleted. Notice that statements 1 and 2 are identical except for the first line in each. Statement 1 is a query to determine which rows that statement 2 will delete. The syntax and this example used an INNER JOIN, but you can also use an OUTER JOIN.

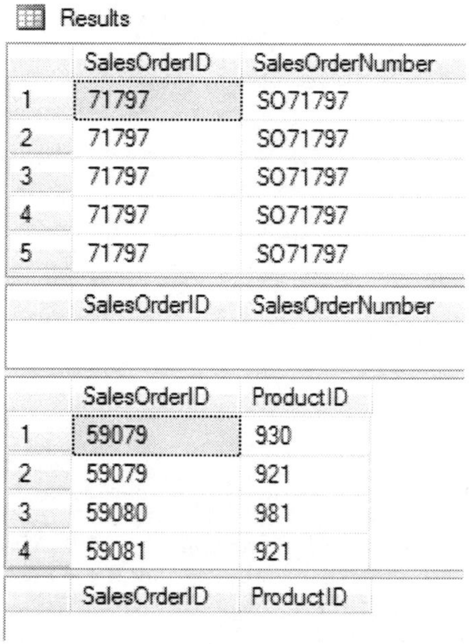
Results

	SalesOrderID	SalesOrderNumber
1	71797	SO71797
2	71797	SO71797
3	71797	SO71797
4	71797	SO71797
5	71797	SO71797

	SalesOrderID	SalesOrderNumber

	SalesOrderID	ProductID
1	59079	930
2	59079	921
3	59080	981
4	59081	921

	SalesOrderID	ProductID

Figure 6-11. *The partial results before and after deleting rows with a join and a subquery*

Statement 5 uses a subquery in the WHERE clause to determine which rows to delete. Again, the code tests the WHERE clause first with a SELECT statement to make sure the correct rows will be deleted.

Another way to delete the rows using a join specifies the table name after the DELETE keyword instead of specifying the alias. Using the alias ensures that the DELETE part of the statement is tied to the SELECT part of the statement. I have seen developers write DELETE statements that inadvertently deleted all rows from a production table because the DELETE part of the statement wasn't really connected to the rest of the statement. I recommend that you always use the technique shown in Listing 6-11 to avoid deleting all the rows in a table by mistake. Here is an example that is really a DELETE statement and a SELECT statement when the intention is just a DELETE statement:

```
DELETE dbo.demoSalesOrderDetail
SELECT d.SalesOrderID
FROM dbo.demoSalesOrderDetail AS d
INNER JOIN dbo.demoSalesOrderHeader AS h ON d.SalesOrderID = h.SalesOrderID
WHERE h.SalesOrderNumber = 'SO71797';
```

Truncating

A way to quickly delete all the rows from a table is to use the TRUNCATE TABLE statement. This is a very fast way to empty a large table. Although deleting rows requires that the user account have DELETE permission on the table, truncating a table requires the user be in the dbo or db_ddladmin database roles or the sysadmin server role. Generally, users running an application will not be members of these powerful roles. Here is the syntax:

```
TRUNCATE TABLE <table1>
```

Listing 6-12 demonstrates how to use TRUNCATE. If you didn't run Listing 6-9 to create the tables, do that first before typing and running the code in Listing 6-12.

Listing 6-12. *Truncating Tables*

```
USE AdventureWorks2012;
GO

--1
SELECT SalesOrderID, OrderDate
FROM dbo.demoSalesOrderHeader;

--2
TRUNCATE TABLE dbo.demoSalesOrderHeader;

--3
SELECT SalesOrderID, OrderDate
FROM dbo.demoSalesOrderHeader;
```

Figure 6-12 shows the results before and after truncating the table. One of the reasons that TRUNCATE is so much more powerful than DELETE is that it actually drops and re-creates the table behind the scenes. That is much quicker than deleting all the rows, but no WHERE clause is allowed with TRUNCATE. The TRUNCATE statement can be used only when you intend to empty the table.

	SalesOrderID	OrderDate
1	43659	2005-07-01 00:00:00.000
2	43660	2005-07-01 00:00:00.000
3	43661	2005-07-01 00:00:00.000
4	43662	2005-07-01 00:00:00.000
5	43663	2005-07-01 00:00:00.000
6	43664	2005-07-01 00:00:00.000
	SalesOrderID	OrderDate

Figure 6-12. *The results before and after truncating*

Deleting data is a very risky operation. It's why database administrators consider a good backup strategy an important part of their jobs. Practice what you have learned about deleting data by completing Exercise 6-2.

■ **Note** In reality, a TRUNCATE TABLE operation is a bit more complicated than a simple drop and recreate. After issuing the TRUNCATE TABLE command SQL Server will deallocate the data pages in a task called a *deferred drop*. The reason for this is to ensure SQL Server doesn't run out of available memory part way through the truncation.

For more information, see Paul Randall's comments at `www.sqlskills.com/BLOGS/PAUL/post/A-SQL-Server-DBA-myth-a-day-(1930)-TRUNCATE-TABLE-is-non-logged.aspx`.

EXERCISE 6-2

Use the AdventureWorks2012 database to complete this exercise. Before starting the exercise, run Listing 6-9 to recreate the demo tables. You can find the solutions in the Appendix.

1. Write a query that deletes the rows from the dbo.demoCustomer table where the LastName values begin with the letter *S*.

2. Delete the rows from the dbo.demoCustomer table if the customer has not placed an order or if the sum of the TotalDue from the dbo.demoSalesOrderHeader table for the customer is less than $1,000.

3. Delete the rows from the dbo.demoProduct table that have never been ordered.

Updating Existing Rows

Updating data is a very important part of T-SQL but requires extreme caution. Only deleting rows, which was discussed in the previous section, requires more care. Well, maybe that's not true; you could actually drop tables or entire databases accidentally. Within applications, the user will usually be working with one row at a time. For example, they may be viewing a screen that displays and allows editing of one employee, one department, or one order. Automated processes often update data in entire tables or many rows at one time. In this section, you will learn how to use the UPDATE statement to update existing rows in several scenarios, including single tables, joins, and aggregates. Run the code in Listing 6-9 to repopulate the tables you will use for the examples in this section.

Using the UPDATE Statement

To update existing rows in a table, use the UPDATE statement. Usually you will add a WHERE clause to make sure that you update only the appropriate rows. Often database administrators have to restore backups of databases to get back data that has been accidentally updated because the WHERE clause was incorrect or missing. Here is the syntax of the UPDATE statement:

```
UPDATE <table1>
SET <col1> = <new value1>,<col2> = <new value2>
[WHERE <condition>]
```

You can use expressions, literal values, or other columns to update existing data. Developers often think that updating data must be done one row at a time. I have talked to many developers who insist that they must update one row at a time because some of the rows must be updated with one value and some with another. In those cases, maybe they could write an UPDATE statement for each business rule or use the CASE function but not perform one update for each row. Type in and execute the code in Listing 6-13 to learn how to update data.

Listing 6-13. Updating Data in a Table

```
USE AdventureWorks2012;
GO

IF  EXISTS (SELECT * FROM sys.objects
    WHERE object_id = OBJECT_ID(N'[dbo].[demoPerson]')
    AND type in (N'U'))
DROP TABLE [dbo].[demoPerson]
GO

SELECT * INTO dbo.demoPerson
FROM Person.Person
WHERE Title in ('Mr.', 'Mrs.', 'Ms.')

--1
SELECT BusinessEntityID, NameStyle, Title
FROM dbo.demoPerson
ORDER BY BusinessEntityID;

--2
UPDATE dbo.demoPerson
SET NameStyle = 1;

--3
SELECT BusinessEntityID, NameStyle, Title
FROM dbo.demoPerson
ORDER BY BusinessEntityID;

--4
UPDATE dbo.demoPerson
SET NameStyle = 0
WHERE Title = 'Ms.';

--5
SELECT BusinessEntityID, NameStyle, Title
FROM dbo.demoPerson
ORDER BY BusinessEntityID;
```

Figure 6-13 shows the results before and after the updates. Query 1 just displays a few rows from the table. Statement 2 updates all the rows in the table changing the NameStyle, a bit column, from 0 to 1. Query 3 shows the result of that change. Statement 4 changes the NameStyle value to 0 for the rows where the Title is *Ms.* And Query 5 displays the final changes.

Results

	BusinessEntityID	NameStyle	Title
1	5	0	Ms.
2	6	0	Mr.
3	13	0	Ms.
4	24	0	Ms.
5	139	0	Mr.

	BusinessEntityID	NameStyle	Title
1	5	1	Ms.
2	6	1	Mr.
3	13	1	Ms.
4	24	1	Ms.
5	139	1	Mr.

	BusinessEntityID	NameStyle	Title
1	5	0	Ms.
2	6	1	Mr.
3	13	0	Ms.
4	24	0	Ms.
5	139	1	Mr.
6	273	1	Mr.

Figure 6-13. The partial results before and after updating

Updating Data with Expressions and Columns

The statements in the previous section updated the dbo.demoCustomer table with literal values. You can also perform updates using expressions or other columns. Developers and database administrators often must perform large updates to data, sometimes on a periodic basis or to fulfill one-time requests. Here is the syntax for this technique:

```
UPDATE <table1>
SET <col1> = <expression>
[WHERE <condition>]
```

Again, you can use expressions, hard-coded values, or other columns in your UPDATE statement. When multiple rows must be updated, such as batch processing that happens after business hours, you should perform updates in sets, not one row at a time. Type in and execute the code in Listing 6-14 to learn how to perform these updates.

Listing 6-14. Update with Expressions, Columns, or Data from Another Table

```
USE AdventureWorks2012;
GO
```

```
IF  EXISTS (SELECT * FROM sys.objects
    WHERE object_id = OBJECT_ID(N'[dbo].[demoPersonStore]')
    AND type in (N'U'))
DROP TABLE [dbo].[demoPersonStore]
GO

CREATE TABLE [dbo].[demoPersonStore] (
[FirstName] [NVARCHAR] (60),
[LastName] [NVARCHAR] (60),
[CompanyName] [NVARCHAR] (60)
);

INSERT INTO dbo.demoPersonStore (FirstName, LastName, CompanyName)
SELECT a.FirstName, a.LastName, c.Name
FROM Person.Person a
JOIN Sales.SalesPerson b
ON a.BusinessEntityID = b.BusinessEntityID
JOIN Sales.Store c
ON b.BusinessEntityID = c.SalesPersonID

--1
SELECT FirstName,LastName, CompanyName,
   LEFT(FirstName,3) + '.' + LEFT(LastName,3) AS NewCompany
FROM dbo.demoPersonStore;

--2
UPDATE dbo.demoPersonStore
SET CompanyName = LEFT(FirstName,3) + '.' + LEFT(LastName,3);

--3
SELECT FirstName,LastName, CompanyName,
    LEFT(FirstName,3) + '.' + LEFT(LastName,3) AS NewCompany
FROM dbo.demoPersonStore;
```

Figure 6-14 shows the results before and after the update. Query 1 displays the data before the update. The NewCompany column contains the expression that will be used in the UPDATE statement. You will find it is useful to display the expression, especially if it is complicated, to make sure that your update will do exactly what you expect. Statement 2 updates the data, changing CompanyName in the dbo.demoPersonStore table to the new value derived from the FirstName and LastName columns. Finally, Query 3 displays the updated data. At this point, the CompanyName should be equivalent to the NewCompany expression.

	FirstName	LastName	CompanyName		NewCompany
1	Tsvi	Reiter	Next-Door Bike Store		Tsv.Rei
2	Linda	Mitchell	Professional Sales and Service		Lin.Mit
3	Jillian	Carson	Riders Company		Jil.Car
4	Michael	Blythe	The Bike Mechanics		Mic.Bly
5	Lynn	Tsoflias	Nationwide Supply		Lyn.Tso

	FirstName	LastName	CompanyName	NewCompany
1	Tsvi	Reiter	Tsv.Rei	Tsv.Rei
2	Linda	Mitchell	Lin.Mit	Lin.Mit
3	Jillian	Carson	Jil.Car	Jil.Car
4	Michael	Blythe	Mic.Bly	Mic.Bly
5	Lynn	Tsoflias	Lyn.Tso	Lyn.Tso

Figure 6-14. The results before and after updating with an expression

Updating with a Join

So far, you have seen how to write UPDATE statements with a single table. When joining, you can update only a single table, but by joining with another table, you can limit the rows to be updated or use the second table to provide the value. Here is the syntax:

```
UPDATE <alias>
SET <col1> = <expression>
FROM <table1> AS <alias>
INNER JOIN <table2> on <alias>.<col2>  = <table2>.<col3>
```

The syntax shows an INNER JOIN, but you could perform an OUTER JOIN if that makes sense for the particular update. Type in and execute the code in Listing 6-15 to learn how to perform an update using this technique.

Listing 6-15. Updating with a Join

```
USE AdventureWorks2012;
GO

--1
SELECT AddressLine1, AddressLine2
FROM dbo.demoAddress;

--2
UPDATE a
SET AddressLine1 = FirstName + ' ' + LastName,
    AddressLine2 = AddressLine1 + ISNULL(' ' + AddressLine2,'')
FROM dbo.demoAddress AS a
INNER JOIN Person.BusinessEntityAddress c ON a.AddressID = c.AddressID
INNER JOIN Person.Person b ON b.BusinessEntityID = c.BusinessEntityID
```

```
--3
SELECT AddressLine1, AddressLine2
FROM dbo.demoAddress;
```

Figure 6-15 shows the results before and after the update. In this case, Statement 2 uses columns from the second table, the Person.Person table, to build an expression to update AddressLine1. The statement uses another expression to move the original AddressLine1 and AddressLine2, if any, to AddressLine2. The dbo.demoAddress table doesn't join directly to the Person.Person table but must join through an intermediary table, Person.BusinessEntityAddress.

⊞ Results

	AddressLine1	AddressLine2
1	1970 Napa Ct.	NULL
2	9833 Mt. Dias Blv.	NULL
3	7484 Roundtree Drive	NULL
4	9539 Glenside Dr	NULL
5	1226 Shoe St.	NULL
6	1399 Firestone Drive	NULL
7	5672 Hale Dr.	NULL
8	6387 Scenic Avenue	NULL

	AddressLine1	AddressLine2
1	Thierry D'Hers	1970 Napa Ct.
2	Vamsi Kuppa	9833 Mt. Dias Blv.
3	Syed Abbas	7484 Roundtree...
4	Mikael Sand...	9539 Glenside Dr
5	Kim Ralls	1226 Shoe St.
6	Belinda New...	1399 Firestone ...
7	Betsy Stadick	5672 Hale Dr.
8	Bob Hohman	6387 Scenic Av...

Figure 6-15. The results before and after updating with a join

Updating with Aggregate Functions

The examples in the previous two sections demonstrated how you can update data using expressions involving literal values, columns, and functions. None of the examples included aggregate functions, however. You may not use expressions containing aggregate functions to update data directly. Type this code to see what happens when you try to use an aggregate function to perform an update:

```
USE AdventureWorks2012;
GO
```

```
UPDATE o
SET SubTotal = SUM(LineTotal)
FROM Sales.SalesOrderHeader AS o INNER JOIN Sales.SalesOrderDetail AS d
ON o.SalesOrderID = o.SalesOrderID;
```

You can isolate an aggregate query into a common table expression and then use the aggregated values to make the updates. Listing 6-16 shows how to use this technique. The first part of the code creates and partially populates a summary table that will be used in the example.

Listing 6-16. Updates with Aggregate Expressions

```
USE AdventureWorks2012;
GO

IF  EXISTS (SELECT * FROM sys.objects
            WHERE object_id = OBJECT_ID(N'[dbo].[demoCustomerSummary]')
                AND type in (N'U'))
DROP TABLE [dbo].[demoCustomerSummary];
GO

CREATE TABLE dbo.demoCustomerSummary (CustomerID INT NOT NULL PRIMARY KEY,
    SaleCount INTEGER NULL,
    TotalAmount MONEY NULL);

GO

INSERT INTO dbo.demoCustomerSummary (CustomerID, SaleCount,TotalAmount)
SELECT BusinessEntityID, 0, 0
FROM dbo.demoPerson;

GO

--1
SELECT CustomerID, SaleCount, TotalAmount
FROM dbo.demoCustomerSummary
WHERE CustomerID in (11621,12798,13589,14465,18623);

--2
WITH Totals AS (
    SELECT COUNT(*) AS SaleCount,SUM(TotalDue) AS TotalAmount,
        CustomerID
    FROM dbo.demoSalesOrderHeader
    GROUP BY CustomerID)
UPDATE c SET TotalAmount = Totals.TotalAmount,
    SaleCount = Totals.SaleCount
FROM dbo.demoCustomerSummary AS c
INNER JOIN Totals ON c.CustomerID = Totals.CustomerID;

--3
SELECT CustomerID, SaleCount, TotalAmount
FROM dbo.demoCustomerSummary
WHERE CustomerID in (11621,12798,13589,14465,18623);
```

Figure 6-16 shows the results before and after the update. This code first creates a table called dbo.demoCustomerSummary. Then the code populates the new table with all the CustomerID values from the dbo.demoCustomer table and zeros in the summary columns. Statement 2 uses a common table expression containing an aggregate query summarizing the sales for each customer. The statement uses the values calculated in the common table expression to update the table. See the "Exploring Derived Tables and Common Table Expressions" section in Chapter 4 to review common table expression. See Chapter 5 to review aggregate queries.

Results

	CustomerID	SaleCount	TotalAmount
1	11621	0	0.00
2	12798	0	0.00
3	13589	0	0.00
4	14465	0	0.00
5	18623	0	0.00

	CustomerID	SaleCount	TotalAmount
1	11621	2	136.1803
2	12798	1	16.5529
3	13589	1	86.7204
4	14465	1	8.0444
5	18623	1	41.1834

Figure 6-16. The results before and after updating with a common table expression

You now know how to update data in existing tables with literal values, expressions, and other columns. Now practice what you have learned by completing Exercise 6-3.

EXERCISE 6-3

Use the AdventureWorks2012 database to complete this exercise. Run the code in Listing 6-9 to recreate tables used in this exercise. You can find the solutions in the Appendix.

1. Write an UPDATE statement that changes all NULL values of the AddressLine2 column in the dbo.demoAddress table to *N/A*.

2. Write an UPDATE statement that increases the ListPrice of every product in the dbo.demoProduct table by 10 percent.

3. Write an UPDATE statement that corrects the UnitPrice and LineTotal of each row of the dbo.demoSalesOrderDetail table by joining the table on the dbo.demoProduct table.

4. Write an UPDATE statement that updates the SubTotal column of each row of the dbo.demoSalesOrderHeader table with the sum of the LineTotal column of the dbo.demoSalesOrderDemo table.

Using Transactions

A *transaction* is a unit of work in SQL Server. Most of the time, a transaction is one statement that inserts, updates, or deletes data. It is possible, however, to define an explicit transaction that includes more than one statement. You can also include SELECT statements in a transaction. Every statement within a transaction must succeed, or the entire transaction fails.

The classic example involves a bank ATM where a customer can transfer money from a savings account to a checking account. Imagine the problems created if an error occurred after the system subtracted the money from the savings account but before the money showed up in the checking account! By using an explicit transaction, any error between the two updates will roll back both of them. If an error occurred, the money would just go back to the savings account like nothing was ever done. This section covers writing multiple statements within explicit transactions, how to commit or roll back transactions, and what happens when transactions last longer than needed.

Writing an Explicit Transaction

The important thing to remember when working with SQL Server is to keep transactions as short as they can be and still do the work. Once a transaction starts, the database engine puts locks on tables involved within the transaction so that the tables usually may not be accessed by another query. For example, don't write an application that begins a transaction and then waits for user input before completing the transaction. The tables could be locked while the user leaves the computer for a lunch break! Here is the syntax for a simple transaction:

```
BEGIN TRAN|TRANSACTION
    <statement 1>
    <statement 2>
COMMIT [TRAN|TRANSACTION]
```

Listing 6-17 demonstrates what happens when a transaction fails. Type in and execute the code.

Listing 6-17. Explicit Transactions

```
USE AdventureWorks2012;
GO

IF  EXISTS (SELECT * FROM sys.objects
            WHERE object_id = OBJECT_ID(N'[dbo].[demoTransaction]')
              AND type in (N'U'))
DROP TABLE [dbo].[demoTransaction];
GO

CREATE TABLE dbo.demoTransaction (col1 INT NOT NULL);
GO
```

```
--1
BEGIN TRAN
    INSERT INTO dbo.demoTransaction (col1) VALUES (1);
    INSERT INTO dbo.demoTransaction (col1) VALUES (2);
COMMIT TRAN

--2
BEGIN TRAN
    INSERT INTO dbo.demoTransaction (col1) VALUES (3);
    INSERT INTO dbo.demoTransaction (col1) VALUES ('a');
COMMIT TRAN

GO
--3
SELECT col1
FROM dbo.demoTransaction;
```

Figure 6-17 shows the results. After running the batch, the query window will display the Messages tab first with an error message. You will have to click the Results tab to see the inserted rows. Transaction block 1 successfully inserts two rows with integer values into the table. Transaction block 2 inserts the value 3 and the value a. Because you can't insert the string value a into a column of type INT, the statement fails. Because the two statements are within the same transaction, the entire transaction rolls back. Query 3 returns the inserted rows, which are only the rows inserted in the first transaction.

Figure 6-17. *The results of using explicit transactions to insert data*

Rolling Back a Transaction

You can purposely roll a transaction back before it is committed by issuing a ROLLBACK command even without an error condition. For example, what if the bank ATM added the money to the checking account before removing it from the savings account and didn't check the savings account balance first? The transaction could roll back the transaction once the balance was checked but before the transaction was committed. Here is the syntax for rolling back a transaction:

```
BEGIN TRAN|TRANSACTION
    <statement 1>
    <statement 2>
ROLLBACK [TRAN|TRANSACTION]
```

In Chapter 7 you will learn how to trap errors and use conditional logic that will allow your code to COMMIT or ROLLBACK based on certain conditions. For now, type in and execute Listing 6-18 to learn how to use the ROLLBACK command.

Listing 6-18. Using a ROLLBACK Command

```
USE AdventureWorks2012;
GO

IF  EXISTS (SELECT * FROM sys.objects
            WHERE object_id = OBJECT_ID(N'[dbo].[demoTransaction]')
              AND type in (N'U'))
DROP TABLE [dbo].[demoTransaction];
GO

CREATE TABLE dbo.demoTransaction (col1 INT NOT NULL);
GO

--1
BEGIN TRAN
    INSERT INTO dbo.demoTransaction (col1) VALUES (1);
    INSERT INTO dbo.demoTransaction (col1) VALUES (2);
COMMIT TRAN


--2
BEGIN TRAN
    INSERT INTO dbo.demoTransaction (col1) VALUES (3);
    INSERT INTO dbo.demoTransaction (col1) VALUES (4);
ROLLBACK TRAN

GO
--3
SELECT col1
FROM dbo.demoTransaction;
```

Figure 6-18 shows the results. Transaction block 1 completes successfully and inserts the two rows in the table. Transaction block 2 contains two valid statements, but because it contains the ROLLBACK command instead of the COMMIT command, the transaction doesn't complete. Query 3 shows that the batch inserts only values 1 and 2 into the table.

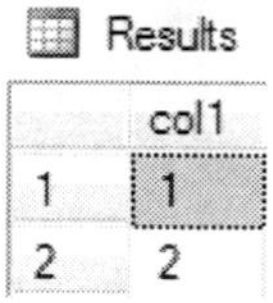

Figure 6-18. The results of a rolled-back transaction

Locking Tables

SQL Server has different *isolation levels* to control how transactions from one connection affect SELECT statements from another connection. Learning about isolation levels is beyond the scope of this book, but this section will demonstrate the default behavior. For this example, you will use two query windows, so follow the instructions carefully.

1. From query window 1, run this code:

```
USE AdventureWorks2012;
GO
IF   EXISTS (SELECT * FROM sys.objects
             WHERE object_id = OBJECT_ID(N'[dbo].[demoTransaction]')
                AND type in (N'U'))
DROP TABLE [dbo].[demoTransaction];
GO

CREATE TABLE dbo.demoTransaction (col1 INT NOT NULL);
GO

BEGIN TRAN
    INSERT INTO dbo.demoTransaction (col1) VALUES (1);
    INSERT INTO dbo.demoTransaction (col1) VALUES (2);
```

2. Switch to window 2, and run this code:

```
USE AdventureWorks2012;
GO
SELECT col1 FROM dbo.demoTransaction;
```

3. At this point, you will see nothing returned from the code from step 2 as it continues to execute. Switch to window 1, and run this code:

```
COMMIT TRAN
```

4. Switch back to window 2 to view the results.

Once you committed the transaction in step 3, the SELECT statement in window 2 could complete. To learn more about locks, transactions, and isolation levels, read *SQL Server 2008 Transact-SQL Recipes* by Joseph Sack (Apress, 2008). You will learn how to add conditional logic to your transactions in Chapter 7. For now, practice what you have learned by completing Exercise 6-4.

EXERCISE 6-4

Use the AdventureWorks2012 database to complete this exercise. Run the following script to create a table for this exercise. You can find the solutions in the Appendix.

```
IF OBJECT_ID('dbo.Demo') IS NOT NULL BEGIN
    DROP TABLE dbo.Demo;
END;
GO
CREATE TABLE dbo.Demo(ID INT PRIMARY KEY, Name VARCHAR(25));
```

1. Write a transaction that includes two INSERT statements to add two rows to the dbo.Demo table.

2. Write a transaction that includes two INSERT statements to add two more rows to the dbo.Demo table. Attempt to insert a letter instead of a number into the ID column in one of the statements. Select the data from the dbo.Demo table to see which rows made it to the table.

Thinking About Performance

SQL Server performs best when working on sets of data instead of one row at a time. Often developers write code that loops through a record set and performs an update or insert for each pass through the loop. The example code in Listing 6-19 demonstrates the difference in performance between the two techniques. Download and run the code from this book's page on www.apress.com. You may need to stop the code execution after a few minutes.

Listing 6-19. The Difference Between the Set-Based and Iterative Approaches

```
USE AdventureWorks2012;
GO
--Create a work table
IF  EXISTS (SELECT * FROM sys.objects
            WHERE object_id = OBJECT_ID(N'[dbo].[demoPerformance]')
                AND type in (N'U'))
DROP TABLE [dbo].[demoPerformance];
GO

CREATE TABLE [dbo].[demoPerformance](
    [SalesOrderID] [int] NOT NULL,
    [SalesOrderDetailID] [int] NOT NULL,
 CONSTRAINT [PK_demoPerformance] PRIMARY KEY CLUSTERED
(
    [SalesOrderID] ASC,
    [SalesOrderDetailID] ASC
)WITH (PAD_INDEX  = OFF, STATISTICS_NORECOMPUTE  = OFF, IGNORE_DUP_KEY = OFF,
    ALLOW_ROW_LOCKS  = ON, ALLOW_PAGE_LOCKS  = ON) ON [PRIMARY]
) ON [PRIMARY]


GO

PRINT 'Insert all rows start';
PRINT getdate();

--Insert all rows from the Sales.SalesOrderDetail table at once
INSERT INTO dbo.demoPerformance(SalesOrderID, SalesOrderDetailID)
SELECT SalesOrderID, SalesOrderDetailID
FROM Sales.SalesOrderDetail;

PRINT 'Insert all rows end';
PRINT getdate();

--Remove all rows from the first insert
TRUNCATE TABLE [dbo].[demoPerformance];

PRINT 'Insert rows one at a time begin';
PRINT getdate();
```

```
--Set up a loop to insert one row at a time
WHILE EXISTS(

    SELECT *
    FROM Sales.SalesOrderDetail AS d LEFT JOIN dbo.demoPerformance AS p
    ON d.SalesOrderID = p.SalesOrderID
        AND d.SalesOrderDetailID = p.SalesOrderDetailID
    WHERE p.SalesOrderID IS NULL) BEGIN


    INSERT INTO dbo.demoPerformance (SalesOrderID,SalesOrderDetailID)
    SELECT TOP 1 d.SalesOrderID, d.SalesOrderDetailID
    FROM Sales.SalesOrderDetail AS d LEFT JOIN dbo.demoPerformance AS p
    ON d.SalesOrderID = p.SalesOrderID
        AND d.SalesOrderDetailID = p.SalesOrderDetailID
    WHERE p.SalesOrderID IS NULL;

END
PRINT 'Insert rows one at a time end';
PRINT getdate();
```

After the code executes or you stop execution after a few minutes, click the Messages tab to see the results (Figure 6-19). Run this statement to see how many rows were actually inserted from the loop:

```
USE AdventureWorks2012;
GO
SELECT COUNT(*) FROM dbo.demoPerformance;
```

The loop inserted about 12,000 rows for me in over 7 minutes! The first INSERT statement, inserting more than 120,000 rows, took less than a second to run.

```
Messages

Insert all rows start
May 30 2011 12:37PM

(121317 row(s) affected)
Insert all rows end
May 30 2011 12:37PM
Insert rows one at a time begin
May 30 2011 12:37PM
```

Figure 6-19. The results of comparing one insert vs. a loop with multiple inserts

Database Cleanup

Run the script in Listing 6-20 to clean up the tables used in this chapter. You can download the script from this book's page at www.apress.com. Alternately, you can reinstall the sample databases by following the instructions in the "Installing the Sample Databases" section in Chapter 1.

Listing 6-20. Deleting Demo Tables

```
USE [AdventureWorks2012];
GO

IF  EXISTS (SELECT * FROM sys.objects
            WHERE object_id = OBJECT_ID(N'[dbo].[demoProduct]')
              AND type in (N'U'))
DROP TABLE [dbo].[demoProduct];
GO

IF  EXISTS (SELECT * FROM sys.objects
            WHERE object_id = OBJECT_ID(N'[dbo].[demoCustomer]')
              AND type in (N'U'))
DROP TABLE [dbo].[demoCustomer];
GO

IF  EXISTS (SELECT * FROM sys.objects
            WHERE object_id = OBJECT_ID(N'[dbo].[demoAddress]')
              AND type in (N'U'))
DROP TABLE [dbo].[demoAddress];
GO

IF  EXISTS (SELECT * FROM sys.objects
            WHERE object_id = OBJECT_ID(N'[dbo].[demoSalesOrderHeader]')
              AND type in (N'U'))
DROP TABLE [dbo].[demoSalesOrderHeader];
GO

IF  EXISTS (SELECT * FROM sys.objects
            WHERE object_id = OBJECT_ID(N'[dbo].[demoSalesOrderDetail]')
              AND type in (N'U'))
DROP TABLE [dbo].[demoSalesOrderDetail];
GO

IF  EXISTS (SELECT * FROM sys.objects
            WHERE object_id = OBJECT_ID(N'[dbo].[demoTransaction]')
              AND type in (N'U'))
DROP TABLE [dbo].[demoTransaction];
GO

IF  EXISTS (SELECT * FROM sys.objects
            WHERE object_id = OBJECT_ID(N'[dbo].[demoCustomerSummary]')
              AND type in (N'U'))
DROP TABLE [dbo].[demoCustomerSummary];
GO

IF  EXISTS (SELECT * FROM sys.objects
            WHERE object_id = OBJECT_ID(N'[dbo].[demoDefault]')
              AND type in (N'U'))
DROP TABLE [dbo].[demoDefault];
```

```
GO

IF  EXISTS (SELECT * FROM sys.objects
            WHERE object_id = OBJECT_ID(N'[dbo].[demoAutoPopulate]')
              AND type in (N'U'))
DROP TABLE [dbo].[demoAutoPopulate];


USE [AdventureWorks2012];
GO

IF  EXISTS (SELECT * FROM sys.objects
            WHERE object_id = OBJECT_ID(N'[dbo].[demoPerformance]')
              AND type in (N'U'))
DROP TABLE [dbo].[demoPerformance];
```

Summary

Writing data modification statements is not difficult once you've mastered the basics of selecting data. These tasks do, however, require much more care because it's possible to unintentionally modify and delete rows or even empty entire tables. Always check the WHERE clause with a SELECT statement first when writing ad hoc statements.

Whenever possible, do modifications on sets of data, not one row at a time. You will often see amazing differences in performance. Many developers learn to operate on one row at a time, but this is not the best way for SQL Server to work.

CHAPTER 7

Understanding T-SQL Programming Logic

Even though the primary purpose of T-SQL is to retrieve and manipulate data, like other programming languages it also contains logic elements. Most of the time you will write T-SQL statements that retrieve or update data, but you can also set up loops and write code with conditional flow. Often database administrators write scripts in T-SQL to perform maintenance tasks that require more than just retrieving or updating data. For example, you might need to write a script that checks the last backup date of all databases on the server or checks the free space of all the databases. Although most administrative tasks are beyond the scope of this book, you may find many uses in your environment for the techniques you learn in this chapter.

Variables

If you have programmed in any other language, you have probably used *variables* in your programs. Variables hold temporary values used to help you in designing programming logic. For example, you might use a variable to hold the results of a calculation, or the results of a string concatenation, or to control the number of times a loop executes.

Declaring and Initializing a Variable

To use a variable, you must first *declare* it. SQL Server 2012 also gives you the option to *initialize* a variable, that is, assign a value to the variable at the same time that you declare it. Versions earlier than SQL Server 2008 required that you assign a value on a separate line. Here is the syntax for declaring a variable and assigning a value at the same time and later in the code:

```
DECLARE @variableName <type>[(size)] = <value1>
SET @variableName = <value2>
```

You assign a value to a variable after you declare it by using the SET statement or by using the SELECT statement. The SET statement lets you work with only one variable at a time. The SELECT statement allows multiple variables to be modified in the same statement. Using a SELECT statement to assign values to multiple variables is more efficient than individual SET statements. In most cases, the difference is so small that you should just write your code using whichever technique you prefer. You can also assign a value to a variable from a column within a query. When doing so, that is the only thing the query can do; the query can't return a result set. Type in and execute Listing 7-1 to learn how to declare and assign variables.

Listing 7-1. Declaring and Using Variables

```
USE AdventureWorks2012;
GO

--1
DECLARE @myNumber INT = 10;
PRINT 'The value of @myNumber';
PRINT @myNumber;
SET @myNumber = 20;
PRINT 'The value of @myNumber';
PRINT @myNumber;
GO

--2
DECLARE @myString VARCHAR(100), @myBit BIT;
SELECT @myString = 'Hello, World', @myBit = 1;
PRINT 'The value of @myString';
PRINT @myString;
PRINT 'The value of @myBit';
PRINT @myBit;
GO

--3
DECLARE @myUnicodeString NVARCHAR(100);
SET @myUnicodeString = N'This is a Unicode String';
PRINT 'The value of @myUnicodeString';
PRINT @myUnicodeString;
GO

--4
DECLARE @FirstName NVARCHAR(50), @LastName NVARCHAR(50);
SELECT @FirstName  = FirstName, @LastName = LastName
FROM Person.Person
WHERE BusinessEntityID = 1;

PRINT 'The value of @FirstName';
PRINT @FirstName;
PRINT 'The value of @LastName';
PRINT @LastName;
GO

--5
PRINT 'The value of @myString';
PRINT @myString;
```

Figure 7-1 shows the results of the script. The script in Listing 7-1 consists of five batches after setting the database context. Batch 1 declares and initializes the local variable @myNumber in one line to the value 10. Local variables in T-SQL begin with the @ symbol and are in scope within the current connection and the current batch. Another line in the batch sets the value of the variable to 20 using the

SET command. The SET command will set the value of only one variable at a time. Using the PRINT command, you can print the value of a variable.

```
Messages
 The value of @myNumber
 10
 The value of @myNumber
 20|
 The value of @myString
 Hello, World
 The value of @myBit
 1
 The value of @myUnicodeString
 This is a Unicode String
 The value of @FirstName
 Ken
 The value of @LastName
 Sánchez
 Msg 137, Level 15, State 2, Line 4
 Must declare the scalar variable "@myString".
```

***Figure 7-1.** The results of declaring and initializing a variable*

Batch 2 demonstrates how you can declare more than one variable on the same line. The batch uses a SELECT statement to assign values to both the variables in the same statement. Batch 3 demonstrates that you set the value of an NVARCHAR string a bit differently. You must begin the string with the uppercase letter *N*. By doing so, SQL Server converts the string to Unicode. If you don't begin the string with *N*, the string will remain as a non-Unicode string, and you may lose any special characters.

In batch 4, the SELECT statement assigns the value of the FirstName and LastName columns to two variables from one row of the Person.Person table. In this case, the WHERE clause restricts the SELECT statement to just one row. If the statement didn't have a WHERE clause or a less restrictive one, the statement would assign the last value returned to the variable.

Batch 5 demonstrates that the variable declared in batch 2 is no longer in scope. Variables go out of scope when the batch completes. Even if there is only one batch in the script, once the code completes, the variable goes out of scope and is no longer in memory.

Using Expressions and Functions with Variables

The previous example demonstrated how to declare and assign a literal value or a value from a query. You can also use any expression and function to assign a value to a variable. For example, you may need to save the count of the rows of a query for later in the script, or you may need to save the value of a file name concatenated to a file path for a maintenance script. Type in and execute the code in Listing 7-2 to learn more about variables.

***Listing 7-2.** Using Expressions and Functions to Assign Variable Values*

```
USE AdventureWorks2012;
GO

--1
DECLARE @myINT1 INT = 10, @myINT2 INT = 20, @myINT3 INT;
SET @myINT3 = @myINT1 * @myINT2;
```

```
PRINT 'Value of @myINT3: ' + CONVERT(VARCHAR,@myINT3);
GO

--2
DECLARE @myString VARCHAR(100);
SET @myString = 'Hello, ';
SET @myString += 'World';
PRINT 'Value of @myString: ' + @myString;
GO

--3
DECLARE @CustomerCount INT;
SELECT @CustomerCount = COUNT(*)
FROM Sales.Customer;
PRINT 'Customer Count: ' + CAST(@CustomerCount AS VARCHAR);

--4
DECLARE @FullName NVARCHAR(152);
SELECT @FullName = FirstName + ISNULL(' ' + MiddleName,'') + ' ' + LastName
FROM Person.Person
WHERE BusinessEntityID = 1;
PRINT 'FullName: ' + @FullName;
```

Figure 7-2 shows the results. Batch 1 declares three integer variables and assigns a value to two of them. The next line uses the SET statement to assign the sum of the two variables to the third one. Finally, to print the label explaining the value and the value on the same line, the code converts the @myINT3 variable to a string.

```
 Messages
   Value of @myINT3: 200
   Value of @myString: Hello, World
   Customer Count: 19820
   FullName: Ken J Sánchez
```

Figure 7-2. The results of using variables with expressions

Batch 2 assigns the value Hello (with a space after it) to the @myString variable. The next line uses the += operator to concatenate another string, *World*, to the variable. The += operator is available in many programming languages as a shorter way to write an assignment. Without the shortcut, the code would look like this:

```
SET @myString = @myString + 'World';
```

Batch 3 assigns the result of the aggregate expression COUNT(*) to the variable @CustomerCount. When assigning a value to a variable from a query, you will assign only one value to a variable. In this case, the query returns only one value, the count of all the rows from the table. The query in Batch 4 also returns one row because of the criteria in the WHERE clause. The query assigns a value to the @FullName variable for one row only.

Using Variables in WHERE and HAVING Clauses

So far, the examples in this book have used literal values in the expressions, also known as *predicates*, in WHERE and HAVING clauses. You will often not know ahead of time what values will be needed, so it makes sense to use variables. Type in and execute the code in Listing 7-3 to learn more about using a variable instead of a literal value in a WHERE or HAVING clause.

Listing 7-3. Using a Variable in a WHERE or HAVING Clause Predicate

```
USE AdventureWorks2012;
GO

--1
DECLARE @ID INT;
SET @ID = 1;

SELECT BusinessEntityID, FirstName, LastName
FROM Person.Person
WHERE BusinessEntityID = @ID;
GO

--2
DECLARE @FirstName NVARCHAR(50);
SET @FirstName = N'Ke%';

SELECT BusinessEntityID, FirstName, LastName
FROM Person.Person
WHERE FirstName LIKE @FirstName
ORDER BY BusinessEntityID;
GO

--3
DECLARE @ID INT = 1;
--3.1
SELECT BusinessEntityID, FirstName, LastName
FROM Person.Person
WHERE @ID = CASE @ID WHEN 0 THEN 0 ELSE BusinessEntityID END;

SET @ID = 0;

--3.2
SELECT BusinessEntityID, FirstName, LastName
FROM Person.Person
WHERE @ID = CASE @ID WHEN 0 THEN 0 ELSE BusinessEntityID END;

GO

--4
DECLARE @Amount INT = 10000;

SELECT SUM(TotalDue) AS TotalSales, CustomerID
```

```
FROM Sales.SalesOrderHeader
GROUP BY CustomerID
HAVING SUM(TotalDue) > @Amount;
```

Figure 7-3 shows the results. Batch 1 declares a variable @ID and assigns the value 1. The query uses the variable in the WHERE clause to restrict the results to just the row from the Person.Person table where the BusinessEntityID is 1. Batch 2 demonstrates how pattern matching with LIKE can be used. The variable contains the wildcard %. The query returns all rows where the FirstName begins with *Ke*.

	BusinessEntityID	FirstName	LastName
1	1	Ken	Sánchez

	BusinessEntityID	FirstName	LastName
1	1	Ken	Sánchez
2	17	Kevin	Brown
3	58	Kendall	Keil
4	105	Kevin	Homer
5	195	Kevin	Liu

	BusinessEntityID	FirstName	LastName
1	1	Ken	Sánchez

	BusinessEntityID	FirstName	LastName
1	285	Syed	Abbas
2	293	Catherine	Abel
3	295	Kim	Abercrombie
4	2170	Kim	Abercrombie
5	38	Kim	Abercrombie

	TotalSales	CustomerID
1	121498.9227	30030
2	169356.0531	29784
3	550658.3836	30076
4	137844.0484	29538
5	625084.409	29615

Figure 7-3. *The partial results of using a variable in the WHERE and HAVING clauses*

Batch 3 uses the variable @ID within a CASE expression in the WHERE clause. The variable starts out with the value 1. Query 3.1 returns only the row in which BusinessEntityID equals 1. Take a closer look at the CASE expression. The variable does not equal 0, so the CASE expression returns the column BusinessEntityID. The variable @ID equals the BusinessEntityID in only one row. In query 3.2, the value of @ID is 0. The CASE expression returns 0 because @ID is equal to 0. Since @ID is equal to 0 and the CASE expression returns 0, the query returns every row. Zero is always equal to zero.

Batch 4 demonstrates that the variables can also be used in the HAVING clause of an aggregate query. Recall from Chapter 5 that you use the HAVING clause to filter the rows after the database engine processes the GROUP BY clause. The query returns only the rows from the Sales.SalesOrderHeader table where the TotalSales value by CustomerID exceeds the value stored in @Amount.

Now that you understand some of the things you can do with variables, practice working with them by completing Exercise 7-1.

EXERCISE 7-1

Use the AdventureWorks2012 database to complete this exercise. You can find the solutions in the Appendix.

1. Write a script that declares an integer variable called @myInt. Assign 10 to the variable, and then print it.

2. Write a script that declares a VARCHAR(20) variable called @myString. Assign "This is a test" to the variable, and print it.

3. Write a script that declares two integer variables called @MaxID and @MinID. Use the variables to print the highest and lowest SalesOrderID values from the Sales.SalesOrderHeader table.

4. Write a script that declares an integer variable called @ID. Assign the value 70000 to the variable. Use the variable in a SELECT statement that returns all the rows from the Sales.SalesOrderHeader table that have a SalesOrderID greater than the value of the variable.

5. Write a script that declares three variables, one integer variable called @ID, an NVARHCAR(50) variable called @FirstName, and a VARCHAR(50) variable called @LastName. Use a SELECT statement to set the value of the variables with the row from the Person.Person table with BusinessEntityID = 1. Print a statement in the "BusinessEntityID: FirstName LastName" format.

6. Write a script that declares an integer variable called @SalesCount. Set the value of the variable to the total count of sales in the Sales.SalesOrderHeader table. Use the variable in a SELECT statement that shows the difference between the @SalesCount and the count of sales by customer.

The IF... ELSE Construct

Use IF along with the optional ELSE keyword to control code flow in your T-SQL scripts. Use IF just as you would in any other programming language to execute a statement or group of statements based on an expression that must evaluate to TRUE or FALSE. For example, you might need to display an error message if the count of the rows in a table is too low. If the count exceeds a given value, your code repopulates a production table.

Using IF

Always follow the keyword IF with a condition that evaluates to TRUE or FALSE. You can follow the condition with the next statement to run on the same line or on the next line. If the condition applies to a group of statements, you will use BEGIN and END to designate which statements are within the IF block. Here is the syntax:

```
IF <condition> <statement>

IF <condition>
    <statement>

IF <condition> BEGIN
    <statement1>
    [<statement2>]
END
```

To make my code more readable and avoid mistakes, I use the first and third methods but avoid the second. For example, I might decide later to add a PRINT statement before the line to execute when the condition is true. In that case, I might accidentally cause the IF to apply just to the PRINT statement by forgetting to go back and add BEGIN and END. Type in and execute the code in Listing 7-4 to learn how to use IF.

Listing 7-4. Using IF to Control Code Execution

```
USE AdventureWorks2012;
GO

--1
DECLARE @Count INT;

SELECT @Count = COUNT(*)
FROM Sales.Customer;

IF @Count > 500 BEGIN
    PRINT 'The customer count is over 500.';
END;
GO

--2
DECLARE @Name VARCHAR(50);

SELECT @Name = FirstName + ' ' + LastName
FROM Person.Person
WHERE BusinessEntityID = 1;

--2.1
IF CHARINDEX('Ken',@Name) > 0 BEGIN
    PRINT 'The name for BusinessEntityID = 1 contains "Ken"';
END;
```

```
--2.2
IF CHARINDEX('Kathi',@Name) > O BEGIN
    PRINT 'The name for BusinessEntityID = 1 contains "Kathi"';
END;
```

Figure 7-4 shows the results. Batch 1 retrieves the count of the rows in the Sales.Customer table. If the count exceeds 500, then the PRINT statement executes. You can use any valid statements within the IF block. These code examples use PRINT statements so that you can easily see the results. Batch 2 assigns the value returned by the expression FirstName + ' ' + LastName to the variable. The 2.1 IF block executes the PRINT statement if the value contains Ken. The 2.2 IF block executes the PRINT statement if the value contains Kathi. Since the value doesn't contain Kathi, nothing prints.

```
 Messages
   The customer count is over 500.
   The name for BusinessEntityID = 1 contains "Ken"
```

Figure 7-4. The results of using IF

Using ELSE

Often you will need to perform an alternate option if the condition you are checking is false. If you are using the BEGIN and END keywords in the IF block, you must close the block first before adding ELSE. Just like IF, you can use BEGIN and END to designate the ELSE block. You can also type the statement on the same line or the next line if you choose. Here is the syntax for many of the ways you can use ELSE:

```
IF <condition> <statement>
ELSE <statement>

IF <condition> BEGIN
    <statement1>
    [<statement2>]
END
ELSE <statement>

IF <condition> BEGIN
    <statement1>
    [<statement2>]
END
ELSE BEGIN
    <statement1>
    [<statement2>]
END
```

The syntax examples show some of the ways you can use ELSE along with IF. You can use BEGIN and END with both or either parts of the construct. Type in and execute Listing 7-5 to learn how to use ELSE.

Listing 7-5. Using ELSE

```
USE AdventureWorks2012;
GO
```

```
--1
DECLARE @Count INT;

SELECT @Count = COUNT(*)
FROM Sales.Customer;

IF @Count < 500 PRINT 'The customer count is less than 500.';
ELSE PRINT 'The customer count is 500 or more.';
GO

--2
DECLARE @Name NVARCHAR(101);

SELECT @Name = FirstName + ' ' + LastName
FROM Person.Person
WHERE BusinessEntityID = 1;

--2.1
IF CHARINDEX('Ken', @Name) > 0 BEGIN
    PRINT 'The name for BusinessEntityID = 1 contains "Ken"';
END;
ELSE BEGIN
    PRINT 'The name for BusinessEntityID = 1 does not contain "Ken"';
    PRINT 'The name is ' + @Name;
END;
--2.2
IF CHARINDEX('Kathi', @Name) > 0 BEGIN
    PRINT 'The name for BusinessEntityID = 1 contains "Kathi"';
END;
ELSE BEGIN
    PRINT 'The name for BusinessEntityID = 1 does not contain "Kathi"';
    PRINT 'The name is ' + @Name;
END;
```

Figure 7-5 shows the results. This listing looks almost like Listing 7-4 except that it contains the ELSE blocks. Batch 1 saves the count of the customers in a variable. This time, if the count is less than 500, the PRINT statement in the IF block executes. In this case, the count exceeds 500, so the PRINT statement in the ELSE block executes. Batch 2 executes the PRINT statement in the IF block of the 2.1 section of code because the value of the variable contains Ken. The 2.2 section of code executes the PRINT statement in the ELSE block because the value of the variable does not contain Kathi.

```
Messages
    The customer count is 500 or more.
    The name for BusinessEntityID = 1 contains "Ken"
    The name for BusinessEntityID = 1 does not contain "Kathi"
    The name is Ken Sánchez
```

Figure 7-5. The results of using ELSE

Using Multiple Conditions

So far, the examples have shown only one condition along with each IF or ELSE. You can include multiple conditions along with AND and OR just like within a WHERE clause. You can also control the logic with parentheses. For example, you may need to execute a statement only if the current day is Monday and the count of the rows in a table exceeds a certain value. Type in and execute the code in Listing 7-6.

Listing 7-6. Using Multiple Conditions with IF and ELSE

```
USE AdventureWorks2012;
GO

--1
DECLARE @Count INT;

SELECT @Count = COUNT(*)
FROM Sales.Customer;

IF @Count > 500 AND DATEPART(dw,getdate()) = 2 BEGIN
    PRINT 'The count is over 500.';
    PRINT 'Today is Monday.';
END
ELSE BEGIN
    PRINT 'Either the count is too low or today is not Monday.';
END;
--2
IF @Count > 500 AND (DATEPART(dw,getdate()) = 2 OR DATEPART(m,getdate())= 5) BEGIN
    PRINT 'The count is over 500.'
    PRINT 'It is either Monday or the month is May.'
END
```

Figure 7-6 shows the results. This listing contains just one batch after setting the database context. IF block 1 checks to see whether the count exceeds 500 and whether the current day of the week is Monday. You may get different results depending on the day of the week you run the code. IF block 2 checks first to see whether the day of the week is Monday or whether the current month is May. The block then checks the count, which must exceed 500. Since both the count exceeds 500 and I executed the code in May, the statements print. Again, you may get different results depending on when you run the code example.

```
Messages
 Either the count is too low or today is not Monday.
 The count is over 500
 It is either Monday or the month is May.
```

Figure 7-6. The results of using multiple conditions with IF

Nesting IF...ELSE

You can nest IF and ELSE blocks inside other IF and ELSE blocks to create even more complex logic. For example, you may need to check to make sure the current date is not a Sunday and execute a statement. Then within the IF block, check to make sure the table has at least a certain number of rows before executing another statement. The BEGIN and END keywords are sometimes optional, but I suggest you include them to make sure that the code is correct and readable. Here are two of the possible syntax examples:

```
IF <condition> BEGIN
    [<statement1>]
    IF <condition> BEGIN
        <statement2>
    END
END

IF <condition> BEGIN
    <statement1>
END
ELSE BEGIN
    [statment2]
    IF <condition> BEGIN
        <statement3>
        [<statement4>]
    END
    ELSE <statement5>
END
```

As you can probably tell, nesting IF blocks can cause your code to become complicated. Be sure to use comments and consistent formatting to aid in your understanding of the code when you come back to it a few months or years after you write it. Type in and execute the code in Listing 7-7 to learn how to nest IF blocks.

Listing 7-7. Using a Nested IF Block

```
USE AdventureWorks2012;
GO

DECLARE @Count INT;

SELECT @Count = COUNT(*)
FROM Sales.Customer;

IF @Count > 500 BEGIN
    PRINT 'The count is over 500.';
    IF DATEPART(dw,getdate())= 2 BEGIN
        PRINT 'Today is Monday.';
    END;
    ELSE BEGIN
        PRINT 'Today is not Monday.';
    END;
END;
```

Figure 7-7 shows the results. Since the count exceeds 500, the code executes the first PRINT statement. Then depending on the day that you execute the code, one of the statements inside the nested IF…ELSE block will print. When writing nested IF blocks, make sure that the logic actually acts in the way you intended.

```
 Messages
    The count is over 500.
    Today is not Monday.
```

Figure 7-7. The results of using a nested IF block

Using IF EXISTS

You can use IF EXISTS to check for the results of a SELECT statement before executing the statements within the IF block. For example, you could check to see whether a certain part number is listed in the parts table. If it is, then based on the results you can choose to begin or end the script or raise an error . You may have noticed IF EXISTS being used in Chapter 6 to check the system tables to make sure a table exists before dropping it. Here is the syntax:

```
IF [NOT] EXISTS(SELECT * FROM <TABLE1> [WHERE <condition>]) BEGIN
    <statement1>
    [<statement2>]
END
```

This is one of the cases where using the asterisk (*) is perfectly acceptable. The database engine just checks to see whether the query will return even one row but doesn't return any rows at all. The EXISTS function returns only TRUE or FALSE. Type in and execute Listing 7-8 to learn how to use IF EXISTS.

Listing 7-8. Using IF EXISTS

```
USE AdventureWorks2012;
GO

--1
IF EXISTS(SELECT * FROM Person.Person WHERE BusinessEntityID = 1) BEGIN
   PRINT 'There is a row with BusinessEntityID = 1';
END
ELSE BEGIN
   PRINT 'There is not a row with BusEntityID = 1';
END;

--2
IF NOT EXISTS(SELECT * FROM Person.Person WHERE FirstName = 'Kathi') BEGIN
   PRINT 'There is not a person with the first name "Kathi".';
END;
```

Figure 7-8 shows the results. Listing 7-8 contains one batch after setting the database context. IF block 1 checks to see whether there is a row in the Person.Person table with BusinessEntityID = 1. You can also use ELSE along with IF EXISTS. IF block 2 uses the NOT keyword to make sure that there isn't a row with the FirstName of Kathi and executes the PRINT statements since there isn't a row with that name.

```
Messages
  There is a row with BusinessEntityID = 1
  There is not a person with the first name "Kathi".
```

Figure 7-8. The results of using IF EXISTS

You should now know how to use IF and ELSE in a number of situations. Practice what you have learned by completing Exercise 7-2.

EXERCISE 7-2

Use the AdventureWorks2012 database to complete this exercise. You can find the solutions in the Appendix.

1. Write a batch that declares an integer variable called @Count to save the count of all the Sales.SalesOrderDetail records. Add an IF block that that prints "Over 100,000" if the value exceeds 100,000. Otherwise, print "100,000 or less."

2. Write a batch that contains nested IF blocks. The outer block should check to see whether the month is October or November. If that is the case, print "The month is " and the month name. The inner block should check to see whether the year is even or odd and print the result. You can modify the month to check to make sure the inner block fires.

3. Write a batch that uses IF EXISTS to check to see whether there is a row in the Sales.SalesOrderHeader table that has SalesOrderID = 1. Print "There is a SalesOrderID = 1" or "There is not a SalesOrderID = 1" depending on the result.

WHILE

Use the WHILE construct to set up *loops*, or code that executes a number of times, in T-SQL. For example, you might have a script that updates 10,000 rows each time within the loop because updating 10,000 rows at a time is more efficient than updating millions of rows at once.

Using a WHILE Loop

The WHILE loop requires a *condition* (an expression that evaluates to true or false) to determine when the looping should stop. If you don't specify a condition, the loop will run until you stop it or some error condition causes it to stop. Here is the syntax:

```
WHILE <condition> BEGIN
    <statement1>
    [<statement2>]
END
```

You can use several different techniques to create the condition that the database engine checks to determine when to exit the loop. One technique is to declare a variable, usually an integer, to be used as a counter. At the beginning of the loop, the code compares the variable to a value. Inside the loop, the code increments the variable. Another common way to control the loop is by using the EXISTS keyword. This might be used if a statement within the loop modifies data in the table used in the EXISTS condition. Type in and execute Listing 7-9 to learn how to use WHILE.

Listing 7-9. *Using WHILE*

```
USE AdventureWorks2012;
GO

--1
DECLARE @Count INT = 1;

WHILE @Count < 5 BEGIN
    PRINT @Count;
    SET @Count += 1;
END;
GO

--2
IF  EXISTS (SELECT * FROM sys.objects
            WHERE object_id = OBJECT_ID(N'dbo.demoContactType')
                AND type in (N'U'))
DROP TABLE dbo.demoContactType;
GO
CREATE TABLE dbo.demoContactType(ContactTypeID INT NOT NULL PRIMARY KEY,
    Processed BIT NOT NULL);
GO
INSERT INTO dbo.demoContactType(ContactTypeID,Processed)
SELECT ContactTypeID, 0
FROM Person.ContactType;
DECLARE @Count INT = 1;
WHILE EXISTS(SELECT * From dbo.demoContactType  WHERE Processed = 0) BEGIN
    UPDATE dbo.demoContactType SET Processed = 1
    WHERE ContactTypeID = @Count;
    SET @Count += 1;
END;
PRINT 'Done!';
```

Figure 7-9 shows the partial results. Batch 1 declares a variable and sets the value to 1 to use as a counter. Once the value of @Count reached 5, the execution exited the loop. It is very important that you set the value of the counter before the WHILE statement. If the value is NULL, then the statement incrementing the value of the counter will not actually do anything since adding one to NULL returns NULL. In this case, the loop will run indefinitely. The other option is to check for a NULL counter variable inside the loop and set the value at that point. The code prints the value of the counter each time through the loop.

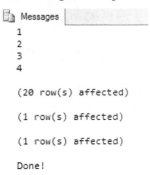

```
Messages
   1
   2
   3
   4

(20 row(s) affected)

(1 row(s) affected)

(1 row(s) affected)

Done!
```

Figure 7-9. The results of using a WHILE loop

The next example contains more than one batch because it creates and populates a table to be updated within the loop. This example also contains a variable called @Count, but the value of @Count doesn't control the execution. This WHILE loop checks to see whether any rows in table dbo.demoContactType have a zero value in the Processed column. Each time through the loop, the code updates any rows with a ContactTypeID equal to the current value of @Count. (I removed all but two of the statements reporting that one row has been updated to save space in Figure 7-9.) When no more rows exist with Processed = 0, the code completes, and the PRINT statement executes. I purposely chose a small table for this example because processing a table row by row is very inefficient.

■ **Note** Keep in mind that row-by-row (or RBAR, "row-by-agonizing-row," as it is known in the SQL community) is inefficient because of the amount of locks SQL Server needs to create and the number of commits. There is no "correct" number in regards to the amount of rows you should commit at any one time. Committing too many rows in one transaction could delay your processing during the commit while growing the transaction log; too few could also slow down execution. The answer is always somewhere in the middle. Plan on testing your batch jobs to judge the best performance.

Using ROWCOUNT

When you run a T-SQL statement, your statement will return, update, insert, or delete all rows meeting the criteria or join condition. By turning on the ROWCOUNT setting, you can specify the number of rows affected by each execution of the statements. The setting stays in effect for the current connection until it is turned off. This technique may be used in a WHILE loop to process a smaller portion of the rows at a time. Recall the car key analogy in Chapter 6 where the solution was to move all the keys at once instead of one at a time. If the pile of keys is too large to transfer at once, you might make two or three transfers but you wouldn't resort to moving one key at a time. Here is the syntax:

```
SET ROWCOUNT <number|@variable>
SET ROWCOUNT 0
```

To turn off ROWCOUNT, set the value to 0. Type in and execute the code in Listing 7-10 to learn how to use ROWCOUNT.

Listing 7-10. Using SET ROW COUNT to Limit the Number of Rows Affected

```
USE AdventureWorks2012;
GO

IF  EXISTS (SELECT * FROM sys.objects
            WHERE object_id = OBJECT_ID(N'dbo.demoSalesOrderDetail')
              AND type in (N'U'))
DROP TABLE dbo.demoSalesOrderDetail;
GO
CREATE TABLE dbo.demoSalesOrderDetail(SalesOrderID INT NOT NULL,
    SalesOrderDetailID INT NOT NULL, Processed BIT NOT NULL);
GO
SET ROWCOUNT 0;

INSERT INTO dbo.demoSalesOrderDetail(SalesOrderID,SalesOrderDetailID,Processed)
SELECT SalesOrderID, SalesOrderDetailID, 0
FROM Sales.SalesOrderDetail;
PRINT 'Populated work table';

SET ROWCOUNT 50000;
WHILE EXISTS(SELECT * From dbo.demoSalesOrderDetail  WHERE Processed = 0) BEGIN

    UPDATE dbo.demoSalesOrderDetail SET Processed = 1
    WHERE Processed = 0;
    PRINT 'Updated 50,000 rows';
END;
PRINT 'Done!';
```

Figure 7-10 shows the results. The code first creates and populates a copy of the Sales.SalesOrderDetail table. A statement changes the ROWCOUNT to 50,000 so the UPDATE statement inside the loop will update only 50,000 rows at a time. Once there are no rows left with the value zero in the Processed column, the loop completes. Be careful when writing a loop like this. If the WHERE clause that makes sure that the statement includes only the rows that need to be updated is missing, the loop will continue indefinitely. That's because it will otherwise keep updating the same rows over and over. Notice that I include the SET ROWCOUNT 0 line before the code to create the table. By default, ROWCOUNT is turned off, so the insert works as expected the first time. Without turning off ROWCOUNT, the INSERT statement inserts only 50,000 rows the second time you run it.

```
Messages

(121317 row(s) affected)
Populated work table

(50000 row(s) affected)
Updated 50,000 rows

(50000 row(s) affected)
Updated 50,000 rows

(21317 row(s) affected)
Updated 50,000 rows
Done!
```

Figure 7-10. The results of using the ROWCOUNT setting

Nesting WHILE Loops

Just as you can nest IF blocks, you can create WHILE loops within WHILE loops. You can also nest IF blocks within WHILE loops and WHILE loops within IF blocks. The important thing to remember when your T-SQL scripts become more complex is to keep your formatting consistent and add comments to your code. You may understand what your code does when you write it, but you may have a hard time figuring it out months or years later when you need to troubleshoot a problem or make a change. Type in and execute Listing 7-11 to learn how to nest WHILE loops.

Listing 7-11. Using a Nested WHILE Loop

```
DECLARE @OuterCount INT = 1;
DECLARE @InnerCount INT;

WHILE @OuterCount < 10 BEGIN
    PRINT 'Outer Loop';
    SET @InnerCount = 1;
    WHILE @InnerCount < 5 BEGIN
        PRINT '    Inner Loop';
        SET @InnerCount += 1;
    END;
    SET @OuterCount += 1;
END;
```

Figure 7-11 shows the results. The PRINT statements show which loop is executing at the time. Make sure that you reset the value of the inner loop counter in the outer loop right before the inner loop. Otherwise, the inner loop will not run after the first time because the counter is already too high.

```
Messages
Outer Loop
        Inner Loop
        Inner Loop
        Inner Loop
        Inner Loop
Outer Loop
        Inner Loop
        Inner Loop
        Inner Loop
        Inner Loop
Outer Loop
        Inner Loop
        Inner Loop
        Inner Loop
        Inner Loop
Outer Loop
```

Figure 7-11. The results of running a nested WHILE loop

Exiting a Loop Early

Most of the time a WHILE loop continues until the controlling condition returns false. You can also cause code execution to exit early by using the BREAK statement. Usually you will include a nested IF statement that controls when the BREAK statement will execute. One reason you might want to use BREAK is if you decide not to include a controlling condition at the top of the loop and include the condition in an IF block instead. The condition may be a query checking to see whether any rows remain to be updated. Type in and execute the code in Listing 7-12 to learn how to use BREAK.

Listing 7-12. Using BREAK

```
DECLARE @Count INT = 1;

WHILE @Count < 50  BEGIN
    PRINT @Count;
    IF @Count = 10 BEGIN
        PRINT 'Exiting the WHILE loop';
        BREAK;
    END;
    SET @Count += 1;
END;
```

Figure 7-12 shows the results. If the code didn't include the BREAK statement, the loop would print the numbers from 1 to 49. Instead, the loop exits when it reaches 10.

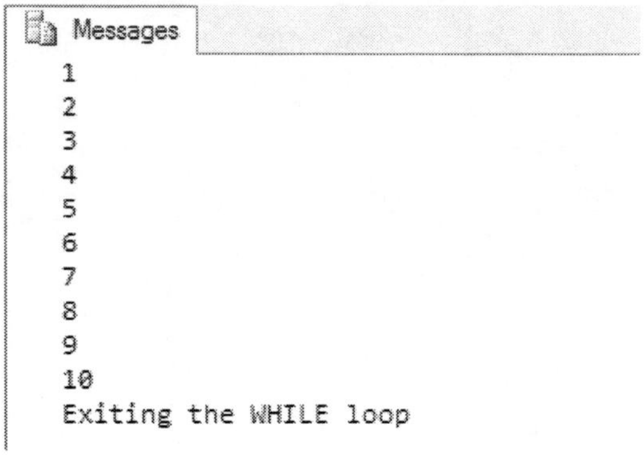

```
Messages
1
2
3
4
5
6
7
8
9
10
Exiting the WHILE loop
```

Figure 7-12. The results of using the BREAK command

Using CONTINUE

The CONTINUE command causes the loop to continue at the top. In other words, the code following the CONTINUE statement doesn't execute. Generally, you will find the CONTINUE within an IF block nested inside the WHILE loop. Type in and execute Listing 7-13 to learn how to use CONTINUE.

Listing 7-13. Using CONTINUE in a WHILE Loop

```
DECLARE @Count INT = 1;

WHILE @Count < 10 BEGIN
    PRINT @Count;
    SET @Count += 1;
    IF @Count = 3 BEGIN
        PRINT 'CONTINUE';
        CONTINUE;
    END;
    PRINT 'Bottom of loop';
END;
```

Figure 7-13 shows the results. Each time though the loop, the PRINT statement at the bottom of the loop executes except for the time when the counter equals 3. Notice that the counter increments before the IF block. If the counter incremented at the bottom of the loop, then the loop would execute indefinitely.

```
Messages
1
Bottom of loop
2
CONTINUE
3
Bottom of loop
4
Bottom of loop
5
Bottom of loop
6
Bottom of loop
7
Bottom of loop
8
Bottom of loop
9
Bottom of loop
```

Figure 7-13. The results of using CONTINUE in a WHILE loop

Now that you know how to write code with a WHILE loop, practice what you have learned by completing Exercise 7-3.

EXERCISE 7-3

Use the AdventureWorks2012 database to complete this exercise. You can find the solutions in the Appendix.

1. Write a script that contains a WHILE loop that prints out the letters *A* to *Z*. Use the function CHAR to change a number to a letter. Start the loop with the value 65. Here is an example that uses the CHAR function:

   ```
   DECLARE @Letter CHAR(1);
   SET @Letter = CHAR(65);
   PRINT @Letter;
   ```

2. Write a script that contains a WHILE loop nested inside another WHILE loop. The counter for the outer loop should count up from 1 to 100. The counter for the inner loop should count up from 1 to 5. Print the product of the two counters inside the inner loop.

3. Change the script in question 2 so the inner loop exits instead of printing when the counter for the outer loop is evenly divisible by 5.

4. Write a script that contains a WHILE loop that counts up from 1 to 100. Print "Odd" or "Even" depending on the value of the counter.

Error Handling

No matter what language you are programming in, there is always the possibility of error conditions that your code must handle. T-SQL has two ways to deal with errors, both of which you will learn about in this section. If you are writing T-SQL code within an application (for example, with a .NET language), your program will probably deal with the errors. If, however, you are writing a T-SQL script, you will handle errors at the T-SQL level. You can do both; you can handle errors within T-SQL and decide what you want sent back to the calling application.

Often the source of an error in T-SQL is a problem with an update or insert. For example, you might try to insert a row into a table that violates the primary key constraint by inserting a row with a duplicate key value. Other errors occur because of nondata reasons, such as divide-by-zero errors, for example.

Using @@ERROR

The traditional way to trap errors in T-SQL is to check the value of the @@ERROR function, formerly called a *global variable*. The @@ERROR function returns a number greater than zero if an error exists. Type in and execute the code in Listing 7-14 to learn how to use this method of error handling.

Listing 7-14. Using @@ERROR to Handle Errors

```
USE AdventureWorks2012;
GO

--1
DECLARE @errorNo INT;
PRINT 1/0;
SET @errorNo = @@ERROR;
IF @errorNo > 0 BEGIN
    PRINT 'An error has occurred.'
    PRINT @errorNo;
    PRINT @@ERROR;
END;

GO


--2
DECLARE @errorNo INT;
DROP TABLE testTable;
SET @errorNo = @@ERROR;
IF @errorNo > 0 BEGIN
    PRINT 'An error has occurred.'
    PRINT @errorNo;
    PRINT @@ERROR;
END;
GO

--3
DECLARE @errorNo INT;
SET IDENTITY_INSERT Person.ContactType ON;
INSERT INTO Person.ContactType(ContactTypeID,Name,ModifiedDate)
VALUES (1,'Accounting Manager',GETDATE());
```

```
SET @errorNo = @@ERROR;
IF @errorNo > 0 BEGIN
    PRINT 'An error has occurred.';
    PRINT @errorNo;
END;
```

Figure 7-14 shows the results. Even if you don't use the error trapping, the error prints on the screen in red, and the database engine returns an error message to the client. Notice that the code saves the value of the @@ERROR function before doing anything else. That is because, once another statement runs, the value of @@ERROR changes. Just by accessing it, the value goes back to zero. By saving the value in a local variable, you can check to see whether the value exceeds zero and deal with the error, in this case, just printing the value. You could roll back a transaction or halt the execution of the batch.

```
Messages
Msg 8134, Level 16, State 1, Line 4
Divide by zero error encountered.
An error has occurred.
8134
0
Msg 3701, Level 11, State 5, Line 4
Cannot drop the table 'testTable', because it does not exist
or you do not have permission.
An error has occurred.
3701
0
Msg 2627, Level 14, State 1, Line 5
Violation of PRIMARY KEY constraint 'PK_ContactType_ContactTypeID'.
Cannot insert duplicate key in object 'Person.ContactType'. The duplicate key value is (1).
The statement has been terminated.
An error has occurred.
2627
```

***Figure 7-14.** The results of using @@ERROR to trap errors*

Batch 1 attempts to divide by zero. Batch 2 tries to drop a table that doesn't exist. Batch 3 inserts a row into the Person.ContactType table but violates the primary key so the row can't be inserted.

Using GOTO

T-SQL allows you to use GOTO statements to cause code execution to jump to a label in another part of the code where processing continues after the label. I recommend that you reserve GOTO for handling errors and don't turn your T-SQL batches into "spaghetti code" with GOTO. Type in and execute the code in Listing 7-15 to learn how to use GOTO.

***Listing 7-15.** Using GOTO*

```
DECLARE @errorNo INT;

PRINT 'Beginning of code.'
PRINT 1/0;
SET @errorNo = @@ERROR;
IF @errorNo > 0 GOTO ERR_LABEL;
PRINT 'No error';
ERR_LABEL:
PRINT 'At ERR_LABEL';
```

Figure 7-15 shows the results. Because of the divide-by-zero error, the code skips over one of the PRINT statements and jumps to the label. T-SQL doesn't have a "return" statement, so at that point, you could include other GOTO statements and labels to control handling errors.

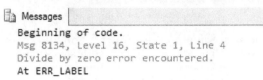

```
Beginning of code.
Msg 8134, Level 16, State 1, Line 4
Divide by zero error encountered.
At ERR_LABEL
```

Figure 7-15. The results of using GOTO

Using TRY ... CATCH

I recommend using the TRY…CATCH error handling construct over the older method of checking the value of @@ERROR. The TRY…CATCH error handling method is similar to the error handling in other programming languages such as C# and VB .NET. Along with this new method, you use several functions that provide information about the error. You can also avoid sending an error message to the client if you choose. Here is the syntax:

```
BEGIN TRY
    <statements that might cause an error>
END TRY
BEGIN CATCH
    <statements to access error information and deal with the error>
END CATCH
```

Table 7-1 lists the new functions you use along with TRY…CATCH. One benefit is that the functions retain their values while in the CATCH block. You can access the values as many times as needed. Once outside of the CATCH block, the values of the error functions revert to NULL.

Table 7-1. The Error Functions

Function	Purpose
ERROR_NUMBER()	Provides the error number. This was the only information you could get in previous releases.
ERROR_SEVERITY()	Provides the severity of the error. The severity must exceed 10 in order to be trapped.
ERROR_STATE()	Provides the state code of the error. This refers to the cause of the error.
ERROR_PROCEDURE()	Returns the name of a stored procedure or trigger that caused the error.
ERROR_LINE()	Returns the line number that caused the error.
ERROR_MESSAGE()	Returns the actual text message describing the error.

Listing 7-16 demonstrates how to use TRY…CATCH. Type in and execute the code to learn how to use it.

Listing 7-16. Using TRY…CATCH

```
USE AdventureWorks2012;
GO

--1
BEGIN TRY
    PRINT 1/0;
END TRY
BEGIN CATCH
    PRINT 'Inside the Catch block';
    PRINT ERROR_NUMBER();
    PRINT ERROR_MESSAGE();
    PRINT ERROR_NUMBER();
END CATCH
PRINT 'Outside the catch block';
PRINT ERROR_NUMBER()
GO

--2
BEGIN TRY
    DROP TABLE testTable;
END TRY
BEGIN CATCH
    PRINT 'An error has occurred.'
    PRINT ERROR_NUMBER();
    PRINT ERROR_MESSAGE();
END CATCH;
```

Figure 7-16 shows the results. One difference between TRY…CATCH and @@ERROR is that you can print the error numbers and messages multiple times within the CATCH block. The values reset to NULL once execution leaves the CATCH block. When using TRY…CATCH, the error will not print at all unless you purposely print it. It is possible to just ignore the error.

```
 Messages
  Inside the Catch block
  8134
  Divide by zero error encountered.
  8134
  Outside the catch block

  An error has occurred.
  3701
  Cannot drop the table 'testTable', because it does not
 exist or you do not have permission.
```

Figure 7-16. The results of using TRY…CATCH

Viewing Untrappable Errors

TRY…CATCH can't trap some errors. For example, if the code contains an incorrect table or column name or a database server is not available, the entire batch of statements will fail, and the error will not be trapped. One interesting way to work around this problem is to encapsulate calls within stored procedures and then call the stored procedure inside the TRY block. You will learn about stored procedures in Chapter 8. Database administrators might use the stored procedure technique for management jobs, for example, checking the job history on each server. If one server is down, the database administrator would want the code to continue to check the other servers. Type in and execute Listing 7-17 to see some examples.

Listing 7-17. Untrappable Errors

```
USE AdventureWorks2012;
GO

--1
PRINT 'Syntax error.';
GO
BEGIN TRY
    SELECT FROM Sales.SalesOrderDetail;
END TRY
BEGIN CATCH
    PRINT ERROR_NUMBER();
END CATCH;
GO

--2
PRINT 'Invalid column.';
GO
BEGIN TRY
    SELECT ABC FROM Sales.SalesOrderDetail;
END TRY
BEGIN CATCH
    PRINT ERROR_NUMBER();
END CATCH;
```

Figure 7-17 shows the results. I put the PRINT statements before each TRY…CATCH block in separate batches because they wouldn't print along with these incorrect statements. Example 1 is a syntax error; the SELECT list is empty. Example 2 contains an invalid column name.

```
Messages
  Syntax error.
  Msg 156, Level 15, State 1, Line 2
  Incorrect syntax near the keyword 'FROM'.
  Invalid column.
  Msg 207, Level 16, State 1, Line 2
  Invalid column name 'ABC'.
```

Figure 7-17. The results of running untrappable errors

Using RAISERROR

By using TRY…CATCH, you can avoid having an error message return to the client application, basically "trapping" the error. Sometimes you might want to return a different error or return an error to the client when one doesn't exist. For example, you might want to return an error message to a client when the code tries to update a nonexistent row. This wouldn't cause a database error, but you might want to cause an error to fire anyway from SQL Server to the client application. You can use the RAISERROR function to raise an error back to the client. Here is the syntax:

```
RAISERROR(<message>,<severity>,<state>)
```

The RAISERROR function has several other optional parameters that provide additional functionality, but for a first look, these three parameters may be all you need. You can create reusable custom error messages by using the sp_addmessage stored procedure or just use a variable or hard-coded string with RAISERROR. Type in and execute Listing 7-18 to learn how to use RAISERROR.

Listing 7-18. *Using RAISERROR*

```
USE master;
GO

--1 This code section creates a custom error message
IF EXISTS(SELECT * FROM sys.messages where message_id = 50002) BEGIN
    EXEC sp_dropmessage 50002;
END
GO
PRINT 'Creating a custom error message.'
EXEC sp_addmessage 50002, 16,
   N'Customer missing.';
GO

USE AdventureWorks2012;
GO
--2
IF NOT EXISTS(SELECT * FROM Sales.Customer
          WHERE CustomerID = -1) BEGIN
   RAISERROR(50002,16,1);
END
GO

--3
BEGIN TRY
    PRINT 1/0;
END TRY
BEGIN CATCH
    IF ERROR_NUMBER() = 8134 BEGIN
        RAISERROR('A bad math error!',16,1);
    END;
END CATCH;
```

Figure 7-18 shows the results. You can provide either a message number or a message string for the message parameter. Batch 1 sets up a custom error message that you can use later when raising an error as in Batch 2. Batch 3 returns a different error to the client than the one that actually happened. Since the code returned an ad hoc error message, the database engine supplied the default number, 50000. The second parameter, severity, ranges from 1 to 25. When under 11, the message is a warning or information. You might want to build a dynamic error based on what happened in your code. If you would like to do this, make sure you save the message in a variable. You can't build the message dynamically inside the RAISERROR function. See the Books Online article "Database Engine Error

Severities" to learn more about error severities, but you will generally use 16 for errors correctable by the user. The state parameter is an integer between 1 and 255. You can use state to define where in the code the error occurred.

```
Messages
Creating a custom error message.
Msg 50002, Level 16, State 1, Line 4
Customer missing.
Msg 50000, Level 16, State 1, Line 9
A bad math error!
```

Figure 7-18. The results of using RAISERROR

Using TRY…CATCH with Transactions

You can use TRY…CATCH to make sure that transactions complete successfully so that the transaction may be rolled back if necessary. Include the transaction in the TRY block. Type in and execute Listing 7-19, which shows a simple example.

Listing 7-19. Using TRY…CATCH with a Transaction

```
--1
CREATE TABLE #Test (ID INT NOT NULL PRIMARY KEY);
GO

--2
BEGIN TRY
    --2.1
    BEGIN TRAN
        --2.1.1
        INSERT INTO #Test (ID)
        VALUES (1),(2),(3);
        --2.1.2
        UPDATE #Test SET ID = 2 WHERE ID = 1;
    --2.2
    COMMIT
END TRY

--3
BEGIN CATCH
    --3.1
    PRINT ERROR_MESSAGE();
    --3.2
    PRINT 'Rolling back transaction';
    ROLLBACK;
END CATCH;
```

Figure 7-19 shows the error message and the transaction rolled back. Statement 2.1.2 attempts to set the value ID to 2 in the row where it equals 1. This violates the primary key; you can't have two rows with the value 2. If the entire transaction had been successful, the COMMIT statement would have committed the transaction. Instead, the CATCH block fired, giving you the chance to handle the error.

```
 Messages
 (3 row(s) affected)

 (0 row(s) affected)
 Violation of PRIMARY KEY constraint 'PK__#Test_____3214EC2768F3BA8F'.
 Cannot insert duplicate key in object 'dbo.#Test'. The duplicate key value is (2).
 Rolling back transaction
```

Figure 7-19. The results of using TRY...CATCH with a transaction

Using THROW Instead of RAISERROR

New in SQL Server 2012 is the THROW statement. You'll find using THROW to be much simpler than using RAISERROR. For example, the error number in the THROW statement doesn't have to exist in sys.messages. Also, the formatting for the error string can be any string format. Here is the syntax:

```
THROW [ { error_number | message | state } ] [ ; ]
```

Keep in mind the statement prior to the THROW command must end in a semicolon. Any error occurring in the THROW statement will cause the batch execution to end. Listing 7-20 shows a basic THROW command. The severity will always be 16. Figure 7-20 shows the output.

Listing 7-20. Simple THROW statement

```
THROW 999999, 'This is a test error.', 1
```

```
 Messages
 Msg 999999, Level 16, State 1, Line 1
 This is a test error.
```

Figure 7-20. Results of THROW statement

Now let's see how to use the THROW statement in a transaction. For this example, you'll attempt to insert a duplicate row into the Person.PersonPhone table. Run the script in Listing 7-21. Figure 7-21 shows the output. Feel free to change the error message to anything you want.

Listing 7-21. Using THROW in a transaction

```
BEGIN TRY
INSERT INTO Person.PersonPhone (BusinessEntityID, PhoneNumber, PhoneNumberTypeID)
VALUES (1, '697-555-0142', 1);
END TRY
BEGIN CATCH
THROW 999999, 'I will not allow you to insert a duplicate value.', 1;
END CATCH
```

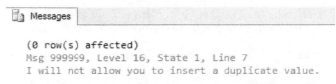

```
(0 row(s) affected)
Msg 999999, Level 16, State 1, Line 7
I will not allow you to insert a duplicate value.
```

Figure 7-21. Results of THROW statement in a transaction

As you can see, the THROW statement is easy to use and extremely customizable. The command is especially useful for those unusual application errors that SQL Server may not be aware of or may not explain with a clearly expressive message indicating the content of the error. As always, though, try to keep your error messages easily understandable and detailed enough to help diagnose the error.

Trapping and handling errors is a very important part of T-SQL. If anything can go wrong, it often will. Practice what you have learned by completing Exercise 7-4.

EXERCISE 7-4

Use AdventureWorks2012 to complete this exercise. You can find the solutions in the Appendix.

1. Write a statement that attempts to insert a duplicate row into the HumanResources.Department table. Use the @@ERROR function to display the error.

2. Change the code you wrote in question 1 to use TRY...CATCH. Display the error number, message, and severity.

3. Change the code you wrote in question 2 to raise a custom error message instead of the actual error message.

Temporary Tables and Table Variables

Temporary, or *temp*, tables and table variables allow you to save data in short-lived table structures that you can use in your scripts. For example, you may need to save the results of complicated calculations for further processing. The use of temp tables and table variables is controversial. You can find many articles and newsgroup discussions stating that no one should ever use these structures. In my opinion, temp tables and table variables are just more tools that you can use if you need them. I have found that they often allow me to break extremely complicated queries into smaller, more manageable pieces— sometimes with better performance.

Creating Local Temp Tables

Temp tables look and behave just like regular tables except that they live in the tempdb database instead of a user database like AdventureWorks2012. The tempdb database is one of the system databases required for SQL Server. SQL Server also uses tempdb as a work area for sorting and other behind-the-scene tasks.

To create a local temp table, preface the table name with the number sign (#). Only the connection in which the table was created can see a local temp table. Chapter 9 covers creating tables with the

CREATE TABLE command, but you have learned how to use the SELECT INTO syntax to create a table. You have also typed in numerous CREATE TABLE statements to create work tables for examples and exercises in Chapter 6. Here is the minimum syntax to create a local temp table using the CREATE TABLE command:

```
CREATE TABLE #tableName (<col1> <data type>,<col2> <data type>)
```

Temp tables can have anything that a regular table has, such as primary keys, defaults, and indexes. Type in and execute the code from Listing 7-22 to learn how to create a temp table.

Listing 7-22. Creating and Populating Local Temp Table

```
USE AdventureWorks2012;
GO
CREATE TABLE #myCustomers(CustomerID INT, FirstName VARCHAR(25),
    LastName VARCHAR(25));
GO

INSERT INTO #myCustomers(CustomerID,FirstName,LastName)
SELECT C.CustomerID, FirstName, LastName
FROM Person.Person AS P INNER JOIN Sales.Customer AS C
ON P.BusinessEntityID = C.PersonID;

SELECT CustomerID, FirstName, LastName
FROM #myCustomers;

DROP TABLE #myCustomers;
```

Figure 7-22 shows the results. The code first uses the CREATE TABLE command to create the table, #myCustomers. This example is very simple. The command could define a primary key, CustomerID, and define that the FirstName and LastName columns should not contain NULL values. The script could include an ALTER TABLE command to add an index. The script populates the table with a regular insert statement, inserting the rows from a join on two tables. The SELECT statement looks like any other SELECT statement. Finally, the DROP TABLE command destroys the table. Even though the table will drop automatically when the connection closes, it's a good practice to drop temp tables when you are done using them.

	CustomerID	First Name	Last Name
1	29485	Catherine	Abel
2	29486	Kim	Abercrombie
3	29487	Humberto	Acevedo
4	29484	Gustavo	Achong
5	29488	Pilar	Ackerman
6	28866	Aaron	Adams
7	13323	Adam	Adams
8	21139	Alex	Adams
9	29170	Alexandra	Adams
10	19419	Allison	Adams
11	11971	Amanda	Adams
12	26746	Amber	Adams
13	16845	Andrea	Adams

Figure 7-22. The partial results of creating and populating a temp table

Creating Global Temp Tables

You can create two kinds of temp tables: local and global. When creating a local temp table, you can access the table only within the connection where it was created. When the connection closes, the database engine destroys the temp table. When creating a global temp table, any connection can see the table. When the last connection to the temp table closes, the database engine destroys the temp table. Global temp tables begin with two number signs. Type in and execute the code from Listing 7-23 to learn how to create a global temp table. Don't close the query window when you're done.

Listing 7-23. Creating and Populating a Global Temp Table

```
USE AdventureWorks2012;
GO
CREATE TABLE ##myCustomers(CustomerID INT, FirstName VARCHAR(25),
    LastName VARCHAR(25));
GO

INSERT INTO ##myCustomers(CustomerID,FirstName,LastName)
SELECT C.CustomerID, FirstName,LastName
FROM Person.Person AS P INNER JOIN Sales.Customer AS C
ON P.BusinessEntityID = C.PersonID;

SELECT CustomerID, FirstName, LastName
FROM ##myCustomers;

--Run the drop statement when you are done
--DROP TABLE ##myCustomers;
```

By using two number signs (##) in the name, you create a global temp table. Open another query window, and type the same SELECT statement to see that you can access the table from another connection. The results will look the same as Figure 7-22. Be sure to drop temp tables, especially global temp tables, when you no longer need them.

You won't find many reasons to use global temp tables. For example, suppose that an application creates a global temp table. If another user runs the same code to create the global temp table with the same name while the first temp table exists, an error will occur. I have actually seen this error happen in a commercially available application!

Creating Table Variables

Table variables became available in SQL Server 2000. At that time, many T-SQL developers decided they should always use table variables instead of temp tables because of a myth about them. Many developers believe that table variables exist in memory instead of tempdb, but that is not the case. Table variables do live in tempdb. Here is the syntax for creating a table variable:

```
DECLARE @tableName TABLE (<col1> <data type>,<col2> <data type>)
```

Because a table variable is a variable, it follows the same scoping rules as other variables. Table variables go out of scope at the end of the batch, not when the connection closes, and you can't perform an ALTER TABLE command to give the table variable nonclustered indexes or make any changes to the definition of a table variable once it is declared. Table variables are fine for small tables that you won't need after running the batch. Temp tables are the better choice for tables with large numbers of rows that could benefit from nonclustered indexes or when you need to use the table after the batch is done. Type in and execute Listing 7-24 to learn how to use a table variable.

Listing 7-24. Creating and Populating Table Variable

```
USE AdventureWorks2012;

DECLARE @myCustomers TABLE (CustomerID INT, FirstName VARCHAR(25),
    LastName VARCHAR(25))

INSERT INTO @myCustomers(CustomerID,FirstName,LastName)
SELECT C.CustomerID, FirstName,LastName
FROM Person.Person AS P INNER JOIN Sales.Customer AS C
ON P.BusinessEntityID = C.PersonID;

SELECT CustomerID, FirstName, LastName
FROM @myCustomers;
```

The results are identical to those in Figure 7-22. Again, if you need to save a very large number of rows temporarily, you may find that a temporary table is a better choice. Another reason you might want to use a temp table is that you can create it with a SELECT INTO statement, which is not possible with a table variable. The advantage of a SELECT INTO is that you don't need to know the column names and data types up front. See the "Creating and Populating a Table in One Statement" section in Chapter 6 for more information.

Using a Temp Table or Table Variable

You may be wondering why you might need to use a temporary table. For example, in many human resource system databases, most of the tables have history and future rows. The tables have effective dates and effective sequences. The effective sequences determine the valid row for a given date for a given employee. Instead of figuring out the effective date and effective sequence for each employee over and over in my scripts, I create a temporary table to hold that information.

Another way I use temp tables is to store a list of values for filtering queries. For example, suppose a user can select one value or more values to filter a report. The reporting application sends a comma-delimited list of values to a stored procedure. You can add each value from the comma-delimited list to a temp table or table variable and then use that table to filter the report results. You will learn about stored procedures in Chapter 9. Listing 7-25 shows how to use a table variable populated from a list of values. Type in and execute the code.

Listing 7-25. Using a Temp Table to Solve a Query Problem

```
USE AdventureWorks2012;
GO

--1
DECLARE @IDTable TABLE (ID INT);
DECLARE @IDList VARCHAR(2000);
DECLARE @ID INT;
DECLARE @Loc INT;

--2
SET @IDList = '16496,12506,11390,10798,2191,11235,10879,15040,3086';

--3
SET @Loc = CHARINDEX(',',@IDList);
--4
WHILE @Loc > 0 BEGIN
    --4.1
    SET @ID = LEFT(@IDList,@Loc-1);
    --4.2
    SET @IDList = SUBSTRING(@IDList,@Loc +1,2000);
    --4.3
    INSERT INTO @IDTable(ID)
    VALUES (@ID);
    --4.4
    SET @Loc = CHARINDEX(',',@IDList);
END;
--5
IF LEN(@IDList) > 0 BEGIN
    SET @ID = @IDList;
    INSERT INTO @IDTable(ID)
    VALUES (@ID);
END;

--6
SELECT BusinessEntityID, FirstName, LastName
FROM Person.Person AS p
INNER JOIN @IDTable ON p.BusinessEntityID = ID;
```

Figure 7-23 shows the results. Code section 1 declares four variables: @IDTable, which is a table variable; @IDList to hold the comma-delimited list sent from the application; @ID to hold one individual value from the list; and @Loc to hold the location of the comma. Statement 2 sets the value of @IDList, which represents the list of values sent by the application.

Results

	BusinessEntityID	FirstName	LastName
1	16496	Gabriel	Mitchell
2	12506	Alejandro	Liang
3	2191	Alfredo	Fuentes Espinosa
4	10798	Katherine	Smith
5	11235	Isabella	Martin
6	11390	Christy	Tang
7	3086	Stephanie	Ward
8	10879	Jenna	Hall
9	15040	Eduardo	Bell

Figure 7-23. *The results of using a table variable*

The code finds each ID value from the comma-delimited string and stores the value in the table variable. Statement 3 finds the location of the first comma in the list and stores the location in `@Loc`. Code section 4 is a `WHILE` loop. Inside the `WHILE` loop, statement 4.1 stores the first value in the `@ID` variable, and statement 4.2 removes that value along with the comma from `@IDList` based on the value of `@Loc`. Statement 4.3 inserts the value stored in `@ID` into the table variable, `@IDTable`. Finally, at the bottom of the loop, statement 4.4 locates the next comma, resetting the value of `@Loc`. The loop continues as long as the code continues to find a comma in `@IDList`. Once the loop completes, the last value is most likely still in `@IDList`. Code section 5 checks the length of `@IDList` and inserts the last value into the table variable. Query 6 joins the `@IDTable` to the Person.Person table, effectively using `@IDTable` as a filter.

Using a Temp Table or Table Variable as an Array

An *array* is a collection of values used in many programming languages. T-SQL doesn't have an array structure, but programmers sometimes use temp tables or table variables as arrays. I often use this method in my administrative scripts to perform a backup or check the space used on each database on a server, for example. Listing 7-26 demonstrates how you might use a table variable as an array. Type in and execute the code to learn how to use this technique.

Listing 7-26. *Using an "Array"*

```
--1
SET NOCOUNT ON;
GO

--2
DECLARE @IDTable TABLE(ArrayIndex INT NOT NULL IDENTITY,
    ID INT);
DECLARE @RowCount INT;
```

```
DECLARE @ID INT;
DECLARE @Count INT = 1;

--3
INSERT INTO @IDTable(ID)
VALUES(500),(333),(200),(999);

--4
SELECT @RowCount = COUNT(*)
FROM @IDTable;

--5
WHILE @Count <= @RowCount BEGIN
    --5.1
    SELECT @ID = ID
    FROM @IDTable
    WHERE ArrayIndex = @Count;
    --5.2
    PRINT CAST(@COUNT AS VARCHAR) + ': ' + CAST(@ID AS VARCHAR);
    --5.3
    SET @Count += 1;
END;
```

Figure 7-24 shows the results. Statement 1 sets the NOCOUNT property to ON. This will remove the messages showing how many each statement affects. In this case, the messages just get in the way. Code section 2 declares the variables used in this example. The table variable, @IDTable, contains an identity column called ArrayIndex. See Chapter 6 for more information about identity columns. Statement 3 populates @IDTable with several values. Since the database engine populates the INDEX column automatically, you now have a two-dimensional "array." Statement 4 populates the @RowCount variable with the number of rows in @IDTable. Code section 5 is a WHILE loop that runs once for each row in @IDTable. During each iteration of the loop, statement 5.1 sets the value of @ID with the ID column from @IDTable corresponding to the ArrayIndex column matching @Count. Statement 5.2 prints the @Count and @ID values, but you could do whatever you need to do instead of just printing the values. Statement 5.3 increments the @Count.

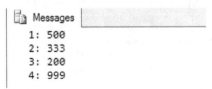

```
Messages
   1: 500
   2: 333
   3: 200
   4: 999
```

Figure 7-24. The results of using an "array"

Temp tables and table variables are just more tools in your T-SQL tool belt, but use them wisely.

Using a Cursor

Another way to loop through a result set is by using a cursor. This is a very controversial topic, especially for beginners. Developers frequently overuse cursors and end up writing poorly performing code. I'll cover cursors so that you are familiar with them and so that you understand the example in the

"Thinking About Performance" section. Type in and execute the code from Listing 7-27, which shows a simple example.

Listing 7-27. Using a Cursor

```
USE AdventureWorks2012;
GO

--1
DECLARE @ProductID INT;
DECLARE @Name NVARCHAR(25);

--2
DECLARE products CURSOR FAST_FORWARD FOR
    SELECT ProductID, Name
    FROM Production.Product;

--3
OPEN products;

--4
FETCH NEXT FROM products INTO @ProductID, @Name;

--5
WHILE @@FETCH_STATUS = 0 BEGIN
    --5.1
    PRINT @ProductID;
    PRINT @Name;
    --5.2
    FETCH NEXT FROM products INTO @ProductID, @Name;
END

--6
CLOSE products;
DEALLOCATE products;
```

Figure 7-25 shows the results. Code section 1 declares variables that will be used later in the code. Statement 2 declares the cursor. The cursor must have a name and a SELECT statement. I included the option FAST_FORWARD to improve the performance. See Books Online if you are interested in learning more about cursor options. Statement 3 opens the cursor so that it is ready for access. Statement 4 reads the first row from the cursor into the variables. There must be one variable for each column selected in the cursor definition. The WHILE loop checks the status of the last read of the cursor. As long as the value is zero, the loop continues. Section 5.1 prints out the variables, but you could do anything you need to do at this point. Statement 5.2 is very important; it reads the next row. Without statement 5.2, the WHILE loop would continue indefinitely. Finally, section 6 cleans up the cursor. Cursors are another tool at your disposal, but use them only when another better-performing option is not available. Developers often use cursors to update one row at a time, which is usually a very bad idea.

```
Messages
1
Adjustable Race
879
All-Purpose Bike Stand
712
AWC Logo Cap
3
BB Ball Bearing
2
Bearing Ball
877
Bike Wash - Dissolver
316
Blade
843
Cable Lock
952
```

Figure 7-25. The partial results of using a cursor

Complete Exercise 7-5 to practice what you have learned about temporary tables and table variables.

EXERCISE 7-5

Use the AdventureWorks2012 database to complete this exercise. You can find the solutions in the Appendix.

1. Create a temp table called #CustomerInfo that contains CustomerID, FirstName, and LastName columns. Include CountOfSales and SumOfTotalDue columns. Populate the table with a query using the Sales.Customer, Person.Person, and Sales.SalesOrderHeader tables.

2. Change the code written in question 1 to use a table variable instead of a temp table.

3. Create a table variable with two integer columns, one of them an IDENTITY column. Use a WHILE loop to populate the table with 1,000 random integers using the following formula. Use a second WHILE loop to print the values from the table variable one by one.

```
CAST(RAND() * 10000 AS INT) + 1
```

Thinking About Performance

This chapter focuses on the logic features available T-SQL instead of retrieving or updating data. Depending on the task at hand, you may or may not need to use this functionality. Often you may need to write or support very complex T-SQL scripts that run once each night. The performance of these scripts is not as critical as that of the performance of T-SQL code in an application or a report, but over time you may have to rewrite several to perform better. For example, a programmer from a software vendor writes a custom program that creates a denormalized table of information from a financial system. That table is needed by many other systems in the enterprise. The program as originally written takes more than an hour to run. Luckily, you have access to the original source code and find that the program populated this table one row and one column at a time. Another way of writing the code and having it run much faster is by using a set-based approach and inserting or updating all the rows at once from each source table instead of one row at a time.

The following example compares two ways to solve a typical problem. The first uses a cursor solution and the second a set-based approach. The requirements are to calculate sales totals by order year, order month, and TerritoryID. The report must also show the total sales for the previous month in the same row. Every territory, year, and month possible must appear on the report even if there are no sales for a particular combination. To save typing, you might want to download the code from this book's page at www.apress.com. Listing 7-28 uses a cursor and two nested WHILE loops to create a temp table with the totals. On my laptop, the code took 19 seconds to run.

Listing 7-28. Using a Cursor to Populate a Report

```
USE AdventureWorks2012;
GO

DECLARE @Year INT;
DECLARE @Month INT;
DECLARE @TerritoryID INT;
DECLARE @Total MONEY;
DECLARE @PreviousTotal MONEY;
DECLARE @FirstYear INT;
DECLARE @LastYear INT;
DECLARE @BeginDate DATETIME;
DECLARE @EndDate DATETIME;

CREATE TABLE #Totals(OrderYear INT, OrderMonth INT,
    TerritoryID INT, TotalSales MONEY,
    PreviousSales MONEY);

SELECT @FirstYear = MIN(YEAR(OrderDate)),
    @LastYear = MAX(YEAR(OrderDate))
FROM Sales.SalesOrderHeader;

DECLARE Territory CURSOR FAST_FORWARD FOR
    SELECT TerritoryID
    FROM Sales.SalesTerritory;

OPEN Territory;
FETCH NEXT FROM Territory INTO @TerritoryID;
WHILE @@FETCH_STATUS = 0 BEGIN
    SET @Year = @FirstYear;

    WHILE @Year <= @LastYear BEGIN
        SET @Month = 1;
        WHILE @Month <= 12 BEGIN
```

```
            SET @BeginDate = CAST(@Year AS VARCHAR) + '/' +
                CAST(@Month AS VARCHAR) + '/1';
            SET @EndDate = DATEADD(M,1,@BeginDate);
            SET @Total = 0;
            SELECT @Total = SUM(LineTotal)
            FROM Sales.SalesOrderDetail AS SOD
            INNER JOIN Sales.SalesOrderHeader AS SOH
            ON SOD.SalesOrderID = SOH.SalesOrderID
            WHERE TerritoryID = @TerritoryID
                AND OrderDate >= @BeginDate AND OrderDate < @EndDate;

            SET @PreviousTotal = 0;
            SET @EndDate = @BeginDate;
            SET @BeginDate = DATEADD(M,-1,@BeginDate);

    SELECT @PreviousTotal = SUM(LineTotal)
            FROM Sales.SalesOrderDetail AS SOD
            INNER JOIN Sales.SalesOrderHeader AS SOH
            ON SOD.SalesOrderID = SOH.SalesOrderID
            WHERE TerritoryID = @TerritoryID
                AND OrderDate >= @BeginDate AND OrderDate < @EndDate;

            INSERT INTO #Totals(TerritoryID, OrderYear,
            OrderMonth,TotalSales, PreviousSales)
            SELECT @TerritoryID, @Year, @Month,
            ISNULL(@Total,0), ISNULL(@PreviousTotal,0);

            SET @Month +=1;
        END; -- Month loop
        SET @Year += 1;
    END; -- Year Loop
    FETCH NEXT FROM Territory INTO @TerritoryID;
END; -- Territory cursor
CLOSE Territory;
DEALLOCATE Territory;

SELECT OrderYear, OrderMonth, TerritoryID,
    TotalSales, PreviousSales
FROM #Totals
ORDER BY OrderYear, OrderMonth, TerritoryID;

SELECT OrderYear, OrderMonth, TerritoryID,
    TotalSales, PreviousSales
FROM #Totals
WHERE TerritoryID = 1 AND TotalSales <> 0 AND PreviousSales <> 0
ORDER BY OrderYear, OrderMonth;

DROP TABLE #Totals;
```

The code in Listing 7-28 uses a cursor-based approach to populate a temp table for the report. The code creates a cursor that loops through the TerritoryID values. Inside the cursor loop, a WHILE loop of months is nested inside a WHILE loop of possible years. The code performs the calculations and inserts a row within the innermost loop. Finally, after the loops complete, two SELECT statements display the results. This code actually performs better than other code I have seen. It is not unusual to see code that not only loops through the territories but also loops through all the sales. Now try the example in Listing 7-29, which produces the same results much faster (about 1 second on my laptop).

Listing 7-29. Populating a Report with a Set-Based Approach

```
USE AdventureWorks2012;
GO

--1
CREATE TABLE #Totals(TerritoryID INT, OrderYear INT, OrderMonth INT,
    TotalSales MONEY, PreviousSales MONEY
    );

--2
CREATE TABLE #SalesMonths(MonthNo INT);

--3
INSERT INTO #SalesMonths(MonthNo)
VALUES (1),(2),(3),(4),(5),(6),(7),(8),(9),(10),(11),(12);

--4
WITH SalesYears AS (
    SELECT YEAR(OrderDate) AS OrderYear
    FROM Sales.SalesOrderHeader
    GROUP BY YEAR(OrderDate)
    )
INSERT INTO #Totals(OrderYear, OrderMonth, TerritoryID,
    TotalSales, PreviousSales)
SELECT OrderYear, MonthNo,TerritoryID, 0 AS TotalSales,0 AS PreviousSales
FROM SalesYears, Sales.SalesTerritory, #SalesMonths
ORDER BY OrderYear, MonthNo, TerritoryID;

--5
WITH Totals AS (
    SELECT SUM(LineTotal) AS TotalSales,
        YEAR(OrderDate) AS OrderYear,
        MONTH(OrderDate) AS OrderMonth, TerritoryID
    FROM Sales.SalesOrderDetail AS SOD
    INNER JOIN Sales.SalesOrderHeader AS SOH
        ON SOD.SalesOrderID = SOH.SalesOrderID
    GROUP BY YEAR(OrderDate), MONTH(OrderDate), TerritoryID
)
UPDATE #Totals SET TotalSales = Totals.TotalSales
FROM #Totals INNER JOIN Totals ON #Totals.OrderYear = Totals.OrderYear
    AND #Totals.OrderMonth = Totals.OrderMonth
    AND #Totals.TerritoryID = Totals.TerritoryID;
--6
WITH Totals AS (
    SELECT SUM(LineTotal) AS TotalSales,
        YEAR(DATEADD(M,1,OrderDate)) AS OrderYear,
```

```
        MONTH(DATEADD(M,1,OrderDate)) AS OrderMonth, TerritoryID
    FROM Sales.SalesOrderDetail AS SOD
    INNER JOIN Sales.SalesOrderHeader AS SOH
        ON SOD.SalesOrderID = SOH.SalesOrderID
    GROUP BY YEAR(DATEADD(M,1,OrderDate)),
            MONTH(DATEADD(M,1,OrderDate)), TerritoryID
)
UPDATE #Totals SET PreviousSales = Totals.TotalSales
FROM #Totals INNER JOIN Totals ON #Totals.OrderYear = Totals.OrderYear
    AND #Totals.OrderMonth = Totals.OrderMonth
    AND #Totals.TerritoryID = Totals.TerritoryID;

--7
SELECT OrderYear, OrderMonth, TerritoryID,
    TotalSales, PreviousSales
FROM #Totals
ORDER BY OrderYear, OrderMonth, TerritoryID;

--8
SELECT OrderYear, OrderMonth, TerritoryID,
    TotalSales, PreviousSales
FROM #Totals
WHERE TerritoryID = 1 AND TotalSales <> 0 AND PreviousSales <> 0
ORDER BY OrderYear, OrderMonth;
DROP TABLE #Totals;
DROP TABLE #SalesMonths;
```

Figure 7-26 shows the results of Listing 7-29. Statement 1 creates a temp table to hold the results. Statement 2 creates a temp table, #SalesMonths. Statement 3 populates the #SalesMonths table with the numbers 1 through 12. Statement 4 contains a CTE, SalesYears, listing all the unique years in the Sales.SalesOrderHeader table. The SELECT statement in statement 4 joins the SalesYears, #SalesMonths, and Sales.SalesTerritory tables in a Cartesian product that inserts every possible combination into a temp table, #Totals. It fills in zeros for the TotalSales and PreviousSales columns. Statement 5 updates the TotalSales column of the #Totals table with the sum of the LineTotal column. Statement 6 updates the PreviousSales column of the #Totals table. Statement 7 displays all the rows in the #Totals table. Statement 8 displays a subset of the rows that actually have some sales.

Results

	OrderYear	OrderMonth	TerritoryID	TotalSales	PreviousSales
1	2005	1	1	0.00	0.00
2	2005	1	2	0.00	0.00
3	2005	1	3	0.00	0.00
4	2005	1	4	0.00	0.00
5	2005	1	5	0.00	0.00
6	2005	1	6	0.00	0.00
7	2005	1	7	0.00	0.00
8	2005	1	8	0.00	0.00

	OrderYear	OrderMonth	TerritoryID	TotalSales	PreviousSales
1	2005	8	1	599134.932	237832.001
2	2005	9	1	475574.0354	599134.932
3	2005	10	1	373105.8705	475574.0354
4	2005	11	1	1125729.286	373105.8705
5	2005	12	1	782592.7034	1125729.286
6	2006	1	1	355332.483	782592.7034
7	2006	2	1	943283.055	355332.483
8	2006	3	1	536683.345	943283.055

Figure 7-26. The partial results of the set-based approach

The point of this example is to show that most of the time a set-based approach can be found and is more efficient. It may take more practice and experience before you come up with this solution, but the more you work with T-SQL, the better you will get.

Summary

If you know one programming language, you will probably find the second and third language even easier to learn because the logic is the same. You will generally have ways to execute or avoid executing lines of code based on certain criteria. You will have ways to repeatedly execute lines code of code by looping. Whether or not you decide to implement this logic in T-SQL scripts will depend on the design of your application, the standards in your shop, or your personal preferences.

This chapter covered using variables, conditional logic, looping, and temporary table structures. In Chapter 9, you will use what you have learned in this chapter to create stored procedures, user-defined functions, and more.

CHAPTER 8

Working with XML

Beginning with SQL Server 2005, Microsoft added the XML data type, the XQuery language, and several new functions for working with XML data. XML stands for Extensible Markup Language, and it looks a lot like HTML except that it generally contains data. Companies often use XML to exchange data between incompatible systems or with their vendors and customers. SQL Server also extensively uses XML data to store query plans.

Fully covering XML support in SQL Server would take another complete book, so I'll just briefly discuss it here. In the past, to work with XML, databases stored the XML data in TEXT columns. The database was just a storage place for the XML data. There was nothing to validate the XML data or to query just part of the XML data. To learn about SQL Server support for XML in depth, check out the book *Pro SQL Server 2008 XML* by Michael Coles (Apress, 2008).

Converting XML into Data Using OPENXML

There are primarily two ways of handling XML. Either you need to convert an XML document into a rowset (table) or you have a rowset and want to convert it into a XML document. Converting an XML document into a rowset is called *shredding* and this is the purpose of the OPENXML command. OPENXML must also be used in conjunction with two other commands: sp_xml_preparedocument and sp_xml_removedocument. The first command loads the XML document into memory; this process is expensive and takes one-eighth of SQL Server's total memory. The command sp_xml_removedocument removes the XML from SQL Server memory and should always be executed at the very end of the transaction. Listing 8-1 shows how this done and Figure 8-1 shows the results from the query.

Listing 8-1. OPENXML Query

```
DECLARE @hdoc int
DECLARE @doc varchar(1000) = N'
<Products>
<Product ProductID="32565451" ProductName="Bicycle Pump">
    <Order ProductID="32565451" SalesID="5" OrderDate="2011-07-04T00:00:00">
        <OrderDetail OrderID="10248" CustomerID="22" Quantity="12"/>
        <OrderDetail OrderID="10248" CustomerID="11" Quantity="10"/>
    </Order>
</Product>
<Product ProductID="57841259" ProductName="Bicycle Seat">
    <Order ProductID="57841259" SalesID="3" OrderDate="2011-08-16T00:00:00">
```

```
          <OrderDetail OrderID="54127" CustomerID="72" Quantity="3"/>
        </Order>
</Product>
</Products>';

EXEC sp_xml_preparedocument @hdoc OUTPUT, @doc

SELECT *
FROM OPENXML(@hdoc, N'/Products/Product');

EXEC sp_xml_removedocument @hdoc;
```

▦ Results

	id	parentid	nodetype	localname	prefix	namespaceuri	datatype	prev	text
1	2	0	1	Product	NULL	NULL	NULL	NULL	NULL
2	3	2	2	ProductID	NULL	NULL	NULL	NULL	NULL
3	28	3	3	#text	NULL	NULL	NULL	NULL	32565451
4	4	2	2	ProductName	NULL	NULL	NULL	NULL	NULL
5	29	4	3	#text	NULL	NULL	NULL	NULL	Bicycle Pump
6	5	2	1	Order	NULL	NULL	NULL	NULL	NULL
7	6	5	2	ProductID	NULL	NULL	NULL	NULL	NULL
8	30	6	3	#text	NULL	NULL	NULL	NULL	32565451
9	7	5	2	SalesID	NULL	NULL	NULL	NULL	NULL
10	31	7	3	#text	NULL	NULL	NULL	NULL	5
11	8	5	2	OrderDate	NULL	NULL	NULL	NULL	NULL
12	32	8	3	#text	NULL	NULL	NULL	NULL	2011-07-04T00:00:00

Figure 8-1. Partial results of the OPENXML query

■ **Note** OPENXML, sp_xml_preparedocument, and sp_xml_removedocument are still available in SQL 2012 but are legacy commands. Newer methods such as nodes(), value(), and query() take advantage of the XML data type and are recommended over OPENXML and FORXML. These newer methods are discussed later in the chapter.

Notice that SQL Server predefines the columns in the rowset. These column names are based on the XML *edge table format*. This format is the default structure for XML represented in table format. Luckily you can modify the column output in order to customize your rowset definitions. You accomplish this by specifying the optional WITH clause in your select statement. Listing 8-2 runs the same OPENXML query but includes the WITH clause and Figure 8-2 shows the results of the OPENXML query.

Listing 8-2. OPENXML Query Using the WITH Clause

```
DECLARE @hdoc int
DECLARE @doc varchar(1000) = N'
<Products>
<Product ProductID="32565451" ProductName="Bicycle Pump">
    <Order ProductID="32565451" SalesID="5" OrderDate="2011-07-04T00:00:00">
        <OrderDetail OrderID="10248" CustomerID="22" Quantity="12"/>
```

```
            <OrderDetail OrderID="10248" CustomerID="11" Quantity="10"/>
        </Order>
    </Product>
    <Product ProductID="57841259" ProductName="Bicycle Seat">
        <Order ProductID="57841259" SalesID="3" OrderDate="2011-08-16T00:00:00">
            <OrderDetail OrderID="54127" CustomerID="72" Quantity="3"/>
        </Order>
    </Product>
</Products>';

EXEC sp_xml_preparedocument @hdoc OUTPUT, @doc

SELECT *
FROM OPENXML(@hdoc, N'/Products/Product/Order/OrderDetail')
WITH (CustomerID int '@CustomerID',
      ProductID int '../@ProductID',
      ProductName varchar(30) '../../@ProductName',
      OrderID int '@OrderID',
      Orderdate varchar(30) '../@OrderDate');

EXEC sp_xml_removedocument @hdoc;
```

Results

	CustomerID	ProductID	ProductName	OrderID	Orderdate
1	22	32565451	Bicycle Pump	10248	2011-07-04T00:00:00
2	11	32565451	Bicycle Pump	10248	2011-07-04T00:00:00
3	72	57841259	Bicycle Seat	54127	2011-08-16T00:00:00

Figure 8-2. Results of the OPENXML query using the WITH clause

In Listing 8-2 you defined the rowpattern as /Products/Product/Order/OrderDetail. You also included the optional ColPattern for each row in the WITH clause. By including the ColPattern you are telling SQL Server to process the XPath using attribute-centric mapping, which is the default method. Another method of mapping XML documents is using element-centric mapping. You'll look at both methods next. Listing 8-3 shows how to access data using attribute-centric mapping; notice the "1" parameter in the OPENXML statement. Figure 8-3 shows the results.

Listing 8-3. Attribute-Centric Mapping

```
DECLARE @hdoc int
DECLARE @doc varchar(1000) = N'
<Orders>
    <Order OrderID="123458">
        <ProductID>32565451</ProductID>
        <ProductName>Bicycle Pump</ProductName>
        <SalesID>5</SalesID>
                <OrderDetail>
                        <CustomerID>22</CustomerID>
                        <Quantity>12</Quantity>
                </OrderDetail>
```

```
    </Order>
</Orders>';

EXEC sp_xml_preparedocument @hdoc OUTPUT, @doc

SELECT *

FROM OPENXML(@hdoc, N'/Orders/Order', 1)

WITH (ProductID int,
      ProductName varchar(30),
          SalesID varchar(10),
          OrderID int,
          CustomerID int);

EXEC sp_xml_removedocument @hdoc;
```

Results

	ProductID	ProductName	SalesID	OrderID	CustomerID
1	NULL	NULL	NULL	123458	NULL

Figure 8-3. Attribute-centric mapping

You've defined your rowpattern as /Orders/Order and, since you're using attribute-centric mapping, your table includes only the OrderID, which is an in-line attribute of the Order element. Notice the OPENXML query also doesn't return the CustomerID, which is an attribute of the OrderDetails element.

Now let's look at the same script but change the OPENXML to element-centric mapping. I've highlighted the change in Listing 8-4. Figure 8-4 shows the output when using element-centric mapping.

Listing 8-4. Element-Centric Mapping

```
DECLARE @hdoc int
DECLARE @doc varchar(1000) = N'
<Orders>
   <Order OrderID="123458">
      <ProductID>32565451</ProductID>
      <ProductName>Bicycle Pump</ProductName>
      <SalesID>5</SalesID>
         <OrderDetail>
                <CustomerID>22</CustomerID>
                <Quantity>12</Quantity>
                </OrderDetail>
   </Order>
</Orders>';

EXEC sp_xml_preparedocument @hdoc OUTPUT, @doc

SELECT *
FROM OPENXML(@hdoc, N'/Orders/Order', 2)
WITH (ProductID int,
      ProductName varchar(30),
```

```
    SalesID varchar(10),
    OrderID int,
    CustomerID int);

EXEC sp_xml_removedocument @hdoc;
```

Results

	ProductID	ProductName	SalesID	OrderID	CustomerID
1	32565451	Bicycle Pump	5	NULL	NULL

Figure 8-4. Element-centric mapping

You're getting closer to parsing all of the XML into the rowset. OPENXML in Listing 8-4 returns all the attributes of the elements under the Order element. It did not return the OrderID attribute of the Order element or any attributes in the OrderDetails element.

How do you return all the attributes in the XML document? You first have to define ColPatterns for each column in the rowset. Doing so will change the parameter to element-centric mapping. Listing 8-5 shows how this works and Figure 8-5 shows the results.

Listing 8-5. Use of ColPattern in the WITH Clause

```
DECLARE @hdoc int
DECLARE @doc varchar(1000) = N'
<Orders>
    <Order OrderID="123458">
        <ProductID>32565451</ProductID>
        <ProductName>Bicycle Pump</ProductName>
        <SalesID>5</SalesID>
            <OrderDetail>
                    <CustomerID>22</CustomerID>
                    <Quantity>12</Quantity>
                    </OrderDetail>
    </Order>
</Orders>';

EXEC sp_xml_preparedocument @hdoc OUTPUT, @doc

SELECT *
FROM OPENXML(@hdoc, N'/Orders/Order/OrderDetail')
WITH (ProductID int '../ProductID',
    ProductName varchar(30) '../ProductName',
    SalesID varchar(10) '../SalesID',
    OrderID int '../@OrderID',
    CustomerID int 'CustomerID');

EXEC sp_xml_removedocument @hdoc;
```

Figure 8-5. Use of ColPattern in WITH clause

You now have all the data. The changes in Listing 8-5 include the ColPattern values but also a change to the rowpattern. The rowpattern is now /Orders/Order/OrderDetail. This allows you to parse the XML document to the lowest element and then work your way up through the XML hierarchy. If any columns are in-line attributes, you will need preface them with an @ sign.

■ **Note** When including ColPatterns for columns in your WITH clause, you don't need to include the mapping parameter in OPENXML. This is because using ColPattern defaults OPENXML to element-centric mapping.

Retrieving Data as XML Using the FOR XML Clause

As mentioned, XML is normally handled in one of two ways. The first way is when you have a XML document and you need to shred it into a table format. For this method, use the OPENXML command. The other way is to convert table data into a XML document using FOR XML.

The FOR XML clause is actually part of a SELECT statement. A SELECT statement returns data from a table in rowset format. Adding the FOR XML clause at the end converts the rowset data into XML format. The command has four modes and each mode provides you a different level of control. The modes determine how much control you want when converting rowset data containing columns and rows into a XML document consisting of elements and attributes. The four modes are RAW, AUTO, EXPLICIT, and PATH. There are also a number of mode options that will be discussed throughout the chapter.

Throughout this chapter I'll be discussing the four modes. Each one provides certain advantages and disadvantages. Table 8-1 gives a brief summary of each.

Table 8-1. FOR XML Modes

MODE	Description
RAW	Easiest to use but provides the least flexibility. Each row creates a single element.
AUTO	Similar to RAW but provides more flexibility. Each column returned is an element and each referenced table with a column in the SELECT clause is an element.
EXPLICIT	Difficult to use but provides improved granularity for creating complex XML documents. Allows you to mix attributes and elements but requires specific syntax structure in the SELECT clause.
PATH	It is recommended to use the PATH mode instead of EXPLICIT. This mode provides similar functionality but with less complexity.

FOR XML RAW

The RAW mode is the simplest mode but provides the least flexibility when generating XML from rowsets. Listing 8-6 shows an example; this mode is an excellent means to quickly generate XML documents from tables. Figure 8-6 shows the initial output and Listing 8-7 shows the results of clicking on the XML hyperlink.

Listing 8-6. *Generating XML Using the FOR XML RAW Command*

```
USE AdventureWorks2012;
GO

SELECT TOP 5 FirstName
FROM Person.Person
FOR XML RAW;
```

Results

XML_F52E2B61-18A1-11d1-B105-00805F49916B
1   `<row FirstName="Syed"/><row FirstName="Catherine"/><row FirstName="Kim"/><row FirstName="Kim"/><row FirstName="Kim"/>`

Figure 8-6. *Using FOR XML RAW*

Listing 8-7. *XML Output Using the FOR XML RAW Command*

```
<row FirstName="Syed" />
<row FirstName="Catherine" />
<row FirstName="Kim" />
<row FirstName="Kim" />
<row FirstName="Kim" />
```

As you can tell from the output in Listing 8-7, RAW mode produces a single node "row" for each row returned and each element has a column-based attribute. By default, RAW mode produces an attribute-centric XML document. Remember that attribute-centric XML consists of inline attributes. Also, each node is named row, which is not very helpful when describing the contents of the XML data. To create an element-centric XML document with a more friendly node name, you will need to include the ELEMENTS option along with a node definition. Listing 8-8 shows an example.

Listing 8-8. *Creating Element-Centric XML Using XML RAW*

```
--Run this query

USE AdventureWorks2012;
GO

SELECT TOP 5 FirstName, LastName
FROM Person.Person
FOR XML RAW ('NAME'), ELEMENTS
```

The following is some of the output:

```
<NAME>
  <FirstName>Syed</FirstName>
  <LastName>Abbas</LastName>
</NAME>
<NAME>
  <FirstName>Catherine</FirstName>
  <LastName>Abel</LastName>
</NAME>
<NAME>
  <FirstName>Kim</FirstName>
  <LastName>Abercrombie</LastName>
</NAME>
<NAME>
  <FirstName>Kim</FirstName>
  <LastName>Abercrombie</LastName>
</NAME>
<NAME>
  <FirstName>Kim</FirstName>
  <LastName>Abercrombie</LastName>
</NAME>
```

In Listing 8-8 the FOR XML RAW clause takes NAME as an input. This defines the node name. The ELEMENTS option converts the columns from attributes to elements within the NAME node.

■ **Note** It is possible to mix attribute-centric mapping with element-centric mapping using FOR XML. To do so requires using nested FOR XML queries. Nested FOR XML queries are beyond the scope of this book. Actually, using the PATH option with nested FOR XML is considered better practice than using the EXPLICIT option. You can get more information at http://msdn.microsoft.com/en-us/library/bb510436(v=SQL.110).aspx.

Keep in mind that even with the ability to use FOR XML RAW to create attribute-centric XML or element-centric XML, the mode still limits your ability to form complex XML documents. FOR XML RAW is well-suited for testing or creating simple XML documents. For more complex XML documents, you will want to work with the other available modes.

FOR XML AUTO

Another option is AUTO mode. This mode is similar to RAW (and just as easy to use) but produces a more complex XML document based on your SELECT query. AUTO creates an element for each table in the FROM clause that has a column in the SELECT clause. Each column in the SELECT clause is represented as an attribute in the XML document. Look at Listing 8-9 to see an example of FOR XML in use. Some example output follows the listing.

Listing 8-9. Using AUTO Mode

```
--Execute the query

USE AdventureWorks2012;
GO

SELECT CustomerID, LastName, FirstName, MiddleName
FROM Person.Person AS p
INNER JOIN Sales.Customer AS c ON p.BusinessEntityID = c.PersonID
FOR XML AUTO;
```

The following is an example of the output that you'll get from executing the query in Listing 8-9:

```
<c CustomerID="29485">
  <p LastName="Abel" FirstName="Catherine" MiddleName="R." />
</c>
<c CustomerID="29486">
  <p LastName="Abercrombie" FirstName="Kim" />
</c>
<c CustomerID="29487">
  <p LastName="Acevedo" FirstName="Humberto" />
</c>
<c CustomerID="29484">
  <p LastName="Achong" FirstName="Gustavo" />
</c>
<c CustomerID="29488">
  <p LastName="Ackerman" FirstName="Pilar" />
</c>
<c CustomerID="28866">
  <p LastName="Adams" FirstName="Aaron" MiddleName="B" />
</c>
<c CustomerID="13323">
  <p LastName="Adams" FirstName="Adam" />
</c>
<c CustomerID="21139">
  <p LastName="Adams" FirstName="Alex" MiddleName="C" />
</c>
<c CustomerID="29170">
  <p LastName="Adams" FirstName="Alexandra" MiddleName="J" />
</c>
<c CustomerID="19419">
  <p LastName="Adams" FirstName="Allison" MiddleName="L" />
</c>
```

Listing 8-10 shows how AUTO mode converted the tables Customer and Person into elements. SQL Server was intelligent enough to link the corresponding columns as attributes in the respective elements. For example, CustomerID is a column in the Sales.Customer table so AUTO mode created CustomerID as an attribute in the Customer element. The AUTO mode would continue to expand the XML document for each table and column you add to the query.

Now add the ELEMENTS option like you did with RAW mode to see how it affects the XML output.

Listing 8-10. Using AUTO Mode with ELEMENTS Option

```
--Run the query

USE AdventureWorks2012;
GO

SELECT CustomerID, LastName, FirstName, MiddleName
FROM Person.Person AS Person
INNER JOIN Sales.Customer AS Customer ON Person.BusinessEntityID = Customer.PersonID
FOR XML AUTO, ELEMENTS;
```

The following is some of the query output from Listing 8-10:

```
<Customer>
  <CustomerID>29485</CustomerID>
  <Person>
    <LastName>Abel</LastName>
    <FirstName>Catherine</FirstName>
    <MiddleName>R.</MiddleName>
  </Person>
</Customer>
<Customer>
  <CustomerID>29486</CustomerID>
  <Person>
    <LastName>Abercrombie</LastName>
    <FirstName>Kim</FirstName>
  </Person>
</Customer>
<Customer>
  <CustomerID>29487</CustomerID>
  <Person>
    <LastName>Acevedo</LastName>
    <FirstName>Humberto</FirstName>
  </Person>
</Customer>
```

Just as in the example using RAW mode, the ELEMENTS option displays columns as elements for each node instead of the default attribute mapping. One difference is the exclusion of the ElementName option that you saw in the previous RAW mode (RAW(NAME)). You can leave this out because AUTO mode automatically names the nodes after the name of each table; in fact, you will receive a syntax error if you try to use the option.

FOR XML EXPLICIT

The most complicated means to convert table data into XML is by using the FOR XML EXPLICIT mode, but with complexity comes flexibility and control. The complexity lies in the rigorous requirement that you structure your SELECT clause so that the output forms a *universal table*.

As you can see from previous examples, XML is based on hierarchies. Listing 8-11 shows a Customer element or node and under Customer is a sub-element called Person. Person is a child element of Customer. In order to create a similar XML document using the EXPLICIT mode, you need to define this relationship in the universal table. This is done by creating two columns called Tag and Parent. Think of this as the relationship between manager and employee. A manager would have a tag ID of 1 and the employee would have a tag ID of 2. Since you are only concerned about the manager level in the hierarchy, the manager would have a parent of 0 (NULL) but the employee would have a parent of 1. Listing 8-11 shows a simple example.

Listing 8-11. Using XML FOR EXPLICIT

```
--Run the query

USE AdventureWorks2012;
GO

SELECT 1 AS Tag,
       NULL       AS Parent,
       CustomerID AS [Customer!1!CustomerID],
       NULL       AS [Name!2!FName],
       NULL       AS [Name!2!LName]
FROM Sales.Customer AS C
INNER JOIN Person.Person AS P
ON  P.BusinessEntityID = C.PersonID
UNION
SELECT 2 AS Tag,
       1 AS Parent,
       CustomerID,
       FirstName,
       LastName
FROM Person.Person P
INNER JOIN Sales.Customer AS C
ON P.BusinessEntityID = C.PersonID
ORDER BY [Customer!1!CustomerID], [Name!2!FName]
FOR XML EXPLICIT;
```

The results are as follows:

```
<Customer CustomerID="11000">
  <Name FName="Jon" LName="Yang" />
</Customer>
<Customer CustomerID="11001">
  <Name FName="Eugene" LName="Huang" />
</Customer>
<Customer CustomerID="11002">
  <Name FName="Ruben" LName="Torres" />
</Customer>
<Customer CustomerID="11003">
  <Name FName="Christy" LName="Zhu" />
</Customer>
<Customer CustomerID="11004">
  <Name FName="Elizabeth" LName="Johnson" />
</Customer>
<Customer CustomerID="11005">
  <Name FName="Julio" LName="Ruiz" />
</Customer>
```

By using the UNION statement you can define different Tag and Parent values in each SELECT clause. This allows you to nest the XML and create hierarchies. In this case you assigned to Customer a Tag of 1 and Parent as NULL. In the next SELECT statement you assigned Name a Tag of 2 and Parent of 1. Table 8-2 shows what the universal table looks like for CustomerID 11008 in Listing 8-11.

Table 8-2. Example Universal Table for the EXPLICIT Mode

Tag	Parent	Customer!1!CustomerID	Name!2!FName	Name!2!LName
1	NULL	11008	NULL	NULL
2	1	NULL	"Rob"	"Verhoff"

In addition to the Tag and Parent values, the ElementName!TagNumber!Attribute defines where in the hierarchy each column exists. The value Customer!1!CustomerID tells you the value belongs with the Customer element, the !1! tells you it is Tag 1 and CustomerID is the attribute.

■ **Note** There is an optional value called Directive when creating the universal table. The format is ElementName!TagNumber!Attribute!Directive. They allow you to control how to encode values (ID, IDREF, IDREFS) and how to map string data to XML (hide, element, elementxsinil, xml, xmltext, and cdata). The details of each can be found at http://msdn.microsoft.com/en-us/library/ms189068(v=SQL.110).aspx or in *Pro T-SQL 2012 Programmer's Guide* (Apress, 2012).

As you can readily see, using the EXPLICIT mode can quickly become cumbersome. What it provides in flexibility it more than makes up in complexity. So for complex XML documents that mix and match attributes and elements, you will want to use the FOR XML PATH mode with nested XML.

FOR XML PATH

As mentioned, if you need to develop complex XML documents from table data, the best tool to use is the FOR XML PATH mode. This is primarily because PATH mode takes advantage of the XPath standard. XPath is a W3C standard for navigating XML hierarchies. XPath includes other useful tools such as XQuery and XPointer.

■ **Note** W3C, or World Wide Web Consortium (www.w3.org), is a group of professionals (both volunteer and paid) who help to define Internet standards. Without a central organization developing standards it would be difficult for the Internet to exist and thrive. XPath is a standard developed for navigating XML documents. This is just one if the items that makes XML such a powerful tool for sharing data between systems around the world running on differing platforms.

Listing 8-12 demonstrates a simple example of the PATH mode. This example runs a SELECT statement against the Prodution.Product table.

Listing 8-12. *Simple FOR XML PATH Query*

```
--Run the query

USE AdventureWorks2012;
GO

SELECT p.FirstName,
       p.LastName,
       s.Bonus,
       s.SalesYTD
FROM Person.Person p
JOIN Sales.SalesPerson s
ON p.BusinessEntityID = s.BusinessEntityID
FOR XML PATH
```

The output from the query in Listing 8-12 will appear as follows:

```
<row>
  <FirstName>Stephen</FirstName>
  <LastName>Jiang</LastName>
  <Bonus>0.0000</Bonus>
  <SalesYTD>559697.5639</SalesYTD>
</row>
<row>
  <FirstName>Michael</FirstName>
  <LastName>Blythe</LastName>
  <Bonus>4100.0000</Bonus>
  <SalesYTD>3763178.1787</SalesYTD>
</row>
<row>
  <FirstName>Linda</FirstName>
  <LastName>Mitchell</LastName>
  <Bonus>2000.0000</Bonus>
  <SalesYTD>4251368.5497</SalesYTD>
</row>
<row>
  <FirstName>Jillian</FirstName>
  <LastName>Carson</LastName>
  <Bonus>2500.0000</Bonus>
  <SalesYTD>3189418.3662</SalesYTD>
</row>
```

Without any modification, the XML PATH mode will create a simple element-centric XML document. Listing 8-12 produces an element for each row. As always, you may want to complicate things a bit. Listing 8-13 demonstrates how you can easily mix and match element and attribute-centric XML document styles.

Listing 8-13. *Defining XML Hierarchy Using PATH Mode*

```
--Run the query

USE AdventureWorks2012;
GO

SELECT p.FirstName "@FirstName",
        p.LastName "@LastName",
            s.Bonus "Sales/Bonus",
            s.SalesYTD "Sales/YTD"
FROM Person.Person p
JOIN Sales.SalesPerson s
ON p.BusinessEntityID = s.BusinessEntityID
FOR XML PATH
```

The following is some example output:

```
<row FirstName="Stephen" LastName="Jiang">
  <Sales>
    <Bonus>0.0000</Bonus>
    <YTD>559697.5639</YTD>
  </Sales>
</row>
<row FirstName="Michael" LastName="Blythe">
  <Sales>
    <Bonus>4100.0000</Bonus>
    <YTD>3763178.1787</YTD>
  </Sales>
</row>
<row FirstName="Linda" LastName="Mitchell">
  <Sales>
    <Bonus>2000.0000</Bonus>
    <YTD>4251368.5497</YTD>
  </Sales>
</row>
<row FirstName="Jillian" LastName="Carson">
  <Sales>
    <Bonus>2500.0000</Bonus>
    <YTD>3189418.3662</YTD>
  </Sales>
</row>
```

If you think the SELECT statement in Listing 8-13 looks familiar, you're right. A similar query was used in Listing 8-5 when navigating an XML document in the OPENXML command using the WITH statement. Keep in mind when mapping columns to a XML document that any column defined with an @ sign becomes an attribute of the node and any column defined with a "/" becomes a separate element. Similar to the OPENXML example, if you add a name value to the PATH mode (FOR XML PATH ('Product'), you can name the root node from "row" to "Product." Listing 8-14 shows what this looks like.

Listing 8-14. Simple FOR XML PATH Query with NAME Option

```
--Run the query

USE AdventureWorks2012;
GO

SELECT ProductID "@ProductID",
       Name "Product/ProductName",
       Color "Product/Color"
FROM Production.Product
FOR XML PATH ('Product')
```

The query output is as follows:

```
<Product ProductID="1">
  <Product>
    <ProductName>Adjustable Race</ProductName>
  </Product>
</Product>
<Product ProductID="2">
  <Product>
    <ProductName>Bearing Ball</ProductName>
  </Product>
</Product>
<Product ProductID="3">
  <Product>
    <ProductName>BB Ball Bearing</ProductName>
  </Product>
</Product>
<Product ProductID="4">
  <Product>
    <ProductName>Headset Ball Bearings</ProductName>
  </Product>
</Product>
<Product ProductID="316">
  <Product>
    <ProductName>Blade</ProductName>
  </Product>
</Product>
```

When choosing from the legacy XML methods, the PATH mode is the preferred means to generate complex XML documents. It allows for granular control of structuring the document but is not overly complicated as the EXPLICIT mode. Beyond the previous legacy modes Microsoft has developed even more robust methods of generating and handling XML in SQL Server.

XML Data Type

Though OPENXML and FOR XML are still available in SQL 2012, you should utilize them mostly for handling legacy code; I suggest working with the newer methods of handling XML documents. Beginning with SQL 2005, you can define a column as XML when creating a table object. Doing so specifically tells SQL

Server to treat the data in the column as XML. You can also use the XML built-in data type when defining variables for stored procedures and functions. Data types are discussed in more detail in Chapter 10. Listing 8-15 creates a sample table with a column defined as a built-in XML data type.

Listing 8-15. Built-in XML Data Type

```
USE tempdb;
GO

CREATE TABLE ProductList (ProductInfo XML);
```

You'll find XML data types scattered throughout the AdventureWorks2012 database. For example, the Person.Person table has two columns defined as XML: AdditionalContactInfo and Demographics. The AdditionalContactInfo column is NULL but is useful for working with XML inserts and updates while the Demographics column shows how the data is, in fact, stored as XML. In the past, this data would be stored as text. Keep in mind the following rules around a column with the XML data type:

- It can't be used as a primary or foreign key.

- You can't convert or cast the column to a text or ntext. It is recommended to use varchar(max) or nvarchar(max). Text and ntext will be deprecated in future versions of SQL Server.

- Column can't be used in a GROUP BY statement.

- The column size can't be greater than 2GB.

Let's now create a table with an XML column and populate it with some data. Type in and execute the code in Listing 8-16.

Listing 8-16. Using XML as a Data Type

```
USE AdventureWorks2012;
GO

--1
CREATE TABLE #CustomerList (CustomerInfo XML);

--2
DECLARE @XMLInfo XML;

--3
SET @XMLInfo = (SELECT CustomerID, LastName, FirstName, MiddleName
FROM Person.Person AS p
INNER JOIN Sales.Customer AS c ON p.BusinessEntityID = c.PersonID
FOR XML PATH);

--4
INSERT INTO #CustomerList(CustomerInfo)
VALUES(@XMLInfo);

--5
SELECT CustomerInfo FROM #CustomerList;
```

```
DROP TABLE #CustomerList;
```

Figure 8-7 shows the results. Statement 1 creates a table with an XML column. Statement 2 declares a variable with the XML data type. Statement 3 saves the information in XML format about each customer from the Sales.Customer and Person.Person tables into a variable. The data comes from the same query that you saw in the previous section. Statement 4 inserts a row into the #CustomerList table using the variable. Query 5 returns the CustomerInfo column from the table without using the FOR XML clause. Since the table stores the data in XML format, the statement looks just like a regular SELECT statement yet returns the data as XML.

Figure 8-7. *The results of using the XML data type*

▓ **Tip** When working with large character data types like XML you no longer should use the text or ntext data types. Both of these data types will be deprecated and replaced with varchar(max) and nvarchar(max). The XML data type can't be converted to text.

XML Methods

XML methods provide ways to handle XML in the XML data type. They allow you to update the XML, convert the XML to rowsets, check whether the XML has nodes, and many other useful options. They provide many of the same functionalities as you saw with the legacy XML commands. Table 8-3 summarizes these methods and I'll discuss each of them.

Table 8-3. *XML Data Type Methods*

Method	Description
query(xquery)	Executes an XQuery against the XML data type. Returns an XML type.
value(xquery, sqltype)	Executes an XQuery against the XML data type and returns a SQL scalar value.
exists(xquery)	Executes an XQuery against the XML data type and returns a bit value representing a criteria of 1 if there is at least one node, 2 if there are no nodes, and NULL if the XML data type in the xquery is NULL.
modify(xml_dml)	Used to update XML stored as the XML data type.
nodes()	This method is what you will use to convert (shred) an XML data type into a rowset (table). If you want to convert XML into a relational form, use this method.

Query Method

Use the query() method when you need to extract elements from an XML data type. You have the capability to extract specific elements and create new XML documents. Listing 8-17 demonstrates the use of a simple query() method you will use in this chapter to build on using some of the other methods.

Listing 8-17. Using the query() Method Against XML Data

```
--Run query

USE AdventureWorks2012;
GO

SELECT Demographics.query('declare namespace ss =
"http://schemas.microsoft.com/sqlserver/2004/07/adventure-works/StoreSurvey";
<Store AnnualSales = "{ /ss:StoreSurvey/ss:AnnualSales }"
       BankName = "{ /ss:StoreSurvey/ss:BankName }" />
') AS Result
FROM Sales.Store;
```

The following is the output:

```
<Store AnnualSales="800000" BankName="United Security" />
<Store AnnualSales="800000" BankName="International Bank" />
<Store AnnualSales="800000" BankName="Primary Bank &amp; Reserve" />
<Store AnnualSales="800000" BankName="International Security" />
<Store AnnualSales="800000" BankName="Guardian Bank" />
```

Listing 8-17 brings up a concept not yet discussed: namespaces. Namespaces can be confusing when first learning XML but the concept is simple. XML uses namespaces to uniquely define element and attribute names in an XML document. The classic example is the element <table>. If the XML document is used by a furniture company, <table> would mean a piece of furniture. If the XML document is used by a company writing data modeling software, <table> would mean a database table. In this case, the furniture company and the data modeling company will use different namespaces. In order to facilitate data transfers and communication, all furniture companies may use the same namespace so that <table> always refers to the same thing.

In your query, you refer to the namespace http://schemas.microsoft.com/sqlserver/2004/07/adventure-works/StoreSurvey. This namespace was defined for you in the stored XML. In this case, the namespace points to a Microsoft site, but namespaces don't have to actually point to anything and there is no validation executed against the XML data as a result of including a namespace. They do have to take the format of a URI and this can sometimes be confusing since namespaces (like the one in the query) point to an actual web site. The namespace in Listing 8-17 must be included in your query because the XML data includes it, which makes typed XML (untyped XML has no schema or namespace association).

Once you declare the required namespace, you can then refer to the XML elements using the namespace prefix. In the previous example, you use the prefix /ss to refer to each element. For example, /ss:StoreSurvey/ss:AnnualSales grabs the AnnualSales element from the XML. The braces symbol {} tell the query() method to insert a value into the output.

■ **Note** XML can be typed or untyped. What this basically means is whether or not the XML document is associated with a schema. A schema helps to define both the elements and the XMLstructure. We won't go into detail of the differences in this chapter but more information can be found at http://msdn.microsoft.com/en-us/library/ms184277(v=SQL.110).aspx.

The value() Method

The value() method uses XQuery against an XML document to return a scalar value. In the value() statement you specify the data type you want returned. Take a look at Listing 8-18 for a quick example using some of the same data you saw earlier in Listing 8-17. Listing 8-18 shows a query and Figure 8-8 shows the results.

Listing 8-18. Using the value() Method

```
USE AdventureWorks2012;
GO

SELECT Demographics.value('declare namespace ss =
"http://schemas.microsoft.com/sqlserver/2004/07/adventure-works/StoreSurvey";
(/ss:StoreSurvey/ss:BankName)[1]', 'varchar(100)') AS Result
FROM Sales.Store
```

Results

	Result
25	Guardian Bank
26	International Bank
27	Primary Bank & Reserve
28	International Security
29	Primary Bank & Reserve
30	International Security
31	International Bank
32	International Bank
33	United Security
34	Reserve Security
35	Primary International
36	Primary Bank & Reserve
37	Reserve Security
38	Primary Bank & Reserve
39	International Security
40	United Security
41	International Bank

Figure 8-8. Partial results of using value() method

Listing 8-18 is similar but only pulls the BankName data from the XML data type. The value() method still declares the namespace and also uses the same XQuery syntax. The difference is the value() method pulls back the data as varchar(100) data type and not as an XML document. The other difference to note is the index [1] in the XQuery text. This is required in order to ensure the expression returns a singleton, or a single example of the value (in the event there are different values for BankName in the XML document).

The exist() Method

The exist() method works similarly to the T-SQL EXIST statement. The method will check to see whether or not a value is true or false. If the value is true, it returns a 1; if the value is false, it returns a 0. If the value is NULL, the method returns NULL. Let's take a look at an example in Listing 8-19 and the results in Figure 8-9.

Listing 8-19. Using the exist() Method

```
USE AdventureWorks2012;
GO

SELECT Demographics.value('declare namespace ss =
"http://schemas.microsoft.com/sqlserver/2004/07/adventure-works/StoreSurvey";
(/ss:StoreSurvey/ss:BankName)[1]', 'varchar(100)') AS LargeAnnualSales
FROM Sales.Store
WHERE Demographics.exist('declare namespace ss =
"http://schemas.microsoft.com/sqlserver/2004/07/adventure-works/StoreSurvey";
/ss:StoreSurvey/ss:AnnualSales [. = 3000000]') = 1
```

Results

	LargeAnnualSales
1	Primary Bank & Reserve
2	Reserve Security
3	Primary International
4	Guardian Bank
5	International Security
6	Primary Bank & Reserve
7	International Bank
8	United Security
9	Reserve Security
10	Primary International
11	Primary Bank & Reserve
12	Guardian Bank
13	International Security
14	Primary International
15	Guardian Bank
16	International Security
17	International Security

Figure 8-9. Partial output of exist() method

Listing 8-19 begins by using the same value method but then uses the exist() method as filter to only return the BankNames with AnnualSales equal to 3 million. Remember the exist() method returns either 1 if true, 0 if false, or NULL if NULL. Since you are requiring a return of all true values, you set the exist() method to equal 1.

The modify() Method

You will use the modify() method if you want to change XML data stored as an XML data type. The modify() method is similar to using update, insert, and delete commands. One primary difference is the modify() method can only be used in a SET clause. Listing 8-20 shows the different ways to use the modify() method to change data in an XML document assigned to a variable.

Listing 8-20. Inserting, Updating, and Deleting XML Using the modify() Method

```
DECLARE @x xml =
'<Product ProductID = "521487">
  <ProductType>Paper Towels</ProductType>
  <Price>15</Price>
  <Vendor>Johnson Paper</Vendor>
  <VendorID>47</VendorID>
  <QuantityOnHand>500</QuantityOnHand>
</Product>'

SELECT @x

/* inserting data into xml with the modify method */
SET @x.modify('
insert <WarehouseID>77</WarehouseID>
into (/Product)[1]')

SELECT @x

/* updating xml with the modify method */
SET @x.modify('
replace value of (/Product/QuantityOnHand[1]/text())[1]
with "250"')

SELECT @x

/* deleting xml with the modify method */
SET @x.modify('
delete (/Product/Price)[1]')

SELECT @x
```

The first SELECT @x statement produces the original XML as it was declared in the variable. Listing 8-21 repeats the statement.

Listing 8-21. Declaring and Selecting XML Data

```
--Run the query

DECLARE @x xml =
'<Product ProductID = "521487">
  <ProductType>Paper Towels</ProductType>
  <Price>15</Price>
  <Vendor>Johnson Paper</Vendor>
  <VendorID>47</VendorID>
  <QuantityOnHand>500</QuantityOnHand>
</Product>'

SELECT @x
```

The query output appears as follows:

```
<Product ProductID="521487">
  <ProductType>Paper Towels</ProductType>
  <Price>15</Price>
  <Vendor>Johnson Paper</Vendor>
  <VendorID>47</VendorID>
  <QuantityOnHand>500</QuantityOnHand>
</Product>
```

The next two statements in Listing 8-22 uses the modify() method to insert a new element into the XML document and then select the variable. The element you insert is the WarehouseID and you insert it under the Product root.

Listing 8-22. Declaring and Inserting XML Data

```
--Run the query

SET @x.modify('
insert <WarehouseID>77</WarehouseID>
into (/Product)[1]')

SELECT @x
```

The results from the INSERT command should look as follows:

```
<Product ProductID="521487">
  <ProductType>Paper Towels</ProductType>
  <Price>15</Price>
  <Vendor>Johnson Paper</Vendor>
  <VendorID>47</VendorID>
  <QuantityOnHand>500</QuantityOnHand>
  <WarehouseID>77</WarehouseID>
</Product>
```

The next two statements update the XML by using the REPLACE command and then select the variable. In this example, you change the OnHandQuantity from 500 to 250. In your XQuery, you have to specify the element as a singleton as well as the path, and you also include the `text()` function. Listing 8-23 shows the query and the results.

Listing 8-23. Declaring and Inserting XML Data

```
--Run the query

SET @x.modify('
replace value of (/Product/QuantityOnHand[1]/text())[1]
with "250"')

SELECT @x
```

The following are the results:

```
<Product ProductID="521487">
  <ProductType>Paper Towels</ProductType>
  <Price>15</Price>
  <Vendor>Johnson Paper</Vendor>
  <VendorID>47</VendorID>
  <QuantityOnHand>250</QuantityOnHand>
</Product>
```

The last step in the example shows the `DELETE` statement in the `modify()` method. The query uses the familiar `DELETE` statement along with the XQuery path. In this example, you completely remove the Price element from the XML document. Again, you have to specify the singleton value of [1] in your path. Listing 8-24 shows the query.

Listing 8-24. *Declaring and Inserting XML Data*

```
--Run the query

SET @x.modify('
delete (/Product/Price)[1]')

SELECT @x
```

And the following is the output:

```
<Product ProductID="521487">
  <ProductType>Paper Towels</ProductType>
  <Vendor>Johnson Paper</Vendor>
  <VendorID>47</VendorID>
  <QuantityOnHand>500</QuantityOnHand>
</Product>
```

Node Method

The final method we'll discuss is the `node` method. This method is used when shredding XML stored as a data type into a relational format. Listing 8-25 shows a brief example that we'll discuss in detail. Figure 8-10 shows the partial result of executing the code in the listing.

Listing 8-25. Shredding XML Using the node() Method

```
USE AdventureWorks2012;
GO

SELECT Name,
       SalesPersonID,
       AnnualSales.query('.') AS XMLResult
FROM Sales.Store
CROSS APPLY
Demographics.nodes('declare namespace ss =
"http://schemas.microsoft.com/sqlserver/2004/07/adventure-works/StoreSurvey";
/ss:StoreSurvey/ss:AnnualSales') AS NodeTable(AnnualSales)
```

▦ Results

	Name	SalesPersonID	XMLResult
1	Next-Door Bike Store	279	<p1:AnnualSales xmlns:p1="http://schemas.micros...
2	Professional Sales and Service	276	<p1:AnnualSales xmlns:p1="http://schemas.micros...
3	Riders Company	277	<p1:AnnualSales xmlns:p1="http://schemas.micros...
4	The Bike Mechanics	275	<p1:AnnualSales xmlns:p1="http://schemas.micros...
5	Nationwide Supply	286	<p1:AnnualSales xmlns:p1="http://schemas.micros...
6	Area Bike Accessories	281	<p1:AnnualSales xmlns:p1="http://schemas.micros...
7	Bicycle Accessories and Kits	283	<p1:AnnualSales xmlns:p1="http://schemas.micros...
8	Clamps & Brackets Co.	275	<p1:AnnualSales xmlns:p1="http://schemas.micros...
9	Valley Bicycle Specialists	277	<p1:AnnualSales xmlns:p1="http://schemas.micros...
10	New Bikes Company	279	<p1:AnnualSales xmlns:p1="http://schemas.micros...
11	Vinyl and Plastic Goods Corporation	282	<p1:AnnualSales xmlns:p1="http://schemas.micros...
12	Top of the Line Bikes	288	<p1:AnnualSales xmlns:p1="http://schemas.micros...
13	Fun Toys and Bikes	281	<p1:AnnualSales xmlns:p1="http://schemas.micros...
14	Great Bikes	283	<p1:AnnualSales xmlns:p1="http://schemas.micros...
15	Metropolitan Sales and Rental	275	<p1:AnnualSales xmlns:p1="http://schemas.micros...

Figure 8-10. Partial result of using the node() method

The first part of the statement executes a familiar SELECT statement against the table. Note that the only way to retrieve data using the node() is to use another XML method. You can use query(), value(), exists(), and nodes() to get the result, but you can't use the modify() method. For example, the following code shows the section from Listing 8-25 in which the columns are defined in the SELECT clause:

```
SELECT Name,
       SalesPersonID,
       AnnualSales.query('.') AS XMLResult
       FROM Sales.Store
```

I've provided the column with the aliases of AnnualSales and XMLResult. The XMLResult alias will be used for the column name while the AnnualSales alias will be used as the name for the table created by the node() method.

The second section of the statement begins with the CROSS APPLY command and then the actual node() method statement. The CROSS APPLY command (shown next) allows for the nodes() table to be input for the query() method and then have results combined into a single table.

```
CROSS APPLY
Demographics.nodes('
declare namespace ss = "http://schemas.microsoft.com/sqlserver/2004/07/adventure-
works/StoreSurvey";
/ss:StoreSurvey/ss:AnnualSales') AS NodeTable(AnnualSales)
```

The actual node() method format should look familiar by now. You again declare your namespace and access the elements using the XQuery path. When using the node() method, you need to alias the virtual table (in this case NodeTable) and reference the virtual column name in the table, AnnualSales.

EXERCISES

Use the AdventureWorks2012 database to complete these exercises.

1. Use OPENXML to produce a table from the following XML document. Make sure you return all elements and attributes. (HINT: You will need to use the rowpattern option.)

```
<Company>
    <Employee EmployeeID="56">
        <Department>Accounting</Department>
        <YearsofService>10</YearsofService>
        <ManagerID>5</ManagerID>
            <PayScale>
                    <PayLevelID>8</PayLevelID>
                    <YearlyBonusPct>2.5</YearlyBonusPct>
                    </PayScale>
    </Employee>
</Company>
```

2. Write a SELECT query with a FOR XML clause that pulls the Name and ListPrice from the Production.Product table. Use the same query but display the results as attribute-centric.

3. Modify the following SELECT statement to use the PATH mode. Make FirstName and LastName an attribute of Person and make JobTitle and Gender elements under a node called Employee.

```
SELECT p.FirstName, p.LastName, e.JobTitle, e.Gender
FROM Person.Person p
JOIN HumanResources.Employee e
ON p.BusinessEntityID = e.BusinessEntityID
```

4. Use the XML declared in the variable for Listing 8-18 for the following exercises:

a. Use the modify() method to delete the QuantityOnHand.

b. Use the modify() method to insert an element named VendorZipCode. Give it a value of 63512.

c. Use the `modify()` method to update the VendorID to a value of 65.

Summary

This chapter only scratches the surface of SQL Server's capabilities in handling XML data. The XML data and its associated methods allow much greater flexibility and control than the legacy OPENXML and FOR XML commands. I strongly suggest using the new methods of `value()`, `modify()`, `exist()`, and `nodes()` over the legacy commands especially when implementing the XML data type.

CHAPTER 9

Moving Logic to the Database

So far, you have worked exclusively with tables by using Data Manipulation Language (DML) statements. You have learned to manipulate data by inserting new rows and updating or deleting existing rows. You can use many other objects in a SQL Server database to make your database applications more efficient and secure. This chapter teaches you how to add restrictions to tables and to create other objects that help to enforce key business rules. In this chapter, you will learn about Data Definition Language (DDL) statements and learn about constraints on tables, views, stored procedures, user-defined functions, and user-defined types. You will also learn about triggers, special objects that fire when data is modified. Because SQL Server provides so many choices for creating these objects, this chapter doesn't attempt to explore every possible option. The chapter does, however, provide enough detail to teach you most of what you will encounter on your journey to becoming an expert T-SQL developer.

Tables

SQL Server and other database systems store data in tables. You have learned how to retrieve data from tables as well as how to insert, update, and delete data. Specifically, you learned how to create temporary tables in Chapter 7 and how to create tables using the SELECT INTO and CREATE TABLE syntax in Chapter 6. You might think of a table as just a way to store data, but you can also enforce some business rules based on constraints built into the table definition.

As a beginning T-SQL developer, you will most likely write T-SQL code against a database already in place, possibly from a software vendor or one created by a design team using data-modelling software to create the tables. Although your job description may not include writing scripts to create tables, you do need to understand how the table definition controls what data you can insert into a table and how you can update the data. This section covers many options available when creating or altering tables such as computed columns, primary keys, foreign keys, and other constraints. The point of this section is not to get you to memorize how to add keys and constraints but to understand the implications of having them in place.

Tip By using SQL Server Management Studio, you can script the commands to create existing tables and other objects in the database. This is a great way to learn how to write scripts and learn the syntax. To script the definition, right-click the object and select the "Script table as" menu.

Adding Check Constraints to a Table

As you know, each column in a table must have a specific data type and usually a maximum size that controls what data can be inserted or updated and whether a column may contain NULL values. For example, you can't add a non-numeric string to an INT column. It is also possible to further control what data you can add by defining check constraints. For example, you may want to restrict the values of a column to a particular range of values.

■ **Note** The NULL and NOT NULL options are also called *constraints*.

Here is the syntax to add a check constraint to a table when creating the table and later with an ALTER TABLE command:

```
--Adding during CREATE TABLE
CREATE TABLE <table name> (<col1> <data type>,<col2> <data type>,
    CONSTRAINT <constraint name> CHECK (<condition>))

--Adding during ALTER TABLE
CREATE TABLE <table name> (<col1> <data type>, <col2> <data type>)
ALTER TABLE <table name> ADD CONSTRAINT <constraint name> CHECK (<condition>)
```

The condition looks much like the criteria in a WHERE clause. Type in and execute the code in Listing 9-1 to learn how to add a constraint.

Listing 9-1. Adding a Check Constraint

```
USE tempdb;
GO
--1
IF OBJECT_ID('table1') IS NOT NULL BEGIN
    DROP TABLE table1;
END;

--2
CREATE TABLE table1 (col1 SMALLINT, col2 VARCHAR(20),
    CONSTRAINT ch_table1_col2_months
    CHECK (col2 IN ('January','February','March','April','May',
        'June','July','August','September','October',
        'November','December')
    )
 );

--3
ALTER TABLE table1 ADD CONSTRAINT ch_table1_col1
    CHECK (col1 BETWEEN 1 and 12);
```

```
PRINT 'January';
--4
INSERT INTO table1 (col1,col2)
VALUES (1,'January');

PRINT 'February';
--5
INSERT INTO table1 (col1,col2)
VALUES (2,'February');

PRINT 'March';
--6
INSERT INTO table1 (col1,col2)
VALUES (13,'March');

PRINT 'Change 2 to 20';
--7
UPDATE table1 SET col1 = 20;
```

Figure 9-1 shows the results. Code section 1 drops the table in case it already exists. Statement 2 creates table1 along with a constraint specifying that the exact months of the year may be entered into col2. Statement 3 adds another constraint to the table, specifying values for col1. Statements 4 to 6 insert new rows into table1. Only statement 5 succeeds because the values in 4 and 6 each violate one of the constraints. If the constraints had not been added to the table, these inserts would have worked. Statement 7 attempts to update the one successful row with an invalid col1. You can see all the error messages in Figure 9-1.

```
📄 Messages
  Janary
  Msg 547, Level 16, State 0, Line 21
  The INSERT statement conflicted with the CHECK constraint "ch_table1_col2_months".
  The conflict occurred in database "tempdb", table "dbo.table1", column 'col2'.
  The statement has been terminated.
  February
  March
  Msg 547, Level 16, State 0, Line 31
  The INSERT statement conflicted with the CHECK constraint "ch_table1_col1".
  The conflict occurred in database "tempdb", table "dbo.table1", column 'col1'.
  The statement has been terminated.
  Change 2 to 20
  Msg 547, Level 16, State 0, Line 36
  The UPDATE statement conflicted with the CHECK constraint "ch_table1_col1".
  The conflict occurred in database "tempdb", table "dbo.table1", column 'col1'.
  The statement has been terminated.
```

Figure 9-1. The results of attempting to violate check constraints

Adding UNIQUE Constraints

You can specify that a column or columns in a table contain unique values. Unlike primary keys, which you will learn more about in the next section, unique columns may contain one NULL value. In the case of multiple columns, you must decide whether to have a constraint on each column or a constraint that covers several columns. In the first case, each column value must be unique; in the second case, the combination of the column values must be unique. You can add UNIQUE constraints to tables when you create them or later with an ALTER TABLE statement. Here is the syntax:

```
--Adding individual constraints
CREATE TABLE <table name> (<col1> <data type> UNIQUE, <col2> <data type> UNIQUE)

--Adding a combination constraint
CREATE TABLE <table name> (<col1> <data type>, <col2> <data type>,
    CONSTRAINT <constraint name> UNIQUE (<col1>,<col2>))

--Add a constraint with ALTER TABLE
CREATE TABLE <table name> (<col1> <data type>, <col2> <data type>)
ALTER TABLE ADD CONSTRAINT <constraint name> UNIQUE (<col1>,<col2>)
```

The first syntax example creates a separate constraint on each column within the CREATE TABLE statement. The other two examples each create one constraint on a combination of the columns. If you don't specify a constraint name as in the first syntax example, SQL Server will come up with a name for you. Listing 9-2 contains example code showing how to create UNIQUE constraints. Type in and execute the code to learn more.

Listing 9-2. Creating Tables with UNIQUE Constraints

```
USE tempdb;
GO
--1
IF OBJECT_ID('table1') IS NOT NULL BEGIN
    DROP TABLE table1;
END;

--2
CREATE TABLE table1 (col1 INT UNIQUE,
    col2 VARCHAR(20), col3 DATETIME);
GO

--3
ALTER TABLE table1 ADD CONSTRAINT
    unq_table1_col2_col3 UNIQUE (col2,col3);

--4
PRINT 'Statement 4'
INSERT INTO table1(col1,col2,col3)
VALUES (1,2,'1/1/2009'),(2,2,'1/2/2009');

--5
PRINT 'Statement 5'
INSERT INTO table1(col1,col2,col3)
VALUES (3,2,'1/1/2009');

--6
PRINT 'Statement 6'
INSERT INTO table1(col1,col2,col3)
VALUES (1,2,'1/2/2009');
```

```
--7
PRINT 'Statement 7'
UPDATE table1 SET col3 = '1/2/2009'
WHERE col1 = 1;
```

Figure 9-2 shows the results. Code section 1 drops the table in case it already exists. Statement 2 creates table1 with three columns. It creates a UNIQUE constraint on col1. Statement 3 adds another UNIQUE constraint on the combination of columns col2 and col3. Statement 4 adds two rows to the table successfully. Statement 5 violates the constraint on col2 and col3. Statement 6 violates the constraint on col1. Statement 7 violates the constraint on col2 and col3 with an UPDATE to the table.

```
Messages
Statement 4
Statement 5
Msg 2627, Level 14, State 1, Line 14
Violation of UNIQUE KEY constraint 'unq_table1_col2_col3'.
Cannot insert duplicate key in object 'dbo.table1'. The duplicate key value is (2, Jan  1 2009 12:00AM).
The statement has been terminated.
Statement 6
Msg 2627, Level 14, State 1, Line 19
Violation of UNIQUE KEY constraint 'UQ__table1__357D0D3FA32C57C2'.
Cannot insert duplicate key in object 'dbo.table1'. The duplicate key value is (1).
The statement has been terminated.
Statement 7
Msg 2627, Level 14, State 1, Line 24
Violation of UNIQUE KEY constraint 'unq_table1_col2_col3'.
Cannot insert duplicate key in object 'dbo.table1'. The duplicate key value is (2, Jan  2 2009 12:00AM).
The statement has been terminated.
```

Figure 9-2. The results of adding UNIQUE constraints

Another interesting thing about UNIQUE constraints is that you will not see them in the Constraints section in SQL Server Management Studio. Instead, you will find them in the Indexes section. When creating a unique constraint, you are actually creating a unique index. Figure 9-3 shows the constraints, as indexes, added to table1.

Figure 9-3. The unique constraints defined on table1 are indexes.

Adding a Primary Key to a Table

Throughout this book, you have read about primary keys. You can use a primary key to uniquely define a row in a table. A primary key must have the following characteristics:

- A primary key may be made of one column or multiple columns, called a *composite key*.

- A table can have only one primary key.

- The values of a primary key must be unique.

- If the primary key is a composite key, the combination of the values must be unique.

- None of the columns making up a primary key can contain NULL values.

I once received a call from a developer asking me to remove the primary key from a table because it was preventing him from inserting rows into a table in one of our enterprise systems. He insisted that the table definition must be wrong. I spent ten minutes explaining that the primary key was preventing him from making a mistake and helped him figure out the correct statements. After this developer moved on to another company, I received almost the identical phone call from his replacement. *Primary keys and other constraints are there to ensure data consistency, not to make your job harder.*

You can add a primary key to a table when you create the table using the CREATE TABLE statement or later by using the ALTER TABLE statement. Here is the syntax:

```
--Single column key
CREATE TABLE <table name> (<column1> <data type> NOT NULL PRIMARY KEY
    [CLUSTERED|NONCLUSTERED] <column2> <data type>)

--Composite key
CREATE TABLE <table name>(<column1> <data type> NOT NULL,
    <column2> <data type> NOT NULL, <column3> <data type>,
    CONSTRAINT <constraint name> PRIMARY KEY [CLUSTERED|NONCLUSTERED]
    (<column1>,<column2>)
)

--Using ALTER TABLE
CREATE TABLE <table name>(<column1> <data type> NOT NULL,
    <column2> <data type>)

ALTER TABLE <table name> ADD CONSTRAINT <primary key name>
    PRIMARY KEY [CLUSTERED|NONCLUSTERED] (<column1>)
```

Take a look at the keys and indexes of the HumanResources.Department table in the AdventureWorks2012 database (see Figure 9-4). When you create a primary key, the database engine automatically creates an index composed of that key. One of the indexes, PK_Department_DepartmentID, is also the primary key composed of the DepartmentID column.

```
⊟ ▦ HumanResources.Department
  ⊞ 🗀 Columns
  ⊟ 🗀 Keys
       🔑 PK_Department_DepartmentID
  ⊞ 🗀 Constraints
  ⊞ 🗀 Triggers
  ⊟ 🗀 Indexes
       ⊞ AK_Department_Name (Unique, Non-Clustered)
       ⊞ PK_Department_DepartmentID (Clustered)
```

Figure 9-4. *The indexes of the HumanResources.Department table*

Listing 9-3 contains some examples that create tables with primary keys, either during the CREATE command or later with the ALTER command. Type in and execute the code to learn more.

Listing 9-3. *Creating Primary Keys*

```
USE tempdb;
GO

--1
IF OBJECT_ID('table1') IS NOT NULL BEGIN
    DROP TABLE table1;
END;

IF OBJECT_ID('table2') IS NOT NULL BEGIN
    DROP TABLE table2;
END;

IF OBJECT_ID('table3') IS NOT NULL BEGIN
    DROP TABLE table3;
END;

--2
CREATE TABLE table1 (col1 INT NOT NULL PRIMARY KEY,
    col2 VARCHAR(10));

--3
CREATE TABLE table2 (col1 INT NOT NULL,
    col2 VARCHAR(10) NOT NULL, col3 INT NULL,
    CONSTRAINT PK_table2_col1col2 PRIMARY KEY
    (col1, col2)
);

--4
CREATE TABLE table3 (col1 INT NOT NULL,
    col2 VARCHAR(10) NOT NULL, col3 INT NULL);

--5
ALTER TABLE table3 ADD CONSTRAINT PK_table3_col1col2
    PRIMARY KEY NONCLUSTERED (col1,col2);
```

Figure 9-5 shows the resulting tables. Code section 1 drops the tables if they already exist in the database. Statement 2 creates table1 with a primary key made of col1. The code doesn't contain the optional keyword CLUSTERED. The keyword CLUSTERED specifies that the primary key is also a clustered index. (See Chapter 1 for more information about clustered and nonclustered indexes.) By default, if no clustered index already exists on the table, as in this case, the primary key will become a clustered index. Because the code in statement 2 didn't specify the primary key constraint name, the database engine named the primary key for you.

Statement 3 creates a composite primary key composed of col1 and col2. You actually don't have to specify NOT NULL when defining the primary key, because SQL Server will change the primary key columns to NOT NULL for you. I prefer to specify the NOT NULL constraint in the CREATE TABLE statement for clarity, especially if I am saving the script. Again, since there is no other clustered index, the primary key will also be a clustered index on table2.

Statement 4 creates table3 without specifying a primary key. Statement 5, an ALTER TABLE statement, adds the primary key, in this case a nonclustered index. The primary key is often a clustered index, but that is not a requirement. You will often see the clustered index composed of a smaller column, such as an INT column, if the primary key contains several large columns. The reason is that the clustered index is automatically part of every other index, so having a "narrow" clustered index saves space in the database, but keep in mind the wider the index the more reads SQL Server will need to perform to retrieve the data and this can have a negative impact on performance.

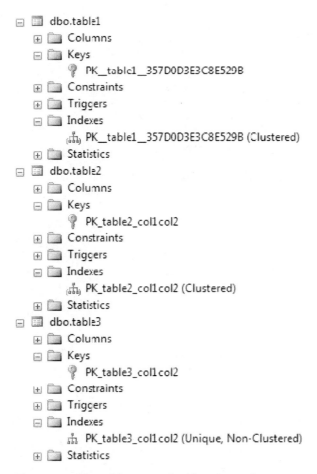

Figure 9-5. The tables created with primary keys

Creating Foreign Keys

You have seen how to join tables on the primary key of one table to the foreign key of another table beginning with Chapter 4. Having foreign keys defined on tables is not a requirement to join tables together but, in addition to performance implications, explicitly defined foreign keys can help enforce what is called *referential integrity*. Referential integrity means that data consistency between tables is maintained. For example, no orders may exist without a valid customer for that order.

Just like primary keys, you can define a foreign key within the CREATE TABLE command or later in an ALTER TABLE statement. Here is the syntax for creating simple foreign keys:

```
--On one column in the CREATE TABLE
CREATE TABLE <table1> (<col1> <data type> FOREIGN KEY REFERENCES <table2> (<col3>))
```

```
--On two columns in the CREATE TABLE
CREATE TABLE <table1> (<col1> <data type>, <col2> <data type>,
    CONSTRAINT <foreign key name> FOREIGN KEY (<col1>,<col2>)
    REFERENCES <table2> (<col3>,<col4>))

--Adding with ALTER table
CREATE TABLE <table1> (<col1> <data type>, <col2> <data type>)
ALTER TABLE <table1> ADD CONSTRAINT <foreign key name> FOREIGN KEY (<col1>)
    REFERENCES <table2> (<col3>))
```

The foreign key refers to the table specified before the keyword REFERENCES. For example, if you were defining the foreign key on the orders table, table2 would be the customers table. The column or columns specified after the REFERENCES keyword generally will be the primary key of that table. If the column or columns referred to are not the primary key, they at least have to be defined as UNIQUE. Type in and execute Listing 9-4, which shows a simple example.

Listing 9-4. Adding a Foreign Key

```
USE tempdb;
GO
--1
IF OBJECT_ID('table2') IS NOT NULL BEGIN
    DROP TABLE table2;
END;

IF OBJECT_ID('table1') IS NOT NULL BEGIN
    DROP TABLE table1;
END;

--2
CREATE TABLE table1 (col1 INT NOT NULL PRIMARY KEY,
    col2 VARCHAR(20), col3 DATETIME);

--3
CREATE TABLE table2 (col4 INT NULL,
    col5 VARCHAR(20) NOT NULL,
    CONSTRAINT pk_table2 PRIMARY KEY (col5),
    CONSTRAINT fk_table2_table1 FOREIGN KEY (col4) REFERENCES table1(col1)
    );
GO

--4
PRINT 'Adding to table1';
INSERT INTO table1(col1,col2,col3)
VALUES(1,'a','1/1/2009'),(2,'b','1/2/2009'),(3,'c','1/3/2009');

--5
PRINT 'Adding to table2';
INSERT INTO table2(col4,col5)
VALUES(1,'abc'),(2,'def');
```

```
--6
PRINT 'Violating foreign key with insert';
INSERT INTO table2(col4,col5)
VALUES (7,'abc');

--7
PRINT 'Violating foreign key with update';
UPDATE table2 SET col4 = 6
WHERE col4 = 1;
```

Figure 9-6 shows the results of adding the foreign key and then violating it. Code section 1 drops table1 and table2 if they exist. Notice that the code drops table2 first. If the drop statements are reversed and you run the code multiple times, it will fail. Note that table1 may not be dropped while the foreign key pointing to it exists. To eliminate this problem, drop table2 first.

Statement 2 creates table1. Statement 3 creates table2 with the foreign key. Statement 4 adds three rows to table1. Statement 5 inserts two valid rows to table2. Any value for col4 must already exist in col1 of table1. Statement 6 attempts to insert a row with the value 7. Since the value 7 doesn't exist in col1 of table1, the statement fails. Statement 7 attempts to update an existing row with an invalid value. The statement fails because the value, 6, doesn't exist in col1 of table1.

```
🔲 Messages

  Adding to table1
  Adding to table2
  Violating foreign key with insert
  Msg 2627, Level 14, State 1, Line 15
  Violation of PRIMARY KEY constraint 'pk_table2'.
  Cannot insert duplicate key in object 'dbo.table2'. The duplicate key value is (abc).
  The statement has been terminated.
  Violating foreign key with update
  Msg 547, Level 16, State 0, Line 20
  The UPDATE statement conflicted with the FOREIGN KEY constraint "fk_table2_table1".
  The conflict occurred in database "tempdb", table "dbo.table1", column 'col1'.
  The statement has been terminated.
```

***Figure 9-6.** The results of adding a foreign key*

Creating Foreign Keys with Delete and Update Rules

You saw in the previous section that foreign keys ensure that only valid values from the referenced table are used. For example, if you have an order table, only valid CustomerID values from the customer table may be used. You can also define what should happen if a customer with orders is deleted from the database. Will all orders also be deleted at the same time? Should SQL Server prevent the customer from being deleted? What about changing the CustomerID in the customer table? Will that change also change the CustomerID in the order table or prevent the change? You can define all that behavior within the foreign key definition. A rule may be set up for deletions and for updates. Here are the possible values:

- CASCADE: Applies the same action to the foreign key table.

- NO ACTION: Prevents the deletion or update and rolls back the transaction.

- SET NULL: Sets the value of the foreign key columns to NULL.

- SET DEFAULT: Sets the value of the foreign key columns to the default values.

Here is the syntax for creating foreign keys with update and delete rules:

```
CREATE TABLE <table1> (<col1> <data type>,<col2> <data type>,
    CONSTRAINT <foreign key name> FOREIGN KEY (<col1>) REFERENCES <table2> (<col3>)
    [ON DELETE [NO ACTION|CASCADE|SET NULL|SET DEFAULT]]
    [ON UPDATE [NO ACTION|CASCADE|SET NULL|SET DEFAULT]])
```

By default, the NO ACTION option applies if no rule is defined. In this case, if you attempt to delete a customer who has placed one or more orders, SQL Server will return an error message and roll back the transaction. To use SET NULL, the columns making up the foreign key must allow NULL values. To use SET DEFAULT, the columns making up the foreign key must have defaults defined. The other requirement is that the default values must be a valid value that satisfies the foreign key. Type in and execute the code in Listing 9-5 to learn how these rules work.

Listing 9-5. Using Update and Delete Rules

```
USE tempdb;
GO
--1
IF OBJECT_ID('table2') IS NOT NULL BEGIN
    DROP TABLE table2;
END;

IF OBJECT_ID('table1') IS NOT NULL BEGIN
    DROP TABLE table1;
END;

--2
CREATE TABLE table1 (col1 INT NOT NULL PRIMARY KEY,
    col2 VARCHAR(20), col3 DATETIME);

--3 default rules
PRINT 'No action by default';
CREATE TABLE table2 (col4 INT NULL DEFAULT 7,
    col5 VARCHAR(20) NOT NULL,
    CONSTRAINT pk_table2 PRIMARY KEY (col5),
    CONSTRAINT fk_table2_table1 FOREIGN KEY (col4) REFERENCES table1(col1)
    );

--4
PRINT 'Adding to table1';
INSERT INTO table1(col1,col2,col3)
VALUES(1,'a','1/1/2009'),(2,'b','1/2/2009'),(3,'c','1/3/2009'),
    (4,'d','1/4/2009'),(5,'e','1/6/2009'),(6,'g','1/7/2009'),
    (7,'g','1/8/2009');

--5
PRINT 'Adding to table2';
INSERT INTO table2(col4,col5)
VALUES(1,'abc'),(2,'def'),(3,'ghi'),
    (4,'jkl');
```

```
--6
SELECT col4, col5 FROM table2;

--7
PRINT 'Delete from table1'
DELETE FROM table1 WHERE col1 = 1;

--8
ALTER TABLE table2 DROP CONSTRAINT fk_table2_table1;

--9
PRINT 'Add CASCADE';
ALTER TABLE table2 ADD CONSTRAINT fk_table2_table1
    FOREIGN KEY (col4) REFERENCES table1(col1)
    ON DELETE CASCADE
    ON UPDATE CASCADE;

--10
PRINT 'Delete from table1';
DELETE FROM table1 WHERE col1 = 1;

--11
PRINT 'Update table1';
UPDATE table1 SET col1 = 10 WHERE col1 = 4;

--12
ALTER TABLE table2 DROP CONSTRAINT fk_table2_table1;

--13
PRINT 'Add SET NULL';
ALTER TABLE table2 ADD CONSTRAINT fk_table2_table1
    FOREIGN KEY (col4) REFERENCES table1(col1)
    ON DELETE SET NULL
    ON UPDATE SET NULL;

--14
DELETE FROM table1 WHERE col1 = 2;

--15
ALTER TABLE table2 DROP CONSTRAINT fk_table2_table1;

--16
PRINT 'Add SET DEFAULT';
ALTER TABLE table2 ADD CONSTRAINT fk_table2_table1
    FOREIGN KEY (col4) REFERENCES table1(col1)
    ON DELETE SET DEFAULT
    ON UPDATE SET DEFAULT;

--17
PRINT 'Delete from table1';
DELETE FROM table1 WHERE col1 = 3;
```

```
--18
SELECT col4, col5 FROM table2;
```

Figure 9-7 shows the information and error messages that result from running the script. Code section 1 drops table1 and table2 if they exist. Statement 2 creates table1. Statement 3 creates table2 with a foreign key referencing table1 with the default NO ACTION rules. In my experience, most of the time the default NO ACTION is in effect preventing updates and deletions from the referenced table, as in statement 3. Statements 4 and 5 add a few rows to the tables. Statement 7 deletes a row from table1. Since that deletion violates the foreign key rules, the statement rolls back and produces an error.

```
 📄 Messages

No action by default
Adding to table1
Adding to table2
Delete from table1
Msg 547, Level 16, State 0, Line 40
The DELETE statement conflicted with the REFERENCE constraint "fk_table2_table1".
The conflict occurred in database "tempdb", table "dbo.table2", column 'col4'.
The statement has been terminated.
Add CASCADE
Delete from table1
Update table1
Add SET NULL
Add SET DEFAULT
Delete from table1
```

Figure 9-7. *The results of applying foreign key rules*

Statement 8 drops the foreign key constraint so that statement 9 can re-create the foreign key with the CASCADE options. Statement 10, which deletes the row from table1 with col1 equal to 1, succeeds. The CASCADE rule also automatically deletes the matching row from table2. (Figure 9-8 shows how table2 looks after population and at the end of the script.) Statement 11 changes the value of col1 in table1 to 10 where the value is equal to 4. The CASCADE rule automatically updates the matching row in table2.

Statement 12 drops the foreign key constraint so that statement 13 can re-create the foreign key with the SET NULL option. Statement 14 deletes a row from table1. The SET NULL rule automatically changes the matching value in table2 to NULL.

Statement 15 drops the foreign key constraint so that statement 16 can re-create the foreign key with the SET DEFAULT option. Statement 17 deletes a row from table1. The SET DEFAULT rule automatically changes the matching value in table2 to the default value 7. Finally, statement 18 displays the rows after all the automatic changes. Review the script again. Except for the INSERT statement, the script contains no other explicit changes to the data in table2. The rule in effect at the time of each data change to table1 automatically made changes to the data in table2.

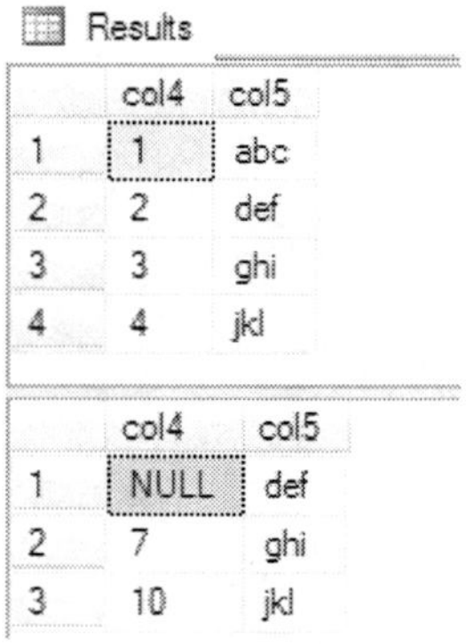

	col4	col5
1	1	abc
2	2	def
3	3	ghi
4	4	jkl

	col4	col5
1	NULL	def
2	7	ghi
3	10	jkl

Figure 9-8. *The results of changes based on foreign key options*

Defining Automatically Populated Columns

You have seen automatically populated columns used in the "Inserting Rows into Tables with Automatically Populating Columns" section in Chapter 6. This section will show you how to define `IDENTITY` columns, `ROWVERSION` columns, `COMPUTED` columns, and columns with `DEFAULT` values. Here are the syntax examples:

```
--IDENTITY
CREATE TABLE <table name> (<col1> INT NOT NULL IDENTITY[(<seed>,<increment>)],
    <col1> <data type>)

--ROWVERSION
CREATE TABLE <table name> (<col1> <data type>,<col2> ROWVERSION)

--COMPUTED column
CREATE TABLE <table name> (<col1> <data type>,<col2> AS <computed column definition>
    [PERSISTED])

--DEFAULT column
CREATE TABLE <table name> (<col1> <data type> DEFAULT <default value or function>)
```

Several rules apply to using these column types:

- A table may contain only one `IDENTITY` column
- By default, `IDENTITY` columns begin with the value 1 and increment by 1. You can specify different values by specifying seed and increment values.
- You may not insert values into `IDENTITY` columns unless the `IDENTITY_INSERT` setting is turned on for the table and session.
- A table may contain only one `ROWVERSION` column.
- The `ROWVERSION` value will be unique within the database.
- You may not insert values into `ROWVERSION` columns.

- Each time you update the row, the ROWVERSION value changes.

- A table may contain multiple COMPUTED columns.

- Do not specify a data type for COMPUTED columns.

- You may not insert values into COMPUTED columns.

- By specifying the option PERSISTED, the database engine stores the value in the table.

- You can define indexes on PERSISTED COMPUTED columns.

- You can specify other non-COMPUTED columns, literal values, and scalar functions in the COMPUTED column definition.

- You do not need to specify a value for a column with a DEFAULT value defined.

- You can use expressions with literal values and scalar functions, but not other column names with DEFAULT value columns.

- If a value is specified for a column with a DEFAULT, the specified value applies.

- If a column with a DEFAULT value specified allows NULL values, you can still specify NULL for the column.

■ **Note** While a sequence does enable you to autopopulate values in a table, it is a database object and is not dependent upon the table. You create SEQUENCES apart from tables and reference them in your INSERT statements.

Listing 9-6 demonstrates creating and populating tables with these automatically populating columns. Type in and execute the code to learn more.

Listing 9-6. Defining Tables with Automatically Populating Columns

```
USE tempdb;
GO

--1
IF OBJECT_ID('table3') IS NOT NULL BEGIN
    DROP TABLE table3;
END;

--2
CREATE TABLE table3 (col1 VARCHAR(10),
    idCol INT NOT NULL IDENTITY,
    rvCol ROWVERSION,
    defCol DATETIME2 DEFAULT GETDATE(),
    calcCol1 AS DATEADD(m,1,defCol),
```

```
        calcCol2 AS col1 + ':' + col1 PERSISTED);
GO

--3
INSERT INTO table3 (col1)
VALUES ('a'), ('b'), ('c'), ('d'), ('e'), ('g');

--4
INSERT INTO table3 (col1, defCol)
VALUES ('h', NULL),('i','1/1/2009');

--5
SELECT col1, idCol, rvCol, defCol, calcCol1, calcCol2
FROM table3;
```

Figure 9-9 shows the results. Statement 1 drops table3 if it exists. Statement 2 creates table3 with one regular column, col1, and several other columns that may be automatically populated. Statement 3 inserts several rows into table3, specifying values only for col1. Statement 4 inserts two more rows, specifying values for col1 and the column with a DEFAULT value, defCol. Notice that the first row inserted in statement 4 specifies NULL for defCol. Statement 5 just returns the results.

If you run the script more than once, you will see that the ROWVERSION column, rvCol, contains different values each time. Notice, also, that in the row where col1 equals h, both devCol and calcCol1 also contain NULL. That is because statement 4 explicitly inserted a NULL value into defCol. Since the value for calcCol1 is based on defCol and any operation on NULL returns NULL, calcCol1 also contains a NULL in that row. Statement 4 inserts a row with another explicit value for defCol, and calcCol1 reflects that as well.

	col1	idCol	rvCol	defCol	calcCol1	calcCo2
1	a	1	0x00000000000007D1	2011-06-06 22:14:22.7300000	2011-07-06 22:14:22.7300000	a:a
2	b	2	0x00000000000007D2	2011-06-06 22:14:22.7300000	2011-07-06 22:14:22.7300000	b:b
3	c	3	0x00000000000007D3	2011-06-06 22:14:22.7300000	2011-07-06 22:14:22.7300000	c:c
4	d	4	0x00000000000007D4	2011-06-06 22:14:22.7300000	2011-07-06 22:14:22.7300000	d:d
5	e	5	0x00000000000007D5	2011-06-06 22:14:22.7300000	2011-07-06 22:14:22.7300000	e:e
6	g	6	0x00000000000007D6	2011-06-06 22:14:22.7300000	2011-07-06 22:14:22.7300000	g:g
7	h	7	0x00000000000007D7	NULL	NULL	h:h
8	i	8	0x00000000000007D8	2009-01-01 00:00:00.0000000	2009-02-01 00:00:00.0000000	i:i

Figure 9-9. The results of populating a table with automatically populating columns

Even though the main purpose of database tables is to store data, you can enforce many business rules by the table definition. Practice what you have learned by completing Exercise 9-1.

```
                                  EXERCISE 9-1
```

Use the AdventureWorks2012 database to complete this exercise. You can find the solutions in the Appendix.

1. Create a table called dbo.testCustomer. Include a CustomerID that is an identity column primary key. Include FirstName and LastName columns. Include an Age column with a check constraint specifying that the value must be less than 120. Include an Active column that is one character with a default of Y and allows only Y or N. Add some rows to the table.

2. Create a table called dbo.testOrder. Include a CustomerID column that is a foreign key pointing to dbo.testCustomer. Include an OrderID column that is an identity column primary key. Include an OrderDate column that defaults to the current date and time. Include a ROWVERSION column. Add some rows to the table.

3. Create a table called dbo.testOrderDetail. Include an OrderID column that is a foreign key pointing to dbo.testOrder. Include an integer ItemID column, a Price column, and a Qty column. The primary key should be a composite key composed of OrderID and ItemID. Create a computed column called LineItemTotal that multiplies Price times Qty. Add some rows to the table.

Views

SQL Server stores data in tables, but you can create objects, called *views*, that you query just like tables. Views don't store data; they are just saved query definitions. Developers can use views to simplify coding. For example, in the AdventureWorks2012 database, the Person.Person table contains name columns for several other tables, such as the HumanResources.Employee table. You could create views to join the Person.Person table to the other tables so that you would always have the name columns available, therefore simplifying queries for reports.

You can also simplify security by using views. You can give a user permission to select data from a view when the user doesn't have permission to select data from the tables comprising the view. This keeps users from seeing or modifying data that they should not access.

■ **Note** An indexed view, also known as a *materialized view*, actually does contain data. SQL Server Express doesn't support indexed views, so this section doesn't cover them. See Books Online for more information about creating and using indexed views.

Creating Views

Creating views is easy. You can create views using most SELECT statements, including those made with common table expressions. For example, you might want to create a view that lists all the customers in the Sales.Customer table from the AdventureWorks2012 database along with their names from the Person.Person table. You could use that view instead of the Sales.Customer table in other queries. Here is the syntax to create, alter, and drop views:

```
CREATE VIEW <view name> AS SELECT <col1>, <col2> FROM <table>
ALTER VIEW <view name> AS SELECT <col1>, <col2> FROM <table>
DROP VIEW <view name>
```

Type in and execute the code in Listing 9-7 to learn how to create and use views.

Listing 9-7. Creating and Using a View

```
USE AdventureWorks2012;
GO


--1
IF OBJECT_ID('dbo.vw_Customer') IS NOT NULL BEGIN
    DROP VIEW dbo.vw_Customer;
END;
GO


--2
CREATE VIEW dbo.vw_Customer AS
    SELECT c.CustomerID, c.AccountNumber, c.StoreID,
        c.TerritoryID, p.FirstName, p.MiddleName,
        p.LastName
    FROM Sales.Customer AS c
    INNER JOIN Person.Person AS p ON c.PersonID = p.BusinessEntityID
GO


--3
SELECT CustomerID,AccountNumber,FirstName,
    MiddleName, LastName
FROM dbo.vw_Customer;

GO


--4
ALTER VIEW dbo.vw_Customer AS
    SELECT c.CustomerID,c.AccountNumber,c.StoreID,
        c.TerritoryID, p.FirstName,p.MiddleName,
        p.LastName, p.Title
    FROM Sales.Customer AS c
    INNER JOIN Person.Person AS p ON c.PersonID = p.BusinessEntityID

GO
```

```
--5
SELECT CustomerID,AccountNumber,FirstName,
    MiddleName, LastName, Title
FROM dbo.vw_Customer
ORDER BY CustomerID;
```

Figure 9-10 shows the results. Code section 1 drops the view if it already exists. Code section 2 creates the view. Notice that the GO statements surround the CREATE VIEW code so that it has its own batch. Any time you create or alter a view, the code must be contained within a batch that has no other code except for comments. Notice that the view begins with the characters vw_, designating that it is a view, not a table. Often companies will have naming conventions such as this; be sure to find out whether your shop requires special naming for views. Statement 3 selects several of the columns from the view. At this point, you could include a WHERE clause, include an ORDER BY clause, or involve the view in an aggregate query if you wanted. Basically, you can treat the view like a table in a SELECT statement. Statement 4 alters the view by adding a column. Statement 5 is another SELECT statement, which includes the new column and an ORDER BY clause.

Results

	CustomerID	AccountNumber	FirstName	MiddleName	LastName
1	29485	AW00029485	Catherine	R.	Abel
2	29486	AW00029486	Kim	NULL	Abercrombie
3	29487	AW00029487	Humberto	NULL	Acevedo
4	29484	AW00029484	Gustavo	NULL	Achong
5	29488	AW00029488	Pilar	NULL	Ackerman
6	28866	AW00028866	Aaron	B	Adams
7	13323	AW00013323	Adam	NULL	Adams
8	21139	AW00021139	Alex	C	Adams

	CustomerID	AccountNumber	FirstName	MiddleName	LastName	Title
1	11000	AW00011000	Jon	V	Yang	NULL
2	11001	AW00011001	Eugene	L	Huang	NULL
3	11002	AW00011002	Ruben	NULL	Torres	NULL
4	11003	AW00011003	Christy	NULL	Zhu	NULL
5	11004	AW00011004	Elizabeth	NULL	Johnson	NULL
6	11005	AW00011005	Julio	NULL	Ruiz	NULL
7	11006	AW00011006	Janet	G	Alvarez	NULL
8	11007	AW00011007	Marco	NULL	Mehta	NULL

Figure 9-10. The results of creating and using a view

To see the view in SQL Server Management Studio, navigate to the Views section of the AdventureWorks2012 database. You will see the newly created view along with several views that ship with the database. Notice that each of the pre-existing views belongs to one of the schemas in the database. Just like tables, you can script out the definition or bring up a graphical designer. Figure 9-11 shows the graphical designer for the view.

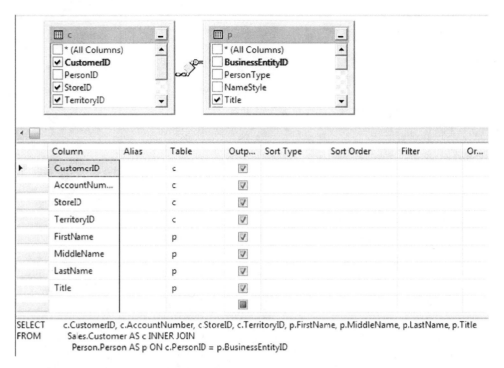

Figure 9-11. *The graphical designer for views*

Avoiding Common Problems with Views

You may decide that you should set up views joining all the tables in the database and just write queries against those views, but there are often problems associated with using views as the main strategy for database development. One problem is the confusion that can result from views created on top of other views. Tracking down logic errors becomes difficult when they are buried in layers of views. If the underlying table structure changes, the view may produce strange results, as shown in Listing 9-8. Make sure that you don't use views in a way that will negatively impact performance. For example, suppose you created a view containing the customers, customer addresses, sales, and sales details tables. If you just wanted a list of customers, you could query the view but you would be also accessing tables you didn't need to view at that time.

Developers often want to add an ORDER BY clause to a view definition. This is actually disallowed except under specific conditions and doesn't make sense because you can always add the ORDER BY clause to the outer query. (To add an ORDER BY to a view definition, you must add the TOP specifier to the view. You will learn about TOP in Chapter 10.) In fact, the database engine doesn't guarantee that the data will be returned in the order specified in the view definition according to the CREATE VIEW topic in SQL Server Books Online. Type in and execute the code in Listing 9-8 to learn more about two common problems with views.

Listing 9-8. *Common Problems Using Views*

```
USE AdventureWorks2012;
GO


--1
IF OBJECT_ID('vw_Dept') IS NOT NULL BEGIN
    DROP VIEW dbo.vw_Dept;
END;
IF OBJECT_ID('demoDept') IS NOT NULL BEGIN
    DROP TABLE dbo.demoDept;
END;

--2
SELECT DepartmentID,Name,GroupName,ModifiedDate
INTO dbo.demoDept
FROM HumanResources.Department;

GO
--3
CREATE VIEW dbo.vw_Dept AS
    SELECT *
    FROM dbo.demoDept;
GO


--4
SELECT DepartmentID, Name, GroupName, ModifiedDate
FROM dbo.vw_Dept;

--5
DROP TABLE dbo.demoDept;
GO


--6
SELECT DepartmentID, GroupName, Name, ModifiedDate
INTO dbo.demoDept
FROM HumanResources.Department;
GO


--7
SELECT DepartmentID, Name, GroupName, ModifiedDate
FROM dbo.vw_Dept;
GO


--8
DROP VIEW dbo.vw_Dept;
GO
```

```
--9
CREATE VIEW dbo.vw_Dept AS
    SELECT TOP(100) PERCENT DepartmentID,
        Name, GroupName, ModifiedDate
    FROM dbo.demoDept
    ORDER BY Name;
GO
```

```
--10
SELECT DepartmentID, Name, GroupName, ModifiedDate
FROM dbo.vw_Dept;
```

Figure 9-12 shows the results. Code section 1 drops the view and a work table in case they already exist. Statement 2 creates the table dbo.demoDept from the HumanResources.Department table. Statement 3 creates a view, dbo.vw_Dept, using the asterisk (*) syntax against the dbo.demoDept table. Statement 4 selects all the rows from the view, and the results look as expected in the first result set.

Statement 5 drops the dbo.demoDept table, and Statement 6 creates and populates the table again but with the columns in a different order. Statement 7 selects the rows from the view, but this time with surprising results. Because the table was dropped and re-created differently, the columns in the view are now mismatched, as shown in the second result set. The Name and GroupName columns are reversed.

Statement 8 drops the view, and statement 9 creates it while attempting to enforce a specific order in the view definition. Statement 10 shows within the final set of results that the ORDER BY clause within the view definition didn't make any difference.

Results

	DepartmentID	Name	GroupName	ModifiedDate
1	1	Engineering	Research and Development	2002-06-01 00:00:00.000
2	2	Tool Design	Research and Development	2002-06-01 00:00:00.000
3	3	Sales	Sales and Marketing	2002-06-01 00:00:00.000
4	4	Marketing	Sales and Marketing	2002-06-01 00:00:00.000
5	5	Purchasing	Inventory Management	2002-06-01 00:00:00.000

	DepartmentID	Name	GroupName	ModifiedDate
1	1	Research and Development	Engineering	2002-06-01 00:00:00.000
2	2	Research and Development	Tool Design	2002-06-01 00:00:00.000
3	3	Sales and Marketing	Sales	2002-06-01 00:00:00.000
4	4	Sales and Marketing	Marketing	2002-06-01 00:00:00.000
5	5	Inventory Management	Purchasing	2002-06-01 00:00:00.000

	DepartmentID	Name	GroupName	ModifiedDate
1	1	Engineering	Research and Development	2002-06-01 00:00:00.000
2	2	Tool Design	Research and Development	2002-06-01 00:00:00.000
3	3	Sales	Sales and Marketing	2002-06-01 00:00:00.000
4	4	Marketing	Sales and Marketing	2002-06-01 00:00:00.000
5	5	Purchasing	Inventory Management	2002-06-01 00:00:00.000

Figure 9-12. The results of demonstrating some common problems with views

Manipulating Data with Views

So far, you have seen how you can use views to select data. You can also modify the data of a table by updating a view as long as the view meets several requirements:

- Modifying the data of a view by inserting or updating may affect only one base table.

- You may not delete data from a view that consists of more than one table.

- The columns updated must be directly linked to updateable table columns; in other words, you can't update a view column based on an expression or an otherwise non-updatable column.

- Inserts into views are possible only if all columns that require a value are exposed through the view.

As you can see, modifying data through views can be much more complicated than through tables, especially if the view is made of more than one table. Type in and execute the code in Listing 9-9 to learn how to update data using views.

Listing 9-9. Modifying Data Through Views

```
USE AdventureWorks2012;
GO


--1
IF OBJECT_ID('dbo.demoCustomer') IS NOT NULL BEGIN
    DROP TABLE dbo.demoCustomer;
END;
IF OBJECT_ID('dbo.demoPerson') IS NOT NULL BEGIN
    DROP TABLE dbo.demoPerson;
END;
IF OBJECT_ID('dbo.vw_Customer') IS NOT NULL BEGIN
    DROP VIEW dbo.vw_Customer;
END;


--2
SELECT CustomerID, TerritoryID, StoreID, PersonID
INTO dbo.demoCustomer
FROM Sales.Customer;

SELECT BusinessEntityID, Title, FirstName, MiddleName, LastName
INTO dbo.demoPerson
From Person.Person;
GO


--3
CREATE VIEW vw_Customer AS
    SELECT CustomerID, TerritoryID, PersonID, StoreID,
        Title, FirstName, MiddleName, LastName
    FROM dbo.demoCustomer
    INNER JOIN dbo.demoPerson ON PersonID = BusinessEntityID;
```

```
GO

--4
SELECT CustomerID, FirstName, MiddleName, LastName
FROM dbo.vw_Customer
WHERE CustomerID IN (29484,29486,29489,100000);

--5
PRINT 'Update one row';
UPDATE dbo.vw_Customer SET FirstName = 'Kathi'
WHERE CustomerID = 29486;
--6
GO
PRINT 'Attempt to update both sides of the join'
GO
UPDATE dbo.vw_Customer SET FirstName = 'Franie',TerritoryID = 5
WHERE CustomerID = 29489;

--7
GO
PRINT 'Attempt to delete a row';
GO
DELETE FROM dbo.vw_Customer
WHERE CustomerID = 29484;

--8
GO
PRINT 'Insert into dbo.demoCustomer';
INSERT INTO dbo.vw_Customer(TerritoryID,
    StoreID, PersonID)
VALUES (5,5,100000);

--9
GO
PRINT 'Attempt to insert a row into demoPerson';
GO
INSERT INTO dbo.vw_Customer(Title, FirstName, LastName)
VALUES ('Mrs.','Lady','Samoyed');

--10
SELECT CustomerID, FirstName, MiddleName, LastName
FROM dbo.vw_Customer
WHERE CustomerID IN (29484,29486,29489,100000);

--11
SELECT CustomerID, TerritoryID, StoreID, PersonID
FROM dbo.demoCustomer
WHERE PersonID = 100000;
```

Since this code will produce some errors, view the error messages and then click the Results tab (see Figure 9-13). Code section 1 drops the two tables and the view involved in this script if they exist. Code section 2 creates the two tables, dbo.demoPerson and dbo.demoCustomer, using SELECT INTO statements. Since the two tables must be in place before the view is created, the code to create dbo.vw_Customer is in a separate batch. Statement 4 shows how three of the rows look before the data is manipulated and is the first result set in Figure 9-13. Statement 5 changes the first name of one row from *Kim* to *Kathi*. This statement succeeds because the update affects only one of the tables.

Statement 6 attempts to update two of the columns. Because the FirstName column is from one base table and TerritoryID is from a different base table, the update fails. Statement 7 attempts to delete a row from the view but fails. Deletions will work only if the view consists of one base table.

Statement 8 successfully inserts one row into the dbo.demoCustomer table through the view. Statement 9 attempts to insert a row into dbo.demoPerson but fails because the view does not expose the non-NULL column, BusinessEntityID, and there is no way to add a valid value. Statements 10 and 11 show the results of the script. The script updated only one row and added one row to dbo.demoCustomer through the view.

	CustomerID	FirstName	MiddleName	LastName
1	29484	Gustavo	NULL	Achong
2	29486	Kim	NULL	Abercrombie
3	29489	Frances	B.	Adams

	CustomerID	FirstName	MiddleName	LastName
1	29484	Gustavo	NULL	Achong
2	29486	Kathi	NULL	Abercrombie
3	29489	Frances	B.	Adams

	CustomerID	TerritoryID	StoreID	PersonID
1	30119	5	5	100000

Figure 9-13. The results of manipulating data through a view

Developers can use views to simplify database programming, but care must be taken to avoid performance and logic problems. Practice what you have learned by completing Exercise 9-2.

EXERCISE 9-2

Use the AdventureWorks2012 database to complete this exercise. You can find the solutions in the Appendix.

1. Create a view called dbo.vw_Products that displays a list of the products from the Production.Product table joined to the Production.ProductCostHistory table. Include columns that describe the product and show the cost history for each product. Test the view by creating a query that retrieves data from the view.

2. Create a view called dbo.vw_CustomerTotals that displays the total sales from the TotalDue column per year and month for each customer. Test the view by creating a query that retrieves data from the view.

User-Defined Functions

You learned about the built-in functions available in SQL Server in Chapter 3. You can also create your own T-SQL user-defined functions (UDFs) that you can use in the same ways as the built-in functions. You will learn about two types of user-defined functions in this chapter: *scalar valued*, which return one value, and *table-valued*, which return record sets. By using UDFs, you can reuse code to simplify development and hide complex logic.

Creating User-Defined Scalar Functions

A scalar function returns one value and may take one or more parameters. You can create your own scalar functions to simplify your code. For example, your application may have a complex calculation that appears in many queries. Instead of including the formula in every query, you can create and include the function in your queries instead. Keep these facts about scalar UDFs in mind:

- UDFs can be used almost anywhere in a T-SQL statement.

- UDFs can accept one or more parameters.

- UDFs return one value.

- UDFs can use logic such as IF blocks and WHILE loops.

- UDFs can access data, though this is not a good idea.

- UDFs can't update data.

- UDFs can call other functions.

- The UDF definition must include a return value.

You may have noticed that scalar-valued UDFs can access data, but this is not a good use of UDFs. UDFs should generally not be dependent on the tables in a particular database. They should be reusable as possible. Another problem with UDFs that access data is that the performance can be very poor, especially when used inline in a T-SQL query. The queries within the function run for each row in the outer query. Here is the syntax for creating, altering, and deleting user-defined scalar functions:

```
CREATE FUNCTION <scalar function Name> (<@param1> <data type1>,
    <@param2> <data type2>)
RETURNS <data type> AS
BEGIN
    <statements>
    RETURN <value>
END

ALTER FUNCTION <scalar function Name> ([<@param1> <data type>,
    <@param2> <data type>])
RETURNS <data type> AS
BEGIN
    <statements>
    RETURN <value>
END

DROP FUNCTION <scalar function name>
```

Listing 9-10 demonstrates how to create and use user-defined functions. Type in and execute the code to learn more.

Listing 9-10. Creating and Using User-Defined Scalar Functions

```
USE AdventureWorks2012;
GO


--1
IF OBJECT_ID('dbo.udf_Product') IS NOT NULL BEGIN
    DROP FUNCTION dbo.udf_Product;
END;
IF OBJECT_ID('dbo.udf_Delim') IS NOT NULL BEGIN
    DROP FUNCTION dbo.udf_Delim;
END;
GO


--2
CREATE FUNCTION dbo.udf_Product(@num1 INT, @num2 INT) RETURNS INT AS
BEGIN

    DECLARE @Product INT;
    SET @Product = ISNULL(@num1,0) * ISNULL(@num2,0);
    RETURN @Product;

END;
GO


--3
CREATE FUNCTION dbo.udf_Delim(@String VARCHAR(100),@Delimiter CHAR(1))
    RETURNS VARCHAR(200) AS
BEGIN
    DECLARE @NewString VARCHAR(200) = '';
    DECLARE @Count INT = 1;

    WHILE @Count <= LEN(@String) BEGIN
        SET @NewString += SUBSTRING(@String,@Count,1) + @Delimiter;
        SET @Count += 1;
    END

    RETURN @NewString;
END
GO


--3
SELECT StoreID, TerritoryID,
    dbo.udf_Product(StoreID, TerritoryID) AS TheProduct,
    dbo.udf_Delim(FirstName,',') AS FirstNameWithCommas
FROM Sales.Customer AS c
INNER JOIN Person.Person AS p ON c.PersonID= p.BusinessEntityID ;
```

Figure 9-14 shows the results. Code section 1 drops the UDFs in case they already exist. Code section 2 creates the UDFs dbo.udf_Product and dbo.udf_Delim. The dbo.udf_Product UDF takes two INT parameters. Inside the UDF, the two parameters are multiplied together after correcting for NULL values. The code saves the product in a variable, @Product, which is returned.

The second UDF, dbo.udf_Delim, takes two parameters: @String, which is a VARCHAR(100), and @Delimiter, which is a one-character string. Inside the definition, a loop builds a new string inserting the delimiter after each character in the original string. The function returns the new string. Query 3 uses the new functions in the SELECT list, multiplying the StoreID by the TerritoryID and adding commas to the FirstName column. Each of these function are database agnostic; you could add them to any database.

Results

	StoreID	TerritoryID	TheProduct	FirstNameWithCommas
1	294	4	1176	C,a,t,h,e,r,i,n,e,
2	296	3	888	K,i,m,
3	298	2	596	H,u,m,b,e,r,t,o,
4	292	5	1460	G,u,s,t,a,v,o,
5	300	9	2700	P,i,l,a,r,
6	NULL	4	0	A,a,r,o,n,
7	NULL	4	0	A,d,a,m,
8	NULL	1	0	A,l,e,x,
9	NULL	4	0	A,l,e,x,a,n,d,r,a,
10	NULL	7	0	A,l,l,i,s,o,n,
11	NULL	4	0	A,m,a,n,d,a,

Figure 9-14. The results of using two user-defined scalar functions

Using Table-Valued User-Defined Functions

The second type of UDF returns a record set instead of one value. You can't use this type of UDF inline within a query, but you can use it in place of a table or save the results into a temp table or table variable for use later in your script.

The AdventureWorks2012 database contains one example of a table-valued UDF. This function accepts a @PersonID value and returns information about the contact. Using SSMS, navigate to the AdventureWorks2012 database, and drill down to the dbo.ufnGetContactInformation function via Programmability ➤ Functions ➤ Table-valued Functions. Once you reach the function, right-click and choose Script Function as ➤ Create to ➤ New Query Editor Window. You will see why this is a function instead of a view. Because the Person.Person table contains information about contacts from many different tables, the function uses logic to figure out which query to run to pull the information. You can't define logic like that in a view, so that is why the AdventureWorks2012 developers chose to create the table-valued UDF.

To work with a table-valued UDF, you can select from it like a table or use the CROSS APPLY operator to join the function to another table. Here is the syntax:

```
SELECT <col1>,<col2> FROM <schema>.<udf name>(<@param>)
SELECT <col1>,<col2> FROM <table1> CROSS APPLY <udf name>(<table1>.<col3>)
```

Listing 9-11 demonstrates using the dbo.ufnGetContactInformation function. Type in and execute to learn more.

Listing 9-11. Using a Table-Valued UDF

```
USE AdventureWorks2012;
GO

--1
SELECT PersonID,FirstName,LastName,JobTitle,BusinessEntityType
FROM dbo.ufnGetContactInformation(1);

--2
SELECT PersonID,FirstName,LastName,JobTitle,BusinessEntityType
FROM dbo.ufnGetContactInformation(7822);

--3
SELECT e.BirthDate, e.Gender, c.FirstName,c.LastName,c.JobTitle
FROM HumanResources.Employee as e
CROSS APPLY dbo.ufnGetContactInformation(e.BusinessEntityID ) AS c;

--4
SELECT sc.CustomerID,sc.TerritoryID,c.FirstName,c.LastName
FROM Sales.Customer AS sc
CROSS APPLY dbo.ufnGetContactInformation(sc.PersonID) AS c;
```

Figure 9-15 shows the partial results. Query 1 calls the UDF with the parameter 1. The logic inside the UDF determines that BusinessEntityID 1 belongs to an employee and returns that information. Query 2 calls the UDF with parameter 7822. The logic inside the UDF determines that this BusinessEntityID belongs to a customer and returns the appropriate information. Query 3 uses the CROSS APPLY operator to join the HumanResources.Employee table to the UDF. Instead of supplying an individual value to find one name, the query supplies the BusinessEntityID column of the HumanResources.Employee table to the function. Columns from the UDF and the table appear in the SELECT list. Query 4 uses CROSS APPLY to join the UDF on the Sales.Customer table. Another option, OUTER APPLY, returns rows even if a NULL value is passed to the UDF, similar to an OUTER JOIN.

Results

	PersonID	FirstName	LastName	JobTitle		BusinessEntityType
1	1	Ken	Sánchez	Chief Executive Officer		Employee

	PersonID	FirstName	LastName	JobTitle	BusinessEntityType
1	7822	Faith	Hughes	NULL	Consumer

	BirthDate	Gender	FirstName	LastName	JobTitle
1	1963-03-02	M	Ken	Sánchez	Chief Executive Officer
2	1965-09-01	F	Terri	Duffy	Vice President of Engineering
3	1968-12-13	M	Roberto	Tamburello	Engineering Manager
4	1969-01-23	M	Rob	Walters	Senior Tool Designer
5	1946-10-29	F	Gail	Erickson	Design Engineer
6	1953-04-11	M	Jossef	Goldberg	Design Engineer
7	1981-03-27	M	Dylan	Miller	Research and Developmen...
8	1980-07-06	F	Diane	Margheim	Research and Developmen...

	CustomerID	TerritoryID	FirstName	LastName
1	11000	9	Jon	Yang
2	11001	9	Eugene	Huang
3	11002	9	Ruben	Torres
4	11003	9	Christy	Zhu
5	11004	9	Elizabeth	Johnson
6	11005	9	Julio	Ruiz
7	11006	9	Janet	Alvarez

Figure 9-15. The partial results of using a table-valued UDF

You will probably find many reasons to write scalar-valued user-defined functions. Table-valued UDFs are not as common. You can also create user-defined functions with a .NET language. Creating functions with a .NET language is beyond the scope of this book. Practice what you have learned about UDFs by completing Exercise 9-3.

EXERCISE 9-3

Use the AdventureWorks2012 database to complete this exercise. You can find the solutions in the Appendix.

1. Create a user-defined function called `dbo.fn_AddTwoNumbers` that accepts two integer parameters. Return the value that is the sum of the two numbers. Test the function.

2. Create a user-defined function called `dbo.Trim` that takes a `VARCHAR(250)` parameter. This function should trim off the spaces from both the beginning and the end of the string. Test the function.

3. Create a function dbo.fn_RemoveNumbers that removes any numeric characters from a VARCHAR(250) string. Test the function. Hint: The ISNUMERIC function checks to see whether a string is numeric. Check Books Online to see how to use it.

4. Write a function called dbo.fn_FormatPhone that takes a string of ten numbers. The function will format the string into this phone number format: "(###) ###-####." Test the function.

Stored Procedures

Stored procedures (sometimes shortened to "procs") are the workhorses of T-SQL. Developers and database administrators use them to increase security as well as encapsulate logic. Stored procedures can contain programming logic, update data, create other objects, and more. Essentially, stored procedures are just saved scripts, and they can do anything that the stored procedure owner can do. Like views, the user of the stored procedure doesn't usually need to have permissions on the tables used within the stored procedure.

■ **Tip** Stored procedures are often used to prevent SQL injection attacks. Hackers employing SQL injection techniques insert SQL commands into web forms that build SQL statements dynamically. Eventually the hacker takes over databases, servers, and networks. This problem is not unique to SQL Server; other database systems have been attacked as well.

Stored procedures and UDFs have many similarities but have some distinct differences. One interesting difference is that they both take parameters, but stored procedures can accept special parameters called OUTPUT parameters. These parameters can be used to get modified values from the stored procedures. UDFs can accept parameters but can return only a single return value. A stored procedure can also return an integer value, usually reporting the success of the stored procedure or some other informational code. Table 9-1 shows some of the differences between stored procedures and UDFs as well as views.

Table 9-1. The Differences Between Stored Procedures and User-Defined Functions

Feature	SP	Scalar UDF	Table UDF	View
Return tabular data	Yes	No	Yes	Yes
Update data	Yes	No	No	No
Create other objects	Yes	No	No	No
Call from a procedure	Yes	Yes	Yes	Yes
Can call a procedure	Yes	No	No	No
Can call a function	Yes	Yes	Yes	Yes
Can call inline	No	Yes	No	No
Use to populate a table	Yes	No	Yes	Yes
Return value required	No	Yes	Yes (table)	N/A
Return value optional	Yes	No	No	N/A
Takes parameters	Yes	Yes	Yes	No
Output parameters	Yes	No	No	No

You will find that creating stored procedures is easy. Here's the syntax to create, alter, drop, and execute a stored procedure:

```
CREATE PROC[EDURE] <proc name> [<@param1> <data type>,<@param2> <data type>] AS
    <statements>
    [RETURN <INT>]

ALTER PROC[EDURE] <proc name> [<@param1> <data type>,<@param2> <data type>] AS
    <statements>
    [RETURN <INT>]

EXEC <proc name> <param values>

DROP PROC[EDURE] <proc name>
```

Some shops require that developers use stored procedures for all database calls from their applications. I have also heard of shops that don't allow stored procedures at all. Chances are you will work with stored procedures at some point in your career. Listing 9-12 shows how to create a stored proc. Type in and execute the code to learn more.

Listing 9-12. Creating and Using a Stored Procedure

```
USE AdventureWorks2012;
GO


--1
IF OBJECT_ID('dbo.usp_CustomerName') IS NOT NULL BEGIN
    DROP PROC dbo.usp_CustomerName;
END;
GO


--2
CREATE PROC dbo.usp_CustomerName AS
    SELECT c.CustomerID,p.FirstName,p.MiddleName,p.LastName
    FROM Sales.Customer AS c
    INNER JOIN Person.Person AS p on c.PersonID = p.BusinessEntityID
    ORDER BY p.LastName, p.FirstName,p.MiddleName ;

    RETURN 0;
GO


--3
EXEC dbo.usp_CustomerName
GO


--4
ALTER PROC dbo.usp_CustomerName @CustomerID INT AS
    SELECT c.CustomerID,p.FirstName,p.MiddleName,p.LastName
    FROM Sales.Customer AS c
    INNER JOIN Person.Person AS p on c.PersonID = p.BusinessEntityID
    WHERE c.CustomerID = @CustomerID;

    RETURN 0;
GO

--5
EXEC dbo.usp_CustomerName @CustomerID = 15128;
```

Figure 9-16 shows the results. Code section 1 drops the stored procedure if it already exists. Code section 2 creates the stored procedure, dbo.usp_CustomerName. The proc simply joins the Sales.Customer table to the Person.Person table and returns several columns from those tables. Notice that the query includes the ORDER BY clause. Unlike views, the ORDER BY clause will actually return the rows in the order specified. Statement 3 calls the proc with the EXEC command. Code section 4 changes the stored proc by adding a parameter and using that parameter in a WHERE clause. Statement 5 calls the modified proc supplying a value for the @CustomerID parameter. You could have left out the name of the parameter when you called the stored procedure in this case. Supplying the name of the parameter makes the code easier to read and understand.

Results

	CustomerID	FirstName	MiddleName	LastName
1	29485	Catherine	R.	Abel
2	29486	Kim	NULL	Abercrombie
3	29487	Humberto	NULL	Acevedo
4	29484	Gustavo	NULL	Achong
5	29488	Pilar	NULL	Ackerman
6	28866	Aaron	B	Adams

	CustomerID	FirstName	MiddleName	LastName
1	15128	Angelica	NULL	Barnes

Figure 9-16. The partial results of using a stored procedure

Using Default Values with Parameters

SQL Server requires that you supply a value for each parameter unless you define a default value for the parameter. When a parameter has a default value, you can skip the parameter when you call the stored procedure. In that case, you will have to name the other parameters, not just rely on the position in the list. Once you use a named parameter when calling the stored procedure, you must continue naming parameters. You may want to get in the habit of naming the parameters anyway because it makes your code easier to understand. Here is the syntax for creating a stored procedure with default value parameters:

```
CREATE PROC[EDURE] <proc name> <@param1> <data type> = <default value> AS
    <statements>
    [return <value>]
```

Listing 9-13 shows how to use default value parameters. Type in and execute the code to learn more.

Listing 9-13. Using Default Value Parameters

```
USE AdventureWorks2012;
GO

--1
IF OBJECT_ID('dbo.usp_CustomerName') IS NOT NULL BEGIN
    DROP PROC dbo.usp_CustomerName;
END;
GO

--2
CREATE PROC dbo.usp_CustomerName @CustomerID INT = -1 AS
    SELECT c.CustomerID,p.FirstName,p.MiddleName,p.LastName
    FROM Sales.Customer AS c
    INNER JOIN Person.Person AS p on c.PersonID = p.BusinessEntityID
    WHERE @CustomerID = CASE @CustomerID WHEN -1 THEN -1 ELSE c.CustomerID END;

    RETURN 0;
GO
```

```
--3
EXEC dbo.usp_CustomerName 15128;

--4
EXEC dbo.usp_CustomerName ;
```

Figure 9-17 shows the results. Code section 1 drops the stored proc if it exists. Code section 2 creates the stored proc along with the parameter @CustomerID and the default value –1. In this case, if the user calls the stored proc without a value for @CustomerID, the stored proc will return all the rows. Statement 3 calls the stored proc with a value, and the stored proc returns the one matching row. Statement 4 calls the stored proc without the parameter value, and the stored proc returns all the rows.

	CustomerID	FirstName	MiddleName	LastName
1	15128	Angelica	NULL	Barnes

	CustomerID	FirstName	MiddleName	LastName
1	11196	Alfredo	NULL	Romero
2	11014	Sydney	NULL	Bennett
3	11182	Stephanie	NULL	Torres
4	11170	Carol	T	Howard
5	11144	Edward	NULL	Hernandez
6	11084	Lucas	NULL	Phillips
7	11062	Noah	D	Powell
8	11022	Ethan	G	Zhang

Figure 9-17. The partial results of using a default value parameter

Using the OUTPUT Parameter

You can use an OUTPUT parameter to get back a value from a stored proc. This is one of those gray areas where you may decide to use a scalar-value UDF with a return value instead. In my opinion, if the logic is not portable to any database, use a stored procedure. Save scalar-valued UDFs for truly database-agnostic uses. Here is the syntax for creating and using an OUTPUT parameter with a stored proc:

```
CREATE PROC[EDURE] <proc name> <@param> <data type> OUTPUT AS
    <statements>
    [return <value>]
GO

DECLARE <@variable> <data type>
EXEC <proc name> [<@param> =] <@variable> OUTPUT
PRINT <@variable>
```

You can include as many parameters as you need, and your OUTPUT parameter can pass a value to the stored proc as well as return a value. Type in and execute Listing 9-14 to learn how to use an OUTPUT parameter.

Listing 9-14. Using an OUTPUT Parameter

```
USE AdventureWorks2012;
GO

--1
IF OBJECT_ID('dbo.usp_OrderDetailCount') IS NOT NULL BEGIN
    DROP PROC dbo.usp_OrderDetailCount;
END;
GO
--2
CREATE PROC dbo.usp_OrderDetailCount @OrderID INT,
    @Count INT OUTPUT AS

    SELECT @Count = COUNT(*)
    FROM Sales.SalesOrderDetail
    WHERE SalesOrderID = @OrderID;

    RETURN 0;
GO

--3
DECLARE @OrderCount INT;
--4
EXEC usp_OrderDetailCount 71774, @OrderCount OUTPUT;
--5
PRINT @OrderCount;
```

Code section 1 drops the stored proc if it exists. Code section 2 creates the stored proc, dbo.usp_OrderDetailCount, along with two parameters, @OrderID and @Count. The first parameter accepts a SalesOrderID value. The second parameter is the OUTPUT parameter, which returns the count of the orders for that SalesOrderID. Statement 3 creates a variable, @OrderCount, to be used as the OUTPUT parameter. Statement 4 calls the stored proc with the value for @OrderID and the variable for the @Count parameter. In statement 5, the final value of @Count from inside the stored procedure saved to the variable @OrderCount prints in the Message window. The call to the stored proc could also have looked like this:

```
EXEC dbo.usp_OrderDetailCount @OrderID = 71774, @Count = @OrderCount OUTPUT.
```

One mistake that developers often make is to forget to use the OUTPUT keyword when calling the stored proc. To get the modified parameter value back, you must use OUTPUT.

Saving the Results of a Stored Proc in a Table

One very popular use of a stored procedure is to save the results in a temp or work table for later processing. When saving the results of a stored proc in a table, define the table define ahead of time. All the columns must be in place and of compatible data types. Here is the syntax for inserting the rows returned from a stored procedure into a table:

```
INSERT [INTO] <table name> EXEC <stored proc> [<@param value>]
```

Listing 9-15 shows how to save the results of a proc into a table. Type in and execute the code to learn more.

Listing 9-15. Inserting the Rows from a Stored Proc into a Table

```
USE AdventureWorks2012;
GO

--1
IF OBJECT_ID('dbo.tempCustomer') IS NOT NULL BEGIN
    DROP TABLE dbo.tempCustomer;
END
IF OBJECT_ID('dbo.usp_CustomerName') IS NOT NULL BEGIN
    DROP PROC dbo.usp_CustomerName;
END;
GO

--2
CREATE TABLE dbo.tempCustomer(CustomerID INT, FirstName NVARCHAR(50),
    MiddleName NVARCHAR(50), LastName NVARCHAR(50))
GO

--3
CREATE PROC dbo.usp_CustomerName @CustomerID INT = -1 AS
    SELECT c.CustomerID,p.FirstName,p.MiddleName,p.LastName
    FROM Sales.Customer AS c
    INNER JOIN Person.Person AS p on c.PersonID = p.BusinessEntityID
    WHERE @CustomerID = CASE @CustomerID WHEN -1 THEN -1 ELSE c.CustomerID END;

    RETURN 0;
GO

--4
INSERT INTO dbo.tempCustomer EXEC dbo.usp_CustomerName;

--5
SELECT CustomerID, FirstName, MiddleName, LastName
FROM dbo.tempCustomer;
```

Figure 9-18 shows the results. Code section 1 drops the table and stored proc if they exist. Statement 2 creates the table dbo.tempCustomer, matching up columns and data types. They don't need to have the same names as the stored proc, but they should have the same number of columns, in the same order, and of compatible data types. Code section 3 creates the stored procedure. Statement 4 calls the stored proc while at the same time storing the results in dbo.tempCustomer. Query 5 returns the results.

Results

	CustomerID	FirstName	MiddleName	LastName
1	29485	Catherine	R.	Abel
2	29486	Kim	NULL	Abercrombie
3	29487	Humberto	NULL	Acevedo
4	29484	Gustavo	NULL	Achong
5	29488	Pilar	NULL	Ackerman
6	28866	Aaron	B	Adams
7	13323	Adam	NULL	Adams
8	21139	Alex	C	Adams
9	29170	Alexandra	J	Adams
10	19419	Allison	L	Adams
11	11971	Amanda	P	Adams

Figure 9-18. The results of saving the results of a stored proc into a table

Using a Logic in Stored Procedures

So far, you have seen stored procs that don't do much more than run queries, but stored procedures are capable of so much more. You can include conditional code, loops, error trapping, object creation statements, and more within stored procedures. Listing 9-16 shows an example. Type in and execute the code to learn more.

Listing 9-16. Using Logic in a Stored Procedure

```
USE tempdb;
GO

--1
IF OBJECT_ID('usp_ProgrammingLogic') IS NOT NULL BEGIN
    DROP PROC usp_ProgrammingLogic;
END;
GO

--2
CREATE PROC usp_ProgrammingLogic AS
    --2.1
    CREATE TABLE #Numbers(number INT NOT NULL);
    --2.2
    DECLARE @count INT;
    SET @count = ASCII('!');

    --2.3
    WHILE @count < 200 BEGIN
        INSERT INTO #Numbers(number) VALUES (@count);
        SET @count = @count + 1;
    END;
```

349

```
    --2.4
    ALTER TABLE #Numbers ADD symbol NCHAR(1);
    --2.5
    UPDATE #Numbers SET symbol = CHAR(number);

    --2.6
    SELECT number, symbol FROM #Numbers
GO
--3

EXEC usp_ProgrammingLogic;
```

Figure 9-19 shows the results. This stored proc creates a table of numbers and the ASCII symbol for each number. This is a simple example just to give you an idea of what you can do. Anything you have learned in this book can be encapsulated within a stored procedure.

	number	symbol
1	33	!
2	34	"
3	35	#
4	36	$
5	37	%
6	38	&
7	39	'
8	40	(
9	41	)

Figure 9-19. The partial results of using a stored procedure with programming logic

CLR Integration

T-SQL is a powerful tool for handling relational data. It is the primary tool for talking to a SQL Server database, but even a tool as powerful and flexible as T-SQL has limitations. For example, if you want to run large aggregate computations on relational data, T-SQL may not be the best tool. CLR (Common Language Runtime) allows for executing .NET languages such as Visual C++, Visual C#, and Visual Basic .NET in procedures, functions, or triggers. In fact, CLR is used by some SQL Server spatial data types (GEOMETRY and GEOGRAPHY) and complex functions (encryption). Without the use of .NET code these data types and functions could not exist using standard T-SQL.

So when should you use CLR and when should you use T-SQL? Though a simplified answer, CLR is best used when you need to perform difficult procedural logic on data. T-SQL is great at selecting, deleting, and updating data but what happens to that data in between is where CLR comes into play. For example, CLR is especially suited for functions. Functions accept data as input but once a function has the data, computations are performed on the data to produce an output. During the computation process there is no need to access the database.

Creating a CLR object in SQL Server is a basically a three-step process. The first step is to create a DLL based on the developed code. You do this in a tool like Visual Studio. To build the application you can download a copy of Visual Studio Express for C# from Microsoft at www.microsoft.com/visualstudio/en-us/products/2010-editions/visual-csharp-express. Once the application is built you then create an *assembly*. Much like an extended stored procedure, CLR uses application DLLs but instead of the DLL residing on the server outside of SQL Server, the DLL is embedded into an assembly that becomes a SQL Server object. The third step is to create the SQL Server object (stored procedure, function, UDF) by referencing the assembly.

Let's look at a useful example that walks through these steps. The example in Listing 9-17 will create a CLR stored procedure used to create a strong, eight-character password based off of two hash keys selected from a table. Although the procedure for building an application DLL is beyond the scope of this chapter, I am including the C# code. Following it is the C# code used to build the application DLL.

Listing 9-17. C# Code for Generating Passwords

```csharp
using System;
using System.Collections.Generic;
using System.ComponentModel;
using System.Data;
using System.Linq;
using System.Text;
using System.IO;
using System.Data.SqlClient;
using System.Data.SqlTypes;

public partial class pwdGen
{
    // private DataSet myDataset;
    private string cString;
    //private int myRow;
    private string key1;
    private string key2;
    //private string mySeed = "HashKeyMe";
    private SqlConnection mySqlConnection;
    private SqlDataAdapter myAdapter;
    string txtUser = "";
    string txtServer = "";
    string password;
    //string letters =
        "abcdefghijkmnopqrstuvwxyzABCDEFGHIJKLMNOPQRSTUVWXYZ23456789!@#$%^&*():;?<>";
    string lcase = "abcdefghijkmnopqrstuvwxyz";
    string ucase = "ABCDEFGHJKLMNOPQRSTUVWXYZ";
    string ncase = "23456789";
    string scase = "!@#[$%]^{&}*(<)?>";
    bool OLD = true;
    bool NEW = false;


    private void LoadData()
    {
        mySqlConnection =
          new SqlConnection(
          "server=HOME-PC" +
          ";database=TEST" +
```

351

```
        ";Integrated Security=SSPI");
    mySqlConnection.Open();
    // build the sql select string
    cString = "SELECT Key1, Key2 FROM tblHashCode";
    //myDataset = ConnectToData(cString, "KeyCodes");
    DataSet dataset;
    myAdapter = new SqlDataAdapter();
    myAdapter.TableMappings.Add("Table", "KeyCodes");
    SqlCommand myCommand = new SqlCommand(cString, mySqlConnection);
    myAdapter.SelectCommand = myCommand;
    dataset = new DataSet("KeyCodes");
    myAdapter.Fill(dataset);

}


private void generate()
{
    string buffer;
    string buffer2;
    string tempbuffer;
    char[] seed = new char[1];
    char[] tempchar = new char[1];
    char[] myTemp = new char[1];
    int i = 0;
    int m = 0;
    int c = 0;
    int temp = 0;
    int bufferval = 0;
    int systemsval = 0;
    bool direction;

    buffer = key1 + txtUser.ToLower();
    buffer2 = key2 + txtServer.ToLower();

    m = txtServer.Length % 2;
    if (m == 0)
    {
        direction = true;
    }
    else
    {
        direction = false;
    }

    // semi random seed
    tempchar[0] = buffer[0];
    for (int x = 1; x < buffer.Length; x++)
    {
        tempchar[0] = (char)(tempchar[0] ^ buffer[x]);
    }
```

```
for (int x = 1; x < buffer2.Length; x++)
{
    tempchar[0] = (char)(tempchar[0] ^ buffer2[x]);
}
seed = tempchar;

// pre-process buffers to make 8 character password
i = 0;
tempbuffer = "";

for (int x = 0; x < buffer.Length; x++)
{
    if (i == 8) i = 0;
    //if (tempbuffer[i] == buffer[x]) tempbuffer[i]++;
    if (x >= 8)
    {
        myTemp[0] = (char)(myTemp[0] ^ buffer[x]);
    }
    else
    {
        myTemp[0] = (char)(seed[0] ^ buffer[x]);
    }
    tempbuffer = tempbuffer + myTemp[0];
    i++;
}
buffer = tempbuffer;

i = 0;
tempbuffer = "";

for (int x = 0; x < buffer2.Length; x++)
{
    if (i == 8) i = 0;
    if (x >= 8)
    {
        myTemp[0] = (char)(myTemp[0] ^ buffer2[x]);
    }
    else
    {
        myTemp[0] = (char)(seed[0] ^ buffer2[x]);
    }
    i++;
    tempbuffer = tempbuffer + myTemp[0];
}
buffer2 = tempbuffer;

// cycle the buffers against each other and generate modulii
c = 0;
m = 0;
password = "";

for (int x = 0; x < 2; x++)
```

```
{
    if (OLD)
    {
        if (c >= buffer2.Length) c = 0;
        if (m >= buffer.Length) m = 0;
        bufferval = buffer[m];
        systemsval = buffer2[c];
    }
    if (direction)
    {
        // Lowercase letter
        if (NEW)
        {
            c++;
            m++;
            if (c >= buffer2.Length) c = 0;
            if (m >= buffer.Length) m = 0;
            bufferval = buffer[m];
            systemsval = buffer2[c];
        }
        temp = (bufferval * systemsval) % 25;
        myTemp[0] = lcase[Math.Abs(temp)];
        password = password + myTemp[0];

        // Uppercase letter
        if (NEW)
        {
            c++;
            m++;
            if (c >= buffer2.Length) c = 0;
            if (m >= buffer.Length) m = 0;
            bufferval = buffer[m];
            systemsval = buffer2[c];
        }
        temp = (bufferval * systemsval) % 25;
        myTemp[0] = ucase[Math.Abs(temp)];
        password = password + myTemp[0];

        // Number character
        if (NEW)
        {
            c++;
            m++;
            if (c >= buffer2.Length) c = 0;
            if (m >= buffer.Length) m = 0;
            bufferval = buffer[m];
            systemsval = buffer2[c];
        }
        temp = (bufferval * systemsval) % 8;
        myTemp[0] = ncase[Math.Abs(temp)];
        password = password + myTemp[0];
```

```
        // Special letter
        if (NEW)
        {
            c++;
            m++;
            if (c >= buffer2.Length) c = 0;
            if (m >= buffer.Length) m = 0;
            bufferval = buffer[m];
            systemsval = buffer2[c];
        }
        temp = (bufferval * systemsval) % 17;
        myTemp[0] = scase[Math.Abs(temp)];
        password = password + myTemp[0];
}
else
{
        // Uppercase letter
        if (NEW)
        {
            c++;
            m++;
            if (c >= buffer2.Length) c = 0;
            if (m >= buffer.Length) m = 0;
            bufferval = buffer[m];
            systemsval = buffer2[c];
        }
        temp = (bufferval * systemsval) % 25;
        myTemp[0] = ucase[Math.Abs(temp)];
        password = password + myTemp[0];

        // Special letter
        if (NEW)
        {
            c++;
            m++;
            if (c >= buffer2.Length) c = 0;
            if (m >= buffer.Length) m = 0;
            bufferval = buffer[m];
            systemsval = buffer2[c];
        }
        temp = (bufferval * systemsval) % 17;
        myTemp[0] = scase[Math.Abs(temp)];
        password = password + myTemp[0];

        // Number character
        if (NEW)
        {
            c++;
            m++;
            if (c >= buffer2.Length) c = 0;
            if (m >= buffer.Length) m = 0;
            bufferval = buffer[m];
```

```
                    systemsval = buffer2[c];
            }
            temp = (bufferval * systemsval) % 8;
            myTemp[0] = ncase[Math.Abs(temp)];
            password = password + myTemp[0];

            // Lowercase letter
            if (NEW)
            {
                c++;
                m++;
                if (c >= buffer2.Length) c = 0;
                if (m >= buffer.Length) m = 0;
                bufferval = buffer[m];
                systemsval = buffer2[c];
            }
            temp = (bufferval * systemsval) % 25;
            myTemp[0] = lcase[Math.Abs(temp)];
            password = password + myTemp[0];
        }
        if (OLD)
        {
            c++;
            m++;
        }
    }

}


// below is the sp
[Microsoft.SqlServer.Server.SqlProcedure]
public static void generatePassword(string user, string svr, out string pwd)
{
    pwdGen objpwd = new pwdGen();
    objpwd.txtUser = user;
    objpwd.txtServer = svr;
    objpwd.password = "";
    objpwd.loadData();
    objpwd.generate();
    pwd = objpwd.password;

}

}
```

Understanding the C# code to the nth degree is not important, but there are two things to notice. Firstly, the only T-SQL being executed is the T-SQL used to select from the table in the LoadData() function, as highlighted in Listing 9-18. Once the data is pulled from SQL Server, the C# logic takes over.

Listing 9-18. LoadData() Function

```
private void LoadData()
{
    mySqlConnection =
      new SqlConnection(
      "server=HOME-PC" +
      ";database=TEST" +
      ";Integrated Security=SSPI");
    mySqlConnection.Open();
    // build the sql select string
    cString = "SELECT Key1, Key2 FROM tblHashCode";
    //myDataset = ConnectToData(cString, "KeyCodes");
    DataSet dataset;
    myAdapter = new SqlDataAdapter();
    myAdapter.TableMappings.Add("Table", "KeyCodes");
    SqlCommand myCommand = new SqlCommand(cString, mySqlConnection);
    myAdapter.SelectCommand = myCommand;
    dataset = new DataSet("KeyCodes");
    myAdapter.Fill(dataset);

}
```

This LoadData() function creates a connection to my server named HOME-PC and database named TEST. If you want to run this code, you will need to modify these values to reflect your specific configuration. The T-SQL performs a SELECT on the tblHashCode. The script for creating this table is in Listing 9-20.

The other item of note is the declaration of the stored procedure at the end of code. This declaration is important because you will need to refer to it later when creating the assembly in SQL Server. Listing 9-19 shows how the stored procedure declaration is created.

Listing 9-19. SqlProcedure Call in C#

```
[Microsoft.SqlServer.Server.SqlProcedure]
    public static void generatePassword(string user, string svr, out string pwd)
    {
        pwdGen objpwd = new pwdGen();
        objpwd.txtUser = user;
        objpwd.txtServer = svr;
        objpwd.password = "";
        objpwd.loadData();
        objpwd.generate();
        pwd = objpwd.password;
```

Once you build the DLL in Visual Studio, you can focus on preparing the SQL Server environment. As mentioned, the C# code references a server, database, and table. You'll need to configure these based on how you modified the original code. In my case, the server is called HOME-PC, the database is called TEST, and the table is called tblHashCode. The table has two columns: key1 and key2. Listing 9-20 creates the table.

Listing 9-20. Create tblHashCode

```
USE test;

CREATE TABLE [dbo].[tblKeyCode](
    [Key1] [varchar](100) NOT NULL,
    [Key2] [varchar](100) NOT NULL
) ON [PRIMARY];

INSERT INTO tblHashCode
VALUES('ApressPublishing', 'ScottShaw');
```

Listing 9-20 creates a table called tblHashCode and inserts two values into the table. These two values can be anything you want and will be used by the code to generate the password. If you change either one of the values, the application will generate a different password. Next, you will create the assembly and the stored procedure. Listing 9-21 takes care of those two tasks.

Listing 9-21. Create Assembly and Storted Procedure

```
ALTER DATABASE test SET TRUSTWORTHY ON;

USE test;
GO

CREATE ASSEMBLY [PasswordGenerator]
AUTHORIZATION [sys]
FROM N'C:\Projects\PasswordGenerator\bin\Release\PasswordGenerator.dll'
WITH PERMISSION_SET = EXTERNAL_ACCESS;

CREATE PROC sp_passwordgenerator(@uname NVARCHAR(50),@srv NVARCHAR(50),@pwd1 NVARCHAR(50)
OUTPUT)
AS EXTERNAL name PasswordGenerator.pwdGen.generatePassword;
```

You first set the database to trustworthy mode since you are creating an assembly with the EXTERNAL ACCESS permission. You will need to change the directory path for the DLL to wherever it is stored on your own system. The CREATE PROCEDURE command specifies all the necessary input and output variables and references the name and methods for the application. Once the stored procedure is successfully created, you can execute it like any other stored procedure. Listing 9-22 shows an example execution. Figure 9-20 shows the results.

Listing 9-22. Executing a CLR Stored Procedure

```
DECLARE @return_status sysname;
DECLARE @pwd1 nvarchar(50);
DECLARE @srv nvarchar(50);
DECLARE @user nvarchar(50);
SET  @srv='HOME-PC';
SET @user ='scott';
EXEC sp_passwordgenerator @user,@srv,@pwd1 output;
SELECT @pwd1;
```

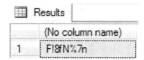

Figure 9-20. *Results of sp_passwordgenerator*

Developers can use stored procedures for all database calls. Database administrators can set up stored procedures as scheduled jobs for batch processing or for reports. CLR is now used in SQL Server as a replacement for extended stored procedures. Developers can use CLR to embed .NET languages in usable SQL Server objects like stored procedures, functions, and data types. Now that you have seen many of the possibilities of using stored procedures, complete Exercise 9-4 to practice what you have learned.

EXERCISE 9-4

Use the AdventureWorks2012 database to complete this exercise. You can find the solutions in the Appendix.

1. Create a stored procedure called dbo.usp_CustomerTotals instead of a view from question 2 in Exercise 9-2. Test the stored procedure.

2. Modify the stored procedure created in question 1 to include a parameter @CustomerID. Use the parameter in the WHERE clause of the query in the stored procedure. Test the stored procedure.

3. Create a stored procedure called dbo.usp_ProductSales that accepts a ProductID for a parameter and has an OUTPUT parameter that returns the total number sold for the product. Test the stored procedure.

User-Defined Data Types

Within a database, you can create user-defined data types. User-defined data types (UDTs) are nothing more than native data types that you have given a specific name. This enables you to make sure that a particular type of column is consistently defined throughout the database. For example, databases often contain ZIP code and phone number columns as UDTs.

Take a look at the UDTs defined for the AdventureWorks2012 database by navigating to Programmability ➤ Types ➤ User-Defined Data Types. If you double-click the Phone data type, you can see the graphical editor for the type (see Figure 9-21).

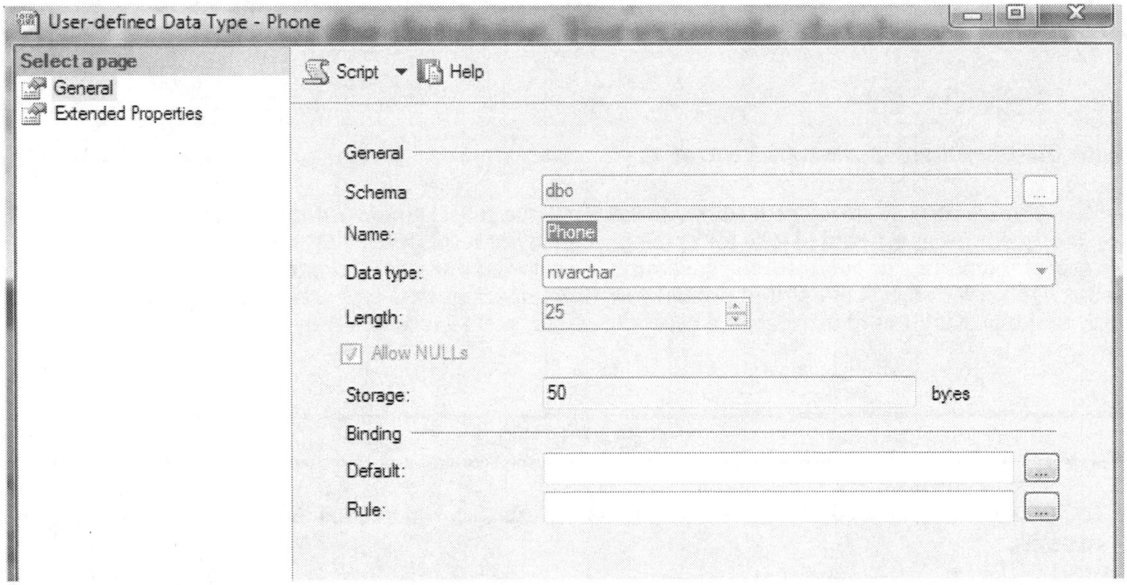

Figure 9-21. The properties of the

The Phone data type is an NVARCHAR(25) that allows NULL values. The Binding section for Default and Rule are blank. In previous versions of SQL Server, you could create defaults and rules that were then applied to columns or UDTs, but the binding features have been deprecated and should not be used. Once you have the data type defined, you can use it when defining columns in tables as any other data type. Here is the syntax for creating a UDT:

```
CREATE TYPE <type name> FROM <native type and size> [NULL|NOT NULL]
```

Listing 9-23 shows how to create a UDT. Type in and execute the code to learn more.

Listing 9-23. Creating a User-Defined Type

```
USE AdventureWorks2012;
GO
IF  EXISTS (
    SELECT * FROM sys.types st
    JOIN sys.schemas ss ON st.schema_id = ss.schema_id
    WHERE st.name = N'CustomerID' AND ss.name = N'dbo') BEGIN

    DROP TYPE dbo.CustomerID;
END;
GO

CREATE TYPE dbo.CustomerID FROM INT NOT NULL;
```

Now that the new UDT exists, you can use it when defining new tables. Another type of object is called a *user-defined type*. This type must be created with a .NET language called a CLR data type. CLR types can contain multiple properties and can contain methods.

Triggers

Triggers are a very powerful feature of SQL Server. As with most powerful things, they can also cause many problems. Triggers are like a special type of stored procedure that runs whenever data is modified. You can define triggers on tables that fire when new rows are inserted or when existing rows are updated or deleted. Triggers can insert data into auditing tables, roll back the current update, or even modify the row that caused the trigger to fire in the first place. Obviously, they can have an impact on performance, and care must be taken so that triggers are not used in a way that causes them to fire repeatedly because of one update.

Any code within a trigger must be very efficient. The transaction that caused the trigger to fire can't complete until the trigger is successfully completed. One common use of triggers is to enforce *referential integrity*, or the primary key/foreign key relationships between tables. For example, a trigger that fires when a customer is deleted from the customer table might delete all the orders for that customer. In actuality, this use of triggers is not necessary. Database designers can use foreign key constraints to take care of situations like this.

Traditionally, triggers were defined only on tables. Triggers defined on a database or on a server are called DDL triggers. These fire when operations such as creating a table or adding a login are performed. They can be used to prevent these operations or log them, for example.

Since this is a beginning book, it doesn't cover creating triggers. Just be aware that triggers often exist in databases and are frequently the cause of performance or logic problems that are difficult to track down.

Thinking About Performance

This chapter covers many ways that you can add logic to the database to enforce business rules or make development easier. One common problem is using UDFs that access data inline in a query. The database engine will have to execute the function for each row of the query. Listing 9-24 illustrates this point. Run the first part of the code to create the objects. Then run query 3 and see how long it takes. Run query 4 and see how long that query takes.

Listing 9-24. Performance Issues with UDFs

```
--RUN THIS FIRST
USE AdventureWorks2012;
GO

IF OBJECT_ID('dbo.udf_ProductTotal') IS NOT NULL BEGIN
    DROP FUNCTION dbo.udf_ProductTotal;
END;
GO

CREATE FUNCTION dbo.udf_ProductTotal(@ProductID INT,@Year INT) RETURNS MONEY AS
BEGIN

    DECLARE @Sum MONEY;

    SELECT @Sum = SUM(LineTotal)
    FROM Sales.SalesOrderDetail AS sod
    INNER JOIN Sales.SalesOrderHeader AS soh
            ON sod.SalesOrderID = soh.SalesOrderID
```

```
        WHERE ProductID = @ProductID AND YEAR(OrderDate) = @Year;

        RETURN ISNULL(@Sum,0);

END;
GO
--TO HERE

--3 Run this by itself to see how long it takes
SELECT ProductID, dbo.udf_ProductTotal(ProductID, 2004) AS SumOfSales
FROM Production.Product
ORDER BY SumOfSales DESC;

--4 Run this by itself to see how long it takes
WITH Sales AS (
    SELECT SUM(LineTotal) AS SumOfSales, ProductID,
        YEAR(OrderDate) AS OrderYear
    FROM Sales.SalesOrderDetail AS sod
    INNER JOIN Sales.SalesOrderHeader AS soh
        ON sod.SalesOrderID = soh.SalesOrderID
    GROUP BY ProductID, YEAR(OrderDate)
)
SELECT p.ProductID, ISNULL(SumOfSales,0) AS SumOfSales
FROM Production.Product AS p
LEFT OUTER JOIN Sales ON p.ProductID = Sales.ProductID
    AND OrderYear = 2004
ORDER BY SumOfSales DESC;
```

On my laptop, query 3 takes 6 or 7 seconds to run, and query 4 takes 1 second. Since the user-defined function must access the Sales.SalesOrderDetail table once for every product, it takes a lot of resources. Unfortunately, the execution plans, if you choose to compare them, don't accurately reflect the difference. On my computer, query 4 takes 100 percent of the resources in the execution plans, but I know that is not true since query 4 runs so much faster.

Database Cleanup

You have created quite a few objects during this chapter. You can either run the script in Listing 9-25 (also available on the catalogue page for this book at www.apress.com) to clean up the objects from the examples or reinstall the sample databases according to the instructions in the "Installing the Sample Databases" section in Chapter 1.

Listing 9-25. Database Cleanup

```
USE AdventureWorks2012;
GO

IF OBJECT_ID('vwCustomer') IS NOT NULL BEGIN
    DROP VIEW vwCustomer;
END;
```

```sql
IF OBJECT_ID('vw_Dept') IS NOT NULL BEGIN
    DROP VIEW dbo.vw_Dept;
END;

IF OBJECT_ID('demoDept') IS NOT NULL BEGIN
    DROP TABLE dbo.demoDept;
END;
IF OBJECT_ID('dbo.demoCustomer') IS NOT NULL BEGIN
    DROP TABLE dbo.demoCustomer;
END;
IF OBJECT_ID('dbo.demoPerson') IS NOT NULL BEGIN
    DROP TABLE dbo.demoPerson;
END;

IF OBJECT_ID('dbo.vw_Customer') IS NOT NULL BEGIN
    DROP VIEW dbo.vw_Customer;
END;

IF OBJECT_ID('dbo.udf_Product') IS NOT NULL BEGIN
    DROP FUNCTION dbo.udf_Product;
END;

IF OBJECT_ID('dbo.udf_Delim') IS NOT NULL BEGIN
    DROP FUNCTION dbo.udf_Delim;
END;

IF OBJECT_ID('dbo.usp_CustomerName') IS NOT NULL BEGIN
    DROP PROC dbo.usp_CustomerName;
END;

IF OBJECT_ID('dbo.usp_OrderDetailCount') IS NOT NULL BEGIN
    DROP PROC dbo.usp_OrderDetailCount;
END;

IF OBJECT_ID('dbo.tempCustomer') IS NOT NULL BEGIN
    DROP TABLE dbo.tempCustomer;
END

IF OBJECT_ID('dbo.usp_CustomerName') IS NOT NULL BEGIN
    DROP PROC dbo.usp_CustomerName;
END;

IF OBJECT_ID('usp_ProgrammingLogic') IS NOT NULL BEGIN
    DROP PROC usp_ProgrammingLogic
END;

IF OBJECT_ID('dbo.CustomerID') IS NOT NULL BEGIN
    DROP TYPE dbo.CustomerID
END;

IF OBJECT_ID('dbo.udf_ProductTotal') IS NOT NULL BEGIN
    DROP FUNCTION dbo.udf_ProductTotal;
```

```
END;

IF OBJECT_ID ('dbo.testCustomer') IS NOT NULL BEGIN
    DROP TABLE dbo.testCustomer;
END;

IF OBJECT_ID('dbo.testOrder') IS NOT NULL BEGIN
    DROP TABLE dbo.testOrder;
END;

IF OBJECT_ID('dbo.testOrderDetail') IS NOT NULL BEGIN
    DROP TABLE dbo.testOrderDetail;
END;

IF OBJECT_ID('dbo.vw_Products') IS NOT NULL BEGIN
    DROP VIEW dbo.vw_Products;
END;

IF OBJECT_ID('dbo.vw_CustomerTotals') IS NOT NULL BEGIN
    DROP VIEW dbo.vw_CustomerTotals;
END;

IF OBJECT_ID('dbo.fn_AddTwoNumbers') IS NOT NULL BEGIN
    DROP FUNCTION dbo.fn_AddTwoNumbers;
END;

IF OBJECT_ID('dbo.Trim') IS NOT NULL BEGIN
    DROP FUNCTION dbo.Trim;
END

IF OBJECT_ID('dbo.fn_RemoveNumbers') IS NOT NULL BEGIN
     DROP FUNCTION dbo.fn_RemoveNumbers;
END;
IF OBJECT_ID('dbo.fn_FormatPhone') IS NOT NULL BEGIN
    DROP FUNCTION dbo.fn_FormatPhone;
END;

IF OBJECT_ID('dbo.usp_CustomerTotals') IS NOT NULL BEGIN
    DROP PROCEDURE dbo.usp_CustomerTotals;
END;

IF OBJECT_ID('dbo.usp_ProductSales') IS NOT NULL BEGIN
    DROP PROCEDURE dbo.usp_ProductSales;
END;

IF  EXISTS (
    SELECT * FROM sys.types st
    JOIN sys.schemas ss ON st.schema_id = ss.schema_id
    WHERE st.name = N'CustomerID' AND ss.name = N'dbo') BEGIN

    DROP TYPE [dbo].[CustomerID];
END;
```

```
DROP DATABASE [TEST];
```

Summary

SQL Server contains many ways to enforce business rules and ensure data integrity. You can set up primary and foreign keys, constraints, and defaults in table definitions. You can create user-defined functions, stored procedures, views, and user-defined data types to add other ways to enforce business rules. You have many options that you can use to make development simpler and encapsulate logic. Each new version of SQL Server adds new data types and functions. Chapter 10 covers some of the new data types added with SQL Server 2012. The new updates to data types related to geography and geometry are especially interesting.

CHAPTER 10

Working with Data Types

You have learned how to retrieve data from SQL Server tables in a number of ways: through simple queries, through joins, with functions, and more. You have learned to manipulate data, write scripts, and create database objects. Essentially, you have learned the T-SQL basics. Not only have you learned these skills, but you have learned to think about the best way to solve a problem, not just the easy way.

This chapter introduces some of the more interesting and complex data types available in SQL Server 2012. You will learn about sparse columns, CLR data types (HIERARCHYID, GEOMETRY, and GEOGRAPHY), enhanced date and time data types, large-value data types (MAX), and FILESTREAM data. Some of these, such as the CLR data types, are nothing like the traditional data types you have been using throughout this book. This chapter provides a glimpse of these interesting new data types.

Chapters 1 through 9 covered the important skills you need to become a proficient T-SQL developer. Since this chapter covers "bonus material," it doesn't contain exercises. I encourage you to practice working with any of the new data types that interest you or that you think will be beneficial in your job.

Large-Value String Data Types (MAX)

Older versions of SQL Server used NTEXT and TEXT data types to represent large values. Microsoft has deprecated those types, which means that in some future release of SQL Server, NTEXT and TEXT will no longer work. For now, however, the deprecated data types still work in SQL Server 2012. Going forward, you should replace these data types with VARCHAR(MAX) and NVARCHAR(MAX).

The TEXT and NTEXT data types have many limitations. For example, you can't declare a variable of type TEXT or NTEXT, use them with most functions, or use them within most search criteria. The MAX data types represent the benefits of both the regular string data types and the TEXT and NTEXT data types when storing large strings. They allow you to store large amounts of data and offer the same functionality of the traditional data types.

When creating string data types, you supply a number of characters. Instead of supplying a number, use the word MAX when the data is going to surpass the maximum normally allowed. Table 10-1 lists the differences between the string value data types.

Table 10-1. The String Data Types

Name	Type	Maximum Characters	Character Set
CHAR	Fixed width	8,000	ASCII
NCHAR	Fixed width	4,000	Unicode
VARCHAR	Variable width	8,000	ASCII
NVARCHAR	Variable width	4,000	Unicode
TEXT	Variable width	$2^{31} - 1$	ASCII
NTEXT	Variable width	$2^{30} - 1$	Unicode
VARCHAR(MAX)	Variable width	$2^{31} - 1$	ASCII
NVARCHAR(MAX)	Variable width	$2^{30} - 1$	Unicode

You work with the MAX string data types just like you do with the traditional types for the most part. Type in and execute Listing 10-1 to learn how to work with the MAX types.

Listing 10-1. Using VARCHAR(MAX)

```
--1
CREATE TABLE #maxExample (maxCol VARCHAR(MAX),
    line INT NOT NULL IDENTITY PRIMARY KEY);
GO

--2
INSERT INTO #maxExample(maxCol)
VALUES ('This is a varchar(max)');

--3
INSERT INTO #maxExample(maxCol)
VALUES (REPLICATE('aaaaaaaaaa',9000));

--4
INSERT INTO #maxExample(maxCol)
VALUES (REPLICATE(CONVERT(VARCHAR(MAX),'bbbbbbbbbb'),9000));

--5
SELECT LEFT(MaxCol,10) AS Left10,LEN(MaxCol) AS varLen
FROM #maxExample;

GO
DROP TABLE #maxExample;
```

Figure 10-1 shows the results. Statement 1 creates a temp table, #maxExample, with a VARCHAR(MAX) column. Statement 2 inserts a row into the table with a short string. Statement 3 inserts a row using the REPLICATE function to create a very large string. If you look at the results, the row inserted by statement 3 contains only 8,000 characters. Statement 4 also inserts a row using the REPLICATE function. This time the statement explicitly converts the string to be replicated to a VARCHAR(MAX). That is because, without explicitly converting it, the string is just a VARCHAR. The REPLICATE function, like most string functions, returns the same data types as supplied to it. To return a VARCHAR(MAX), the function must receive a VARCHAR(MAX). Statement 5 uses the LEFT function to return the first ten characters of the value stored in the maxCol column, demonstrating that you can use string functions with VARCHAR(MAX). Attempting to use LEFT on a TEXT column will just produce an error. It uses the LEN function to see how many characters the column stores in each row. Only 8,000 characters of the row inserted in statement 3 made it to the table since the value wasn't explicitly converted to VARCHAR(MAX) before the REPLICATE function was applied.

Results

	Left10	varLen
1	This is a	22
2	aaaaaaaaaa	8000
3	bbbbbbbbbb	90000

Figure 10-1. *The results of using the VARCHAR(MAX) data type*

If you get a chance to design a database, you may be tempted to make all your string value columns into MAX columns. Microsoft recommends that you use the MAX data types only when it is likely that you will exceed the 8,000- or 4,000-character limits. To be most efficient, size your columns to the expected data.

Large-Value Binary Data Types

You probably have less experience with the data types that store binary data. You can use BINARY, VARBINARY, and IMAGE to store binary data including files such as images, movies, and Word documents. The BINARY and VARBINARY data types can hold up to 8,000 bytes. The IMAGE data type, also deprecated, holds data that exceeds 8,000 bytes, up to 2GB. In SQL Server versions 2005 and greater, always use the VARBINARY(MAX) data type, which can store up to 2GB of binary data, instead of IMAGE.

Creating VARBINARY(MAX) Data

To store data into a VARBINARY(MAX) column, or any of the binary data columns, you can use the CONVERT or CAST function to change string data into binary. Using a program written in a .NET language or any language type that supports working with SQL Server 2012, you can save actual files into VARBINARY(MAX) columns. In this simple demonstration, you will add data by converting string data. Type in and execute Listing 10-2 to learn more.

Listing 10-2. Using VARBINARY(MAX) Data

```
USE AdventureWorks2012;


--1
IF OBJECT_ID('dbo.BinaryTest') IS NOT NULL BEGIN
    DROP TABLE dbo.BinaryTest;
END;

--2
CREATE TABLE dbo.BinaryTest (DataDescription VARCHAR(50),
    BinaryData VARBINARY(MAX));

GO

--3
INSERT INTO dbo.BinaryTest (DataDescription,BinaryData)
VALUES ('Test 1', CONVERT(VARBINARY(MAX),'this is the test 1 row')),
    ('Test 2', CONVERT(VARBINARY(MAX),'this is the test 2 row'));

--4
SELECT DataDescription, BinaryData, CONVERT(VARCHAR(MAX), BinaryData)
FROM dbo.BinaryTest;
```

Figure 10-2 shows the results. Code section 1 drops the dbo.BinaryTest table if it already exists. Statement 2 creates the dbo.BinaryTest table containing the BinaryData column of type VARBINARY(MAX). Statement 3 inserts two rows. To insert data into the BinaryData column, it must be converted into a binary type. Query 4 displays the data. To read the data, the statement converts it back into a string data type.

	DataDescription	BinaryData	(No column name)
1	Test 1	0x7468697320697320746865207465737420312072...	this is the test 1 row
2	Test 2	0x7468697320697320746865207465737420322072...	this is the test 2 row

Figure 10-2. The results of using a VARBINARY(MAX) column

Using FILESTREAM

Often database applications involving files, such as images or Word documents, store just the path to the file in the database and store the actual file on a share in the network. This is more efficient than storing large files within the database since the file system works more efficiently than SQL Server with streaming file data. This solution also poses some problems. Since the files live outside the database, you have to make sure they are secure. You can't automatically apply the security setup in the database to the files. Another issue is backups. When you back up a database, how do you make sure that the backups of the file shares are done at the same time so that the data is consistent in case of a restore?

The FILESTREAM object solves these issues by storing the files on the file system but making the files become part of the database. You do this by adding the word FILESTREAM to the VARBINARY(MAX) column.

The SQL Server instance must be configured to allow FILESTREAM data, and the database must have a file group defined. AdventureWorks2012 has the file group defined, and if you installed your SQL Server instance according to the instructions in Chapter 1, the configuration should be in place.

For this demonstration, you will need to find the folder on your computer that stores the file data. Inside the Object Explorer in SQL Server Management Studio, right-click the AdventureWorks2012 database and choose Properties. Click the Files page and scroll until you can see the file location of the FileStreamDocuments folder. Figure 10-3 shows the location on my system.

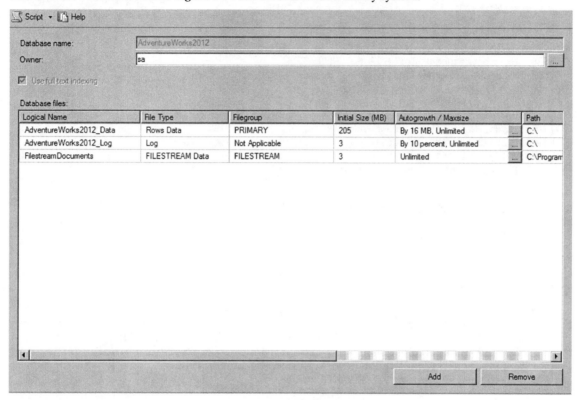

Figure 10-3. The location of the FileStreamDocuments folder on my system

■ **Note** If you didn't enable FILESTREAM during the initial install you can still enable FILESTREAM through the SQL Server Configuration Manager. The tool is located in under the SQL Server 2012 folder in your Windows Programs folders in the Start menu. When you open the tool you'll need to select the properties for the instance and then enable FILESTREAM. SQL Server Books Online has clear instructions on how to accomplish this at http://msdn.microsoft.com/en-us/library/cc645923(v=SQL.110).aspx.

If you don't see a FILESTREAM file, you can simply add one by clicking on the Add button. Name it whatever name you want but be sure to select Filestream data from the file type drop-down and then add the directory path to where you want SQL Server to create the files. Now that you have a working FILESTREAM data file, run the code in Listing 10-3.

Listing 10-3. Working with a FILESTREAM Column

```
USE AdventureWorks2012;


--1
IF OBJECT_ID('dbo.NotepadFiles') IS NOT NULL BEGIN
    DROP TABLE dbo.NotepadFiles;
END;

--2
CREATE table dbo.NotepadFiles(Name VARCHAR(25),
    FileData VARBINARY(MAX) FILESTREAM,
    RowID UNIQUEIDENTIFIER ROWGUIDCOL
        NOT NULL UNIQUE DEFAULT NEWSEQUENTIALID())

--3
INSERT INTO dbo.NotepadFiles(Name,FileData)
VALUES ('test1.txt', CONVERT(VARBINARY(MAX),'This is a test')),
    ('test2.txt', CONVERT(VARBINARY(MAX),'This is the second test'));

--4
SELECT Name,FileData,CONVERT(VARCHAR(MAX),FileData), RowID
FROM dbo.NotepadFiles;
```

Figure 10-4 shows the results. Code section 1 drops the NotepadFiles table in case it already exists. Statement 2 creates the NotepadFiles table. The Name column holds the file name. The FileData column is the FILESTREAM column. To create the FILESTREAM column, specify the FILESTREAM keyword when creating a VARBINARY(MAX) column. The RowID column is a special data type called ROWGUIDID. The NEWSEQUENTIALID function populates the RowID column. This function creates a unique value for each row, which is required when using FILESTREAM data.

	Name	FileData	(No column name)	RowID
1	test1.txt	0x54686973206973206120746573374	This is a test	278EB51A-ADF3-E011-8C8A-0800273864D9
2	test2.txt	0x546869732069732074686520736563636F6E6420746573374	This is the second test	288EB51A-ADF3-E011-8C8A-0800273864D9

Figure 10-4. The results of populating a FILESTREAM column

Statement 3 inserts two rows into the table. The data to be inserted into the FileData column must be of type VARBINARY(MAX) so the statement converts it. Statement 4 shows the results. The FileData column displays the binary data. By converting it to VARCHAR(MAX), you can read the data. Navigate to the appropriate folder on your system. You should see a Documents folder as well as the database files for all the databases hosted on the instance. Inside the Documents folder is a folder with a unique identifier name; this folder corresponds to the Production.Documents table since it has a FILESTREAM column. Figure 10-5 shows the Documents folder on my system.

Figure 10-5. *The Documents folder*

If you navigate further down to the actual files, you will see two files that can be opened in Notepad. When working with a production database, the user would have an application that opens the file through calls to SQL Server with the appropriate program, not by navigating to the actual file.

When you delete a row from the NotepadFiles table, the corresponding file on disk will also disappear. If you drop the table, the entire folder will disappear. Run this code, and then check the Documents folder once again.

```
DROP TABLE NotepadFiles;
CHECKPOINT;
```

The database engine doesn't delete the folder until the database commits all transactions to disk, called a *checkpoint*. By running the CHECKPOINT command, you force the checkpoint.

FileTables

Building off from the FILESTREAM technology, SQL Server 2012 provides an exciting new feature called FileTables. FileTables allow you to store files like movies, documents, or music in a SQL Server table but still access them through Windows Explorer or through another application. The fact that these files are stored in SQL Server is transparent to the user but, because they are stored in the database, you get all the benefits of a relational database, such as the ability to query file properties using T-SQL.

Since the data stored in a FileTable is not your normal data, you will need to first tell SQL Server to treat the data differently. You do this by telling SQL Server the data is non-transactional. A FileTable requires a directory name so you create one in your ALTER DATABASE statement. I choose the name FileTableDocuments. After running the ALTER DATABASE script, you are now able to create a FileTable. In my example, I created a FileTable name MyDocuments that points to a directory called Misc Documents. As you'll see later, the Misc Documents folder will be created under the FileTableDocuments folder. Listing 10-4 shows both queries.

Listing 10-4. *Creating a FileTable*

```
USE AdventureWorks2012;
GO

ALTER DATABASE AdventureWorks2012
    SET FILESTREAM ( NON_TRANSACTED_ACCESS = FULL, DIRECTORY_NAME = 'FileTableDocuments');
GO

CREATE TABLE MyDocuments AS FileTable
    WITH (
        FileTable_Directory = 'Misc Documents',
        FileTable_Collate_Filename = SQL_Latin1_General_CP1_CI_AS
```

```
        );
GO
```

One thing to note is when creating the FileTable I needed to change the collation. The AdventureWorks2012 database is case-sensitive and FileTables can't be created in databases with case-sensitive collation. The collation I specified in the CREATE TABLE statement is case-insensitive. Also note I did not include any column names in my CREATE TABLE statement. This is because a FileTable has a default set of columns that can't be altered. These columns refer to key metadata information on the file stored in the table.

Now that you have the FileTable created, you can do the fun part. There are two ways to get to the directory, or contents, of the table. The first way is through SQL Server Management Studio. If you navigate to the Tables folder under the AdventureWorks2012 database, you will notice an additional folder called FileTables. If you expand the folder, you will see the table created in Listing 10-4. Right-click on the table and select "Explore FileTable Directory." Figure 10-6 shows where the FileTable object can be found in SSMS.

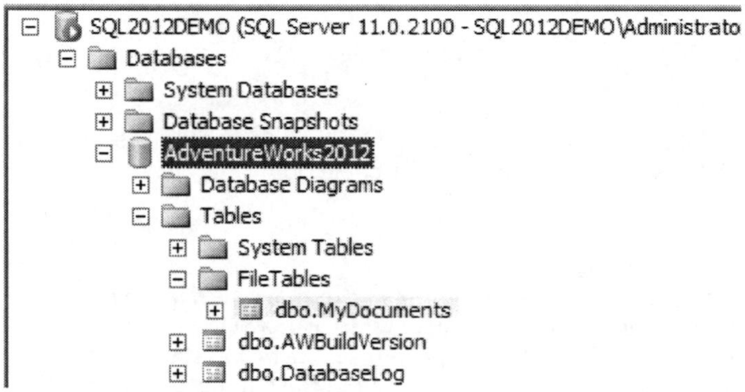

Figure 10-6. *FileTable in SSMS*

Once the folder opens, notice the full path to the directory in the address bar. In my case, the full path is \\Scott-pc\mssqlserver\FileTableDocuments\Misc Documents. This leads to the second method of getting to the folder. You can access this folder by typing the UNC path in the run bar under your Windows Start menu. This is also the path you can share with other users who need to place files in the directory.

Right now the FileTable is empty, as is the folder. You can confirm this by executing a SELECT statement against the table and noticing that no rows are returned. So let's put a file in the folder. You can either create a new file like a .txt file or you can copy an existing file into the directory. In my example, I will right-click on the empty directory and create a blank text file called FileTableTest.txt. Figure 10-7 shows the partial results of my SELECT statement.

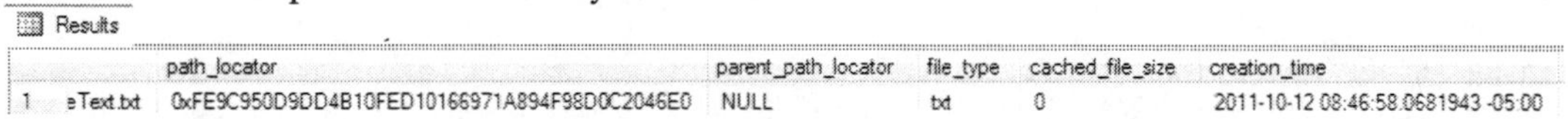

		path_locator	parent_path_locator	file_type	cached_file_size	creation_time
1	≥Text.txt	0xFE9C950D9DD4B10FED10166971A894F98D0C2046E0	NULL	txt	0	2011-10-12 08:46:58.0681943 -05:00

Figure 10-7. *Viewing a document in a FileTable*

You now have a text document stored in a database table, but it can be viewed through Windows Explorer as if it is stored on a filesystem. If you delete the file from the folder, the row will be removed from the table. If you delete the row from the table, the file will be removed from the folder. This means you get all the benefits of a relational database including all the backup and recovery options SQL Server offers but with the simplicity of Windows file navigation.

Enhanced Date and Time

Previous versions of SQL Server have the DATETIME and SMALLDATE time data types for working with temporal data. One big complaint by developers has been that there wasn't an easy way to store just dates or just time. SQL Server 2012 contains several temporal data types. You have a choice of using the DATE and TIME data types as well as the DATETIME2 and DATETIMEOFFSET data types.

Using DATE, TIME, and DATETIME2

You can store just a date or time value by using the new DATE and TIME data types. The traditional DATETIME and SMALLDATETIME data types default to 12 a.m. when you don't specify the time. You can also specify a precision, from zero to seven decimal places, when using the TIME and DATETIME2 data types. Type in and execute Listing 10-5 to learn how to use the new types.

Listing 10-5. Using DATE and TIME

```
USE tempdb;

--1
IF OBJECT_ID('dbo.DateDemo') IS NOT NULL BEGIN
    DROP TABLE dbo.DateDemo;
END;


--2
CREATE TABLE dbo.DateDemo(JustTheDate DATE, JustTheTime TIME(1),
    NewDateTime2 DATETIME2(3), UTCDate DATETIME2);


--3
INSERT INTO dbo.DateDemo (JustTheDate, JustTheTime, NewDateTime2,
    UTCDate)
VALUES (SYSDATETIME(), SYSDATETIME(), SYSDATETIME(), SYSUTCDATETIME());

--4
SELECT JustTheDate, JustTheTime, NewDateTime2, UTCDate
FROM dbo.DateDemo;
```

Figure 10-8 shows the results. Code section 1 drops the dbo.DateDemo table if it already exists. Statement 2 creates the dbo.DateDemo table with a DATE, a TIME, and two DATETIME2 columns. Notice that the TIME and DATETIME2 columns have the precision specified. The default is seven places if a precision is not specified. Statement 3 inserts a row into the table using the new SYSDATETIME function. This function works like the GETDATE function except that it has greater precision than GETDATE. The statement populates the UTCDate column with the SYSUTCDATETIME function, which provides the Coordinated Universal Time (UTC). Statement 4 shows the results. The JustTheDate value shows that even though the SYSDATETIME function populated it, it stored only the date. The JustTheTime values stored only the time with one decimal place past the seconds. The NewDateTime2 column stored both the date and time with three decimal places. The UTCDate column stored the UTC date along with seven decimal places. Since the computer running this demo is in Central time, the time is five hours different.

Results

	JustTheDate	JustTheTime	NewDateTime2	UTCDate
1	2011-08-06	10:09:57.9	2011-08-06 10:09:57.884	2011-08-06 15:09:57.8837890

Figure 10-8. The results of using the new date and time data types

Most business applications won't require the default precision of seven places found with the TIME and DATETIME2 types. Be sure to specify the required precision when creating tables with columns of these types to save space in your database.

Using DATETIMEOFFSET

The new DATETIMEOFFSET data type contains, in addition to the date and time, a time zone offset for working with dates and times in different time zones. This is the difference between the UTC date/time and the stored date. Along with the new data type, several new functions for working with DATETIMEOFFSET are available. Type in and execute Listing 10-6 to learn how to work with this new data type.

***Listing 10-6.** Using the DATETIMEOFFSET Data Type*

```
USE tempdb;

--1
IF OBJECT_ID('dbo.OffsetDemo') IS NOT NULL BEGIN
    DROP TABLE dbo.OffsetDemo;
END;

--2
CREATE TABLE dbo.OffsetDemo(Date1 DATETIMEOFFSET);


--3
INSERT INTO dbo.OffsetDemo(Date1)
VALUES (SYSDATETIMEOFFSET()),
    (SWITCHOFFSET(SYSDATETIMEOFFSET(),'+00:00')),
    (TODATETIMEOFFSET(SYSDATETIME(),'+05:00'));


--4
SELECT Date1
FROM dbo.OffsetDemo;
```

Figure 10-9 shows the results. Code section 1 drops the dbo.OffsetDemo table if it exists. Statement 2 creates the table with a DATETIMEOFFSET column, Date1. Statement 3 inserts three rows into the table using the new functions for working with the new data types. The SYSDATETIMEOFFSET function returns the date and time on the server along with the time zone offset. The computer I am using is five hours behind UTC, so the value -05:00 appears after the current date and time. Using the SWITCHOFFSET function, you can switch a DATETIMEOFFSET value to another time zone. Notice that by switching to

+00:00, the UTC time, the date and time values adjust. By using the TODATETIMEOFFSET function, you can add a time zone to a regular date and time.

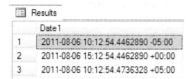

Figure 10-9. The results of using DATETIMEOFFSET

The new data type and functions may be useful to you if you work with data in different time zones. When time changes go into effect, such as Daylight Saving Time, the offsets don't adjust. Keep that in mind if you choose to work with DATETIMEOFFSET.

HIERARCHYID

The HIERARCHYID data type is used to represent hierarchical relationships in data, for example, family trees, organizational charts, or directory structures. This data type is a CLR data type (you were introduced to CLR in Chapter 9), which means that it can contain multiple properties instead of just one value. The HIERARCHYID column also has methods, which means that columns and variables of this type can "do something" and not just contain a value. The HIERARCHYID data type originally shipped with SQL Server 2008, and you can use it even if you don't want to create any custom types.

You learned about joining a table to itself in the "Self-Joins" section in Chapter 4. In older versions of AdventureWorks, the ManagerID column points back to the EmployeeID column in the HumanResources.Employee table. To follow the org chart from this table, you must recursively follow the chain of command from the CEO down each manager-employee path to the lowest employee, which is pretty difficult to do with T-SQL. Chapter 11 covers how to do this in the "Writing Recursive Queries" section. The AdventureWorks2012 database replaces the self-join with OrganizationalNode, a HIERARCHYID column, which is much easier to query.

Viewing HIERARCHYID

If you just write a query to view the OrganizationalNode in the HumanResources.Employee table, you will see binary data. That is because CLR data types are stored as binary values. To view the data in readable form, you must use the ToString method of the type. The OrganizationalLevel column in the table is a computed column based on OrganizationalNode using the GetLevel method. Type in and execute Listing 10-7 to view the data.

Listing 10-7. Viewing the OrganizationalNode

```
USE AdventureWorks2012;
GO

SELECT BusinessEntityID,
    SPACE((OrganizationLevel) * 3) + JobTitle AS Title,
    OrganizationNode, OrganizationLevel,
    OrganizationNode.ToString() AS Readable
FROM HumanResources.Employee
ORDER BY Readable;
```

Figure 10-10 shows the partial results. As mentioned, the OrganizationalNode data is meaningless unless you use the ToString method as in the Readable column. By using the SPACE function to indent the JobTitle column from the table to produce the Title column in the results and by sorting on the Readable column, you can see the relationships between the job titles in the data.

Results

	BusinessEntityID	Title	OrganizationNode	OrganizationLevel	Readable
1	1	Chief Executive Officer	0x	0	/
2	2	Vice President of Engineering	0x58	1	/1/
3	3	Engineering Manager	0x5AC0	2	/1/1/
4	4	Senior Tool Designer	0x5AD6	3	/1/1/1/
5	5	Design Engineer	0x5ADA	3	/1/1/2/
6	6	Design Engineer	0x5ADE	3	/1/1/3/
7	7	Research and Development Manager	0x5AE1	3	/1/1/4/
8	8	Research and Development Engineer	0x5AE158	4	/1/1/4/1/
9	9	Research and Development Engineer	0x5AE168	4	/1/1/4/2/
10	10	Research and Development Manager	0x5AE178	4	/1/1/4/3/
11	11	Senior Tool Designer	0x5AE3	3	/1/1/5/
12	12	Tool Designer	0x5AE358	4	/1/1/5/1/
13	13	Tool Designer	0x5AE368	4	/1/1/5/2/
14	14	Senior Design Engineer	0x5AE5	3	/1/1/6/
15	15	Design Engineer	0x5AE7	3	/1/1/7/
16	16	Marketing Manager	0x68	1	/2/
17	17	Marketing Assistant	0x6AC0	2	/2/1/

Figure 10-10. The partial results of querying the HumanResources.Employee table

The very first node in the hierarchy is the CEO, or Chief Executive Officer, of the company, represented as a slash (/) in the Readable column. The level for the CEO is 0, which you can see in the computed column OrganizationLevel. Several employees have an OrganizationLevel of 1; these employees report directly to the CEO. If you scroll down through all the results, you will see that these have a value, 1 through 6, in between two slashes. The Vice President of Engineering is the first node in level 1. The Marketing Manager is the second node in level 1. Each of these employees has other employees reporting to them. Those employees have a level of 2. For example, the Engineering Manager reports to the Vice President of Engineering and has a Readable value of /1/1/. Four employees report to the Engineering Manager. These employees all have Readable values that begin with /1/1/ along with an additional value, 1 through 4.

Creating a Hierarchy

As you can see from the previous example, querying hierarchical data using HIERARCHYID is not difficult. Maintaining the data, however, is much more challenging. To add a new value or update existing values, you must use the built-in methods of the data type. If you have worked with nodes and pointers in other programming languages, you will find this to be very similar. To learn how to insert nodes using these methods to create hierarchical data, type in and execute the code in Listing 10-8.

Listing 10-8. Creating a Hierarchy with HIERARCHYID

```
Use tempdb;


--1
IF OBJECT_ID('SportsOrg') IS NOT NULL BEGIN
    DROP TABLE SportsOrg;
END;


--2
CREATE TABLE SportsOrg
    (DivNode HIERARCHYID NOT NULL PRIMARY KEY CLUSTERED,
    DivLevel AS DivNode.GetLevel(), --Calculated column
    DivisionID INT NOT NULL,
    Name VARCHAR(30) NOT NULL);


--3
INSERT INTO SportsOrg(DivNode,DivisionID,Name)
VALUES(HIERARCHYID::GetRoot(),1,'State');


--4
DECLARE @ParentNode HIERARCHYID, @LastChildNode HIERARCHYID;

--5
SELECT @ParentNode = DivNode
FROM SportsOrg
WHERE DivisionID = 1;

--6
SELECT @LastChildNode = max(DivNode)
FROM SportsOrg
WHERE DivNode.GetAncestor(1) = @ParentNode;
--7
INSERT INTO SportsOrg(DivNode,DivisionID,Name)
VALUES (@ParentNode.GetDescendant(@LastChildNode,NULL),
2,'Madison County');

--8
SELECT DivisionID,DivLevel,DivNode.ToString() AS Node,Name
FROM SportsOrg;
```

Figure 10-11 shows the results. You might be surprised how much code was required just to insert two rows! Code section 1 drops the SportsOrg table if it already exists. Statement 2 creates the SportsOrg table with the DivisionID and Name columns to identify each division or team. The DivNode column is a HIERARCHYID column, and the DivLevel is a computed column. Statement 3 inserts the first row, the root, into the table. Take a close look at the INSERT statement. Instead of inserting a value into DivNode, the statement uses the name of the data type along with the GetRoot method. Of course, since the DivLevel is computed column, you don't insert anything into the column.

	DivisionID	DivLevel	Node	Name
1	1	0	/	State
2	2	1	/1/	Madison County

Figure 10-11. The results of creating a hierarchy

To insert the second and subsequent nodes, you have to use the GetDescendant method of the parent node. You also have to determine the last child of the parent. Statement 4 declares two variables needed to accomplish this. Statement 5 saves the parent into a variable. Statement 6 saves the last child of the parent into a variable. In this case, there are no children just yet. Statement 7 inserts the row using the GetDescendant method. If the second argument is NULL, the method returns a new child that is greater than the child node in the first argument. Finally, query 8 displays the data.

Using Stored Procedures to Manage Hierarchical Data

Working with HIERARCHYID can be pretty complicated, as shown in the previous section. If you decide to use this data type in your applications, I recommend that you create stored procedures to encapsulate the logic and make coding your application much easier. Listing 10-9 contains a stored procedure to add new rows to the table. Type in and execute the code to learn more.

Listing 10-9. Using a Stored Procedure to Insert New Nodes

```
USE tempdb;
GO


--1
IF OBJECT_ID('dbo.usp_AddDivision') IS NOT NULL BEGIN
    DROP PROC dbo.usp_AddDivision;
END;
IF OBJECT_ID('dbo.SportsOrg') IS NOT NULL BEGIN
    DROP TABLE dbo.SportsOrg;
END;
GO


--2
CREATE TABLE SportsOrg
    (DivNode HierarchyID NOT NULL PRIMARY KEY CLUSTERED,
    DivLevel AS DivNode.GetLevel(), --Calculated column
    DivisionID INT NOT NULL,
    Name VARCHAR(30) NOT NULL);
GO


--3
INSERT INTO SportsOrg(DivNode,DivisionID,Name)
VALUES(HIERARCHYID::GetRoot(),1,'State');
GO
```

```
--4
CREATE PROC usp_AddDivision @DivisionID INT,
    @Name VARCHAR(50),@ParentID INT AS

    DECLARE @ParentNode HierarchyID, @LastChildNode HierarchyID;

    --Grab the parent node
    SELECT @ParentNode = DivNode
    FROM SportsOrg
    WHERE DivisionID = @ParentID;

    BEGIN TRANSACTION
        --Find the last node added to the parent
        SELECT @LastChildNode = max(DivNode)
        FROM SportsOrg
        WHERE DivNode.GetAncestor(1) = @ParentNode;
        --Insert the new node using the GetDescendant function
        INSERT INTO SportsOrg(DivNode,DivisionID,Name)
        VALUES (@ParentNode.GetDescendant(@LastChildNode,NULL),
            @DivisionID,@Name);
    COMMIT TRANSACTION;
GO


--5
EXEC usp_AddDivision 2,'Madison County',1;
EXEC usp_AddDivision 3,'Macoupin County',1;
EXEC usp_AddDivision 4,'Green County',1;
EXEC usp_AddDivision 5,'Edwardsville',2;
EXEC usp_AddDivision 6,'Granite City',2;
EXEC usp_AddDivision 7,'Softball',5;
EXEC usp_AddDivision 8,'Baseball',5;
EXEC usp_AddDivision 9,'Basketball',5;
EXEC usp_AddDivision 10,'Softball',6;
EXEC usp_AddDivision 11,'Baseball',6;
EXEC usp_AddDivision 12,'Basketball',6;
EXEC usp_AddDivision 13,'Ages 10 - 12',7;
EXEC usp_AddDivision 14,'Ages 13 - 17',7;
EXEC usp_AddDivision 15,'Adult',7;
EXEC usp_AddDivision 16,'Preschool',8;
EXEC usp_AddDivision 17,'Grade School League',8;
EXEC usp_AddDivision 18,'High School League',8;

--6
SELECT DivNode.ToString() AS Node,
    DivisionID, SPACE(DivLevel * 3) + Name AS Name
FROM SportsOrg
ORDER BY DivNode;
```

Figure 10-12 shows the results. Code section 1 drops the stored procedure and table if they already exist. Statement 2 creates the table, and statement 3 inserts the root as in the previous section. Code section 4 creates the stored procedure to insert new nodes. The stored procedure requires the new DivisionID and Name values along with the DivisionID of the parent node. Inside the stored proc, an explicit transaction contains the code to grab the last child node and perform the insert. If this were part of an actual multiuser application, it would be very important to make sure that two users didn't accidentally insert values into the same node position. By using an explicit transaction, you avoid that problem. Code section 5 calls the stored procedure to insert each node. Finally, query 6 retrieves the data from the SportsOrg table. The query uses the same technique from the previous section utilizing the SPACES function to format the Name column results.

	Node	DivisionID	Name
1	/	1	State
2	/1/	2	Madison County
3	/1/1/	5	Edwardsville
4	/1/1/1/	7	Softball
5	/1/1/1/ˉ/	13	Ages 10 - 12
6	/1/1/1/2/	14	Ages 13 - 17
7	/1/1/1/3/	15	Adult
8	/1/1/2/	8	Baseball
9	/1/1/2/ˉ/	16	Preschoo
10	/1/1/2/2/	17	Grade School League
11	/1/1/2/3/	18	High School League
12	/1/1/3/	9	Basketball
13	/1/2/	6	Granite City
14	/1/2/1/	10	Softball
15	/1/2/2/	11	Baseball
16	/1/2/3/	12	Basketball
17	/2/	3	Macoupin County
18	/3/	4	Green County

Figure 10-12. The results of using a stored procedure to insert new rows

Deleting a node is easy; you just delete the row. Unfortunately, there is nothing built into the HIERARCHYID data type to ensure that the children of the deleted nodes are also deleted or moved to a new parent. You will end up with orphaned nodes if the deleted node was a parent node. You can also move nodes, but you must make sure that you move the children of the moved nodes as well. If you decide to include the HIERARCHYID in your applications, be sure to learn about this topic in depth before you design your application. See Books Online for more information about how to work with HIERARCHYID.

Spatial Data Types

In the previous section, you learned about the CLR data type HIERARCHYID. SQL Server 2012 has two other CLR data types, GEOMETRY and GEOGRAPHY, also known as the *spatial* data types. The GEOMETRY data type might be used for a warehouse application to store the location of each product in the warehouse. The

GEOGRAPHY data type can be used to store data that can be used in mapping software. You may wonder why two types exist that both store locations. The GEOMETRY data type follows a "flat Earth" model, with basically X, Y, and Z coordinates. The GEOGRAPHY data type represents the "round Earth," storing longitude and latitude. These data types implement international standards for spatial data.

Using GEOMETRY

By using the GEOMETRY type, you can store points, lines, and polygons. You can calculate the difference between two shapes, determine whether they intersect, and much more. Just like HIERARCHYID, the database engine stores the data as a binary value. GEOMETRY also has many built-in methods for working with the data. Type in and execute Listing 10-10 to learn how to use the GEOMETRY data type with some simple examples.

Listing 10-10. Using the GEOMETRY Data Type

```
USE tempdb;
GO

--1
IF OBJECT_ID('dbo.GeometryData') IS NOT NULL BEGIN
    DROP TABLE dbo.GeometryData;
END;

--2
CREATE TABLE dbo.GeometryData (
    Point1 GEOMETRY, Point2 GEOMETRY,
    Line1 GEOMETRY, Line2 GEOMETRY,
    Polygon1 GEOMETRY, Polygon2 GEOMETRY);

--3
INSERT INTO dbo.GeometryData (Point1, Point2, Line1, Line2, Polygon1, Polygon2)
VALUES (
    GEOMETRY::Parse('Point(1 4)'),
    GEOMETRY::Parse('Point(2 5)'),
    GEOMETRY::Parse('LineString(1 4, 2 5)'),
    GEOMETRY::Parse('LineString(4 1, 5 2, 7 3, 10 6)'),
    GEOMETRY::Parse('Polygon((1 4, 2 5, 5 2, 0 4, 1 4))'),
    GEOMETRY::Parse('Polygon((1 4, 2 7, 7 2, 0 4, 1 4))'));

--4
SELECT Point1.ToString() AS Point1, Point2.ToString() AS Point2,
    Line1.ToString() AS Line1, Line2.ToString() AS Line2,
    Polygon1.ToString() AS Polygon1, Polygon2.ToString() AS Polygon2
FROM dbo.GeometryData;

--5
SELECT Point1.STX AS Point1X, Point1.STY AS Point1Y,
    Line1.STIntersects(Polygon1) AS Line1Poly1Intersects,
    Line1.STLength() AS Line1Len,
    Line1.STStartPoint().ToString() AS Line1Start,
    Line2.STNumPoints() AS Line2PtCt,
```

```
    Polygon1.STArea() AS Poly1Area,
    Polygon1.STIntersects(Polygon2) AS Poly1Poly2Intersects
FROM dbo.GeometryData;
```

Figure 10-13 shows the results. Code section 1 drops the dbo.GeometryData table if it already exists. Statement 2 creates the table along with six GEOMETRY columns each named for the type of shape it will contain. Even though this example named the shape types, a GEOMETRY column can store any of the shapes; it is not limited to one shape. Statement 3 inserts one row into the table using the Parse method. Query 4 displays the data using the ToString method so that you can read the data. Notice that the data returned from the ToString method looks just like it does when inserted. Query 5 demonstrates a few of the methods available for working with GEOMETRY data. For example, you can display the X and Y coordinates of a point, determine the length or area of a shape, determine whether two shapes intersect, and count the number of points in a shape.

Results

	Point1	Point2	Line1	Line2	Polygon1	Polygon2
1	POINT (1 4)	POINT (2 5)	LINESTRING (1 4, 2 5)	LINESTRING (4 1, 5 2, 7 3, 10 6)	POLYGON ((1 4, 2 5, 5 2, 0 4, 1 4))	POLYGON ((1 4, 2 7, 7 2, 0 4, 1 4))

	Point1X	Point1Y	Line1Poly1Intersects	Line1Len	Line1Start	Line2PtCt	Poly1Area	Poly1Poly2Intersects
1	1	4	1	1.4142135623731	POINT (1 4)	4	4	1

Figure 10-13. *The results of using the GEOMETRY type*

Using GEOGRAPHY

The GEOGRAPHY data type is even more interesting than the GEOMETRY type. With the GEOGRAPHY type, you can store longitude and latitude values for actual locations or areas. Just like the GEOMETRY type, you can use several built-in methods to work with the data. You can also extract the data in a special XML format that can be used along with Microsoft's Virtual Earth application. Unfortunately, integrating the GEOMETRY data with the Virtual Earth is beyond the scope of this book. To learn more about creating Virtual Earth applications with SQL Server Geometry data, see the book *Beginning Spatial with SQL Server 2008* by Alastair Aitchison (Apress, 2009).

The AdventureWorks2012 database contains one GEOMETRY column in the Person.Address table. Type in and execute the code in Listing 10-11 to learn more.

Listing 10-11. *Using the GEOGRAPHY Data Type*

```
USE AdventureWorks2012;
GO


--1
DECLARE @OneAddress GEOGRAPHY;

--2
SELECT @OneAddress = SpatialLocation
FROM Person.Address
WHERE AddressID = 91;
--3
SELECT AddressID,PostalCode, SpatialLocation.ToString(),
    @OneAddress.STDistance(SpatialLocation) AS DiffInMeters
FROM Person.Address
WHERE AddressID IN (1,91, 831,11419);
```

Figure 10-14 shows the results. Statement 1 declares a variable, @OneAddress, of the GEOGRAPHY type. Statement 2 assigns one value to the variable. Query 3 displays the data including the AddressID, the PostalCode, and the SpatialLocation.ToString method. The DiffInMeters column displays the distance between the location saved in the variable to the stored data. Notice that the difference is zero when comparing a location to itself.

▦ Results

	AddressID	PostalCode	(No column name)	DiffInMeters
1	1	98011	POINT (-122.164644615406 47.7869921906598)	25366.6874166672
2	91	98104	POINT (-122.391164430965 47.6176669267707)	0
3	831	06510	POINT (-72.9550181450784 41.3589413896096)	3924885.39255556
4	11419	98366	POINT (-122.72771089643 47.575135985628)	25748.07917586

Figure 10-14. *The results of using the GEOGRAPHY data type*

Viewing the Spatial Results Tab

When you select GEOMETRY or GEOGRAPHY data in the native binary format, another tab shows up in the results. This tab displays a visual representation of the spatial data. Type in and execute Listing 10-12 to see how this works.

Listing 10-12. *Viewing Spatial Results*

```
--1
DECLARE @Area GEOMETRY;

--2
SET @Area = geometry::Parse('Polygon((1 4, 2 5, 5 2, 0 4, 1 4))');

--3
SELECT @Area AS Area;
```

After running the code, click the "Spatial results" tab. Figure 10-15 shows how this should look. This tab will show up whenever you return spatial data in the binary format in a grid.

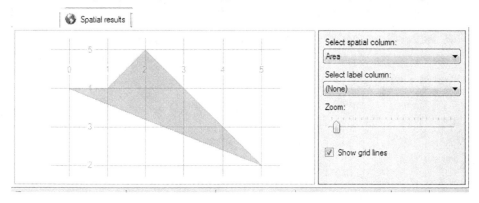

Figure 10-15. *The "Spatial results" tab*

385

Although the spatial data types are very interesting, they also require specialized knowledge to take full advantage of them. I encourage you to learn more if you think that your applications can benefit from these new data types.

Circular Arcs

SQL Server 2012 includes a number of enhancements to both the geography and the geometry features. These new features demonstrate the increasing need for advanced spatial capabilities in relational databases. One of these new features is the introduction of circular arcs. Simply put, circular arcs allow for curved lines between any two points. You can also combine straight and curved lines for even more complex shapes. Figure 10-16 shows some examples.

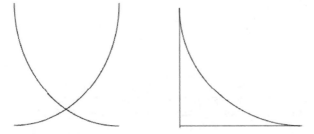

Figure 10-16. *Example shapes using curved and straight lines*

To create these shapes you will use the CIRCULARSTRING command. This command requires you to define at least three points along the circular arc: a beginning, a point anywhere along the segment, and an end. The total amount of points along the arc will always be odd and you are allowed to have the last point be the same as the first. Listing 10-13 shows how you would use the CIRCULARSTRING command to create a single curved line. You can combine multiple curved or straight lines using the COMPOUNDCURVE command. When combining lines whether curved or straight, the beginning of the next line must always be the endpoint of the previous line. Figure 10-17 shows the output from the two SELECT statements in the listing.

Listing 10-13. *Example of curved lines using CIRCULARSTRING and COMPOUNDCURVE*

```
DECLARE @g geometry;

SET @g = geometry:: STGeomFromText('CIRCULARSTRING(1 2, 2 1, 4 3)', 0);
SELECT @g.ToString();

SET @g = geometry::STGeomFromText('
COMPOUNDCURVE(
CIRCULARSTRING(1 2, 2 1, 4 3),
CIRCULARSTRING(4 3, 3 4, 1 2))', 0);
SELECT @g AS Area ();
```

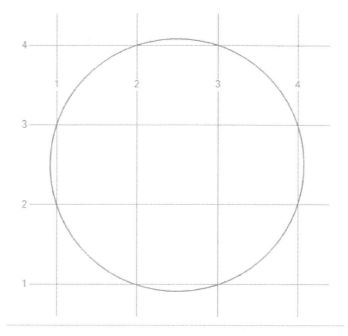

Figure 10-17. Results of using CIRCULARSTRING and COMPOUNDCURVE

The COMPOUNDCURVE command allows you to simply combine multiple curved arcs or create more complicated shapes by combining curved and straight lines. The CIRCULARSTRING command defines each circular arc while the straight lines are defined with only the points along the line. Remember that lines are defined with only two points but curved lines are defined with three. The endpoint of one arc is the starting point of the next. Listing 10-14 shows examples of each. Notice the how the lines in the code for the linear segment don't contain a keyword (I've highlighted them in bold for emphasis). The shape the query generates is shown in Figure 10-18.

Listing 10-14. Example of mixing straight and curved lines using COMPOUNDCURVE

```
DECLARE @g geometry;
SET @g = geometry::STGeomFromText('
COMPOUNDCURVE(
    (2 2, 2 6),
    CIRCULARSTRING(2 6, 4 4, 6 2),
    (6 2, 2 2))', 0);

SELECT @g AS Area;
```

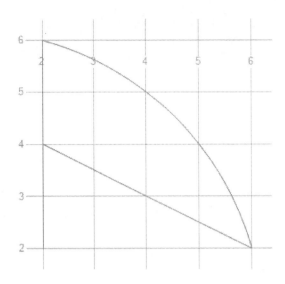

Figure 10-18. *Using COMPOUNDCURVE to mix lines and curved segments*

■ **Note** This chapter only scratches the surface of the available features included in SQL Server 2012 for the geography and geometry data types. SQL Server 2012 includes a large number of additional methods and performance improvement for these data types such as FULLGLOBE and GEOGRAPHY_AUTO_GRID. If your job requires you to understand more or if you are simply curious, I suggest going to
http://msdn.microsoft.com/en-us/library/ff848797(v=SQL.110).aspx for more information.

Sparse Columns

Whenever you store fixed-length data, such as any of the numeric data types and some of the string data types, the data takes up the same amount of space in the database even when storing NULL values. By using the new sparse option, you can significantly reduce the amount of storage for NULL values. The trade-off is that the non-NULL values of sparse columns take up slightly more space than values stored in regular columns, and there is a small performance decrease when retrieving the non-NULL values. To use sparse columns, the option must be specified when creating the table. You can also include a special type of column, called a *column set*, to return all the sparse columns as XML. Type in and execute Listing 10-15 to learn more.

Listing 10-15. Using Sparse Columns

```
USE tempdb;
GO

--1
IF OBJECT_ID('dbo.SparseData') IS NOT NULL BEGIN
    DROP TABLE dbo.SparseData;
END;
GO

--2
CREATE TABLE dbo.SparseData
    (ID INT NOT NULL PRIMARY KEY,
    sc1 INT SPARSE NULL,
    sc2 INT SPARSE NULL,
    sc3 INT SPARSE NULL,
    cs XML COLUMN_SET FOR ALL_SPARSE_COLUMNS);
GO

--3
INSERT INTO dbo.SparseData(ID,sc1,sc2,sc3)
VALUES  (1,1,NULL,3),(2,NULL,1,1),(3,NULL,NULL,1);

--4
INSERT INTO SparseData(ID,cs)
SELECT 4,'<sc2>5</sc2>';

--5
SELECT * FROM dbo.SparseData;

--6
SELECT ID, sc1, sc2, sc3, cs FROM SparseData;
```

Figure 10-19 shows the results. Code section 1 drops the dbo.SparseData table if it exists. Statement 2 creates the table with a primary key column, ID; three sparse integer columns; and the XML column, cs. Statement 3 inserts three rows into the table, leaving out the cs column. Statement 4 inserts a row, but this time only providing values for ID and cs. Query 5 uses the asterisks to return all the columns and rows with surprising results. Instead of returning the individual sparse columns, the cs column provides the sparse data. Query 6 shows that you can still retrieve these columns individually if you need to and validates the cs column. Statement 4 provides a value only for the cs column and not the sparse columns. Query 6 proves that statement 4 inserted the data correctly into the sparse column.

Results

	ID	cs
1	1	<sc1>1</sc1><sc3>3</sc3>
2	2	<sc2>1</sc2><sc3>1</sc3>
3	3	<sc3>1</sc3>
4	4	<sc2>5</sc2>

	ID	sc1	sc2	sc3	cs
1	1	1	NULL	3	<sc1>1</sc1><sc3>3</sc3>
2	2	NULL	1	1	<sc2>1</sc2><sc3>1</sc3>
3	3	NULL	NULL	1	<sc3>1</sc3>
4	4	NULL	5	NULL	<sc2>5</sc2>

Figure 10-19. The results of using sparse columns

Because there is increased overhead when using sparse columns and because non-NULL values of sparse columns take a bit more space, Microsoft suggests that you use this feature only when the data will contain mostly NULL values. SQL Server Books Online contains a table in the "Using Sparse Columns" article showing the percentage of NULL values the data should contain in order to make using the sparse columns beneficial.

To make it easier to work with the new sparse columns, Microsoft introduced a type of index called a *filtered index*. By using a filtered index, you can filter out the NULL values from the sparse columns right in the index.

Summary

By practicing the skills taught in Chapters 1 through 9, you should become a very proficient T-SQL developer. This chapter introduced you to advanced data types available in SQL Server 2012 and how to work with them. You now know that you should not use TEXT, NTEXT, and IMAGE types going forward and that the new MAX data types should be used for very large columns. If you must store files, such as Microsoft Word documents or video, you know about the FILESTREAM option. The new HIERARCHYID type and the spatial types of GEOGRAPHY and GEOMETRY are available for special-purpose applications. You also have a new way to save space when working with tables that have many columns containing mostly NULLs. You now know what these types can do as well as the downsides of using these types. Armed with this knowledge, you can come up with solutions to challenging problems that may not occur to others on your team.

Writing Advanced Queries

In Chapter 10, you learned about some useful data types in SQL Server 2012. In this chapter, you will learn about some of the functions and advanced queries available with these most recent releases. For example, you will learn more about common table expressions (CTEs), how to write a pivot query, how to use the new ranking functions, and more. As a beginning T-SQL developer, you may or may not need this information right away. This chapter doesn't contain any exercises, but I encourage you to experiment and come up with your own examples for any of the features that you are interested in. Consider the information in this chapter as a head start in becoming an expert T-SQL developer.

Advanced CTE Queries

In Chapter 4, you learned to use common table expressions as one of the ways to combine the data from more than one table into one query. In Chapters 5 and 6, you learned how CTEs can simplify many statements. CTEs allow you to isolate part of the query logic or do things you could not ordinarily do, such as use an aggregate expression in an update. In these cases, you could use derived tables (see the "Derived Tables" section in Chapter 4), but now you will learn that CTEs are much more versatile. You can do several things with CTEs that are not possible with derived tables, such as write a recursive query. This section covers these advanced CTE features.

▧ **Caution** The keyword WITH appears in many other statement types. Because of this, a statement containing a CTE must be the first statement in the batch, or the previous statement must end with a semicolon. At this point, Microsoft recommends using semicolons to end T-SQL statements, but it is not required. Some developers start all CTE definitions with a semicolon to avoid errors.

Using Multiple CTEs

You can use CTEs to organize and isolate query logic in order to write complicated queries efficiently. You can't nest CTEs; that is, one CTE can't contain another CTE. You can, however, add multiple CTEs to one query. You might want to do this just to make your query more readable or possibly because writing the query this way will let you avoid creating temp tables or views. Here is the syntax:

```
WITH <cteName1> AS (SELECT <col1> FROM <table1>),
    <cteName2> AS (SELECT <col2> FROM <table2>),
    <cteName3> AS (SELECT <col3> FROM <table3>)
```

```
SELECT <col1>, <col2>, <col3>
FROM <cteName1> INNER JOIN <cteName2> ON <join condition1> ·
INNER JOIN <cteName3> ON <join condition2>
```

Of course, your CTE definitions can contain just about any valid SELECT statement, and your outer query can use the CTEs in any way you need to use them. Type in and execute Listing 11-1 to learn more.

■ **Note** The CTE examples in this chapter create objects in tempdb. Keep in mind that tempdb is recreated each time the SQL service restarts, so if you restart SQL Server, you will need to run the CREATE TABLE statements again.

Listing 11-1. A Query with Multiple Queries in a CTE

```
--1 First, populate the tempdb tables

USE [tempdb];
GO

CREATE TABLE [Employee](
        [EmployeeID] [int] NOT NULL,
        [ContactID] [int] NOT NULL,
        [ManagerID] [int] NULL,
        [Title] [nvarchar](50) NOT NULL);

CREATE TABLE [Contact] (
        [ContactID] [int] NOT NULL,
        [FirstName] [nvarchar](50) NOT NULL,
        [MiddleName] [nvarchar](50) NULL,
        [LastName] [nvarchar](50) NOT NULL);

INSERT INTO tempdb.dbo.Contact (ContactID, FirstName, MiddleName, LastName) VALUES
        (1030,'Kevin','F','Brown'),
        (1009,'Thierry','B','DHers'),
        (1028,'David','M','Bradley'),
        (1070,'JoLynn','M','Dobney'),
        (1071,'Ruth','Ann','Ellerbrock'),
        (1005,'Gail','A','Erickson'),
        (1076,'Barry','K','Johnson'),
        (1006,'Jossef','H','Goldberg'),
        (1001,'Terri','Lee','Duffy'),
        (1072,'Sidney','M','Higa'),
        (1067,'Taylor','R','Maxwell'),
        (1073,'Jeffrey','L','Ford'),
        (1068,'Jo','A','Brown'),
        (1074,'Doris','M','Hartwig'),
        (1069,'John','T','Campbell'),
        (1075,'Diane','R','Glimp'),
        (1129,'Steven','T','Selikoff'),
        (1231,'Peter','J','Krebs'),
```

```
        (1172,'Stuart','V','Munson'),
        (1173,'Greg','F','Alderson'),
        (1113,'David','N','Johnson'),
        (1054,'Zheng','W','Mu'),
        (1007, 'Ovidiu', 'V', 'Cracium'),
        (1052, 'James', 'R', 'Hamilton'),
        (1053, 'Andrew', 'R', 'Hill'),
        (1056, 'Jack', 'S', 'Richins'),
        (1058, 'Michael', 'Sean', 'Ray'),
        (1064, 'Lori', 'A', 'Kane'),
        (1287, 'Ken', 'J', 'Sanchez');

INSERT INTO tempdb.dbo.Employee (EmployeeID, ContactID, ManagerID, Title) VALUES
        (1, 1209, 16,'Production Technician - WC60'),
        (2, 1030, 6,'Marketing Assistant'),
        (3, 1002, 12,'Engineering Manager'),
        (4, 1290, 3,'Senior Tool Designer'),
        (5, 1009, 263,'Tool Designer'),
        (6, 1028, 109,'Marketing Manager'),
        (7, 1070, 21,'Production Supervisor - WC60'),
        (8, 1071, 185,'Production Technician - WC10'),
        (9, 1005, 3,'Design Engineer'),
        (10, 1076, 185,'Production Technician - WC10'),
        (11, 1006, 3,'Design Engineer'),
        (12, 1001, 109,'Vice President of Engineering'),
        (13, 1072, 185,'Production Technician - WC10'),
        (14, 1067, 21,'Production Supervisor - WC50'),
        (15, 1073, 185,'Production Technician - WC10'),
        (16, 1068, 21,'Production Supervisor - WC60'),
        (17, 1074, 185,'Production Technician - WC10'),
        (18, 1069, 21,'Production Supervisor - WC60'),
        (19, 1075, 185,'Production Technician - WC10'),
        (20, 1129, 173,'Production Technician - WC30'),
        (21, 1231, 148,'Production Control Manager'),
        (22, 1172, 197,'Production Technician - WC45'),
        (23, 1173, 197,'Production Technician - WC45'),
        (24, 1113, 184,'Production Technician - WC30'),
        (25, 1054, 21,'Production Supervisor - WC10'),
        (109, 1287, NULL, 'Chief Executive Officer'),
        (148, 1052, 109, 'Vice President of Production'),
        (173, 1058, 21, 'Production Supervisor - WC30'),
        (184, 1056, 21, 'Production Supervisor - WC30'),
        (185, 1053, 21, 'Production Supervisor - WC10'),
        (197, 1064, 21, 'Production Supervisor - WC45'),
        (263, 1007, 3, 'Senior Tool Designer');

--2 Now run the CTE query

USE tempdb;
WITH
Emp AS(
    SELECT e.EmployeeID, e.ManagerID,e.Title AS EmpTitle,
```

393

```
            c.FirstName + ISNULL(' ' + c.MiddleName,'') + ' ' + c.LastName AS EmpName
    FROM Employee AS e
    INNER JOIN Contact AS c
    ON e.ContactID = c.ContactID
    ),
Mgr AS(
    SELECT e.EmployeeID AS ManagerID,e.Title AS MgrTitle,
            c.FirstName + ISNULL(' ' + c.MiddleName,'') + ' ' + c.LastName AS MgrName
    FROM Employee AS e
    INNER JOIN Contact AS c
    ON e.ContactID = c.ContactID
    )
SELECT EmployeeID, Emp.ManagerID, EmpName, EmpTitle, MgrName, MgrTitle
FROM Emp INNER JOIN Mgr ON Emp.ManagerID = Mgr.ManagerID
ORDER BY EmployeeID;
```

Figure 11-1 shows the partial results. Each CTE must have a name, followed by the keyword AS and the definition in parentheses. Separate the CTE definitions with a comma. This query, from the tempdbdatabase, contains a CTE for the employees, Emp, and a CTE for the managers, Mgr. Within each CTE, the Employee table joins the Contact table. By writing the query using CTEs, the outer query is very simple. You just join the Mgr CTE to the Emp CTE just as if they were regular tables or views.

	EmployeeID	ManagerID	EmpName	EmpTitle	MgrName	MgrTitle
1	2	6	Kevin F Brown	Marketing Assistant	David M Bradley	Marketing Manager
2	5	263	Thierry B DHers	Tool Designer	Ovidiu V Cracium	Senior Tool Designer
3	6	109	David M Bradley	Marketing Manager	Ken J Sanchez	Chief Executive Officer
4	7	21	JoLynn M Dobney	Production Supervisor - WC60	Peter J Krebs	Production Control Manager
5	8	185	Ruth Ann Ellerbrock	Production Technician - WC10	Andrew R Hill	Production Supervisor - WC10
6	10	185	Barry K Johnson	Production Technician - WC10	Andrew R Hill	Production Supervisor - WC10
7	12	109	Terri Lee Duffy	Vice President of Engineering	Ken J Sanchez	Chief Executive Officer
8	13	185	Sidney M Higa	Production Technician - WC10	Andrew R Hill	Production Supervisor - WC10
9	14	21	Taylor R Maxwell	Production Supervisor - WC50	Peter J Krebs	Production Control Manager
10	15	185	Jeffrey L Ford	Production Technician - WC10	Andrew R Hill	Production Supervisor - WC10
11	16	21	Jo A Brown	Production Supervisor - WC60	Peter J Krebs	Production Control Manager
12	17	185	Doris M Hartwig	Production Technician - WC10	Andrew R Hill	Production Supervisor - WC10
13	18	21	John T Campbell	Production Supervisor - WC60	Peter J Krebs	Production Control Manager
14	19	185	Diane R Glimp	Production Technician - WC10	Andrew R Hill	Production Supervisor - WC10
15	20	173	Steven T Selikoff	Production Technician - WC30	Michael Sean Ray	Production Supervisor - WC30
16	21	148	Peter J Krebs	Production Control Manager	James R Hamilton	Vice President of Production
17	22	197	Stuart V Munson	Production Technician - WC45	Lori A Kane	Production Supervisor - WC45
18	23	197	Greg F Alderson	Production Technician - WC45	Lori A Kane	Production Supervisor - WC45
19	24	184	David N Johnson	Production Technician - WC30	Jack S Richins	Production Supervisor - WC30
20	25	21	Zheng W Mu	Production Supervisor - WC10	Peter J Krebs	Production Control Manager

Figure 11-1. The partial results of multiple CTEs in one statement

Calling a CTE Multiple Times

Just as you can have multiple CTE definitions within one statement, you can call a CTE multiple times within one statement. This is not possible with a derived table, which can be used only once within a statement. (See Chapter 4 for more information about derived tables.) A CTE could be used in a self-join, in a subquery, or in any valid way of using a table within a statement. Here are two syntax examples:

```
--self-join
WITH <cteName> AS (SELECT <col1>, <col2> FROM <table1>)
SELECT a.<col1>, b.<col1>
FROM <cteName> AS a
INNER JOIN <cteName> AS b ON <join condition>

--subquery
WITH <cteName> AS (SELECT <col1>, <col2> FROM <table1>)
SELECT <col1>
FROM <cteName>
WHERE <col2> IN (SELECT <col2>
    FROM <cteName> INNER JOIN <table1> ON <join condition>)
```

Type in and execute Listing 11-2 to see some examples. The self-join produces the same results as those in the previous section.

Listing 11-2. Calling a CTE Multiple Times Within a Statement

```
USE tempdb;

WITH
Employees AS(
    SELECT e.EmployeeID, e.ManagerID,e.Title,
        c.FirstName + ISNULL(' ' + c.MiddleName,'') + ' ' +  c.LastName AS EmpName
    FROM Employee AS e
    INNER JOIN Contact AS c
    ON e.ContactID = c.ContactID
    )
SELECT emp.EmployeeID, emp.ManagerID, emp.EmpName, emp.Title AS EmpTitle,
   mgr.EmpName as MgrName, mgr.Title as MgrTitle
FROM Employees AS Emp INNER JOIN Employees AS Mgr
ON Emp.ManagerID = Mgr.EmployeeID;

--2
WITH Employees AS (
    SELECT e.EmployeeID, e.ManagerID,e.Title,
        c.FirstName + ISNULL(' ' + c.MiddleName,'') + ' ' +  c.LastName AS EmpName
    FROM Employee AS e
    INNER JOIN Contact AS c
    ON e.ContactID = c.ContactID)
SELECT EmployeeID, ManagerID, EmpName, Title
FROM Employees
WHERE EmployeeID IN (SELECT EmployeeID
    FROM Employees AS e
```

```
    INNER JOIN AdventureWorks2012.HumanResources.Employee AS er2 ON e.ManagerID =
er2.BusinessEntityID
        WHERE er2.MaritalStatus = 'M');
```

Figure 11-2 shows the partial results. Statement 1 defines just one CTE, joining Employee to Contact. The outer query calls the CTE twice, once with the alias Emp and once with the alias Mgr. Statement 2 defines the same CTE. In this case, however, the outer query uses the CTE as the main table and also within a subquery.

Results

	EmployeeID	ManagerID	EmpName	EmpTitle		MgrName	MgrTitle
1	2	6	Kevin F Brown	Marketing Assistant		David M Bradley	Marketing Manager
2	5	263	Thierry B DHers	Tool Designer		Ovidiu V Cracium	Senior Tool Designer
3	6	109	David M Bradley	Marketing Manager		Ken J Sanchez	Chief Executive Officer
4	7	21	JoLynn M Dobney	Production Supervisor - WC60		Peter J Krebs	Production Control Manager
5	8	185	Ruth Ann Ellerbrock	Production Technician - WC10		Andrew R Hill	Production Supervisor - WC10
6	10	185	Barry K Johnson	Production Technician - WC10		Andrew R Hill	Production Supervisor - WC10
7	12	109	Terri Lee Duffy	Vice President of Engineering		Ken J Sanchez	Chief Executive Officer
8	13	185	Sidney M Higa	Production Technician - WC10		Andrew R Hill	Production Supervisor - WC10

	EmployeeID	ManagerID	EmpName	Title
1	2	6	Kevin F Brown	Marketing Assistant
2	5	263	Thierry B DHers	Tool Designer
3	6	109	David M Bradley	Marketing Manager
4	8	185	Ruth Ann Ellerbrock	Production Technician - WC10
5	9	3	Gail A Erickson	Design Engineer
6	13	185	Sidney M Higa	Production Technician - WC10
7	14	21	Taylor R Maxwell	Production Supervisor - WC50
8	17	185	Doris M Hartwig	Production Technician - WC10

Figure 11-2. The partial results of using a CTE twice in one statement

Joining a CTE to Another CTE

Another very interesting feature of CTEs is the ability to call one CTE from another CTE definition. This is not recursion, which you will learn about in the "Writing a Recursive Query" section. Calling one CTE from within another CTE definition allows you to base one query on a previous query. Here is a syntax example:

```
WITH <cteName1> AS (SELECT <col1>, <col2> FROM <table1>),
    <cteName2> AS (SELECT <col1>, <col2>, <col3>
        FROM <table3> INNER JOIN <cteName1> ON <join condition>)
SELECT <col1>, <col2>, <col3> FROM <cteName2>
```

The order in which the CTE definitions appear is very important. You can't call a CTE before it is defined. Type in and execute the code in Listing 11-3 to learn more.

Listing 11-3. *Joining a CTE to Another CTE*

```
USE tempdb;


--1
IF OBJECT_ID('dbo.JobHistory') IS NOT NULL BEGIN
    DROP TABLE dbo.JobHistory;
END;

--2
CREATE TABLE JobHistory(
    EmployeeID INT NOT NULL,
    EffDate DATE NOT NULL,
    EffSeq INT NOT NULL,
    EmploymentStatus CHAR(1) NOT NULL,
    JobTitle VARCHAR(50) NOT NULL,
    Salary MONEY NOT NULL,
    ActionDesc VARCHAR(20)
 CONSTRAINT PK_JobHistory PRIMARY KEY CLUSTERED
(
    EmployeeID, EffDate, EffSeq
));

GO

--3
INSERT INTO JobHistory(EmployeeID, EffDate, EffSeq, EmploymentStatus,
    JobTitle, Salary, ActionDesc)
VALUES
    (1000,'07-31-2008',1,'A','Intern',2000,'New Hire'),
    (1000,'05-31-2009',1,'A','Production Technician',2000,'Title Change'),
    (1000,'05-31-2009',2,'A','Production Technician',2500,'Salary Change'),
    (1000,'11-01-2009',1,'A','Production Technician',3000,'Salary Change'),
    (1200,'01-10-2009',1,'A','Design Engineer',5000,'New Hire'),
    (1200,'05-01-2009',1,'T','Design Engineer',5000,'Termination'),
    (1100,'08-01-2008',1,'A','Accounts Payable Specialist I',2500,'New Hire'),
    (1100,'05-01-2009',1,'A','Accounts Payable Specialist II',2500,'Title Change'),
    (1100,'05-01-2009',2,'A','Accounts Payable Specialist II',3000,'Salary Change');

--4
DECLARE @Date DATE = '05-02-2009';

--5
WITH EffectiveDate AS (
        SELECT MAX(EffDate) AS MaxDate, EmployeeID
        FROM JobHistory
        WHERE EffDate <= @Date
        GROUP BY EmployeeID
    ),
    EffectiveSeq AS (
```

```
        SELECT MAX(EffSeq) AS MaxSeq, j.EmployeeID, MaxDate
        FROM JobHistory AS j
        INNER JOIN EffectiveDate AS d
            ON j.EffDate = d.MaxDate AND j.EmployeeID = d.EmployeeID
        GROUP BY j.EmployeeID, MaxDate)
SELECT j.EmployeeID, EmploymentStatus, JobTitle, Salary
FROM JobHistory AS j
INNER JOIN EffectiveSeq AS e ON j.EmployeeID = e.EmployeeID
    AND j.EffDate = e.MaxDate AND j.EffSeq = e.MaxSeq;
```

Figure 11-3 shows the results. I based this example on a system that I have worked with for several years. Many of the tables in this system contain history information with an effective date and an effective sequence. The system adds one row to these tables for each change to the employee's data. For a particular effective date, the system can add more than one row along with an incrementing effective sequence. To display information valid on a particular date, you first have to figure out the latest effective date before the date in mind and then figure out the effective sequence for that date. At first glance, you might think that just determining the maximum date and maximum sequence in one aggregate query should work. This doesn't work because the maximum sequence in the table for an employee may not be valid for a particular date. For example, the employee may have four changes and, therefore, four rows for an earlier date and only one row for the latest date.

	EmployeeID	Employment Status	Job Title	Salary
1	1000	A	Intern	2000.00
2	1100	A	Accounts Payable Specialist II	3000.00
3	1200	T	Design Engineer	5000.00

Figure 11-3. The results of calling one CTE from another CTE definition

Code section 1 drops the JobHistory table if it already exists. Statement 2 creates the JobHistory table including a primary key composed of EmployeeID, EffDate, and EffSeq. Statement 3 inserts several rows into the table. Notice that the statement inserts one row for each change even if the changes happen on the same date. Statement 4 declares and initializes a variable, @Date, which will be used in the WHERE clause in Statement 5. You can change the value of this variable to validate the results for different dates.

Statement 5 contains the SELECT statement. The first CTE, EffectiveDate, just determines the maximum EffDate from the JobHistory table for each employee that is valid for the @Date value. The second CTE, EffectiveSeq, joins the JobHistory table to the EffectiveDate CTE to find the maximum EffSeq for each employee for the date determined in the previous CTE, EffectiveDate. Finally, the outer query joins the JobHistory table on the EffectiveSeq CTE to display the valid data for each employee on the date stored in @Date.

Using the Alternate CTE Syntax

I prefer naming all the columns within the CTE definition, but you can also specify the column names outside the definition. There is no advantage to either syntax, but you should be familiar with both. Here is the syntax:

```
WITH <cteName> (<col1>, <col2>) AS (
    SELECT <col3>,<col4> FROM <table1>)
SELECT <col1>,<col2> FROM <cteName>
```

When using this technique, the column names defined outside the definition must be used in the outer query. If you have an expression within the definition, you don't have to give the expression an alias. Type in and execute the code in Listing 11-4 to practice this technique.

Listing 11-4. *Writing a Query with the Alternate CTE Syntax*

```
USE tempdb;

WITH Emp (EmployeeID, ManagerID, JobTitle,EmpName) AS
    (SELECT e.EmployeeID, e.ManagerID,e.Title,
        c.FirstName + ISNULL(' ' + c.MiddleName,'') + ' ' + c.LastName
    FROM Employee AS e
    INNER JOIN Contact AS c
    ON e.ContactID = c.ContactID)
SELECT Emp.EmployeeID, ManagerID, JobTitle, EmpName
FROM Emp;
```

Figure 11-4 shows the partial results. All the columns must be listed in parentheses between the CTE name and the definition. Only the columns listed are valid. Either syntax will work; it is just a matter of preference.

	EmployeeID	ManagerID	JobTitle	EmpName
1	2	6	Marketing Assistant	Kevin F Brown
2	5	263	Tool Designer	Thierry B DHers
3	6	109	Marketing Manager	David M Bradley
4	7	21	Production Supervisor - WC60	JoLynn M Dobney
5	8	185	Production Technician - WC10	Ruth Ann Ellerbrock
6	9	3	Design Engineer	Gail A Erickson
7	10	185	Production Technician - WC10	Barry K Johnson
8	11	3	Design Engineer	Jossef H Goldberg
9	12	109	Vice President of Engineering	Terri Lee Duffy
10	13	185	Production Technician - WC10	Sidney M Higa
11	14	21	Production Supervisor - WC50	Taylor R Maxwell
12	15	185	Production Technician - WC10	Jeffrey L Ford
13	16	21	Production Supervisor - WC60	Jo A Brown
14	17	185	Production Technician - WC10	Doris M Hartwig
15	18	21	Production Supervisor - WC60	John T Campbell
16	19	185	Production Technician - WC10	Diane R Glimp
17	20	173	Production Technician - WC30	Steven T Selikoff

Figure 11-4. *The partial results of using the named column CTE syntax*

Writing a Recursive Query

Recursive code, in any programming language, is code that calls itself. Programmers use this technique to follow paths in tree or directory structures. When following the paths in these structures, the code must start at the root, follow each path to the end, and back up again to the next path repeatedly. In T-SQL, you can use the same technique in a CTE. Let's use the same Employee table created in tempdb at the beginning of the chapter to demonstrate how to use a recursive CTE. The self-join found in that table represents a hierarchical structure. To view the entire hierarchy, you must start at the root, the CEO of the company, and follow every possible manager-employee path down to the lowest person. Here is the syntax for writing a recursive CTE:

```
WITH <cteName> (<col1>, <col2>, <col3>, level)
AS
(
    --Anchor member
    SELECT <primaryKey>,<foreignKey>,<col3>, 0 AS level
    FROM <table1>
    WHERE <foreignKey> = <startingValue>
    UNION ALL
    --Recursive member
    SELECT a.<primaryKey>,a.<foreignKey>,a.<col3>, b.level + 1
    FROM <table1> AS a
    INNER JOIN <cteName> AS b
        ON a.<foreignKey>  = b.<primaryKey>
)
SELECT <col1>,<col2>,<col3>,level
FROM <cteName> [OPTION (MAXRECURSION <number>)]
```

To write the recursive CTE, you must have an anchor member, which is a statement that returns the top of your intended results. This is like the root of the directory. Following the anchor member, you will write the recursive member. The recursive member actually joins the CTE that contains it to the same table used in the anchor member. The results of the anchor member and the recursive member join in a UNION ALL query. Type in and execute the code in Listing 11-5 to see how this works.

Listing 11-5. A Recursive CTE

```
USE tempdb;

WITH OrgChart (EmployeeID, ManagerID, Title, Level,Node)
    AS (SELECT EmployeeID, ManagerID, Title, 0,
            CONVERT(VARCHAR(30),'/') AS Node
        FROM Employee
        WHERE ManagerID IS NULL
        UNION ALL
        SELECT a.EmployeeID, a.ManagerID,a.Title, b.Level + 1,
            CONVERT(VARCHAR(30),b.Node +
                CONVERT(VARCHAR,a.ManagerID) + '/')
        FROM Employee AS a
        INNER JOIN OrgChart AS b ON a.ManagerID = b.EmployeeID
    )
SELECT EmployeeID, ManagerID, SPACE(Level * 3) + Title AS Title, Level, Node
FROM OrgChart
```

```
ORDER BY Node;
```

Figure 11-5 shows the results. The anchor member selects the EmployeeID, ManagerID, and Title from the Employee table for the CEO. The CEO is the only employee with a NULL ManagerID. The level is zero. The node column, added to help sorting, is just a slash. To get this to work, the query uses the CONVERT function to change the data type of the slash to a VARCHAR(30) because the data types in the columns of the anchor member and recursive member must match exactly. The recursive member joins Employee to the CTE, OrgChart. The query is recursive because the CTE is used inside its own definition. The regular columns in the recursive member come from the table, and the level is one plus the value of the level returned from the CTE. To sort in a meaningful way, the node shows the ManagerID values used to get to the current employee surrounded with slashes. This looks very similar to the node used in the HierarchyID example in Chapter 10.

	EmployeeID	ManagerID	Title	Level	Node
1	109	NULL	Chief Executive Officer	0	/
2	6	109	Marketing Manager	1	/109/
3	12	109	Vice President of Engineering	1	/109/
4	148	109	Vice President of Production	1	/109/
5	3	12	Engineering Manager	2	/109/12/
6	4	3	Senior Tool Designer	3	/109/12/3/
7	9	3	Design Engineer	3	/109/12/3/
8	11	3	Design Engineer	3	/109/12/3/
9	263	3	Senior Tool Designer	3	/109/12/3/
10	5	263	Tool Designer	4	/109/12/3/263/
11	21	148	Production Control Manager	2	/109/148/
12	7	21	Production Supervisor - WC60	3	/109/148/21/
13	14	21	Production Supervisor - WC50	3	/109/148/21/
14	16	21	Production Supervisor - WC60	3	/109/148/21/
15	18	21	Production Supervisor - WC60	3	/109/148/21/
16	25	21	Production Supervisor - WC10	3	/109/148/21/
17	173	21	Production Supervisor - WC30	3	/109/148/21/

Figure 11-5. The partial results of a recursive query

The query runs the recursive member repeatedly until all possible paths are selected; that is, until the recursive member no longer returns results. In case of an incorrectly written recursive query that will run forever, the recursive member will run only 100 times by default unless you specify the MAXRECURSION option to limit how many times the query will run. To alter the query in Listing 11-5 to a potential unending loop, change a.ManagerID = b.EmployeeID to a.EmployeeID = b.EmployeeID.

Just because the default MAXRECURSION value is 100 doesn't mean that a recursive query will return only 100 rows. In this example, the anchor returns the CEO, EmployeeID 109. The first time the recursive member runs, the results include all employees who report to 109. The next call returns the employees reporting to the employees returned in the last call, and so on. The values from one call feed the next call. This process will quickly exceed the MAXRECURSION value and the query will generate an error. If you

401

want to see what an unending recursive query loop looks like, change the MAXRECURSION value to 0. Keep in mind that you will need to manually terminate the query since it will never actually complete.

Instead of filtering the anchor to find the CEO, you can supply any ManagerID value. If you specify a particular manager, instead of starting at the CEO, the results will start at the subordinates of the ManagerID supplied. On your own, change the criteria in the anchor member, and rerun the query to see what happens.

Writing recursive queries is an advanced skill you may or may not need right away. Luckily, if you do need to write a recursive query, you will know where to find a simple example.

The OUTPUT Clause

You learned how to manipulate data in Chapter 6. The OUTPUT clause allows you to see or even save the modified values when you perform a data manipulation statement. The interesting thing about OUTPUT is that data manipulation statements don't normally return data except for the number of rows affected. By using OUTPUT, you can retrieve a result set of the data in the same statement that updates the data. You can see the result set in the query window results or return the result set to a client application.

Using OUTPUT to View Data

When using OUTPUT, you can view the data using the special tables DELETED and INSERTED. You may wonder why there is not an UPDATED table. Instead of an UPDATED table, you will find the old values in the DELETED table and the new values in the INSERTED table. Here are the syntax examples for using the OUTPUT clause for viewing changes when running data manipulation statements:

```
--Update style 1
UPDATE a SET <col1> = <value>
OUTPUT deleted.<col1>,inserted.<col1>
FROM <table1> AS a

--Update style 2
UPDATE <table1> SET <col1> = <value>
OUTPUT deleted.<col1>, inserted.<col1>
WHERE <criteria>

--Insert style 1
INSERT [INTO] <table1> (<col1>,<col2>)
OUTPUT inserted.<col1>, inserted.<col2>
SELECT <col1>, <col2>
FROM <table2>

--Insert style 2
INSERT [INTO] <table1> (<col1>,<col2>)
OUTPUT inserted.<col1>, inserted.<col2>
VALUES (<value1>,<value2>)

--Delete style 1
DELETE [FROM] <table1>
OUTPUT deleted.<col1>, deleted.<col2>
WHERE <criteria>
```

```
--DELETE style 2
DELETE [FROM] a
OUTPUT deleted.<col1>, deleted.<col2>
FROM <table1> AS a
```

Probably the trickiest thing about using OUTPUT is figuring out where in the statement to include it. Type in and execute the code in Listing 11-6 to learn more about OUTPUT.

Listing 11-6. *Viewing the Manipulated Data with OUTPUT*

```
USE AdventureWorks2012;
GO

--1
IF OBJECT_ID('dbo.Customers') IS NOT NULL BEGIN
    DROP TABLE dbo.Customers;
END;

--2
CREATE TABLE dbo.Customers (CustomerID INT NOT NULL PRIMARY KEY,
    Name VARCHAR(150),PersonID INT NOT NULL)
GO

--3
INSERT INTO dbo.Customers(CustomerID,Name,PersonID)
OUTPUT inserted.CustomerID,inserted.Name
SELECT c.CustomerID, p.FirstName + ' ' + p.LastName,PersonID
FROM Sales.Customer AS c
INNER JOIN Person.Person AS p
ON c.PersonID = p.BusinessEntityID;

--4
UPDATE c SET Name = p.FirstName +
    ISNULL(' ' + p.MiddleName,'') + ' ' + p.LastName
OUTPUT deleted.CustomerID,deleted.Name AS OldName, inserted.Name AS NewName
FROM dbo.Customers AS c
INNER JOIN Person.Person AS p on c.PersonID = p.BusinessEntityID;

--5
DELETE FROM dbo.Customers
OUTPUT deleted.CustomerID, deleted.Name, deleted.PersonID
WHERE CustomerID = 11000;
```

Figure 11-6 shows the partial results. Unfortunately, you can't add an ORDER BY clause to OUTPUT, and the INSERT statement returns the rows in a different order than the UPDATE statement. Code section 1 drops the dbo.Customers table if it already exists. Statement 2 creates the dbo.Customers table. Statement 3 inserts all the rows when joining the Sales.Customer table to the Person.Person table. The OUTPUT clause, located right after the INSERT clause, returns the CustomerID and Name. Statement 4 modifies the Name column by including the MiddleName in the expression. The DELETED table displays the Name column data before the update. The INSERTED table displays the Name column after the update. The UPDATE clause includes aliases to differentiate the values. Statement 5 deletes one row from the table. The OUTPUT clause displays the deleted data.

403

	CustomerID	Name
1	11000	Jon Yang
2	11001	Eugene Huang
3	11002	Ruben Torres
4	11003	Christy Zhu
5	11004	Elizabeth Johnson
6	11005	Julio Ruiz
7	11006	Janet Alvarez
8	11007	Marco Mehta

	CustomerID	OldName	NewName
1	29485	Catherine Abel	Catherine R. Abel
2	29486	Kim Abercrombie	Kim Abercrombie
3	29487	Humberto Acevedo	Humberto Acevedo
4	29484	Gustavo Achong	Gustavo Achong
5	29488	Pilar Ackerman	Pilar Ackerman
6	28866	Aaron Adams	Aaron B Adams
7	13323	Adam Adams	Adam Adams
8	21139	Alex Adams	Alex C Adams

	CustomerID	Name	PersonID
1	11000	Jon V Yang	13531

Figure 11-6. The partial results of viewing the manipulated data with OUTPUT

Saving OUTPUT Data to a Table

Instead of displaying or returning the rows from the OUTPUT clause, you might need to save the information in another table. For example, you may need to populate a history table or save the changes for further processing. Here is a syntax example showing how to use INTO along with OUTPUT:

```
INSERT [INTO] <table1> (<col1>, <col2>)
OUTPUT inserted.<col1>, inserted.<col2>
INTO <table2>
SELECT <col3>,<col4>
FROM <table3>
```

Type in and execute the code in Listing 11-7 to learn more.

Listing 11-7. *Saving the Results of OUTPUT*

```
USE AdventureWorks2012;

--1
IF OBJECT_ID('dbo.Customers') IS NOT NULL BEGIN
    DROP TABLE dbo.Customers;
END;

IF OBJECT_ID('dbo.CustomerHistory') IS NOT NULL BEGIN
    DROP TABLE dbo.CustomerHistory;
END;

--2
CREATE TABLE dbo.Customers (CustomerID INT NOT NULL PRIMARY KEY,
    Name VARCHAR(150),PersonID INT NOT NULL)

CREATE TABLE dbo.CustomerHistory(CustomerID INT NOT NULL PRIMARY KEY,
    OldName VARCHAR(150), NewName VARCHAR(150),
    ChangeDate DATETIME);
GO

--3
INSERT INTO dbo.Customers(CustomerID, Name, PersonID)
SELECT c.CustomerID, p.FirstName + ' ' + p.LastName,PersonID
FROM Sales.Customer AS c
INNER JOIN Person.Person AS p
ON c.PersonID = p.BusinessEntityID;

--4
UPDATE c SET Name = p.FirstName +
    ISNULL(' ' + p.MiddleName,'') + ' ' + p.LastName
OUTPUT deleted.CustomerID,deleted.Name, inserted.Name, GETDATE()
INTO dbo.CustomerHistory
FROM dbo.Customers AS c
INNER JOIN Person.Person AS p on c.PersonID = p.BusinessEntityID;

--5
SELECT CustomerID, OldName, NewName,ChangeDate
FROM dbo.CustomerHistory;
```

Figure 11-7 shows the partial results. Code section 1 drops the dbo.Customers and
dbo.CustomerHistory tables if they already exist. Code section 2 creates the two tables. Statement 3
populates the dbo.Customers table. Statement 4 updates the Name column for all of the rows. By
including OUTPUT INTO, the CustomerID along with the previous and current Name values are saved into
the table. The statement also populates the ChangeDate column by using the GETDATE function.

Results

	CustomerID	OldName	NewName	ChangeDate
1	11000	Jon Yang	Jon V Yang	2011-09-10 12:36:56.820
2	11001	Eugene Huang	Eugene L Huang	2011-09-10 12:36:56.820
3	11002	Ruben Torres	Ruben Torres	2011-09-10 12:36:56.820
4	11003	Christy Zhu	Christy Zhu	2011-09-10 12:36:56.820
5	11004	Elizabeth Johnson	Elizabeth Johnson	2011-09-10 12:36:56.820
6	11005	Julio Ruiz	Julio Ruiz	2011-09-10 12:36:56.820
7	11006	Janet Alvarez	Janet G Alvarez	2011-09-10 12:36:56.820
8	11007	Marco Mehta	Marco Mehta	2011-09-10 12:36:56.820
9	11008	Rob Verhoff	Rob Verhoff	2011-09-10 12:36:56.820
10	11009	Shannon Carlson	Shannon C Carlson	2011-09-10 12:36:56.820
11	11010	Jacquelyn Suarez	Jacquelyn C Suarez	2011-09-10 12:36:56.820
12	11011	Curtis Lu	Curtis Lu	2011-09-10 12:36:56.820
13	11012	Lauren Walker	Lauren M Walker	2011-09-10 12:36:56.820
14	11013	Ian Jenkins	Ian M Jenkins	2011-09-10 12:36:56.820
15	11014	Sydney Bennett	Sydney Bennett	2011-09-10 12:36:56.820
16	11015	Chloe Young	Chloe Young	2011-09-10 12:36:56.820
17	11016	Wyatt Hill	Wyatt L Hill	2011-09-10 12:36:56.820

Figure 11-7. The partial results of saving the OUTPUT data into a table

The MERGE Statement

The MERGE statement, also known as *upsert,* allows you to synchronize two tables with one statement. For example, you would normally need to perform at least one UPDATE, one INSERT, and one DELETE statement to keep the data in one table up-to-date with the data from another table. By using MERGE, you can perform the same work more efficiently (assuming that the tables have the proper indexes in place) with just one statement. The drawback is that MERGE is more difficult to understand and write than the three individual statements. One potential use for MERGE—where taking the time to write the MERGE statements really pays off—is loading data warehouses and data marts. Here is the syntax for a simple MERGE statement:

```
MERGE <target table>
USING <source table name>|(or query>) AS alias [(column names)]
ON (<join criteria>)
WHEN MATCHED [AND <other critera>]
THEN UPDATE SET <col> = alias.<value>
WHEN NOT MATCHED BY TARGET [AND <other criteria>]
THEN INSERT (<column list>) VALUES (<values>) -- row is inserted into target
WHEN NOT MATCHED BY SOURCE [AND <other criteria>]
THEN DELETE -- row is deleted from target
[OUTPUT $action, DELETED.*, INSERTED.*];
```

At first glance, the syntax may seem overwhelming. Basically, it defines an action to perform if a row from the source table matches the target table (WHEN MATCHED), an action to perform if a row is missing in the target table (WHEN NOT MATCHED BY TARGET), and an action to perform if an extra row is in the target table (WHEN NOT MATCHED BY SOURCE). The actions to perform on the target table can be anything you need to do. For example, if the source table is missing a row that appears in the target table (WHEN NOT MATCHED BY SOURCE), you don't have to delete the target row. You could, in fact, leave out that part of the statement or perform another action. In addition to the join criteria, you can also specify any other criteria in each match specification. You can include an optional OUTPUT clause along with the $action option. The $action option shows you which action is performed on each row. Include the DELETED and INSERTED tables in the OUTPUT clause to see the before and after values. The MERGE statement must end with a semicolon. Type in and execute the code in Listing 11-8 to learn how to use MERGE.

Listing 11-8. *Using the MERGE Statement*

```
USE AdventureWorks2012;

--1
IF OBJECT_ID('dbo.CustomerSource') IS NOT NULL BEGIN
    DROP TABLE dbo.CustomerSource;
END;
IF OBJECT_ID('dbo.CustomerTarget') IS NOT NULL BEGIN
    DROP TABLE dbo.CustomerTarget;
END;

--2
CREATE TABLE dbo.CustomerSource (CustomerID INT NOT NULL PRIMARY KEY,
    Name VARCHAR(150), PersonID INT NOT NULL);
CREATE TABLE dbo.CustomerTarget (CustomerID INT NOT NULL PRIMARY KEY,
    Name VARCHAR(150), PersonID INT NOT NULL);

--3
INSERT INTO dbo.CustomerSource(CustomerID,Name,PersonID)
SELECT CustomerID,
    p.FirstName + ISNULL(' ' + p.MiddleName,'') + ' ' + p.LastName,
    PersonID
FROM Sales.Customer AS c
INNER JOIN Person.Person AS p ON c.PersonID = p.BusinessEntityID
WHERE c.CustomerID IN (29485,29486,29487,10299);

--4
INSERT INTO dbo.CustomerTarget(CustomerID,Name,PersonID)
SELECT CustomerID, p.FirstName  + ' ' + p.LastName, PersonID
FROM Sales.Customer AS c
INNER JOIN Person.Person AS p ON c.PersonID = p.BusinessEntityID
WHERE c.CustomerID IN (29485,29486,21139);

--5
SELECT CustomerID, Name, PersonID
FROM dbo.CustomerSource
ORDER BY CustomerID;
```

```
--6
SELECT CustomerID, Name, PersonID
FROM dbo.CustomerTarget
ORDER BY CustomerID;

--7
MERGE dbo.CustomerTarget AS t
USING dbo.CustomerSource AS s
ON (s.CustomerID = t.CustomerID)
WHEN MATCHED AND s.Name <> t.Name
THEN UPDATE SET Name = s.Name
WHEN NOT MATCHED BY TARGET
THEN INSERT (CustomerID, Name, PersonID) VALUES (CustomerID, Name, PersonID)
WHEN NOT MATCHED BY SOURCE
THEN DELETE
OUTPUT $action, DELETED.*, INSERTED.*;--semi-colon is required

--8
SELECT CustomerID, Name, PersonID
FROM dbo.CustomerTarget
ORDER BY CustomerID;
```

Figure 11-8 shows the results. Code section 1 drops the tables dbo.CustomerSource and dbo.CustomerTarget. Code section 2 creates the two tables. They have the same column names, but this is not a requirement. Statement 3 populates the dbo.CustomerSource table with four rows. It creates the Name column using the FirstName, MiddleName, and LastName columns. Statement 4 populates the dbo.CustomerTarget table with three rows. Two of the rows contain the same customers as the dbo.CustomerSource table. Query 5 displays the data from dbo.CustomerSource, and query 6 displays the data from dbo.CustomerTarget. Statement 7 synchronizes dbo.CustomerTarget with dbo.CustomerSource, correcting the Name column, inserting missing rows, and deleting extra rows by using the MERGE command. Because the query includes the OUTPUT clause, you can see the action performed on each row. Query 8 displays the dbo.CustomerTarget with the changes. The target table now matches the source table.

Results

	CustomerID	Name	PersonID
1	29485	Catherine R. Abel	293
2	29486	Kim Abercrombie	295
3	29487	Humberto Acevedo	297

	CustomerID	Name	PersonID
1	21139	Alex Adams	16724
2	29485	Catherine Abel	293
3	29486	Kim Abercrombie	295

	$action	CustomerID	Name	PersonID	CustomerID	Name	PersonID
1	DELETE	21139	Alex Adams	16724	NULL	NULL	NULL
2	UPDATE	29485	Catherine Abel	293	29485	Catherine R. Abel	293
3	INSERT	NULL	NULL	NULL	29487	Humberto Acevedo	297

	CustomerID	Name	PersonID
1	29485	Catherine R. Abel	293
2	29486	Kim Abercrombie	295
3	29487	Humberto Acevedo	297

Figure 11-8. The results of using MERGE

GROUPING SETS

You learned all about aggregate queries in Chapter 5. Another option, GROUPING SETS, when added to an aggregate query, allows you to combine different grouping levels within one statement. This is equivalent to combining multiple aggregate queries with UNION. For example, suppose you want the data summarized by one column combined with the data summarized by a different column. Just like MERGE, this feature is very valuable for loading data warehouses and data marts. When using GROUPING SETS instead of UNION, you can see increased performance, especially when the query includes a WHERE clause and the number of columns specified in the GROUPING SETS clause increases. Here is the syntax:

```
SELECT <col1>,<col2>,<aggregate function>(<col3>)
FROM <table1>
WHERE <criteria>
GROUP BY GROUPING SETS (<col1>,<col2>)
```

Listing 11-9 compares the equivalent UNION query to a query using GROUPING SETS. Type in and execute the code to learn more.

Listing 11-9. Using GROUPING SETS

```
USE AdventureWorks2012;


--1
SELECT NULL AS SalesOrderID,SUM(UnitPrice)AS SumOfPrice,ProductID
FROM Sales.SalesOrderDetail
WHERE SalesOrderID BETWEEN 44175 AND 44180
GROUP BY ProductID
UNION
SELECT SalesOrderID,SUM(UnitPrice), NULL
FROM Sales.SalesOrderDetail
WHERE SalesOrderID BETWEEN 44175 AND 44180
GROUP BY SalesOrderID;

--2
SELECT SalesOrderID,SUM(UnitPrice) AS SumOfPrice,ProductID
FROM Sales.SalesOrderDetail
WHERE SalesOrderID BETWEEN 44175 AND 44180
GROUP BY GROUPING SETS(SalesOrderID,ProductID);
```

Figure 11-9 shows the partial results. Query 1 is a UNION query that calculates the sum of the UnitPrice. The first part of the query supplies a NULL value for SalesOrderID. That is because SalesOrderID is just a placeholder. The query groups by ProductID, and SalesOrderID is not needed. The second part of the query supplies a NULL value for ProductID. In this case, the query groups by SalesOrderID, and ProductID is not needed. The UNION query combines the results. Query 2 demonstrates how to write the equivalent query using GROUPING SETS.

	SalesOrderID	SumOfPrice	ProductID
1	NULL	3578.27	751
2	NULL	3578.27	752
3	NULL	3578.27	753
4	NULL	3399.99	774
5	NULL	6749.98	777
6	44175	3578.27	NULL
7	44176	3578.27	NULL
8	44177	3374.99	NULL

	SalesOrderID	SumOfPrice	ProductID
1	NULL	3578.27	751
2	NULL	3578.27	752
3	NULL	3578.27	753
4	NULL	3399.99	774
5	NULL	6749.98	777
6	44175	3578.27	NULL
7	44176	3578.27	NULL
8	44177	3374.99	NULL

Figure 11-9. The partial results of comparing UNION to GROUPING SETS

Pivoted Queries

Normally a query displays the data in a way that is similar to how it looks in a table, often with the column headers being the actual names of the columns within the table. A pivoted query displays the values of one column as column headers instead. For example, you could display the sum of the sales by month so that the month names are column headers. Each row would then contain the data by year with the sum for each month displayed from left to right. This section shows how to write pivoted queries with two techniques: CASE and PIVOT.

Pivoting Data with CASE

Many developers still use the CASE function to create pivoted results. (See "The Case Function" section in Chapter 3 to learn more about CASE.) Essentially, you use several CASE expressions in the query, one for each pivoted column header. For example, the query will have a CASE expression checking to see whether the month of the order date is January. If the order does occur in January, supply the total sales value. If not, supply a zero. For each row, the data ends up in the correct column where it can be aggregated. Here is the syntax for using CASE to pivot data:

```
CASE <col1>,SUM(CASE <col3> WHEN <value1> THEN <col2> ELSE 0 END) AS <alias1>,
    SUM(CASE <col3> WHEN <value2> THEN <col2> ELSE 0 END) AS <alias2>,
    SUM(CASE <col3> WHEN <value3> THEN <col2> ELSE 0 END) AS <alias3>
FROM <table1>
GROUP BY <col1>
```

Type in and execute Listing 11-10 to learn how to pivot data using CASE.

Listing 11-10. Using CASE to Pivot Data

```
USE AdventureWorks2012;

SELECT YEAR(OrderDate) AS OrderYear,
ROUND(SUM(CASE MONTH(OrderDate) WHEN 1 THEN TotalDue ELSE 0 END),0)
    AS Jan,
ROUND(SUM(CASE MONTH(OrderDate) WHEN 2 THEN TotalDue ELSE 0 END),0)
    AS Feb,
ROUND(SUM(CASE MONTH(OrderDate) WHEN 3 THEN TotalDue ELSE 0 END),0)
    AS Mar,
ROUND(SUM(CASE MONTH(OrderDate) WHEN 4 THEN TotalDue ELSE 0 END),0)
    AS Apr,
ROUND(SUM(CASE MONTH(OrderDate) WHEN 5 THEN TotalDue ELSE 0 END),0)
    AS May,
ROUND(SUM(CASE MONTH(OrderDate) WHEN 6 THEN TotalDue ELSE 0 END),0)
    AS Jun
FROM Sales.SalesOrderHeader
GROUP BY YEAR(OrderDate)
ORDER BY OrderYear;
```

Figure 11-10 shows the results. To save space in the results, the statement calculates the totals only for the months January through June and uses the ROUND function. The GROUP BY clause contains just the YEAR(OrderDate) expression. You might think that you need to group by month as well, but this query doesn't group by month. It just includes each TotalDue value in a different column depending on the month.

Results

	OrderYear	Jan	Feb	Mar	Apr	May	Jun
1	2005	0.00	0.00	0.00	0.00	0.00	0.00
2	2006	1462449.00	2749105.00	2350568.00	1727690.00	3299799.00	1920507.00
3	2007	1968647.00	3226056.00	2297693.00	2660724.00	3866365.00	2852210.00
4	2008	3359927.00	4662656.00	4722358.00	4269365.00	5813557.00	6004156.00

Figure 11-10. The results of using CASE to create a pivot query

Using the PIVOT Function

Microsoft introduced the PIVOT function with SQL Server 2005. In my opinion, the PIVOT function is more difficult to understand than using CASE to produce the same results. Just like CASE, you have to hardcode the column names. This works fine when the pivoted column names will never change, such as the months of the year. When the query bases the pivoted column on data that changes over time, such as employee or department names, the query must be modified each time that data changes. Here is the syntax for PIVOT:

```
SELECT <groupingCol>, <pivotedValue1> [AS <alias1>], <pivotedValue2> [AS <alias2>]
FROM (SELECT <groupingCol>, <value column>, <pivoted column>) AS <queryAlias>
PIVOT
( <aggregate function>(<value column>)
FOR <pivoted column> IN (<pivotedValue1>,<pivotedValue2>)
) AS <pivotAlias>
[ORDER BY <groupingCol>]
```

The SELECT part of the query lists any nonpivoted columns along with the values from the pivoted column. These values from the pivoted column will become the column names in your query. You can use aliases if you want to use a different column name than the actual value. For example, if the column names will be the month numbers, you can alias with the month names.

This syntax uses a derived table, listed after the word FROM, as the basis of the query. See the "Derived Tables" section in Chapter 4 to review derived tables. Make sure that you only list columns that you want as grouping levels, the pivoted column, and the column that will be summarized in this derived table. Adding other columns to this query will cause extra grouping levels and unexpected results. The derived table must be aliased, so don't forget this small detail.

■ **Tip** It is possible to use a CTE to write this query instead of a derived table. See the article "Create Pivoted Tables in 3 Steps" in *SQL Server Magazine*'s July 2009 issue to learn this alternate method.

Follow the derived table with the PIVOT function. The argument to the PIVOT function includes the aggregate expression followed by the word FOR and the pivoted column name. Right after the pivoted column name, include an IN expression. Inside the IN expression, list the pivoted column values. These will match up with the pivoted column values in the SELECT list. The PIVOT function must also have an alias. Finally, you can order the results if you want. Usually this will be by the grouping level column, but you can also sort by any of the pivoted column names. Type in and execute Listing 11-11 to learn how to use PIVOT.

Listing 11-11. *Pivoting Results with PIVOT*

```
USE AdventureWorks2012;

--1
SELECT OrderYear, [1] AS Jan, [2] AS Feb, [3] AS Mar,
    [4] AS Apr, [5] AS May, [6] AS Jun
FROM (SELECT YEAR(OrderDate) AS OrderYear, TotalDue,
    MONTH(OrderDate) AS OrderMonth
    FROM Sales.SalesOrderHeader) AS MonthData
PIVOT (
    SUM(TotalDue)
    FOR OrderMonth IN ([1],[2],[3],[4],[5],[6])
    ) AS PivotData
ORDER BY OrderYear;

--2
SELECT OrderYear, ROUND(ISNULL([1],0),0) AS Jan,
    ROUND(ISNULL([2],0),0) AS Feb, ROUND(ISNULL([3],0),0) AS Mar,
    ROUND(ISNULL([4],0),0) AS Apr, ROUND(ISNULL([5],0),0) AS May,
    ROUND(ISNULL([6],0),0) AS Jun
FROM (SELECT YEAR(OrderDate) AS OrderYear, TotalDue,
    MONTH(OrderDate) AS OrderMonth
    FROM Sales.SalesOrderHeader) AS MonthData
PIVOT (
    SUM(TotalDue)
    FOR OrderMonth IN ([1],[2],[3],[4],[5],[6])
    ) AS PivotData
ORDER BY OrderYear;
```

Figure 11-11 shows the results. First take a look at the derived table aliased as MonthData in query 1. The SELECT statement in the derived table contains an expression that returns the year of the OrderDate, the OrderYear, and an expression that returns the month of the OrderDate, OrderMonth. It also contains the TotalDue column. The query will group the results by OrderYear. The OrderMonth column is the pivoted column. The query will sum up the TotalDue values. The derived table contains only the columns and expressions needed by the pivoted query.

Results

	OrderYear	Jan	Feb	Mar	Apr	May	Jun
1	2005	NULL	NULL	NULL	NULL	NULL	NULL
2	2006	1462448.8986	2749104.6546	2350568.1264	1727689.5793	3299799.233	1920506.6177
3	2007	1968647.184	3226056.1486	2297692.9898	2660723.7481	3866365.1263	2852209.8283
4	2008	3359927.2196	4662655.6183	4722357.5175	4269365.0103	5813557.453	6004155.7672

	OrderYear	Jan	Feb	Mar	Apr	May	Jun
1	2005	0.00	0.00	0.00	0.00	0.00	0.00
2	2006	1462449.00	2749105.00	2350568.00	1727690.00	3299799.00	1920507.00
3	2007	1968647.00	3226056.00	2297693.00	2660724.00	3866365.00	2852210.00
4	2008	3359927.00	4662656.00	4722358.00	4269365.00	5813557.00	6004156.00

Figure 11-11. *The results of using PIVOT*

The PIVOT function specifies the aggregate expression SUM(TotalDue). The pivoted column is OrderMonth. The IN expression contains the numbers 1–6, each surrounded by brackets. The IN expression lists the values for OrderMonth that you want to show up in the final results. These values are also the column names. Since columns starting with numbers are not valid column names, the brackets surround the numbers. You could also quote these numbers. The IN expression has two purposes: to provide the column names and to filter the results.

The outer SELECT list contains OrderYear and the numbers 1–6 surrounded with brackets. These must be the same values found in the IN expression. Because you want the month abbreviations instead of numbers as the column names, the query uses aliases. Notice that the SELECT list does not contain the TotalDue column. Finally, the ORDER BY clause specifies that the results will sort by OrderYear.

The results of query 2 are identical to the results from the pivoted results using the CASE technique in the previous section. This query uses the ROUND and ISNULL functions to replace NULL with zero and round the results.

Numbers Table

Many T-SQL developers and some DBAs use what is a called a numbers table to help with some advanced queries involving ranges of data. A numbers table is simply a table containing a sequential list of numbers. The amount of numbers you put in the table is dependent on how many numbers you may need and how large you want the table. As an example, let's create a numbers table with 500,000 rows; this should be enough for almost any task. First, you create the table. The table contains only one column with a clustered index on the column. Listing 11-12 shows the script for creating the table.

Listing 11-12. Creating a Numbers Table

```
USE tempdb;

CREATE TABLE tblNumbers
    (num     INT NOT NULL
    ,CONSTRAINT pk_tblNumbers PRIMARY KEY CLUSTERED(num) WITH FILLFACTOR = 100
    );
```

In this case, you created the table in tempdb. Normally, depending on your use of the table, you will want to either create it in model database or in any user database needing a numbers table. The preferred method is to create a new database used exclusively to store DBA objects or custom T-SQL code. You would then script out this utility database and create on every new server. Put a primary key constraint on the column to avoid any chance of duplicate rows. You also create a fillfactor equal to 100 since you won't be inserting or deleting rows into the table.

The second step now is to populate the table with sequential numbers. Listing 11-13 populates the tblNumbers with values 1-500,000. Although there are many ways to do this, you'll generate the values by using the recursive CTE technique discussed earlier in the chapter.

Listing 11-13. Populating a Numbers Table

```
WITH    cte0 AS (SELECT 1 AS c UNION ALL SELECT 1),
        cte1 AS (SELECT 1 AS c FROM cte0 a, cte0 b),
        cte2 AS (SELECT 1 AS c FROM cte1 a, cte1 b),
        cte3 AS (SELECT 1 AS c FROM cte2 a, cte2 b),
        cte4 AS (SELECT 1 AS c FROM cte3 a, cte3 b),
        cte5 AS (SELECT 1 AS c FROM cte4 a, cte4 b),
        nums AS (SELECT row_number() OVER (ORDER BY c) AS n FROM cte5)
```

```
INSERT INTO tblNumbers(num)
    SELECT n FROM nums
    WHERE n <= 500000
```

So now that you have a table with sequential numbers from 1 to 500,000, what are some things you can do with it? You can use it as a method to create a calendar table for the current year. Listing 11-14 shows the code to create the table. Figure 11-12 shows the partial output.

Listing 11-14. *Creating a Calendar Table*

```
USE tempdb;
GO

    SELECT dt, DATENAME( dw, dt )
      FROM ( SELECT DATEADD( d, num - 1, CAST( CAST( YEAR( CURRENT_TIMESTAMP )
                    * 10000 + 101 AS  VARCHAR(8) ) AS DATETIME ) )
               FROM tblNumbers ) D ( dt )
      WHERE YEAR( dt ) = 2011 ;
```

Results

	dt	(No column name)
1	2011-01-01 00:00:00.000	Saturday
2	2011-01-02 00:00:00.000	Sunday
3	2011-01-03 00:00:00.000	Monday
4	2011-01-04 00:00:00.000	Tuesday
5	2011-01-05 00:00:00.000	Wednesday
6	2011-01-06 00:00:00.000	Thursday
7	2011-01-07 00:00:00.000	Friday
8	2011-01-08 00:00:00.000	Saturday
9	2011-01-09 00:00:00.000	Sunday
10	2011-01-10 00:00:00.000	Monday
11	2011-01-11 00:00:00.000	Tuesday
12	2011-01-12 00:00:00.000	Wednesday
13	2011-01-13 00:00:00.000	Thursday
14	2011-01-14 00:00:00.000	Friday
15	2011-01-15 00:00:00.000	Saturday

Figure 11-12. *Partial output of the calendar table*

Another use for numbers table is to parse an array of string values separated by commas. These are common in CSV files sometimes used in data imports. In this example, you will define in a variable a short list of string values separated by commas. The code in Listing 11-15 will take this variable and use the value from the numbers table in the SUBSTRING( ) function. The output is shown in Figure 11-13.

Listing 11-15. Parsing a Comma-Delimited List

```
USE tempdb;
GO

DECLARE @p VARCHAR(50)
SET @p = 'ABCDE,FG,HIJ,KLMNO,PQR,STUV,WX,YZ'

SELECT SUBSTRING( ',' + @p + ',', num + 1,
                CHARINDEX( ',', ',' + @p + ',', num + 1 ) - num - 1 ) AS "value"
    FROM tblNumbers
    WHERE SUBSTRING( ',' + @p + ',', num, 1 ) = ','
      AND num < LEN( ',' + @p + ',' ) ;
```

Results

	value
1	ABCDE
2	FG
3	HIJ
4	KLMNO
5	PQR
6	STUV
7	WX
8	YZ

Figure 11-13. Results of parsing a comma-delimited list

A numbers table is invaluable for any serious T-SQL programmer. The table helps to simplify many complex problems while also increasing performance by avoiding cursors. I recommend creating a numbers table either in a database specifically used for data management or in each user database. If you create the table in the model database, the table will be created each time you create a user database. Still, keep in mind the size of the table and only populate it with the amount of values you think you will ever need.

■ **Note** There are more uses for a numbers table than can be discussed here. For more details see Brandon Galderisi's article at www.sqlservercentral.com/articles/T-SQL+Aids/64696/. Jeff Moden and Itzic Ben Gan also have some excellent discussions concerning the implementations of numbers tables for everyday use.

Database Cleanup

Run the script in Listing 11-16 to clean up the tables used in this chapter. You can download the script from this book's page at www.apress.com. Alternately, you can reinstall the sample databases by following the instructions in the "Installing the Sample Databases" section in Chapter 1. There is no need to clean up databases created in tempdb. These will be removed once you restart SQL Server.

Listing 11-16. Demo Table Cleanup

```
USE AdventureWorks2012;
GO

IF OBJECT_ID('dbo.Customers') IS NOT NULL BEGIN
    DROP TABLE dbo.Customers;
END;
IF OBJECT_ID('dbo.CustomerHistory') IS NOT NULL BEGIN
    DROP TABLE dbo.CustomerHistory;
END;
IF OBJECT_ID('dbo.CustomerSource') IS NOT NULL BEGIN
    DROP TABLE dbo.CustomerSource;
END;
IF OBJECT_ID('dbo.CustomerTarget') IS NOT NULL BEGIN
    DROP TABLE dbo.CustomerTarget;
END;
IF OBJECT_ID('dbo.Sales') IS NOT NULL BEGIN
    DROP TABLE dbo.Sales;
END;
```

Summary

This chapter covered how to write advanced queries using some T-SQL features supported in SQL Server 2012. Starting with Chapter 4, you saw how CTEs, or common table expressions, can help you solve query problems without resorting to temporary tables or views. In this chapter, you learned several other ways to use CTEs, including how to display hierarchical data with a recursive CTE. With the OUTPUT clause, you can return or store the data involved in data manipulation statements. If you will be involved with loading data warehouses, you can use the MERGE and GROUPING SET features to improve performance. You learned two ways to write pivot queries, using CASE and using the new PIVOT function. Finally, you learned how to use a numbers table to simply complex queries and increase performance by avoiding the use of cursors.

Although the material in this chapter is not required knowledge for beginning T-SQL developers, it will be very beneficial to you to keep these techniques in mind. As you gain more experience, you will often find ways to take advantage of these features.

CHAPTER 12

Where to Go Next?

I hope you have enjoyed learning about T-SQL as much as I have enjoyed writing about it. Not everyone is cut out to be a T-SQL developer; it helps to really enjoy writing code. Programming is not something you can just learn and be done with it. You will continue to learn new techniques as long as you are programming T-SQL. The other thing you can count on is that Microsoft will continue to add new features to SQL Server, including new T-SQL features, giving you more to learn about. In fact, this book describes numerous, completely new T-SQL enhancements only found in SQL Server 2012. I can guarantee the next SQL Server release will have even more.

You may have read this book from cover to cover, typing in all the sample code and performing the exercises found in most of the chapters. If you are like me, you may have just skipped around looking for specific knowledge as you needed it, using the book as a reference. Either way, you would have found simple examples that showed you how to use a specific feature or solve a particular problem. Each chapter used techniques from the previous chapters to solve more complex query problems as the book progressed.

I began writing T-SQL queries 12 years ago. I had a book that was about four inches thick on my desk that contained just about everything I needed to know about SQL Server at the time, including T-SQL. I remember constantly looking up how to join tables, write aggregate queries, or perform updates until, eventually, I just knew the syntax. As I learned even more techniques, the syntax I knew continued to grow, and the syntax I had to look up constantly changed. Since then, Microsoft has introduced several new versions of SQL Server, expanding the feature set each time. I would probably need four or five books the size of my old reference to cover everything offered with SQL Server today.

Online Resources

Besides having a great reference book in your hands, what other ways can you learn? A wealth of knowledge is available for free on the Web. You can post questions on newsgroups and forums; read articles, blogs, and white papers; and even view videos explaining how to write T-SQL code. Someone else has already posted an answer, blog, or article that covers just about anything you could ever want to know. Here are some of my favorite sites featuring SQL Server information:

- www.sqlservercentral.com

- www.sqlteam.com

- www.microsoft.com/sqlserver/en/us/community.aspx

- www.sql-server-performance.com/

- http://sqlblog.com/

- `http://sqlserverpedia.com/`

- `www.sqlshare.com/`

- `www.mssqltips.com/`

- `http://sqlcat.com/`

At the time of this writing, social networking sites such as Facebook, LinkedIn, and Twitter make the news every day. These sites provide yet another way to get answers to questions by discussing the issues with colleagues across the world. For example, if you send a SQL Server question on Twitter and use hashtag #sqlhelp, you'll get professionals from around the world willing to answer your question.

Because of printing and shipping costs and the impact of online resources, publishers are moving print magazines to online services only. I suspect that over time we will see less and less paper and even more online subscription resources. You'll also want to take advantage of e-books, which can be quickly downloaded onto your reader and are much less expensive to purchase than physical books.

Conferences

If you get the chance to attend a conference such as Professional Association for SQL Server (PASS), PASS SQLRally, DevTeach/SQLTeach, TechEd, or one of the other conferences featuring SQL Server presentations, be sure to take advantage of the opportunity. The great thing about attending conferences is that you get a chance to talk with the gurus and experts as well as listen to the presentations. You also get to meet other people who face many of the same issues that you do and learn about the solutions they have developed. Conferences can get you out of your day-to-day environment, get you refreshed, and get you excited about the future.

Just as more and more traditionally printed material now appears on the Internet, you can also attend virtual conferences via the Web. SQL Server World User Group hosts two or three virtual conferences each year (`www.sswug.org/`). The advantage to virtual conferences over in-person conferences is in cost savings and lack of travel. The disadvantage, of course, is not getting to meet the speakers and other attendees face-to-face. Either way, attending conferences is a great way to learn about SQL Server.

User Groups

Many metropolitan areas have user groups dedicated to programming languages or using certain software. These groups often provide pizza, prizes, and educational presentations at meetings held on a scheduled basis. To find a list of user groups that are associated with PASS, go to `www.sqlpass.org`. User group membership is usually free. A few dedicated volunteers run most user groups, and sponsors, such as recruiting firms or software vendors, often pay for the food and provide prizes. Not only is attending user group meetings a great way to learn T-SQL and other SQL Server topics, but you may also meet your next employer at a user group meeting!

Also keep an eye out for SQLSaturday events. These events are part of PASS but are arranged by local user groups. They occur throughout the year in various locations around the world. A SQLSaturday event is an entire Saturday of SQL presentations and—the best part—it's free! To see if there is a SQLSaturday scheduled near you, go to `www.sqlsaturday.com/` and check it out.

Vendors

Even though they may have an ulterior motive, such as getting you to buy a product, vendors creating software for SQL Server developers and database administrators often provide a wealth of information. Vendors have educational web sites, webinars, newsletters, and online books all for free. Some of the software vendors employ high-profile SQL Server experts who speak at user group meetings and conferences to provide education to the SQL Server community.

Books

Even though there are many online resources available to you, nothing beats a great book that you can carry with you on an airplane or a bus. You now have the choice to buy the physical book, download the book as a computer file, or read the book on a subscription device such as a Kindle or Nook. The great thing about books by Apress authors, regardless of how you access the books, is that they are written by developers and database administrators who have worked at real jobs—just like you. Apress authors can pass along the benefit of their experience as well as their knowledge.

If you need to get started learning a language or need to really focus on a particular area, a well-organized book will save you a lot of time vs. hunting down resources on the Web. When learning a new programming language, follow the examples from cover to cover at first. Then, once you are familiar with the language, save your book as a reference for when you need more information about a particular topic.

Classes

If you live in a metropolitan area, many training centers offer SQL Server courses. These classes are a great way to get you started with new language, especially if you learn better in person than with a book or video. Another benefit is being able to ask the instructor questions, often even after the class is over by e-mail. Like conferences, getting out of the regular work environment helps you focus and learn. I encourage you to attend training classes, especially if your employer is willing to foot the bill.

SQL Server Books Online

Refer to SQL Server Books Online often. I am constantly surprised to learn new ways to use T-SQL features from taking a look at Books Online when I thought I already knew all there was to know about a feature. I often use Books Online as a starting point and then see how someone else explains the same concept in a book or article.

One thing that I don't like about Books Online is how the syntax is presented. The syntax examples include every possible option, making it, in my opinion, difficult to understand. I usually skip down to the example code to figure it out. I hope you learned a lot by the way this book presented the syntax examples, showing only what you needed to see to learn the particular topic at hand.

Practice, Practice, and More Practice

The only way to really learn T-SQL is by doing it. You can have an entire bookshelf filled with T-SQL books, attend conferences and classes, ask questions, and surf the Web, but you won't learn T-SQL without practicing it yourself. I am reminded of a recent TV episode of *The Big Bang Theory* where one of the characters thought he could learn to swim by just reading about swimming on the Web. The more you practice and experiment, the faster you will learn.

This book is full of examples and exercises that you can use to experiment. What will happen if you tweak this query, or how can you change that query so that it runs more efficiently? Keep working at it; keep learning.

Teach Someone Else

I am always amazed at how much I learn when I must explain a concept to another developer or write about a T-SQL topic. To use a feature, you have to understand it, but to teach it, you have to know it at an entirely different level. I have learned so much by writing this book, not only about the process of writing a book, but about writing T-SQL code. I have been surprised that writing a query one way didn't really give me the performance increase I expected. I have learned about an optional parameter or a different way to use a particular feature. To explain a concept to you, I had to really think about how the query works, not just how to make it work.

I have learned a lot writing this book. Thank you for learning along with me.

Index

▆ D

▒ E

T

U

Y, Z

CPSIA information can be obtained at www.ICGtesting.com
Printed in the USA
LVOW071503050712

288896LV00003B/2/P